ABSTRACTS
of
CARROLL COUNTY NEWSPAPERS
1831–1846

Items Taken from the Newspapers of *The Carrolltonian* and *Baltimore & Frederick Advertiser, The Democrat & Carroll County Republican* [Westminster] and *The Regulator & Taneytown Herald*

BY

Marlene Bates AND
Martha Reamy

INDEX BY
Bill Reamy

HERITAGE BOOKS
2010

HERITAGE BOOKS

AN IMPRINT OF HERITAGE BOOKS, INC.

Books, CDs, and more—Worldwide

For our listing of thousands of titles see our website
at
www.HeritageBooks.com

Published 2010 by
HERITAGE BOOKS, INC.
Publishing Division
100 Railroad Ave. #104
Westminster, Maryland 21157

International Standard Book Numbers
Paperbound: 978-1-58549-114-8
Clothbound: 978-0-7884-8575-6

PREFACE

The Historical Society of Carroll County has been a repository for local history for almost half a century. In 1939, a handful of concerned citizens saved the Shellman House from demolition and started an archives to house the written record of Carroll County's past. Over the years, the archives has grown to include four sets of Carroll County newspapers from 1833 to 1988, family histories, church and cemetery records, the Tracy Land Records, books and other documents on local history, ephemera, daybooks and ledgers and over 2000 photographs.

This growth is due to the awareness on the part of Carroll Countians of the importance of their history and heritage. Recognizing these documents as connections to the past and as links to the present and future, generous citizens have donated these written records to be cared for in perpetuity.

The Historical Society's responsibility, therefore, is to not only care for and store this material, but to also make it available to all people. Publications such as this allow for the information to be disseminated in an orderly, logical and nation-wide manner. Now, every genealogist, historian and researcher will have these abstracts available to him.

And that is the Historical Society of Carroll County's ultimate goal: to educate each and every one of us about our heritage.

Joanne Manwaring,
Curator
1988

iii

INTRODUCTION

This volume is composed of abstracts of genealogical information from available newspapers printed in Carroll County, Maryland area from 1831 until 1846.   We have included vital records,
legal notices, advertisements, land sales and political events--
anything that might be of interest to a genealogical researcher.

Most of these original newspapers are located at the
Historical Society of Carroll County in Westminster, Maryland,
and this project could not have been completed without the assistance of Joanne Manwaring, curator.

Other newspapers were located in their original form and on
microfilm at the following facilities: Hanover Public Library,
Hanover, Pennsylvania; Maryland State Archives, Annapolis, Maryland; The Maryland Historical Society, Baltimore, Maryland; and
the Library of Congress in Washington, D.C.   One issue of the
Taneytown Regulator at the Huntington Beach Library in Huntington
Beach, California, inaccessible to us, has been omitted from this
work.

The largest volume of newspapers available for this time
period was the Westminster Carrolltonian.   Most of the abstracts
were done from originals at the Historical Society of Carroll
County, but many issues were incomplete.   Even microfilmed issues
found in other repositories oftentimes were not complete.

The following information pertains to the various papers
abstracted and was taken from "A Check List of the Carroll County
Press" published by J. Leland Jordan, Westminster, Maryland,
January 1937.

☞   [WESTMINSTER]   THE CARROLLTONIAN and Baltimore & Frederick
Advertiser was established at Westminster, the first issue appeared 28 June 1833, by John Klinehoff Longwell, editor and
publisher. $2.00 per year; 6 columns; page 13 3/4 x 20 3/4
inches.   Publication day changed from Friday to Saturday 20 July
1833.   In 1837 it changed to 7 columns; page 16x21 inches.   Friday publication was resumed with Vol. III, No. 45.   In 1838 the
name of the newspaper was changed from THE CARROLLTONIAN to the
WESTMINSTER CARROLLTONIAN.   In October 1844, Francis T. Kerr
became associated with Longwell and the firm became known as the
Francis T. Kerr Company. Following Kerr's death in 1846, George
D. Miller became editor and publisher. Longwell and Miller sold
the paper to William H. Grammer in 1848, who continued as editor
and publisher until 8 June 1855, when the paper ceased
publication.

☞   [WESTMINSTER] THE DEMOCRAT & CARROLL COUNTY REPUBLICAN was
established at Westminster and the first issue appeared Thursday,
?? March 1838, by William Shipley. It began as a 6-column page,
later increased to 7 columns. Subscriptions were $2.00 per year

v

It was sold to Joseph M. Parke in April 1840. Parke continued until a partnership was formed with Josiah T. H. Bringman, a native of Gettysburg, Pennsylvania, 12 March 1846. The paper was then changed to THE CARROLL COUNTY DEMOCRAT.

☞ THE REGULATOR & TANEYTOWN HERALD was established at Taneytown, first issue appearing 15 May 1830, Samuel P. Davidson editor and publisher. John K. Longwell purchased the paper in 1832 and began the publication of [Taneytown] THE MARYLAND RECORDER, 5 columns; 13x20 inch page; $2.00 per year.

Our thanks to all of the repositories above who made it possible for us to do this volume, especially to The Historical Society of Carroll County, and to Bob Barns for the use of his Carroll County newspaper notebooks.

Marlene Bates &
Martha Reamy
Compilers
Carroll County, MD
1988

THE
CARROLLTONIAN.

CARROLL COUNTY NEWSPAPERS - REFERENCE LISTING

HSCC - Historical Society of Carroll County, 210 East Main
    Street, Westminster, Maryland 21157
MSA - Maryland State Archives, 350 Rowe Blvd., Annapolis,
    Maryland, 21401
HPL - Hanover Public Library, Library Place, Hanover,
    Pennsylvania 17331
LC - Library of Congress, Newspaper Division, Washington, D.C.

All issues are full, except when denoted p, which refers to
partial issues only available, followed by page numbers.

[WESTMINSTER] CARROLLTONIAN -- HSCC, original issues:
July 12, 1833 to March 15 & December 6 & 20 1834; February 21 &
March 7, 1835 (p 1&2); March 14 & 28 & April 11, 1835; May 2 to
30, June 13 & September 5, 1835; September 19 & October 3, 1835
(p 1&2); October 24, 1835; April 9 to 23, May 13 & 27, June 10 &
17, 1836; June 24, 1836 (p 1&2); July 1 & 22, 1836; July 29, 1836
(p 1&2); August 12, 1836; August 19 & September 9, 1836 (p 1&2);
October 7 & 14, 1836; October 21, 1836 (p 1&2); October 28 to
December 2, 1836; December 23 1836 (p 1&2-top half only). April
14, 1837 (time capsule issue); September 22, 1837 (p 1&2);
October 6 to December 8, 22 & 29, 1837 (p 1&2). January 12,
1838; January 19 to April 27 & May 11, 1838 (p 1&2); August 10 &
17, 1838 (p 3&4 incomplete); September 7, 1738 (p 1&2); October
5, 1838 (p 3&4 partly illegible); October 12 to 26, 1838 (p 1&2);
November 2 & 9 1838 (part of 3&4 missing); November 16 to 30,
1838 & January 4, 1839 (p 1&2); January 25, 1839; February 8 &
22, 1839 (p 1&2); March 1 & 8, 1839 (part of 3&4 missing); March
22 & April 5, 1839 (p 1&2); April 12, 1839; April 26 & May 3,
1839 (p 1&2); May 10 to 31, 1839 (part of 3&4 missing); June 14,
1839 (p 1&2); June 21, 1839 (part of 3&4 missing); June 28 to
August 16, 1839 (p 1&2); August 23, 1839; August 30 to September
20, October 4 to November 1 & 15, 1839 (p 1&2); November 22, 1839
(part of 3&4 missing); January 10 to February 7, 1840 (p 1&2);
February 14, 1840; February 21, 28 & March 13 to April 24, 1840
(p 1&2); May 15 & 22, 1840; May 29 to July 3, 1840 (p 1&2); July
10, 1840; July 17 to August 7, 21 & September 4, 18, 25 & October
2, 16 to November 6, 1840 (p 1&2); November 13, 1840; November
20, 1840 (p 1&2); December 4 & 11, 1840; December 25, 1840.
January 1, 1841 (p 1&2); January 15, 1841; January 22 to February
5, 1841 (p 1&2); February 12, 1841 (part of 3&4 missing);
February 26 & March 26 & April 2, 1841 (p 1&2); April 9, 1841;
April 16, 1841 (part of 3&4 missing); April 23, 1841 (p 1&2);
April 30 & May 21, 28 & June 4, 1841 (part of 3&4 missing); June
11 to July 2, 1841 (p 1&2); July 9, 1841; July 16 to August 27,
1841 (p 1&2); September 10 & 24, 1841; October 8 to December 3,
1841 (p 1&2); December 17, 1841; December 24, 1841 (p 1&2).
January 7 to 28 & February 11 to March 4, 1842 (p 1&2); September

16, 1842; October 7 & December 30,1842 (p 1&2); February 3 to 24, 1843 (p 1&2); March 24, April 7 & May 12, 19 & June 16, 1843 (p 1&2); July 21, 1843; September 1, 22 & 29, 1843 (p 1&2); October 4, 1844; May 8, 22 to June 19, 1846 (p. 1&2).

The same issues above found at HSCC   have been micro-filmed by MSA and each repository has a copy of the microfilm. M4375-80 (6 reels) The following issues appear on microfilm, but the originals are no longer available at Carroll County: July 5, 1833; February 6 & March 5, 1836 (p 1&2); March 12, 1836; March 28, 1836 (p 1&2); November 25 & December 2, 1836 (p 1&2); April 13, 1838 (includes only 1 column of p 4); October 4, 1843. On microfilm only December 7, 1833, page 4 is missing; the original complete issue is at HSCC. December 6, 1834, page 1 is repeated before page 4 appears.

HPL - issues available on microfilm only. When researching news-papers on microfilm in the state of Pennsylvania, no numbers are used to designate reels. Each reel is identified by the name of the township or city and year only. This is not the microfilm identified above made by MSA; we have not been able to locate the original copies of these papers. [WESTMINSTER] CARROLLTONIAN. All issues are full (4 pages) unless otherwise noted. August 21, 1840; November 12 & 19 & December 3, 10, 17, 31, 1841. January 7, 21, 28 & February 11, 18, March 11, May 27, 1842; June 3 & 10, 1842 (p 1 missing); June 24 to August 5, 1842; August 26, September 9 to 30, 1842; October 14 & 21, 1842.

THE REGULATOR & TANEYTOWN HERALD   LC - Originals August 2 & 23, 1831; Huntington Beach Library, Huntington, California one issue only June 16, 1830.

DEMOCRAT & CARROLL COUNTY REPUBLICAN   LC-Original February 20, 1840; MHS-Originals August 9 & September 20, 1838; August 7, 1845.

ABBREVIATIONS

Adm'r = Administrator   co = county
d/o = daughter of   dec'd = deceased
Ex'r = Executor   inst. = instant
s/o = son of   Tr. = Trustee
ulto. = ultimate, used in reference to last month,
        (inst. referring to current month)

BEAVER, Adam of Baltimore Co. died Tuesday last, 66 years old.
STEVENSON, Mary Ann (Miss) died Wednesday last, Westminster in 32nd year
of her age. (July 12 obit.-died of Scrofula or "Kings Evil", which began
at age 13. After amputation of a foot, the disease again cropped up, and
only her faith sustained her to the end.)
Collection to be made to aid the fire victims in Cumberland. James SMITH,
C. BIRNIE, & John M'CALEB, Committee (Taneytown).
Meeting of 3rd District citizens held at Hamlet GILLESPIE's, of persons
opposed to dismemberment of said county. Edward W. DORSEY, chairman,
Henry BUSSARD, secretary.
Congressional Candidates: William Cost JOHNSON & George C. Washington-
Montgomery & parts of Frederick District; James DIXON & Francis THOMAS-
Frederick, Washington & Allegany District. (It was published that Mr.
WASHINGTON withdrew from the race 9 September 1833.)

12 July 1833
ARNOLD, Anthony H., persons who gave their notes at his sale are notified
that they have been left at the Westminster Savings institution for
collection. Jacob REESE, Treasurer.
BIRNIE, C. of Thorndale, near Taney-town has two short-horn bulls by the
names of Brilliant & President to let to cows; also Saxony Ram Lambs,
common Sheep, bull calves & Heifers for sale.
DELL, John Nicholas: dec'd. of Frederick Co. sale of his estate, farm where
Jacob DELL resides, adjoins land of Philip NICODEMUS & David BROWN; 60
acres with log house & barn. George WARFIELD,Trustee.
FORRY, S. Dr. Offers professional services in Westminster.
HOLMES, Abraham of Baltimore Co., dec. Jacob REESE, administrator.
RITTER, Lewis cautions persons against selling goods or loaning money to
his wife, Anna RITTER on his account.
SHIPLEY, William Jr. $50 reward for person who entered his stable yard and
inflicted unfeeling & inhuman injury to a cow.
SHERMAN, Elizabeth will no longer give indulgence toward debtors.
WENTZ, George dec. of Frederick Co., Jacob REESE, administator.
New County Meeting: At house of S. SULTZER in Taney-Town, Col. Thomas
HOOK, chairman; Abraham LIGHTENWALTER, asst. chairman; James M'KILLIP &
George A. FARQUHAR, secretaries. Attending: Washington VAN BIBBER,
David KEPHART & William ROBERTS.
Sheriff Candidates: Mathias E. BARTGIS & Thomas GURLEY (Frederick Co.)
Meeting Jackson Reform Party: Held in Taney-Town District at home of John
NULL. John JONES, chairman; Dr. William B. GWINN, secretary. Committee:
John B. BOYLE, William SHAW, Michael NULL, Thomas JONES, Moses SHAW Jr.,
Samuel NAILL, John MEERING Sen., Thomas HICKLEY, Lewis PETERS, Capt.
George CRABBS, David BUFFINGTON, Tobias COVER, David HAPE, John WHITE,
John ADELSPERGER, Peter HULL, Jacob FEESER, William FISHER & Johnson
JAMISON.
Meeting Jackson Reform Party: Held in Westminster District, Isaac SHRIVER,
Esq. chairman, E. CRUMBACKER, secretary. Delelgates: Jesse SLINGLUFF,
Elijah BOND, George WARFIELD, Jacob GROVE, Nicholas H. BROWN, John A.
BYERS, George REINHART, John KUHN Jr., Thomas HAINES, Jacob LANDES,
Jacob SHAFFER, David GRIMAN, Michael MORELOCK, Joseph WEAVER, David
KEEFER, John FISHER, Isaac SHRIVER, Benjamin YINGLING, Nimrod FRIZZLE,
William SHIPLEY & Basil HAYDEN.
Congressional Candidate: Madison NELSON, Frederick, Washington & Allegany
District.

July 20, 1833
BEAVER, Martin of Baltimore Co., dec., Jacob REESE, administrator.

July 20, 1833
MAULSBY, John H. Lt., eldest son of Col. J. D. MAULSBY, Harford County,
  drowned Saturday last, near New Castle DE. Was to enter Navy.
NEVINS, Rev. Mr. of Baltimore, to preach in Westminster tomorrow.
REEVER, Abraham, wife Catharine has left my bed & board without cause,
  is determined to pay no debts of hers.
Applicants for the benefit of insolvent laws: Robert ANDERSON, William
  DELL, Samuel FITZGERALD, Zacchariah DANNER.
Manchester Celebration: 57th Anniversary of Independence, July 4th.
  Attended by the Manchester Blues, held on the property of Col. A. SHOWER.
  Rev. Jacob ALBERT opened with prayer, Declaration of Independence read by
  Henry E. BELTZ, patriotic oration by Joseph M. PARKE, prayer by Rev.
  Jacob GEIGER. Dinner prepared by William CRUMRINE. Volunteer toasts
  by: Capt. Solomon MYERLY, Henry BELTZ, Benjamin KLINEFELTER, Dr.
  SHOWER for nullification of offspring of disappointed ambition, Jacob
  FRANKFORTER Washington, Charles MILLER, Esq., George EVERHART, Joseph
  GONTER, Levy MAXWELL, Jacob FRICK, Jacob SWEM, Jacob HOUCK, David
  FRANKFORTER, Jacob SELLER (blacksmith), "The defenders of our country,
  may their hearts of steel strike fire on the anvil of Liberty," Henry E.
  BELTZ, William CRUMRINE, "May fortune resemble the bottle & bowl, &
  stand by the man who cannot stand by himself," Samuel S. PARKE, Jacob
  LINAWEAVER, Elias BUCKINGHAM (ensign), John MATTHIAS, John P. FRICK,
  Samuel KLINEFELTER, Jacob N. MILLER, Jacob SAUL, James MC CUTCHEN,
  Godfrey KNELIER, Peter LINAWEAVER, Henry LYFORD, Abraham KUNTZ. Jacob T.
  GILT. John H. WORTHINGTON our worthy guest, James TURNER former
  representative of Baltimore County.

27 July 1833
CLOUGH, (?), the murderer escaped from the Mount Holly (PA) prison, with
  500 persons in pursuit was recaptured in the evening in a swamp. He was
  to have been executed yesterday.
M'PHERSON, David M. formerly of Gettysburg now publisher at St. Clairs-
  ville, Ohio.
NICHOL, Adam of Frederick, Md. on Saturday last, 23d ult, fell from the
  bow of a flat boat near Zanesville (Ohio) and drowned.

3 August 1833
BARTGIS, Mathias E. candidate for sheriff of Frederick Co.
BELL, Isaac looking for stray cow from farm about 2 miles below Westminster
  on Baltimore Turnpike; small, mouse-colored cow with crumpled horns,
  white underbelly & large bush at end of her tail.
BRIENS, Messrs. awarded damages sustained by the passage of Canal through
  their lands in Washington Co. Counsel for Canal: B. PRICE, James DIXON,
  R. H. HENDERSON & Walter JONES. Esq. for BRIENs: J. J. MERRICK, William
  PRICE & Frederick A. SCHLEY.
CROFT, John of Rocksdale Woolen Factory will buy wool at Mr. Jacob REESE's
  or Mr. H. YINGLING's store (Westminster) and Jessie MANNING's store,
  Joshua ALLGER's, Mr. WEAVER's tavern & at Samuel HERMAN's store in
  Reisterstown, George MATTER, Esq. in Manchester & John MURRAY's store
  in Hampstead.
CROWL, Michael removing to the west selling farm in Frederick Co. 1/4
  mile east of turnpike from Westminster to Littlestown, 1 1/2 miles from
  former; 87 1/2 acres, log house, log barn & springhouse.
DODDS, Robert Dr. died at his residence in New Windsor Saturday a.m. last
  at 10 1/2 o'clock, after a long illness, 48th year of his age & buried on
  the Monday after in Union-Town.
GERNAND, Emanuel, blue dyer, carpet & coverlid manufacturer. Opposite
  Dr. Willis' office, nearly opposite Mr. H. FORRY's tavern. Served
  apprenticeship with G. M. CONRADT of Frederick. Wool taken in exchange
  for work; also looking for an apprentice.

3 August 1833

MATHIAS, Jacob, seeks journeyman, tanning & currying business-Westminster.
MOTTER, Lewis & others petitioned General Assembly to nulify the charter of
    Westminster, Taney-town & Emmitsburg Turnpike Co.
MULLAN, Jonathan died 24 July, 5 years old, son of Edward & Ann MULLAN of
    Baltimore County.
RASIN, Unit in Westminster for few days to collect his accounts. Can be
    found at Mr. Philip JONES'.
REESE, Jacob: Selling flaxseed, one-horse Dearborn & Yankee Clocks.
SMITH, Solomon, dec'd., property sale. Land in Frederick County on the
    road leading from Westminster to Taney-Town, adjoining Frizzlesburg; 84
    acres with log dwelling house, log barn & other out-houses. Jacob
    MATHIAS, Trustee. (Oct. 5, 1833 edition: amount of sale $1187.37 1/2.)
WENTZ, George, dec. of Frederick Co. sale of estate near Westminster on
    Gettysburg Turnpike, 4 acres, new 2-story brick house, brick outbuilding
    & log barn & 30 acres adjoining. Sold disencumbered of title of dower of
    the widow. Jacob REESE, Trustee.
Letters held at Westminster Post Office 1 July: John ARTHUS, Andrew J.
    BROOKS, William BURGOON, Frederick BAUCHMAN Esq., Nicholas BOSST, John
    C. COLEHEN, FRENER & his partner, J. FLEGLE Esq., John FERRIS, Esq., John
    GRIMES, John GREENHOLTZ, Peter HENRY, Mrs. Elizabeth KEYS, Jacob KEMP,
    William KONE, Robert LUCAS, Jacob MYERLEY Esq., Joel OGBOIN, William
    ORPUT, Susannah POWELL, Unit RASIN, Adam SHANER, Solomon STOCKDALE,
    Joseph SHREEV, John SMITH Jr., John ZILE.   E. CRUMBACKER, Post Master
Letters held at Taneytown 1 July: Peter BOMGARTNER, Daniel BOYLE, Mr.
    BITTROLF, Jacob CLUTZ, Jacob COONCE, Jacob CROOMER, William ELINE,
    Catharine ELDER, Andrew FRITZ, Thomas GARRETT, Peter GALLY, George
    KEEFER, Margaret KOONS, Jacob LAMBERT, George RINEHART, Abraham RECK,
    George B. SHRINER, Jacob SNYDER, Mrs. Susan SHRINER, Mary STEWART,
    William TOY, Jacob WAGONER.   Hugh SHAW Jr., Post Master

10 August 1833

BROWN, Joshua estate sale livestock, farm implements, household furniture.
    David BROWN, executor.
COCKEY, Jushua [sic] held political meeting at his house in Westminster.
    Jesse SLINGLUFF & David KEPHART chairmen, Col. Thomas HOOK & John
    MALEHORN secretaries.
ECKLER, Ulrich, heirs of, dec. of Frederick Co., selling 49 acres near the
    center Westminster, log house & lot at Main & Church Sts. & log house.
    Also back lots in said town & wood lot in Baltimore Co., part of
    "Arnold's Harbor Enlarged", 4 acres. Joshua SMITH, Jr. Trustee
HAHN, Jacob Jr. living on Silver Run near Maus' Mill, Frederick Co.,
    opening a slate quarry, will sell for roofing houses.
JONES, Philip selling mantle clock, bureau & bedstead cheap. (Westm.)
ORENDORF, Samuel (Westminster) selling dry goods, groceries, etc.
SMITH, Samuel, sudden death, a laboring man of Cumberland, Md., Monday
    last week. Was intemperate & 2 days before his death drank "not less
    than a half gallon of apple brandy . . ." Monday a.m. he was taken with
    a cramp in the stomach & about noon he was a corpse.
National Administration, 9th District meeting met at house of William
    WERTENBAKER in New Market. Arthur TANZEY chairman, Roderick DORSEY
    secretary. Committee to meet General Convention in Frederick: Thomas
    NORWOOD, Lemuel BRADENBURGH, Richard HAGEN, Upton WORTHINGTON, Lawrence
    REEL, George W. BEALL, Barnard KEMP, Luke DAVIS, Talbot G. SHIPLEY, Joel
    HALL, John HARDING, Horatio SANK, Henry W. DORSEY, Wilson Lee MC ELFRESH,
    John SMITH of George, Elias W. BOTELAR, Samuel STEVENS, Jesse WRIGHT,
    Lemuel MUSSESTTER, Lemuel GRIFFITH, Lemuel CLAY, John STEVENS, James
    BURTON, Alexander JAMISON, Henry BARNES, John RYNE & Solomon CLARY.
    Committee of Correspondence: Thomas RUCKMAN, James SIMPSON, Samuel

THE CARROLLTONIAN

10 August 1833
WRIGHT, Dr. E. M. MOBBERLY, Thomas ANDERSON, John H. WORTHINGTON & Dr.
J. H. M. SMITH.

17 August 1833.
JONES, Philip selling house & lot in Westminster, occupied as store.
Voters Meeting at Mrs. WOOLREY's Tavern, 4th election district.
Voters Meeting of Taney-Town held at Mr. S. SULTZER's Tavern; James SMITH
  Esq. chairman Dr. Philip KEPHART secretary. Nominating Committee for
  Legislature Evan MC KINSTRY, Esq., Capt. John MATHIAS, Elias GRIMES,
  Esq., John BAUMGARDNER, Esq., Maj. John MC KALEB, Dr. Samuel SWOPE, Upton
  SCOTT, George A. FARQUHAR, Joseph MOORE, Charles A. WRIGHT, Jonathan
  SWITZER, Dr. William B. HEBBARD, Dr. Philip KEPHART, WIlliam HUGHES,
  William SHEPHERD, J. A. MC KALEB.
Nominations Jackson Republican Convention: Hon. Francis THOMAS, Mr. DIXON
  stand as independent, Col. Charles S. SEWALL nominated for Baltimore &
  Harford Cos., Messers. WORTHINGTON & TURNER independents; Dr. RICE of
  Kent Co. for District of Kent, Talbot, Cecil & Queen Anne's.
National Republicans met in Union-town to appoint delegates from 6th Dist.
  at Convention in Frederick 24th inst. Maj. Jacob MATHIAS, chairman, A.F.
  SHRIVER secretary. Committee: Joshua SMITH Jr., Moses SHAW Sr., John
  ROBERTS. John M. FERGUSON, Charles DEVILBISS, James C. ATTEE, Dr. William
  WILLS, A. F. SHRIVER, Washington VAN BIBBER, William ECKER, Abraham
  WAMPLER, Nicholas DURBIN, Frederick BAUGHMAN, Isaac NICODEMUS, Israel
  NORRIS & Daniel ENGLE.

24 August 1833
DAVIS, Benjamin: Ad for Hampstead races run over 600 yd. course.
HOPPE, Frederick late of Frederick Co., dec'd., sale at house of Mr. FORRY
  in Westminster; heirs selling lot of chestnut timber land 33 acres 1 mile
  from Westminster 1/2 mile north of Coleman's Tavern, adjoins land of Mr.
  MALEHORN & property formerly of M'COMBS heirs. J. Henry HOPPE, Agent.

31 August 1833
BLIZZARD, James married to Miss H. OGBORN, both of this county by Rev.
  Daniel ZOLLICKOFFER, Thursday 19th instant.
HAINES, Joseph: Wanted, journeyman to the tanning & currying business,
  subscriber living near Haines' Mill on Little Pipe Creek.
MOTT, Richard Dr. opens practice in New Windsor, relocating from Baltimore
  City, where he has practiced for two years.
SCHLEY, John clerk for the Frederick County court.
Appointments by the Governor & Council for Frederick County: Notaries
  Public- Edward TURBUTT, Frederick; Jacob REESE, Westminster. Additional
  Justices of the Peace- Solomon FORREST, G. W. SANDS. Militia Officers-
  James M. COALE, Aid-de-Camp Brig. Gen. of the 9th Brigade, rank of Major.
  16th Regiment- Lewis KEMP. Col.; James M. SHELMAN, Lt. Col.; Benjamin
  PRICE, Major. 20th Regiment-Thomas SAPPINGTON, Col.; William WILLIS, Lt.
  Col.; Thomas HAMMOND, Major; Mathias E. BARTGIS, Quarter Master of 9th
  Brigade.
Jackson Convention Candidates: House of Delegates, Dr. John W. DORSEY &
  John RIGNEY chairmen, David SCHLEY & John SIFFORD, secretaries. Joseph
  M. PALMER, Abdiel UNKEFER, David SCHLEY & John SIFFORD nominated. Commit.
  to draft resolutions: Christian KEEFER, Nicholas SNIDER, Daniel S. BISER,
  Michael THOMAS, Henry BOTELER, J. BUZZARD, M. BLESSING, John H. CURTIS,
  Dr. William B. GWINN, John WOLF, William WERTENBAKER & John SMITH.
National Republican Convention: Moses WORMAN, Esq. & John MC NEILL chair-
  men. Nelson POE & J. A. M'KALEB secretaries. Nominees: Daniel DUVALL,
  L. P. W. BALCH, Thomas HAMMOND, and John LEE.
Committee Report regarding the contemplated new county. Members: C.
  BIRNIE, William MURRAY, Edward DORSEY, Joshua C. GIST, Thomas HOOK, John

4

31 August 1833
M'KALEB, Archibald DORSEY, William SHEPHERD, M. G. COCKEY, John M'KILLIP,
Joseph STEEL, John BAUMGARTNER, Nicholas ALLGIER, William SHAW of Hugh,
George RICHARDS, William ROBERTS, Frederick RITTER, Samuel GALT, Nicholas
KELLY, George HAWKE, James C. ATLEE, Washington VAN BIBBER, Evan L.
CRAWFORD, Peter HULL, Peter G. JONES, Peter ERB Jr., Jacob SHRIVER,
William BROWN, Evan M'KINSTRY, Bazel D. STEVENSON, Philip ENGLAR, Abraham
BIXLER, Jacob LANDES, William CAPLES, David KEPHART, Joshua SELLMAN,
William B. HEBBARD, John MALEHORN, I. Henry HOPPE, Michael MILLER, John
SWOPE, George WARFIELD, William JORDAN, George CRABBS, Sebastian SULTZER,
John C. KELLY, Andrew HAWKE, David FOUTZ, Jesse SLINGLUFF, Nathan
GORSUCH, Joseph KEEFFER, Abraham NULL (of M.), Jesse L. WARFIELD & George
CASSELL (of John).

7 September 1833
EBAUGH, Jacob: sale of property to be held at Tavern of Benjamin DAVIS in
    Hampstead, 26 miles from Baltimore City, on turnpike road to Hanover.
    Tavern stand & 3 1/4 acres of land occupied by DAVIS with barn & sheds.
    Also 4 lots in Hampstead, also farm of 100 acres with log house within a
    mile of Hampstead. Also new-built paper mill on the Patapsco Falls with
    114 acres & stone house, barn and other out-houes, within 2 1/2 miles of
    Hampstead.
ERB, Charles moving West, selling farm in Frederick County 1 mile west of
    J. Henry HOPPE's store, same distance from George RINEHARD's tavern,
    adjoins land of John MILLER, David WANTZ, Gabriel BOYERS, etc., 105 1/2
    acres, log dwelling house, log barn & springhouse.
KELLER, Jacob Frederick has received a letter from the Counsul General of
    Wurtemburg, being held at Samuel KONIG's in Frederick Co. Ad signed
    Nelson POE of Frederick.
LOWE, William running for sheriff of Frederick County.
PALMER, Mr. withdrawn from the Jackson Delegate ticket of Frederick.
National Republican Meeting, Westminster (7th Dist.): Jacob ZIMMERMAN
    chairman, Joshua SMITH Jr. secretary. Delegates: Jacob MATHIAS, John
    SMITH (of Joshua), George CASSELL Esq., Isaac NICODEMUS, William WILLIS,
    John ROBERTS, A. F. SHRIVER, Jacob FRINGER Jr.
National Republican Meeting, Taney-Town District: William SHEPHERD chair-
    man, Capt. John MATHIAS assistant chairman, David FOUTZ secretary.
Delegates: William SHEPHERD, John MATHIAS, Elias GRIMES, John BAUMGARDNER,
    William B. HEBBARD, Thomas HOOK, George A. FARQUHAR, William HUGHES &
    Ephriam CARMACK.
Sixth Election District Meeting, Taney-Town: Met at S. SULTZER, Esq.'s,
    Evan M'KINSTRY Esq. chairman, James M'GUIGAN secretary. Committee: Maj.
    John M'KALEB, Dr. John SWOPE, Sterling GALT, James SMITH Esq., Isaac
    DERN Esq., John DELAPLANE & John THOMAS.
Congressional Candidates: Roderick DORSEY, Montgomery & parts of Frederick
    Counties.

14 September 1833
BROWN, Nicholas Hall, Westminster, burning a kiln of lime to sell.
CAPLES, Samuel held meeting at his home in Baltimore County.
FITZHUGH, Colonel: Hagerstown, cholera broke out Friday night in Jail. A
    man from the line of the Canal first taken it. Six prisoners have died.
    On it's appearance Col. FITZHUGH, Sheriff released all inmates. A
    colored woman, resident of the town, attacked and died Monday evening.
GEATTY, Henry, house carpenter and cabinet maker, thanks patrons.
RANDOLPH, Edwin, s/o the late P. RANDOLPH of Richmond, committed suicide a
    few days ago in Charlestown, Jefferson County, VA. "Blew his brains out
    by placing the pistol in contact with his forehead."

THE CARROLLTONIAN

14 September 1833
National Republication Convention held at New Market Wednesday last. Dr.
Horace WILSON of Montgomery County chaired, Maj. SIMMONS of Frederick
County assistant chair. William Cost JOHNSON nominated.
Teacher wanted at the Jerusalem Church, Frederick County. See George
MATHIAS or Frederick BACHMAN.

21 September 1833
CRUMBACKER, Virginia died Saturday last, only daughter of Mr. Ephraim
CRUMBACKER, of this place, aged 4 years, 5 months.
OURSLER, Henry, cabinet maker, giving up carpentering business, will
devote himself to cabinet making. Will make sideboards, bureaus,
secretaries, tables, & coffins made in the most expeditious manner.
SHOWERS, Adam Col., died in Baltimore County Thursday evening the 29th
ult., aged 60. He was a useful & upright citizen, who had served his
country faithfully as a legislator & a soldier.
TESLING, Andrew forwarns persons from trusting his wife Elizabeth for
anything on his account as she absconded from his bed & board.
October Elections: For Congress, Montgomery & Frederick Cos., William
Cost JOHNSON, Roderick DORSEY. For Harford & Baltimore Cos., Charles S.
SEWALL, James TURNER, John T. H. WORTHINGTON. House of Delegates,
Frederick County: I. P. W. BALCH, John LEE, Thomas HAMMOND, Daniel
DUVALL, Joseph M. PALMER, David SCHLEY, John SIFFORD, Abdiel UNKETER;
Baltimore County, Hugh ELY, Thomas J. PRICE, John B. HOLMES, Z. H.
WORTHINGTON, E. T. J. WOODWARD, --- GORE, Solomon HILLEN Jr., C. C. LOVE,
John H. CARROLL, -- M'BIAR, Dixon STANSBERRY. Sheriff, Frederick
County, Mathias E. BARTGIS, Thomas GURLEY, Mahlon TALBOTT, Abner
CAMPBELL, William LOWE; Baltimore County, Nathaniel CHILDS, William
POCHIN, John W. WALKER, H. S. SANDERSON.
Congressional Convention: Dr. Horace WILSON of Montgomery, President;
Maj. James SIMMONS, Vice President; Dr. Richard DORSEY & Nicholas
NORRIS, secretaries, all of Frederick Co. Resolutions offered by
Washington BURGESS Esq. of New Market district & Richard I. BOWIE Esq.
of Montgomery. Resolution was negatived then the Montgomery delegation
were invited by Richard J. BOWIE Esq. to retire and a majority of them
withdrew from the convention. Dr. George HUGHES offered resolution &
William Cost JOHNSON Esq. was nominated. W. BURGESS Esq. & Jacob MATHIAS
Esq. made motions. Committee to prepare address to voters of 6th
District, Dr. George HUGHES, J. H. HILLEARY & James DURBIN.
New Party -The Mechanics of Baltimore nominated Maj. Elijah STANSBURY &
Joshua VANSANT as candidates.

28 September 1833
GARNER, Jacob-camp meeting held on his land on Log Cabin Branch, 3 miles
west of Union-town 18 October.
MILTIMORE, Ebenezer of Middleburg, MD has invented a device to lock hind
wheels of stage coaches & vehicles of burthen when going down hill, to
be manufactured by Stockton & Stokes of Baltimore.
ROSE, John, botanic physician, in the house formerly occupied by Jonathan
P. CREAGER, having qualified himself by study & practice is ready to
to attend the sick and afflicted.
SWEARINGTON, Charles Dr.: of Cumberland died by his own hand Tuesday last.
He entered a public house carrying a loaded rifle & fired upon Mr.
THISTLE, a young member of the bar. He then re-loaded and shot himself
dead upon the spot. THISTLE's wound was considered dangerous.
TESLING, Elizabeth informs the public regarding her husband's ad of the
21st instant, that about 3 weeks ago he married his present wife, & never
had either bed or board, except what is hers. Because of money she has
in a savings institution, which she will not let him have, he has

6

THE CARROLLTONIAN

28 September 1833
    absconded from her bed and board. The public should not credit the
    said Andrew TESLING alias FISHER.
WARFIELD, George Esq. appointed post master of new P.O. established at his
    store, Frederick Co. 4 miles from this place. (Westminster)
Election: Contest in upper district Jacksonian race, Mr. THOMAS calls upon
    Dr. William TYLER & John NELSON to appear before the people & make known
    reasons why they oppose his election.

5 October 1833
BALCH, L. P. W. presents his respects to the Jackson candidates, especially
    Joseph Mortimer PALMER, Esq., and invites them to a tete a tete.
BATCH, Stephen B. Rev., D.D. of Georgetown died Sunday morning 22nd ult. as
    he was setting out for the church to perform his duties.
BROWN, Lewis H. of Baltimore Co. married 24 September at the residence of
    Mr. Robert HUDSON, Baltimore Co., by Rev. Mr. WEBSTER, to Miss Susan Ann
    d/o Mr. Horatio HUDSON of Anne Arundel County.
BYERS, John A. stray cow came to his farm near Westminster on the Littles-
    town turnpike. A red Brindle cow with a bell.
MEDTART, Jacob, secretary, Clergy and Lay Delegates of Md and VA of
    Evangelical Lutheran Synod of Md. to meet in Martinsburg, VA.
SHOWER, Adam, late of Baltimore Co., dec., Orphans' Court of Baltimore Co.
    sale of his residence near Manchester. Personal property consists of
    negroes, horses, cows, sheep, etc. & distillery. Jacob SHOWER & George
    SHOWER, Administrators.
STEUART, William M. Esq. a young lawyer of Rockville taking over the
    editorial department of the Rockville American, formerly run by Jesse
    LEACH Esq.
YINGLING, Henry selling fresh oysters & choice liquors.
Elections- Congressional candidates for Montgomery & part of Frederick,
    William Cost JOHNSON, Roderick DORSEY; for Harford & Baltimore Charles S.
    SEWALL, James TURNER, John T. H. WORTHINGTON. House of Delegates
    candidates, Frederick L. P. W. BALCH, John LEE, Thomas HAMMOND, Daniel
    DEWALL, Joseph M. PALMER, David SCHLEY, John SIFFORD, Abdiel UNKETER.
    Baltimore County Hugh ELY, Thomas J. PRICE, John B. HOLMES, Z. H. WORTH-
    INGTON, E. T. J. WOODWARD, --- GORE, Solomon HILLEN Jr., C.C. LOVE, John
    H. CARROLL, ----- M'BLAIR, Dixon STANSBERRY. Sheriff Frederick Co.
    Mathias E. BARTGES, Thomas GURLEY, Mahlon TALBOTT, Abner CAMPBELL,
    William LOWE. Sheriff Baltimore Co. Nathaniel CHILDS, William PECHIN,
    John W. WALKER, H. S. SANDERSON. In paid ad as candidates for sheriff
    of Frederick Co.: Henry HOUCK, James DURBIN Jr., James M. HARDING.
List of Letters held at the Post Office, Westminster 1 Oct. 1833:
    John BANKERT, Mrs. S. BUCKINGHAM, John BELL, Jacob CASHOUR, Regin COOK,
    David DALL, Jacob EBAUGH, Andrew GRAMMER, Mrs. Fanny GREEN, Mrs. Rebecca
    GREEN, David KEEFER, Francis LENARD, Joseph LOGSDON, Jason MOORE, John
    MANNING, Barnard MAGREE, Miss Jennet MC COMB, George REINEHART, (Mr.)
    Unit ROETHICKEN, Peter SOMMER, Philip SEWER, John SHAMER, Rezin STEVENS,
    George STARY, Benjamin SHEEN, James TOWSON, Hiram WINCHESTER, Mrs.
    Hannah WHEELER.
List of Letters held at the Post Office, Taney-Town 1 October 1833: Rev
    Henry AURAND, William CALVERT, Jacob HYTER, Debborah HAYS, Dr. William
    HEBBARD, William KOONS, Mrs. F. S. KEY, William M'KALEB Esq., John
    NANKIVELL, Mary SHRINER, Bernard SHOEMAKER, George SPALDING, Mrs. Maryann
    STORM, Mr. (Miller) SWITZER, Mrs. Mary STEWART, William TOY, Frances
    WIMMS.

12 October 1833
GIRTY, Jacob a celebrated collar-maker until a few days ago, when he was
    attacked by disease & died at Union-town 5 October, aged 73 years. It

7

12 October 1833

is said he has a wife, a son and a sister, living widely scattered. Buried in German Reformed graveyard in Union-town.

THISTLE, Bayard died in Cumberland Thursday morning last, at the home of his grandfather (Maj. John H. BAYARD) at the age of 24, son of George THISTLE. The unfortunate youth was shot in the back by the late Dr. Charles V. SWEARENGEN on the 17th ultmo.

ZIMMERMAN, Jacob & John dissolving their partnership in New Windsor. The business will be carried on by John.

19 October 1833

RINEDOLLAR, Henry, deceased, sale of his farm 2 miles north of Taney-Town, 164 acres, one log house & barn, another house & stable 1/4 mile from first; also wood lot situated in Lind's Bottom 1/2 mile from Taney-Town; also 2 log houses & lot in Taney-Town northeast of the cross street; also selling horses, cows, wagon, ploughs, harrows, windmill, carry-all & hearse, household goods. Louisa RINEDOLLAR & Abraham LIGHTENWALTER, Exs.

WENTZ, George, persons who gave notes at his sale are to pay up.

Westminster Savings Institution officers: William WILLIS President, Jacob REESE Treasurer; Directors: John ROOP, Jacob MATHIAS, William GRUMBINE, Jacob GRAMMER, John KUHN, Andrew POWDER, William CROUSE, Emanuel GERNAND, Michael BARNITZ.

Candidates for sheriff of Frederick County: Henry HOUCK, James DURBIN Jr., James M. HARDING.

26 October 1833

BELT, George Gordon, trustee; sale on an order of Baltimore Co. court of paper mill on Patapsco Falls, 27 miles from Baltimore City, 2 miles from Hampstead. Stone building, 2-stories; 120 acres, stone house with Switzer Barn & outbuildings. Also, tavern stand & store in Hampstead, 2-stories, front of about 60' on the turnpike; 3 acres & log barn. Also 2 vacant lots in Hampstead. Also 100 acre farm 1 mile from Hampstead adjoining land of William MILLVAIN, etc. Log dwelling & out-buildings, etc. Also 20 acres adjoining land of Major STANSBURY, etc. all in wood.

FORRY, S. Dr. selling horse powder to improve wind, strength & appetite of horses. For sale at his drug store in Westminster.

GALLION, John P. closing his business will sell house & lot in Frizzleburg on turnpike from Westminster to Taney-Town, 5 miles from former & 7 from latter. Two-story house with shop attached; 2 acres. Also seasoned wood & wagon-makers tools.

HARTZELL, Jacob, meeting for the purpose of separating Baltimore Co. from the City held at his tavern in Reisterstown.

HOLMES, Jonathan, heirs holding sale by order of Orphans' Court of Balto. Co. on Westminster turnpike, 27 miles from Baltimore. Sale consists of 1 negro man 22 years of age, who is a good blacksmith, 1 woman 37 years old to be sold for a term of years, not to be sold or carried out of MD, also household goods. Also farm 108 acres in Baltimore County, 2 miles from Westminster, near turnpike, adjoins lands of John FISHER, REESE & Richard GORSUCH. Two running streams, 2 houses.

KNOX, William Col. died on Saturday last at his residence near Taney-town after a lingering illness.

TAWNY, Jacob died on Sunday last of Baltimore County.

VANBLARICUM, Michael, tried for the murder of William M'PHERSON, formerly of Gettysburg PA. Found guilty of manslaughter, sentenced to 5 years. Victim was drowned when a canoe they were riding in with ---- LEWIS was deliberately upset by VANBLARICUM. It was suggested that the victim was strangled underwater.

THE CARROLLTONIAN

2 November 1833
CHASE, Aurelia, a negro woman, on trial for the murder of Mrs. Elizabeth
A. DURKEE, wife of Dr. Robert A. DURKEE, of Baltimore City, who died of
arsenic poisoning. The woman was a cook with the family & poisoned the
soup. William H. NORRIS, Esq., was the attorney for the state, J. Mason
CAMPBELL & Alex. CHEVES, Esqs., spoke on behalf of the prisoner as did
R. W. GILL, Esq., Deputy Attorney General. The jury found her guilty.
FORRY, Mr., tavernkeeper in Westminster holding political meeting.
GISE, Adam, of Menallen Township (PA), his house entirely destroyed by fire
Friday last, the roof caught from a spark. The building took fire while
they were attending the funeral of a son of Mr. GISE; that Mr. GISE lying
ill & a daughter were in the house, the daughter not expected to live.
HOPPE, J. H. of Mt. Pleasant has store where you can inquire about register-
ing for the newly opened high school in Mt. Pleasant.
HYDER, Mr. of Union-town, lost deed Tuesday morning last between
Westminster & Union-town, wrapped & tied up in a piece of newspaper.
JONES, William M., of Tobacco Stick (Cambridge, MD), accidently shot his
sister on Thursday of last week.
NICODEMUS, Isaac has given all accounts of persons indebted to him to
Mr. Lot HOKE for collection.
Candidates for sheriff: George BOWLUS, Nicholas SNIDER, John BAUMGARTNER.

9 November 1833
BEARD, J. G. new store in Westminster in room formerly occupied by John S.
MURRAY; opposite David KEEJER's tavern, will carry groceries & liquors,
china, glass & Queens-ware, etc.
CARACHER, Mr. of Warwick township (PA) found dead in his stable 4 miles
from Manhiem, Thursday the 24th inst. after a quarrel with his wife.
Found on the floor with a rope around his neck, it was deducted that he
had been his own executioner. Much addicted to the use of strong drink.
CHASE, Aurelia of Baltimore City, convicted of murder by poison. Sentenced
by Judge BRICE, City Court. (21 Dec. 1833-executed by hanging yesterday.)
COCKEY, J. intending to leave MD disposing of large tavern house in Westminster on the main turnpike from Baltimore to Pittsburg. Also selling
brick house adjoining property of Jacob REESE & an unimproved lot
opposite thereto.
DARBY, John s/o John DARBY of Fayetteville died Saturday last in Taneytown,
aged 6 years.
FLEMING, George, of Carlile PA to publish a collection of Music for Singing
Schools, Societies & Choirs in both Round & Patent Notes. Also apply to
J. H. HICKOK, Lewistown, PA.
KOONTZ, John estate sale by Frederick Co. court of Equity, 202 acres &
large 2-story house with small log house attached, 2 barns. Silver Run
flows through, convenient to Westminster turnpike 1 mile from Silver Run
church & same distance from Joseph WISNER's Tavern, bounded by land of
John DODDERO, Nicholas DILL, etc. John BRUMGARTNER, Trustee.
SCHELL, Joseph, tax collector for 1833 will be at the following locations:
Woodsborough, Mrs. YANTIS' tavern; Liberty, TAYLOR's Tavern; FRANKLIN's
Tavern; Maurer's Mill, New Windsor, WOOD's Tavern; Middleburg, NEALE's
Tavern; Union Bridge, G. A. FARQUHAR's store; Union-town, GLAZIER's
store; Union-town, GLAZIER's Tavern; Union Mills, A. SHRIVER's Tavern,
Westminster; Taney-town, SULTZER's Tavern; Emmitsburg, AGNEW's Tavern;
Mechanics-town, FUNDENBERG's Tavern; Creager's-town, BECKENBAUGH's
Tavern; New-Market, SCHELL's Tavern, Middletown, RICHMOND's Tavern.
(Tax rate one-hundred nineteen cents per $100.) George BALTZELL, late
collector.
TRISLER, George store in Frederick was forcibly entered on Monday night
last. Entrance was forced using an iron lever, which was taken from
the railing round the Court House yard.

9

THE CARROLLTONIAN

9 November 1833
WALLACE, Nelson of Baltimore City, sentenced to death by Judge BRICE in
    City Court, convicted of rape. (21 Dec. 1833, WALLACE hung until dead.)
WELLS, John 17 year old tailors apprentice ran away from Israel HITESHUE.
    Has dark hair & is a remarkable chewer of tobacco.
WOOD, Thomas removing to the western country selling property midway
    between Union-Town & Union-Bridge 2 acres & house, stable & grist &
    saw mill.
(Philadelphia) The steamboat New Philadelphia Rail-Road Line was detained
    by a serious accident on Friday evening last, 17 miles the other side of
    Bordentown. Mr. STEDMAN of NC died, appeared to be traveling alone.
    His remains left at Hightstown. An Episcopal clergyman named WEST had
    his legs broken. A passenger stated that the cars were going at the rate
    of 35 miles an hour. Can this be possible? We called at Mrs. SWORDS &
    at Congress Hall, & learned that Mrs. BARTLETT & child of Washington &
    Mr. CHARLES of St. Louis, all severely injured in an accident Friday last
    on the Amboy Rail Road, were all much better, all of them out of danger.

16 November 1833
BARSTOW, Dr. of Susquehanna Co. PA, was traveling with his family near
    Tunkhannock during a storm of hurricane force when a huge hemlock, 2'
    or more across, was thrown across the road, falling precisely between
    the horses & the carriage, only breaking the tongue of the wagon.
BEARD, J. G. of this place, an infant child of his died Wednesday last.
CATHCART, Dr. of York, PA, keeps a memorandum of every murder in the U.S.
    which came under his notice. There have been 156 murders & suicides in
    the last year, & he considers many may have escaped his observation.
FORRY, Mr. held meeting in Westminster about new county. Jesse MANNING of
    Baltimore & Joseph SMITH of Frederick Co. chairmen.; A. F. SHRIVER &
    J. K. LONGWELL secretaries.
MILLER, George: 50,000 lbs. of pork wanted; also removing to the Western
    country selling 11 acres on turnpike to Taney-town within a half mile of
    Westminster log house, barn, smoke house & salt-house, all nearly new.
WAMPLER, David of this place, died Thursday last.

23 November 1833
CAMPBELL: Mr.: Post Master of Union Town PA, Mail Robbery committed the
    12th inst. mailbag contents taken between Cumberland & UnionTown.
GURLEY, Thomas Jr. & Miss Amanda STULL, both of this county, married
    Thursday 14th inst. by the Rev. Mr. WACHTER.
SHULTZE, imprisoned in the Adams Co. (PA) jail charged with the robbery of
    the house of Mr. WIREMAN, escaped Wednesday the 13th inst. A man
    answering his description (22 years of age & 6'2" tall) was seen
    travelling towards Waynesboro in Franklin Co.
WAGES, Nancy (Miss) of Baltimore County died on Friday last.
Fire at Mifflin Forge PA, between Gettysburg & Chambersburg destroyed
    property of Col. James D. PAXTON & T. STEVENS Wednesday morning last.
African Colonization of this town: Mrs. WILLIS, President; Mrs. VAN
    BIBBER, Vice President; Miss Lucretia VAN BIBBER & Miss Mary Ann
    SHRIVER secretaries. (Westminster)

30 November 1833
BILLINGSLEA, James L. Dr. of Uniontown married to Miss Susan, d/o the late
    Daniel HAINES, on Wednesday last by Rev. Daniel ZOLLICKOFFER.
FISHER, William, merchant, married Miss Jane Alricks, d/o Mr. Harmanus
    BOGGS of Baltimore on Tuesday evening last by Rev. Mr. BRECKENRIDGE.
GEYER, George Jr.: of Gettysburg married to Miss Maria COLE of this place
    on Thursday last by Rev. Mr. GUTELIUS.

10

7 December 1833
DELL, Henry married by Rev. Mr. M'GEE to Miss Sarah WEAVER, both of this
county.
EGE, Michael P. of Pine Grove Furnace married in Carlisle, on the 20th ult.
by Rev. Henry R. WILSON to Miss Jane Louisa d/o Major M'KINNEY of
Shippinsburg. (PA)
HILTLEBRIDLE, Jacob selling farm, intending to remove to the west. In
Frederick Co. 2 1/2 miles from Westminster, near turnpike to Littlestown;
adjoins lands of John FORMWALT, John BEGGS, etc., 97 acres with 2-story
house & 1 1/2 story lot shop building.
JONES, John (of John) late of Frederick Co., deceased, for sale 200 acres,
2-story stone dwelling & small stone kitchen attached. Bank barn, nearly
new, 65x25', with wagon shed & corn crib, spring house. Within 3 miles
of Union Mills, near main road from said Union Mills to Hanover & 6 miles
from latter. Bounded by lands of George GOBLE, John JONES Jr., Felty
ARHART, Henry CRUMRINE etc. John JONES Jr., executor.
LICHTENWALTER, Ephraim David died Friday the 29th ult. at residence of John
SHEETS, near Oxford, Adams Co., PA. Infant s/o Adam LICHTENWALTER of
Frederick Co., aged 9 months 25 days.
OREM, James Jr., his trial removed recently from Cambridge, was this week
in Somerset Co., convicted, sentenced 15 years for passing counterfeit
notes.

14 December 1833
CRUMBINE, William & STEVENSON, Charles getting out of the farming business,
selling personal property, 6 head of horses, etc.
HOLMES, Mrs. Susan, consort of Francis HOLMES of this place died Thursday
last, in the 23d year of her age.
MIDDLEKAUFF, Messers. D. M. & J. A., store in Hagerstown was robbed Monday
last; 2 suspects have been traced on the Baltimore Road.
SHARP, George W., late editor of the "Citizen" married to Miss Caroline R.
d/o Capt. Nicholas SNIDER Tuesday last by Rev. SMITH, all of Frederick.

28 December 1833
Frederick: The grand Jurors of MD in their official capacity visited
the Jail of said county & found it was in a very comfortable & healthy
condition. Those who visited were: Thomas CARLTON, Nicholas NORRIS,
John HEAD, Michael SULLIVAN, Thomas C. BRASHEAR, Joshua SMITH Jr., John
SMITH of George, John YOUNG, Daniel YEISER, John JONES, John SMITH, Jacob
POWDER, Joseph TALBOTT, Joseph WELTY, Edward MC BRIDE, William DURBIN,
James CASTLE, George H. WIESCHE, John LEASE, Peter NICHOLS.

—••●••—
4 January 1834
BANKERT, John, heirs selling farm of 95 acres within 1/2 mile of Union
Mills, near turnpike road leading from Westminster to Littlestown, adjoins lands of Isaac BANKERT, Robert CRAWFORD, Peter ERB &c. Big Pipe
Creek runs through property. 2 log dwelling houses, double barn, stables,
springhouse & other outbuildings. The whole property will be sold to the
widow's interest. J. Henry HOPPE, Agent.
BEAVER, John, sale of 119 acre farm in Baltimore Co., 2 miles from Westmin-
ster; Beaver Run pass through land, adjoins land of Jabe MURRAY & George
TRUMBO.
BIRNIE, C. seeks tenant for farm & a good blacksmith to let a house & shop
on the turnpike. In Thorndale, 3 miles from Taney-town.
DILL, John, tavern owner in Frederick, at which farmers & millers of
Frederick Co, are to meet regarding the repeal of the inspection law.
FEW, James Cornelius, indented apprentice of weaving business ran away from
John HARMAN 12 Nov. 1833. About 19 years of age, 5'6", sandy hair,
wearing black cloth coat & pantaloons & a white fur hat.

THE CARROLLTONIAN

4 January 1834
FISHER, John, Cashier of Bank of Westminster announces dividend.
FOGLE, David, offers house & lot (6 acres, 3 rods) within 300 yards of
  George CRABB's Mill on Big Pipe Creek, Frederick County.
GEIMAN, David, selling tavern stand presently occupied by Michael GREAT; on
  the Baltimore Turnpike 13 miles from the city, near Owings Mills, 2
  story-brick building.
HAYDEN, Bazil, manufacturer of hats thanks customers. Has no particular
  objection to take cash, but will take all kinds of produce in exchange.
HOPPE, J. H. (Mr.) runs store in Mt. Pleasant, Frederick County.
JONES, Philip, selling house & lot in Westminster.
KEEFER, David, tavern owner in Westminster.
KEMP, Henry Col., president of Orphans' Court of Frederick County, died
  Saturday last, in the 71st year of his age.
KUNS, Abraham, has discovered a complete & radical cure for cancer. (Ad)
MURRAY, John S., having determined to move to the Western country, selling
  property in Westminster.
NAIL, Jacob, late of Frederick County, dec'd., executor's sale of farm, 103
  acres; 1/2 mile of the Union Mills, on the main road from the mills to
  Hanover; adjoins lands of Andrew SHRIVER, David LEISTER, Peter ERB, John
  SLYDER &c. Includes tenant house & stable, now in the possession of John
  STONE, Jr. J. Henry HOPPE, executor.
RAITT, Charles H. continues stand No. 123, N. Howard St., Baltimore, 1 door
  from Franklin St., ready to receive all kinds of country produce.
REESE, Jacob, selling chestnut rails & water oak posts & house logs.
STANNER, Adam, late of Frederick County, dec'd., property sale 110 acres;
  said right, title, claim & interest was heretofore conveyed by John DEMAN
  to said dec'd by deed. 3 miles north from the Union Mills in Frederick
  County adjoins lands of John CRUMRINE, Jonathan STANNER &c. Frederick
  TRUMP, trustee.
THOMSON, Samuel Dr., meeting of the owners of Dr. Samuel Thomson's Family
  Rights held in Westminster, Frederick County, subject Botanic System of
  Medicine. Mr. MALEHORN will please provide a room.
Westminster Savings Institution list of officers: William WILLIS, Presi-
  dent; Jacob REESE, Treasurer. Directors: John ROOP, Jacob MATHIAS,
  William GRUMBINE, Jacob GRAMMER, John KUHN, Andrew POWDER, William
  CROUSE, Emanuel GERNAND, and Michael BARNITZ.
Letters remaining at the Post Office at Westminster 1 January 1834: Joseph
  ARNOLD, George BRUCE, Christian BOWERS, John COOK, Elizabeth COOK, Nancy
  ENSEY, George ECKLER, Rev. Jonathan FORREST, James GRAHAM, Charles
  HEAGEA, Jacob KEIM, Henry KNOTE, Elizabeth KEYS, Basil LUCAS, Susanna
  LOVEALL, Thomas MILRAY, Susan MOREHEAD, William MERCER, Ellen MYUH,
  Jacob MEARING, (?) MC CUMSEY, John RHINEHARD, Charles E. ROTTEKEN,
  Abraham RICHARDS, Catharine SHAROTS, George SHRIVER, Jacob SMITH, Henry
  WAMPLER, Emanuel WITHERS.   E. CRUMBACKER, Post Master.
Letters remaining at the Post Office at Taney Town 1 January 1834: Rev.
  Henry AURAND, Jacob BROWN, Elizabeth COVER, Jacob CORRELL Jr., Eliza
  DELOPLANE, Jacob FRINGER, Henry HESS, Rev. George W. KENEY, William KNOX,
  John NULL, John NANKIVELL, Samuel NEWCOMER, Emily J. RINEDOLLAR, George
  RINEHART, Honor RETT, Benjamin SHUNK, George SIX of Philip, Sylvester
  SPALDING, Joshua SEVOYER, William TOY. Hugh SHAW, Jr., Post Master

11 January 1834
AMERMAN, Rev. Mr., will preach in this place tomorrow morning.
BELL, Isaac, selling farm in Baltimore County, about 2 miles from Westmin-
  ster, adjoins lands of John BEAVER, Jabe MURRAY, George TRUMB & others.
  119 acres.
COBLER, Infant died by burning on Christmas day, child of Mrs. Mary & S.
  COBLER of Cumberland.

11 January 1834

DORSEY, Roderick of Frederick received 42 votes to serve on the Counsel to the Governor.

SHRIVER, Edward, attorney & soliciter in chancery. Office in Market Street, 2nd door from southwest corner of Patrick Street, Frederick.

SHRIVER, Francis, adv. for journeyman tanner; near Manchester, Balto. Co.

WILLIS, William, compelled to close his old books, requested all persons indebted to him to settle their accounts.

WINCHESTER, Gen. having resigned his office as President of the Baltimore & Susquehanna Rail Road Co.; James HOWARD, Esq. to succeed him.

18 January 1834

BRUCE, Francis Mrs., widow of the late Francis BRUCE, 5 miles above Cumberland on the National Road, had a fire at her tavern house. Mr. PERCY a boarder lost $500-$600. Fire originated from a stove pipe in the back building.

M'KILIP, Henry, died on Thursday week in Taney-town, youngest s/o James M'KILIP, in the 4th year of his age.

NICODEMUS, Philip, renting storehouse 5 miles west of Westminster; 3 miles east of New Windsor.

ROSE, John, Botanic Physician to deliver medical lecture at the home of Abraham WAMPLER. Thomas WINWOOD, President & John ROSE, Secretary of Tomsonian Group.

VAN BIBBER, Washington, renting farm on which he resides; includes dairy & lime kilns.

WAMPLER, Lewis, selling chestnut rails at residence 1 1/2 miles from Westminster, near Mr. Henry LEISTER's Mill.

WILLIS, Emily Georgiana, died Wednesday morning last, d/o Dr. William WILLIS, aged 4 years & 2 months.

YINGLING, Jacob, added as Director of Westminster Savings Institution.

MD State Temperance Society: Stevenson ARCHER, President; Alexander RANDALL, Secretary; Franklin ANDERSON, Esq. Vice President. Committee: Daniel MURRAY, Richard POTTS & John G. BLANCHARD.

25 January 1834

BEAVER, John, complainant; Elias ROBERTSON, Joseph RITTER & wife defen-dants, resulted in Trustee's public sale by virtue of Baltimore County Court, held at BATSON's Tavern near 24th mile stone on the turnpike from Baltimore to Westminster. James M. BUCHANAN, T. Parkin SCOTT, Trustees.

FEESER, Jacob, died Friday the 10th instant, of Frederick County, aged 70 years, 3 months & 11 days.

GIST, J. found stray cow October last; claim at "Long Farm" near Westminster.

M'IHENNY, A. sale of large brick house & lot, late the residence of Doctor BOYER, in the village of Union-town, Frederick County.

MATTHIAS, Henry, real estate of, late of Frederick County, dec'd, trustee sale of farm & 226 1/4 acres lying in Frederick County, 1 mile northwest from Frederick BACHMAN's mill & same distance from BOWER's Church; ad-joins lands of Peter BIXLER, heirs of the late Joseph MATTHIAS, George MATTHIAS Sr., within 5 miles of Manchester & 8 miles of Westminster. Property to be sold subject to the life estate of Mary MATTHIAS, widow of said deceased. J. Henry HOPPE, Trustee.

NEILSON, Ann Mrs., died Friday night the 17th instant, in the 47th year of her age, at her residence in the vicinity of Reisterstown (Baltimore Co.) after an unusually protracted & painful illness.

OTANN, Edward, superintendent of Baltimore Foundry & F. LUCAS, Jr. Agent.

1 February 1834

BISHOP, Jacob, late of Frederick County, dec'd., trustee's sale of farm, 123 acres, lying in Frederick County, about 2 miles from Union-Town &

THE CARROLLTONIAN

1 February 1834
within 1/2 mile of Westminster & Taney-Town Turnpike; adjoins lands of
David FOUTZ, Esq., Peter SHOEMAKER &c. Jacob MATHIAS, Trustee.
BRAMWELL, George, Esq. appointed Post Master at new Post Office established
at Finksburg.
GOULD, H. H. (Mr.) to open school in this place for improvement in writing
in a few days. He has been teaching in Baltimore.
POWDER, Jacob Sr., house & lot for sale in town of Westminster, nearly
opposite Mr. Jacob YINGLING's tannery.

8 February 1834
BENTLEY, Ann, dec'd, late of Frederick County, residence of dec'd in
Taney-Town for sale. Large 2-story house & lot; also furnishings. Also
property in Middleburg viz: large stone house, log house & lot in said
town, 14 acres adjoining town being part of tract called "Good Intent."
Abraham LICHTENWALTER, Executor.

15 February 1834
ELY, Hugh Col. representative from Baltimore County appealed to members
from the Eastern Shore to vote against the formation of Carroll County
from Baltimore & Frederick Counties as proposed by Mr. CARTER of
Montgomery County.
PRICE, Horatio, opening wagon-making business near the confluence of the 3
turnpikes, Westminster. Will manufacture wagons, ploughs, harrows, etc.

22 February 1834
BURNS, David married Miss Mary Ann d/o Mr. George WINEBRENNER of the
vicinity of Hanover. (PA)
DAY, (?), stone mason, hung himself at a public house in Frederick on
Monday last.
DOW, Lorenzo, preacher, died on Monday last (Georgetown, D.C.); preached in
the American West & Ireland.
DULOP, James Esq. of Chambersburg (PA), elected to the State Legislature
from Franklin County by a larger majority over Robert MACLAY.
POOLE, Daniel J. renting a lime kiln & 80 acres of land, 1 1/2 miles from
Graceham, Frederick Co. Apply 5 miles from Middleburg, near the Monocacy.
STEVENS, Thaddeus Esq. of Gettysburg (PA) has announced as a candidate for
the Vice Presidency.
WIRT, William Hon., Son of Maryland, died at Washington attending the
sessions of the Supreme Court, in the 62nd year of his age.

1 March 1834
CROUT, Hezekiah, commenced tinning business in the shop formerly occupied
by the Widow CROUT. Old pewter will be taken in exchange for ware. Will
attend to the spouting of houses any distance under ten miles.
HEBBARD, Ann (Mrs.) died Tuesday morning week, after an illness of less
than 3 days, consort of Dr. William B. HEBBARD of Frederick County.
RICHARDSON, B. H., Agent for the Young Man's Temperance Society, Balto.

8 March 1834
BOYD, Robert, lumber merchant selling white & yellow pine, Wrightsville,
York County, PA.
CANNON, Minors, formerly assistant Engineer of the steamboat Pocaahontas &
Potomac, & lastly of The Lady of the Lake; murdered by being stabbed &
found lying at Little Water St. between Commerce St. & Rothery's Lane.
Investigation resulted in the commitment of William TAYLOR, who has been
some time trading in oysters between this place & New York in the sloop
Dandy & Abraham HOUSEMAN, a carpenter. CANNON was about 35 years old.
FRINGER, Jacob, renting tavern stand on the Baltimore Turnpike, 1 mile from
Westminster, presently occupied by Mr. John COLEMAN.

14

8 March 1834

HITCHCOCK, I. Irvine, of American Farmer Establishment, No. 16 S. Calvert
St., Baltimore, selling nationwide his annual supply of field & garden
seeds from Europe & his own garden. Publishes the AMERICAN FARMER weekly
at this establishment.

MOTT, Edward Esq., lawyer of Milford, PA, committed suicide by shooting
himself with a pistol.

SHRIVER, Andrew, of Union Mills, will sell or rent store & tavern stand for
many years occupied as a store by Gen. JAMESON, on the turnpike 5 miles
below Westminster; 60-70 acres with large house & barn.

15 March 1834

FISHER, J., Lost Saturday last, on the turnpike road, between Westminster &
Reisterstown, a red morocco wallet. Contained some money, among which is
recollected a 10 & 5 dollar note of the Cumberland Bank of Allegany & 10
dollar note of new emission of the Bank of Westminster. Also sundry
papers among which is a note drawn by George BELTZHOOVER, agent in favor
of John SHOWACRE dated Feb. 1834. Finder will be liberally rewarded upon
returning it to J. FISHER, Bank of Westminster.

FISHER, John, brags in letter to the editor of his sow "Bonnets" who
produced litter totals of 90 piglets between March 1831 & March 1834.

GORSUCH, Richard, died Saturday last, of the vicinity of this place, in the
73d year of his age.

M'KILLIP, John, died monday last in Taney-town, 80th year of his age.

PRICE, Horatio, selling iron in Westminster.

SHRIVER, Isaac, President, Bank of Westminster.

SHRIVER, Isaac, renting tavern stand, formerly occupied by himself &
latterly by Mr. FORRY. Situated in the central part of Westminster.
Includes stables, sheds, &c. with large yard for wagons & carriages.

WEBB, Joseph B., Agricultural inspector for Frederick County.

Franklin Academy: Nathan C. BROOKS, A. M. Principal & Prof. of Languages,
Elisha J. HALL, Prof. of Mathematics. Students: Jeremiah, Jesse & John
AILER, Henry H. & Nehemiah BERRYMAN, Edwin & Christopher C. BROOKS,
Alfred & Allen BUCKINGHAM, Charles S. COLLINS, Isaac N. DICKSON, Henry H.
DUCKER, William FRESH, Edmund C. GARDNER, James JOHNSON, George W. LARSH,
Philip D. THOMAS, Greenberry W. WEAVER, Edward WHEELER - all of
Reisterstown; Charles W. & Edwin BROOKS, John M. CLEMANS, George B.
COFFIN, Charles S. CUTLER, William F. DE LA ROCHE, William K. GARDNER,
William GRAFF, George W. MYERS, James H. ORR, Thomas SPRIGG, William H.
WALL - all of Baltimore; George CLARK, William H. COCKEY, Robert & Silas
W. CONN, Thomas CROMWELL, William F. DEAN, Joshua & William GENT, Henry
GORE, Thomas GRIFFITH, George W. HALL, Ed. J., Fr. & J. M'H. HOLLINGS-
WORTH, William KING, John B. KNIGHT, Frederick H. OWINGS, John PEDEN,
Lenis RUPP, Ebenezer WINWOOD, John W. & Nimrod YINGLING - all of Baltimore
County; Richard & George GIST of Westminster; Nathan & Stephen R. GORE,
Nathan M. HARDEN, Randolph J. SHIPLEY & Jesse S. WORCELL - all of
Freedom. Boarding is $80 per ann. Tuition: Classics $24 per ann.,
mathematics $20 per ann., English branches $12 per ann. Horatio
HOLLINGSWORTH, President, Jno. SUMWALT, Treas., Silas LARSH, M.D.,
Secretary. Trustees - Louis L. DICKSON, M.D., Arthur HILL, William
DWYER, Philip REISTER, Jeremiah DUCKER, John HOLLINGSWORTH.

6 December 1834

BRADY, John; murdered, trial held in Hagerstown November 29th. Patrick
RYAN & wife tried, verdict in each case was not guilty. RYAN is a
contractor on the Chesapeake & Ohio Canal. Deceased was in RYAN's
employment as cook & on the night before his death quarreled with Mrs.
RYAN.

CIRCLE, Barbara (Mrs.), died Sunday last, wife of David CIRCLE of
Westminster District, in the 31st year of her age.

15

6 December 1834

DURBIN, William; now occupies Store House belonging to Francis HENRY, selling dry goods & groceries. (Westminster)

ENSEY, Perry G., intending to remove to the west, selling 1/2 acre of land on which is erected a brick house; also another 1 acre lot adjoining the turnpike from Westminster to Gettysburg. On the same day will be offered a kiln containing 100,000 well burnt brick, household & kitchen furniture & 150 water oak posts, all hewed, & part of them morticed.

FICKLE, Daniel, dec'd, of Frederick County, George CRABBS, administrator.

FISHER, Rachel (Miss), died on Monday last. Her afflictions were great & trying, but it is gratifying to know that she bore all with the humble meekness of the Christian.

FRINGER, Jacob Sr., dec'd, by order of Orphans Court of Frederick County sale of the described property, wagon, carry-all, windmill, sorrel mare, cow, horse gears & farming utensils.

GIST, Joshua, will rent the farm on which he resides, known by the name of "Long Farm", near Westminster, 400 acres. Apply to GIST on Liberty Road, 25 miles from Baltimore.

HARRITT, John, candidate for sheriff.

HULL, Andrew's creditors notified & warned to file their claims before 6 December to receive their dividends. J. Henry HOPPE & John BAUMGARTNER, trustees.

LIND, John, being anxious to remove to the Western country, selling tavern stand in Union-town, Frederick County. Attached are stables, sheds, spring & smoke houses, & warehouse. A room in the house for a shop is now rented for $20 per annum. Also a lot, 8 acres, near Uniontown, under good fencing. Also a lot of timberland, 2 acres, 3/4 of a mile from town. Also 1 town lot, an alley lot. Also 1 coloured boy 11 years old to serve until 21. Also 1 blooded colt, 1 8-day clock, several watches, 2 stoves & pipe, etc. If not sold, tavern stand will be rented.

MC COLLUM, John & GERAND, Emanuel in the Victualling business & furnish first quality Beef every Tuesday & Friday mornings. (Westminster)

PETERS, George, late of Frederick County, executor's sale of farm & tavern stand; on main road from Frederick City to York, about 4 1/2 miles from Taney-town & same distance from Petersburg, (Littlestown); 253 3/4 acres, house & large Switzer barn, understory stone, upperstory logs, large log stable, wagon shed & corn crib & distilery-house. House has been occupied as a public house for 40 years & is extensively known. Lewis PETERS, executor.

PORTER, Gustavus, on the Liberty Road about 2 1/2 miles west of Freedom, holding meeting of the friends on the contemplated new county. Also meeting to be held at Mr. LAMOTT's tavern in Hampstead.

REESE, Jacob, selling 20,000' pine boards, very low for cash.

SHIPLEY, William Jr. wants sawyer. Selling rails, posts, house logs & wood. Has 10,000 chestnut rails, seasoned $52 per thousand, green $26; 1,000 seasoned round & mauled Water Oak posts 6 1/4 cents each. Roanoke Farm, 3 miles south of Westminster on the Washington road.

VAN BIBBER, Washington, runs grist mills with custom of Grinding & Sawing.

VANCE, Valentine of Frederick County, Joseph KEEFER Justice of the Peace testifies that he brought before him a stray sorrel horse.

WELLER, J.'s vegetable rheumatic compound & Indian panacea. Joseph W. BIGGS, M.D., of Graceham & Emanuel GERNAND of Westminster recommend it.

WENTZ, Rachel, renting a part of the brick house & lot in which she now resides; on the Gettysburg turnpike, 1/3 of a mile from the "Forks" of Westminster.

YINGLING, Mary Jane (Miss) departed this transitory existence Tuesday the 25th ultimo, after a short but painfull illness of 3 days; eldest d/o Peter & Sarah YINGLING, near Westminster; 15th year of her age.

20 December 1834

BARNITZ, Michael, spelts wanted at the Westminster Brewery.

BECK, Nimrod, a fire originated in his cabinet shop in Woodsboro, which burned to the ground; threatening the entire eastern section of town.

BOYER, Jacob, died Monday last, one of the oldest citizens of Frederick, who for the last 30 years was crier in the Court of Frederick, in the 80th year of his age.

BRIEN, William Coleman, died at the Antietam Iron Works on the 11th instant; youngest son of the late John BRIEN, 22d year of his age.

CRAPSTSER, William L., meeting held at his tavern near Taney-town in favor of the formation of a New County.

DORSEY, John W. Dr., of Liberty Town, Frederick County, had honorary degree of Doctor of Medicine conferred upon him by the Washington Medical College of Baltimore. He was surgeon in the Navy of the U.S. during the Tripolitan war under Commodore Edward PREBLE.

HEBBARD, E. B., closing store accounts. Pay up.

HICKLEY, Thomas, desirous of removing westward selling his farm of 128 acres, 1 1/2 miles from Taney-town on the turnpike leading to Westminster; adjoins lands of Maj. John MC KALEB, Henry SHRINER &c. Log house with brick back building, log barn, &c.

KINZER, John Jr., of Frederick County married to Ann GORE of Baltimore County on the 2d instant by Rev. Mr. MONROE.

LITTLE, Mr.,meeting of friends of New County held at his tavern in Freedom.

MANNING, John, Baltimore County, deceased, Orphan's Court notice.

MURPHY, John Jr., about to leave Westminster, selling household effects.

POOLE, Eli married to Miss Elizabeth BIGGS by the Rev. David F. SCHAEFFER, both of Frederick County.

SHRIVER, Joseph Esq. of Cumberland married to Henrietta J., eldest d/o James H. CAUSTEN Esq. of Washington on the 4th instant by Rev. Mr. SARGENT. (Washington)

SPRENKLE, Mary; murdered, trial of CONNER commenced in Frederick County Court Wednesday last.

Citizens of Baltimore county convened agreeably to public notice at Mr. PORTER's Tavern, Freedom District. William BROWN Esq. chair, Benjamin DORSEY secretary. Col. Joshua C. GIST, Benjamin DORSEY, Eli BENNETT, William SHIPLEY & Nathan GORSUCH proposed resolutions. Request Messrs. ELY, SHOWER, WISE & ORRICK, members elect of this county to obtain passage of a law for a new county.

—•@•—

21 February 1835

FEESER, Adam Sr., late of Frederick County, trustee's sale of farm 2 1/2 miles from Union Mills, on the main road from Bachman's Mills to Hanover, adjoins lands of Adam FEESER Jr., Valentine EHRHART &c, 111A-2 rods- 25 perches; double log dwelling & barn, wagon shed & stone spring-house. Also selling lot adjoining above farm, 9 3/4 acres; also another lot adjoining farm 26 3/4 acres; also lot 17 1/2 acres adjoining the Hanover road, under good fences. Adam FEESER, Jr., Trustee.

HENRY, Francis, sale at his tavern in Westminster offering a stock of merchandise, store house & lot, brick dwelling, stable; also 2 lots 1/2 acre each situated at the "Forks."

MALEHORN, John, agent for Dr. Samuel THOMSON's medical books for Baltimore County.

14 March 1835

ATLEE, Isaac, will sell or rent house & lot in New Windsor presently occupied by Dr. Jesse L. WARFIELD. Has stable, carriage-house & wood-house.

BEITLER, Daniel, supplies fresh oysters, located opposite Mr. TOPPER's tavern.

14 March 1835
CULBERTSON, J. F., has taken over the Westminster Hotel, formerly occupied
by I. SHRIVER.
DUKEHART, Joseph & Co., Woodenware & Fishing Tackle Warehouse, No. 101 1/2
Baltimore St., between South & Calvert Streets. Carry weavers' shuttles
& Reeds, Nets, Wash-boards, Baskets, Marbles, Tops & Bandy Balls;
Kitchen, Parlor & Smiths' Bellows, etc.
HAINES, Thomas, late of Frederick County, sale late at the late residence
of the said dec'd., near the property known by the name of Mordecai
HAINES' mills, selling all personal property. Catharine HAINES & John
WEAVER, Administrators.
HARDING, James M., candidate for sheriff of Frederick County.
HEBBARD, E. B. Dr., opening store in Westminster has fresh supply of
Medicines & Drugs; offers services of medicine, surgery & obstetrics.
HOUCK, Henry, candidate for sheriff of Frederick County.
KEEFFER, Joseph, renting store room with cellar & warehouse, connected with
his tavern on turnpike from Baltimore to Chambersburg in Frederick
County, near the Silver Run Church. Now occupied as a store by Messrs.
GORE & HOUCK.
KELLER, John, of Westminster, selling blacksmith's tools.
KEPHART, David, seeks young man 14 to 18 years to learn milling business.
Also selling Timothy Hay by the ton. Brick Mill near Union Town.
KOONTZ, George, late of Frederick County, sale of estate consisting of 181
acres, two log dwelling-houses, each 2-stories, large log barn, log
stable & spring house. Land lies on Turnpike from Petersburg to
Westminster near the Silver Run Church, bounded by lands of John FEESER,
Joseph KEEFER, Henry BECHTEL & others. Tract sold subject to the widows
right of dower. Abraham KOONTZ, Trustee.
LAFLUREE, Elizabeth, intending to remove from Westminstser, will sell at
her residence opposite Mr. YINGLING's tannery, mantle clock, sideboard,
tin-plate stove, rifle, pistol, jewellery & show window.
LEISTER, John, removing to the west, selling farm on which he now resides 4
1/2 miles from Westminster & 2 1/2 from Uniontown, on the Westminster &
Hagerstown turnpike; adjoins lands of Daniel MYERS & Joseph MYERS. 289
acres, brick house with 4 rooms on lower floor and 4 rooms above, 2
cellars under the house & a large kitchen attached; large barn, nearly
new, part brick & part stone (120'x30', with an overshute of 7 feet);
wagon, dry, smoke, wash & spring houses. Also a tenant house on the
farm, nearly new. Also selling personal property the same day.
LIGHTNER, Amos, married to Miss Ann FISHER, both of this place, on Tuesday
last by the Rev. Mr. RUTHRAUFF.
LOGUE, Joshua, keeps a supply of the very best candles at Jacob REESE's
store in Westminster.
PEDICORD, Humphrey, selling house & lot on the Westminster Turnpike, 21
miles from Baltimore, 7 miles from Westminster; has 2 stables.
REESE, Jacob, sells Houck's Panacea by Jacob HOUCK of Baltimore.
SHRINER, Jacob, collecting accounts due, Big Pipe Creek.
SHRIVER, Isaac, Esq., President of Temperance Association of Westminster,
calling special meeting where Revd. Mr. SMEADMER invited to speak.
SHRIVER, Isaac, President of the Bank of Westminster.
SHRIVER, Isaac, renting tavern stand formerly occupied by himself &
latterly by Mr. FORRY, in central Westminster. Attached to house are
stables & sheds.
STEVENSON, Basil D., removing to the West, selling farm on which he resides
containing 180 acres, 2 miles south of Westminster in Frederick County.
Buildings all nearly new.
TOPPER, Joseph, Auctioneer, informs the public that he is available for
those who want crying done in the most exquisite manner.

14 March 1835
TRUMBO, Lewis, removing to the western country, selling town property at
the Forks of the 3 turnpikes in Westminster, 1/4 acre, 2-story log house
(rough casted) 18' front, part of which is occupied by a store.
WAMPLER, Abraham, renting tavern stand in Westminster, formerly kept by
subscriber & many others for many years.
WILLIS, William, President of Westminster Savings Institution.
Liberty Fire Company of Baltimore selling old engine. Apply to C. M.
KEYSER, President, Howard St. or David MARTIN, Fayette St., Balto.
Notice to Bridge Builders: Proposals being received to build a Bridge
across Toms Creek, on road from Frederick to Emmittsburg where the old
Bridge now stands, one span of 74'. To be built after the plan of
Williams' Ferry or any other as good. Signed, Frederick TROXEL, Felix B.
TANEY & John GRABILL.
Notice to Bridge Builders: Clerk of Levy Court of Frederick County taking
proposals for construction of bridge over the Catoctin Creek near Toms on
the old Hagerstown road. Apply to Thomas SPRINGER & Solomon FORREST,
Members of the Court or to John MC NEEL.

28 March 1835
BAILE, Eliza, died Sunday last, d/o Ludwick BAILE, Esq. of Westminster
District.
COCKEY, J., having taken HUSSEY's Wheatfield Inn in Baltimore, renting
tavern stand (house) he presently occupies in Westminster.
CROUTE, Hezekiah, will carry on his tinning business on larger scale, also
will attend to the making & putting up of spouting.
DAVIS, Walter, of Wakefield, Westminster District, died Sunday last.
DUKEHART, Valerius, publishers agent, selling anti-Masonic publications.
DURBIN, Nicholas, selling lot of 5 acres near Westminster, adjoining lands
of Joseph ORENDORFF, William & John ROBERTS & DURBIN's farm. 2-story log
house & small frame barn, frame Spring & Wash house.
EDIE, John R., having relinquished duties as Principal of the Union (Westminster) Academy; being about to remove from this place asks payment of
tuition. Mr. THAYER will take charge of the institution.
GAMBLE, William, continues to carry on the Factory on Little Pipe Creek,
known as "Shepherd's Factory," where he will conduct the woollen
manufacturing of cloth, cassinet, flannel, broad blanketing & linsey,
etc. He receives work at Joseph POOLE's, WILSON's stores at Liberty,
Benjamin BOND's tavern on the Liberty Road, MAURER's mill on Sam creek,
Henry KOONS on the Frederick & York road, Hugh SHAW's & John B. BOYLE's
stores in Taneytown, MEHRING's mill in Bruceville, George CRABB's mill on
Big Pipe Creek, David HAPE's & John DELAPLANE's stores in Middleburg, &
John STRAWSBURG's in Johnsville.
HALVERSTADT, Peter, at his late residence selling for cash by virtue of
sundry writs of Fierifaces out of Frederick County Court 50 bushels corn,
a lot of cherry, poplar & maple boards & a lot of slabs, baskets, jugs,
bottles, apple paring machine, etc. Late the property of said HALVER-
STADT--seized & taken at the suits of Jacob ERB, Barbara HESSON, Peter
MOCK & others. Mahlon TALBOTT, Sheriff & Thomas GURLEY.
HIBBERT, Mrs., died Sunday last at the residence of her son near New
Windsor; at an advanced age.
JONES, Margaretta, died Wednesday last, aged 9 years, youngest d/o Mr.
Philip JONES of Westminster; died of "Gangrene of the face, supervening
on scarlet fever."
OURSLER, Henry, cabinet maker at the "Forks" where he manufactures side-
boards, bureaus, secretary, cubboards, tables, coffins, etc.
STEAVENSON, Harriet Frances, died Friday the 20th instant, youngest d/o Mr.
Charles STEAVENSON, aged 8 years, 1 month & 14 days.
THAYER, N. H., renting the two lower rooms of house lately occupied by him.

THE CARROLLTONIAN

28 March 1835
THAYER, Nathaniel H., Principal of Classical & Mathematical School of this
town will unite his school with the Union Acadamy. References:
Washington VAN BIBBER, William WILLIS, Joshua COCKEY, Jacob MATHIAS,
Jacob YINGLING, Jacob REESE, E. CRUMBACKER, John S. MURRAY, S. FORRY, M.
BARNITZ, John K. LONGWELL.
Announcing as Candidates: Hon. James TURNER (of Dug Hill) for Congress in
in District composed of Baltimore & Harford Counties & Col. Anthony
KIMMEL for 6th District for Congress.
Candidates for Sheriff: Henry HOUCK, John HARRITT, Thomas GURLEY, John
BAUMGARTNER & George BOWLUS.
Title of Acts Passed at the Session of 1834-35: An act for the relief of
Margaret DODS of Frederick County. To make valid the partition of real
estate in Frederick county involving Henry CLAGGET & Julia CLAGGETT his
wife of the one part, & Grafton DUVALL & Elizabeth DUVALL his wife of the
other part, 25 June 1821, recorded in Liber J. S. No. 13, folio 545. An
act authorizing Levy Court of Frederick County a sum of money to defray
the funeral expenses of Edward O'BRIEN, a revolutionary soldier. An act
to lay out & open a road from HARNE's Old Field in Baltimore County to
Lisbon in Anne Arundel County. An act for benefit of P. PINCUS of
Baltimore County. An act for benefit of Lydia EVERT, George BRUCE,
Isaac BRUCE & David BRUCE of Frederick County. An act to divorce
Margaret CALAHAN of Frederick from her husband Patrick CALAHAN. An act
for benefit of James CARLIN of Frederick County. An act to make valid a
deed from Bene S. PIGMAN to Henry MOTTER dated 12 June 1834 & recorded in
Liber J. S. No. 20, Folio 226, etc. in Frederick County. An act
authorizing leasing of lands in Baltimore County in which Henry Payson
NORRIS, a minor, is interested.

11 April 1835
BEITLER, Daniel, will commence butchering on Wednesday at his establishment
nearly opposite Mr. TOPPER's tavern.
BILLINGSLEA, J. H., renting tavern stand in Union-town occupied for many
years by David STEM.
CARMICHAEL, William, of Wye, E. Shore, Md. wrote letter to editor in
reference to farming.
DURBIN, Nicholas married on the 2nd instant by the Rev. Jonathan FORREST to
Miss Sophia BAILE, both of Westminster District.
GERNAND, Charlotte, died of Scarlatina; daughter & only child of Mr.
Emanuel GERNAND, of this place, in the 5th year of her age. (no date)
HARRITT, Cecilia Loretta Miss, died in Emmitsburg on the 4th instant,
second d/o Major John HARRITT, in the 23rd year of her age.
HARSNEPE, Alice, deceased of Frederick County. Joshua SMITH, Jr.,
administrator of her personal estate.
HARWOOD, Richard, (of Thomas) died on Saturday last at Annapolis, was
Adjutant General of the State.
MC KEEHAN, Samuel Livingston, late Editor of the Frederick Citizen. . . .
terminated his existence by shooting a pistol ball through his head.
MARTIN, William Bond, Hon., died on the 3d instant, Chief Justice of the
4th Judicial District in the 66th year of his age.
PARKE, Joseph M., principal of Manchester Academy married to Miss Amanda,
d/o George MATTER, Esq. of Manchester by the Rev. Jacob ALBERT.
RICHARDS, George & Richard, selling ground rents of lots in Manchester &
Hampstead in Baltimore County.
WEBSTER, C. W., will commence a school, Brick Meeting Room at the Forks.
WEISER, D. P. & Co., selling 200,000 shingles of the Codorus Navigation &
300,000' of seasoned boards at his market on N. George St., York, Pa.
List of Letters remaining in the Post-Office at Westminster as of 1 July
1835: Jackson BLIZZARD, Mrs. Catharine BOYERS, David CRABBS, Benjamin

11 April 1835
DAVIS, Charles DEVILBISS, Archibald DORSEY, Justes KIEFFER, William M.
KEITH, John MC LAUGHLIN, David MIDDLECOFF, Mrs. Susannah MITTEN, Jacob
NULL, Horatio PRICE, Joshua PLOWMAN, William POWEL, Christopher RANDALS,
David ROOP, Chose RAYNER, Peter SOMMER, John SOUDON, Jacob STONESIFER,
William STEVENSON, John SHAFER, Adam TROFF, Amon TIPTON, Miss Margaret
TAYLOR, Mr. UMBAUGH, Henry WEARHEIM, W. WINCHESTER Esq., Andrew WERBLE, &
Joseph YOUNG.   E. CRUMBACKER, Post Master.
List of Letters remaining in the Post-Office at Taney Town as of 1 April
1835: Henry BLACK, Mary CALDWELL, Jesso. DAVIDSON, William FISHER, Daniel
FUSS, Eliza. GRIBLE, Appolona HEFFNER, John HARNER, Samuel HESS, George
HESS, John HAHN, Abraham HAYS, John HANN, Joseph KOON, Peter KEEFER,
David MARTIN, John MC ALLESTER, Peter MARK, John MAUS, David MERRING,
Abraham NULL, William PAXTON, Samuel RECK, Michael REAVER, Miss Mary SIX,
Peter SHOEMAKER, John SWITZER, David STOUFFER, John WHITELOATHER, James
L. WALKER, & Jacob YAKE. Hugh SHAW, Post Master.
Westminster Savings Institution: Newly-elected officers: John ROOP, Jacob
MATHIAS, Thomas WELLS, John SHAFER, John KUHN Jr., Andrew POUDER, Emanuel
GERNAND, Jacob YINGLING & William KROUSE. Dr. William WILLS, President;
Jacob REESE, Treasurer.
Commissioners appointed Frederick County Court to whether a road should
open beginning at Frizzlesburg on the Taney-town road, then to Samuel
MESSENGER's mill, to the Stone road, and thence to Silver Run Church, to
intersect the Reisterstown turnpike road at or near Joseph KEEFER's
tavern. John SMITH, John BAUMGARTNER & David FOUTZ.
Appointments by the Methodist Protestant Church at Conference in Baltimore
Wednesday last for the Md. District, Dr. John S. REESE, President. Levi
R. REESE & Asa SHINN, Baltimore; William COLLIER, East Baltimore; John W.
PORTER, Georgetown; Augustus WEBSTER, Alexandria; William KESLY, Mt.
Olive; Josiah VARDEN, Tabernacle; Robert WILSON & Henry MYERS, Anne
Arundel; Hugh DOYLE, John W. EVERIST & A. LIPSICUM, Pipe Creek; Nicholas
DORSEY & Eli HINKLE, sup, Reisterstown; Daniel E. REESE Jr. & Victor
WILSON, Deer Creek; Reuben T. BOYD, New Market; Bignel APPELLY, Ship-
pensburg; James CROUSE, Juniate; Isaac WEBSTER & J. M. TALLINTYR,
Williamsport; William SEXSMITH & Augustus G. GROVE, Princes Ann & Snow
Hill; George HERITAGE & William MC GUIGAN, Kent; Samuel RAWLEY & Dr.
Daniel DAVIS, Queen Anne's & Talbot; Joshua RUTLEDGE, Caroline; George D.
HAMILTON & Thomas G. CLAYTON, Dorchester & Sussex; Elias WILLIAMS, Prince
William & Conference Missionary Thomas H. STOCKTON.
Congressional Candidates, 6th District: William C. JOHNSON, James M.
COALE, Anthony KIMMEL, Roderick DORSEY & Abdiel UNKEFER.

2 May 1835
APPLER, Isaac, 2 of his dwellings near Union-town entirely consumed by fire
Monday evening last.
BEEBY, Nancy, seeking information on John HOFFMAN, who resided in Belmont
county, Ohio 1 year ago, left there taking with him her son, named Enoch
BEEBY, about 2 years 8 months old. She would deem it a great kindness to
hear of him. (Gettysburg Sentinel)
CROOK, John, selling 1 lot of ground in Mt. Vernon, 2 1/2 miles south of
New Windsor & 1 miles east of MAURER's mill, 1 1/2 acres & 2-story house
& store house; also lot of ground in same town, 1/4 acre with cabinet-
maker's shop; also wood lot, 4 1/2 acres with house.
GARNER, William Asbury, died in Manchester Friday the 24th ultimo, s/o Mr.
Jarret GARNER, merchant, lately of Union-town, aged 8 years & 8 months.
HEBBARD, Ebenezer B., holding auction of dry goods, groceries, hardware,
bar iron, cast steel, hollow-ware & earthenware, medicines, oils, paints,
etc. & closing partnership of Ebenezer B. HEBBARD & William B. HEBBARD.
KINNER, Jesse, by writs issued by William ZOLLICKEFFER, justice of the
peace for Frederick County, selling at Middleburg all right, title,

21

2 May 1835
    Interest & claim of his to 1 acre of land with improvements, known by Lot
    No. 21, part of Williams' addition to Middleburg. Late property of said
    KINNER, seized & taken at the suits of John DELAPLANE & John CLABAUGH.
LIND, William, sale at his residence near Tany Town, all right title,
    interest and estate of his, of, in and to 63 acres of land, late his
    property, seized and taken at the suit of George WILT & Abraham NULL.
MYERS, George, at Centre Mills Factory on Meadow Branch, cards wool. Will
    receive wool at Mr. BROWN's store, Frizzlesburg; Mr. Jacob MORELOCK's
    tavern, William ROBERTS' store Uniontown, Messrs. SWOPE's store in
    Taneytown, Mr. David BUFFINGTON's mills Big Pipe Creek, Mr. Thomas
    METCALF's Blacksmith's shop.
NORRIS, John, died on the 15th ultimo, at his residence near Middleburg.
PARSONS, Mason, candidate for sheriff for Frederick County.
RAYMOND, James, new residence at the North middle House in the brick row of
    dwellings on Court St., fronting the est [sic] & extending to Second
    Street; office in basement. (Attorney at Law, Frederick)
SHEPHERD, N., of Richmond, VA, informs the public that he is the original
    discoverer of Junkins Ointment & holds the patent. Testimony by: William
    K. NEWMAN of Cumberland; A. I. BARNEY of New Market; J. A. BENTZ of
    Baltimore; Mr. C. HERSTONS of Frederick County; Mr. David BROOKHART
    tavern keeper at Boonsboro; Messrs. L. & R. T. LOWNES merchants at
    Cumberland; C. HERSTENS at Middletown Valley, Frederick County;
    Christopher LONG & John COLE of Frederick County. Sold by: Jacob REESE,
    Westminster; William ROBERTS, Union-Town; Daniel H. SWOPE, Taney-town;
    SHORB & GROVER, Emmitsburg; J. ZIMMERMAN, New-Windsor; Jeremiah DUCKER,
    Reisterstown; John MURRAY, Hampstead; NAILL & ENGLE, Sams Creek; Henry
    STIERS, Middleburg; George COX, Liberty District.
WAMPLER, Lewis, selling 2,000 prime chestnut rails, 1 mile below
    Westminster.
Whig Voters of Taney-town District will meet at SULTZER's Hotel to elect
    delegates for convention at New Market May next. Creagerstown District
    voters will meet at BECKENBAUGH's; New-Market District will meet at
    SCHELL's; Buckeys-town District will meet at Allen SAINS tavern in
    Buckeys-Town; Woodsborough District will meet at Isaac LYNN's tavern in
    Woodsborough; Jefferson District will meet at S. S. CHURCH's tavern in
    Jefferson. Candidates for 6th Congressional District: William C.
    JOHNSON, James M. COALE, Anthony KIMMEL, Roderick DORSEY, Abdiel UNKEFER.
Bank of Westminster, newly elected Directors: Isaac SHRIVER, W. VAN BIBBER,
    Jesse SLINGLUFF, Jacob REESE, Jacob MATHIAS, Andrew POUDER, Abraham
    WAMPLER, David KEPHART, Burgess NELSON & David GEIMAN.

9 May 1835
GOOD, W. A., Secretary, Maryland Classis meeting held at Woodstock, said
    classis will convene 10 May 1835 in Waynesboro, PA.
KEEFER, Frederick, late of Frederick County, Jacob MATHIAS, Administrator.
LEISTER, James, carrying on his carding & fulling business at the Fulling
    mill of David LEISTER, 1 mile from mills of Andrew SHRIVER, Esq. Wool
    taken at the following places: David LEISTER's mill, 1 mile from West-
    minster; Peter HULL's tan-yard, Silver Run; Samuel MESSENGER's mill, Bear
    Branch; Henry CASSELL's mill, Little Pipe Creek; Washington VAN BIBBER's
    mill, Little Pipe Creek; Nimrod STEVENSON's store, Westminster.
POOL, William Henry, died on the 19th ultimo, s/o Mr. Albinos POOL, aged 4
    years & 7 months.
SHIPLEY, William Jr., operates saw mill. Orders left with Mr. George
    WARFIELD at his store, Mr. Jacob REESE or his son George S. D. SHIPLEY in
    the office of Drs. WILLIS & FORRY, Westminster.
WEAVER, ---- Mrs., died Friday morning last, of this place, 98 years old.
Whig Voters: Convened at house of Mr. LINN in Woodsborough. Motion of Mr.
    Philip HINES, George BARRICK (of Jacob) called to chair; Joshua DOUB

9 May 1835
secretary. Committee: Elias CRUTCHLEY, George M. POTTS, S. G. COCKEY,
Dr. T. W. JOHNSON, C. SHRINER & Col. Noah PHILLIPS. Capt. FULTON & Dr.
GOLDSBOROUGH made motions. Committee: Capt. FULTON, Jacob ROOT, David
HINES, Lewis BALTZELL, Dr. GOLDSBOROUGH, George BARRICK of Peter, Gideon
D. CRUMBAUGH, Dr. SIMM & Joseph DELAPLANE.
Whig Voters: Met in Creagerstown at Mr. BECKENBAUGH's tavern. Col. Jacob
CRAMER, chair; William P. JONES, Secretary. Committee: Dr. GOLDSBOROUGH,
Z. KUHN, Valentine SHYROCK, Martin EICHELBERGER & William H. GRIMES.
Committee: Dr. Robert C. CUMMING, William P. JONES, Zebulon KUHN, Warner
T. GRIMES & Valentine SHYROCK.

16 May 1835
ADAMS, William, tried & convicted in Baltimore of murder of Capt. TILDEN,
sentenced by Judge GLENN; execution May 20th.
BALLS, Merritt Mr., employed on Baltimore & Washington Railroad, found
Sunday morning in his chamber at Three Tun Tavern almost dead. He
committed suicide by drinking laudanum. A few days previous he had been
robbed of $200 & that loss is to have induced him to resort to death.
FISHER, John, Cashier of Bank of Westminster, announces dividend.
JUDEK, Mr., about 14 miles from Baltimore on the Reisterstown Road, found
missing trunk on his property cut from the mail stage.
M'COLLUM & GERNAND, dissolved partnership in butchering business.
MONKUR, John C. S. Dr., appointed Professor surgery & surgical Anatomy in
the Washington Medical College of Baltimore.
PEEBLES, Robert H. Dr., died after practicing medicine for 14 years in
Vandalia, Illinois. A native of Shippensburg, PA. Left wife & 1 child.
SHIPLEY, William, died Monday 4th inst., of Freedom District, Balto. Co.
Meeting of Ladies holding Fair at General Church in Westminster: Mrs.
LITTLER, chair & Miss Catharine J. JONES, secretary. Committee: Mr. H.
CROUTE & Mr. N. H. BROWN. Committee: Mrs. VAN BIBBER, Mrs. WILLIS & Miss
M. FISHER & Miss C. J. JONES. Next meeting at Mrs. Jacob POWDER's.
Whig Voters met at S. SULTZER's Hotel in Taneytown. David KEPHART, Esq.,
chair & S. SULTZER, secretary. Delegates: James SMITH, Dr. Samuel SWOPE,
Col. Thomas HOOK, Sterling GALT, Jacob ZUMBRUN, Elias GRIMES, David
FOUTZ, John MATHIAS & Samuel MC KINSTRY.
Whig Voters met at New Market at Enos SCHELL's tavern. Abel RUSSELL, chair
& John LEWIS, asst. chair; Jacob CRONISE, secretary. Committee: Nathan
HAMMOND (of Ormond), Jacob CONISE, Washington BURGESS, Singleton WOETTON,
George P. BUCKEY, Abel RUSSELL, William NORRIS, George PHELPS, William
MORSELL, Nathan NELSON, Abraham JOHNS, Zachariah MC ELFRESH, John KLAY,
Enos SCHELL, John HOUCK & John BARTHOLOW.

23 May 1835
ATKINS, Samuel, who resided about 4 miles northwest of Frederick, 2 members
of his family accidentally poisoned Saturday last. Supposed that arsenic
used by mistake for potash in making bread. Mr. Atkins' mother & 1 of
his children died on Sunday morning.
BRENGLE, L. J., at the Union Mills on Tuesday the 12th inst. married Miss
Eliza, d/o Andrew SHRIVER, Esq. by Rev. Mr. GEIGER, all of this county.
BROWN, Peter H., Esq. has taken charge of the "Frederick Citizen", recently
conducted by the lamented Dr. MC KEEHAM.
MARSDEN, John H. Rev., of Gettysburg, married on Tuesday the 5th instant
Miss Susan, eldest d/o the Rev. S. GRIER of Liberty Township, by Rev. J.
C. WATSON.
RICHARDS, Ann, ran away from John MATHIAS, residing near the Union Bridge
on 12th instant. White girl, indented, 15-16 years, stout & well made.
SPRIGG, Thomas Otho, of Frederick County, should apply to Post-Master at
Ft. Wayne, IN to hear something to his advantage.

23 May 1835
SCHAEFFER, Joseph, manufactures carriages.
THAYER, Nathaniel H., Principal of Manchester Academy. Mr. WEBSTER his
    successor.
Union-Town District, new district out of parts of Taney-town & Westminster
    Districts. Commencing on Beaver Dam, runs in line (excluding Middleburg)
    to SIX's ford on Big Pipe Creek to -----'s Ford 1/ 1/2 miles above
    GROVE's mill & near the Baltimore turnpike; thence to MESSENGER's mill;
    thence to SMITH's tavern, east of Frizzlesburg, crossing the Union-town &
    Westminster turnpike a few rods east of Mr. John LEISTER's; thence to
    HAINES' mill on Little Pike Creek; thence to Mr. Abraham BAILE's; thence
    to Sams Creek; down said stream to place of beginning. Includes Union-
    Town, New Windsor, Union Bridge & Frizzlesburg.
Voters of 14th election district met at house of S. S. CHURCH in Jefferson;
    John CULLER, chair & Dr. E. M. GATTON, secretary. Committee: Dr. T. J.
    MC GILL, G. Cost BISER, Henry KELLER, William NORRED, John ERVIN, J. B.
    HALLER & Christian TABLER. Delegates: Patric MC GILL, Jr., Henry KELLER,
    William LYNCH, William JARBOE, John CULLER, Sr., John COST & Dr. E. M.
    GATTON. Correspondence Committee: Abraham LAKINS, Col. T. JOHNSON, Lewis
    RODERICK, A. BLESSING of (G.), George HOFFMAN, Philson??, Philip CULLER,
    Henry COST, Capt. R. JOHNSON, Christian TABLER, Sr., Capt. John KEFAUVER,
    Joseph CARTZENDAFFER, T. THRASHER. Committee of vigilance: Capt. William
    LAKINS, John NEIGHBOURS, J. B. HALLER, William NORRED, David CULLER, W.
    NEIGHBORS, David STOCKMAN, John CRUM, Martin MILLER, Frederick R. HEMP,
    George W. CRUM, Perry DICE, Sr., Henry GROSS, Sr., Fielder THOMPSON,
    Henry GROSS, Jr., James T. CASTLE, George WILLIAM, Lloyd DORSEY, Thomas
    BOTELER, William LAMAR, Richard CHILCOTE, Nelson HOFFMAN, Isaac SHIPLEY,
    John CULLER, Jr., James TORRANCE, David KELLER, John ERVIN, Jacob DUPLE,
    John SHAEFFER, Jesse M. LITTLE, John COBLENTZ, Lewis EASTERDAY, George
    SHAFER, Peter SHATER, Joseph DANNER, John DANNER, Lloyd LUCKETT, John
    BRUNNER, Col. N. LUCKETT, S. S. CHURCH, Christopher WEAVER, Dr. T. J.
    MC GILL, & Col. William Cost JOHNSON.
Whig Voters of Liberty District met at the Tavern of Joseph L. WAGNER in
    Liberty. Surrat D. WARFIELD, chair & Dr. Richard DORSEY, secretary.
    Committee: Nicholas NORRIS, Thomas HAMMOND, John DUDDERAR, Richard
    SIMPSON, Abraham JONES, Thomas SAPPINGTON & Thomas BARTHOLOW. Delegates:
    Surratt D. WARFIELD, Abraham JONES, Dr. R. DORSEY, Thomas HAMMOND,
    William DUDDERAR, Nicholas NORRIS, William WORMAN, Christopher OWINGS, &
    John C. PHILIPS.

30 May 1835
HENRY, Francis: Joseph M. PALMER, Trustee, selling real estate of Mr. HENRY
    & wife at Isaac SHRIVER's tavern in Westminster. Large house, out houses
    & storehouse; has been used as a public house for some time past & as a
    story by Francis HENRY; also lots #5 & #6 in said town; also lot near
    Westminster conveyed to Mr. HENRY by William GRUMBINE (deed dated 23
    August 1834). Also lots #'s 3 & 4 in Westminster, heretofore sold to
    James CALT by B. S. PIGMAN, Esq. trustee to sell estate of John LOGSDON &
    by the said James GALT sold to Francis HENRY.
HENRY, Francis: sheriff's sale of household goods & a 2-story brick house &
    lot in Westminster; also large store house & lot; & 2 lots of ground
    unimproved; seized & taken in the suit of John M. BARRY & others. For
    Mahlon TALBOTT, Sheriff. Thomas GURLEY.
JONES, William Gwynn, editor of the Baltimore Gazette, arrested yesterday
    morning on charges of having robbed the Post Office of letters containing
    money.
REESE, Jacob, selling dry goods, groceries, hardware, etc. in Westminster.
STEM, David, died Wednesday evening last, innkkeeper of Union-Town, at an
    advanced age.
A New County meeting will be held at MARTEN's Tavern in Middleburg.

30 May 1835
New Market Convention of Delegates, 6th Congressional District; Evan
M'KINSTRY, Esq., President; Jacob MATHIAS & John SIMMONS, Esqs. VPs &
Joseph L. SMITH & Henry KEMP, Secretaries. Maj. William M. STEUART from
Montgomery read proceedings of meeting held at Rockville. Dr. R. DORSEY
of Liberty offered resolution. Washington BURGESS, Esq. nominated
William Cost JOHNSON. Dr. Joshua JONES, Jr. put forth motion that a
committee of 5 draft address to voters; appointed were Dr. J. JONES, Jr.,
Dr. J. MANRO, W. BURGESS, Esq., Dr. William WILLIS & Mr. S. M'KINSTRY.
Jacob MATHIAS, Joseph L. SMITH & Henry KEMP appointed to inform Mr.
JOHNSON of his nomination.
Whig Meeting of voters of 2d district of Frederick County. Cyrus MANTZ,
Esq., chair; William Ogden NILES, secretary. Nelson POE, Esq., explained
purpose of meeting & submitted resolutions seconded by Francis BRENGLE,
Esq. Committee appointed to attend convention: Moses WORMAN, Israel
MYERS, Dr. W. S. MC PHERSON, Jona. GETZENDANNER, Charles H. BURKHART,
Gideon BANTZ, Lewis RAMSBURG, Valentine BIRELY, Abraham KEMP, Patrick
TORMEY, Jacob FAUBEL, Lawrence J. BRENGLE. Central Committee of
Correspondence: Dr. W. B. TYLER, Richard POTTS, Col. G. M. ECHELBERGER,
Col. J. MC PHERSON, Dr. J. BALTZALL, Nicholas H. PITTS, William J. ROSS,
M. B. LUCKET, Charles A. GAMBRILL & George J. FISHER.
Jackson Republican Voters of Hauver's district to meet at Henry NEED's
Tavern, OAT's old stand.
Petersville District Jackson Republican Voters to meet at Tavern of William
KNOX in Burkittsville.
Buckeystown District Jackson Republican Voters met at Allen SAIN's Tavern
in Buckeystown. Col. Daniel DUVALL, chair; W. R. KING, asst. chair;
Joseph L. SMITH, Esq., secretary. Delegates appointed: Dr. Jonathan
MANROA, Joseph L. SMITH, Philemon MC ELFRESH, A. H. BROWN, B. A.
CUNNINGHAM, Henry KEMP, George KEPHART, E. HOWARD, Zadock WINDSOR &
Patrick MURPHY. Delegation to Frederick to nominate candidate for next
General Assembly: Daniel DUVALL, J. G. COBBS, George HASSELBOCK, Conrad
DUDROW, Allen SAIN, Otho THOMAS, Dr. J. LAMBERT, Maj. J. SIMMONS, C.
DANNEHILL, Z. T. WINDSOR, R. B. MURDOCK, M. M. MAHENEY, Samuel JARBOE,
James L. DAVIS & Thomas R. KING. Committee of Correspondence: B. A.
CUNNINGHAM, Dr. J. VAN BUSKIRK, Dr. Jonathan MANROE, James A. JOHNSON,
Thomas L. DAVIS, Charles JOHNSON, Elisha HOWARD & Dr. James JOHNSON.
Whig Voters met at the house of Jacob GLAZIER in Uniontown. Dr. James L.
BILLINGSLEA, chair; Dr. Joshua JONES, secretary. Delegates appointed:
Evan MC KINSTRY, James C. ATLEE, John ROBERTS, Dr. J. JONES, William
SHEPHERD, Daniel ENGLE & John SMITH.

13 June 1835
HEIRD, James, selling a sorrel horse at his tavern on the Westminster &
Littlestown turnpike.
HUNT, Elias, has taken over Cockey's Hotel in Westminster.
MILLER, John Sr., died Thursday morning, 89th year of his age, in
Westminster District.
SHRINER, Henry, deceased, late of Frederick County, sale of late residence
1 1/2 miles from Taney-town, on the main road to Baltimore. Also house
hold goods. At same time & place selling 2-story brick house & lot in
Taneytown, fronting on main street with 2-story brick back building with
double porch; 1/2 acre of ground & outbuildings. George B. & Henry
SHRINER, Jr., Executors.
VICKERS, Benjamin, died 29th May last at his residence in Kent County,
Maryland, in the 74th year of his age.
WINCHESTER, David, deceased of Baltimore County, James Mason CAMPBELL, Adm.

5 September 1835

DAVIS, Phineas, of Baltimore, died Sunday when a train engine that he was driving from Washington to Baltimore ran off the tracks & he died instantly. He was a worker on Locomotive engines used on the B&O Railroad.

EDIE, John R., determined to make this his permanent place of residence, intends opening an Academy for instruction of English & mathematics.

ELLICOTT, Thomas, on trial with charges being brought against him by the Bank of Maryland which Trustees allege $25,000 was paid to him out of bank funds without or for an inadequate consideration. Counsel for Plaintiffs are F. S. KEY, R. JOHNSON, R. W. GILL & A. W. BRADFORD, Esqs. For the defendant, Walter JONES, J. NELSON, O. SCOTT & A. CONSTABLE.

GALLEE, Peter, a stray cow came to him living 1 1/2 miles from MAUS's Mill, near gravel road.

HAINES, Thomas, late of Frederick County, those who gave notes for property purchased, please settle. Catharine HAINES & John WEAVER, Adm.

HARRIS, Washington, selling small farm in Frederick County, about 4 miles west of Taney-town, about 100 acres. Apply to Mr. HARRIS in Emmitsburg, who is determined to sell & remove to the west.

HOOVER, George, deceased of Frederick County, Catharine & Joseph HOOVER, Administrators.

KONE, Henry, issued promissory note to be paid in the completion of a Saw Mill built by William SHIPLEY, Jr. Said KONE has failed to comply with his contract & Mr. SHIPLEY protests against payment of said note.

MC GEE, Thomas, of Frederick Circuit of Methodist Episcopal Church, camp meeting to be held on land of George HOFFMAN, 2 miles from Jefferson.

MILLER, John, camp meeting of Episcopal Methodists on his land, Double Pipe Creek.

REESE, Jacob, having declined the Mercantile business, requests payments.

STIER, H., new store in New Windsor at the corner-house, selling dry goods, groceries, hard, delf, glass & china ware, drugs & medicines.

SCHLEY, Henry & EICHELBERGER, George M., Agents of the Levy Court of Frederick County placing on loan $10,330.

SHRINER, Henry, in pursuance of his last Will & Testament, for sale 1 farm & tavern stand near Taney-town & 38 miles from Baltimore on the turnpike road to Pittsburg. 138 acres, 2-story log house now a tavern & brick dwelling 1 1/2 stories high, a brick Blacksmith shop; 2-story brick Spring-house, 2 paneled gardens, Switzer Barn, nearly new. Also another farm in Baltimore County about 4 miles south of Manchester, near turnpike from Baltimore to Hanover; 132 acres with 2-story house, large log barn & springhouse, all nearly new. To view call on Mr. H. RUBEY, presently residing on premises. George B. & Henry SHRINER, Jr., Executors.

WAMPLER, John, deceased of Frederick County, commissioners to meet to value & divide his real estate. Jacob MATHIAS, William WILLIS, Jacob REESE & Jacob POWDER, Jr., Commissioners.

WEBSTER, C. W., will resume duties of his school on the 31th instant.

WEBSTER, C. W., to open a night school teaching Reading, Writing, Arithmetic, English Grammer & Mathematics, using the Goodwane system of Angular Writing. Scholars to furnish their own light & fuel.

WILLIS & FORRY, drug store selling Baker's Cocoa, superfine rice, flour & Homopathic Chocolate, lemon syrup, Canton ginger syrup, etc.

WINCHESTER, David, deceased, estate sale contiguous to town of Westminster in Frederick County, 230 acres; also a tract called "Legh Castle," 30 acres about 1 mile from Westminster. First property has been in Winchester family for nearly a century. J. Mason CAMPBELL, Trustee.

WINCHESTER, David, deceased, sale of farm behind & contiguous to town of Westminster in Frederick County. 100 acres; sole subject to the estates for their lives & the life of the survivor of Miss Elizabeth & Miss Lydia WINCHESTER in all that part of the farm on which they reside. Life estates embrace mansion house & appurtenances, about 14 acres & attached

5 September 1835
    to them as the right of firewood & pasturage in the rest of the farm.
    Property has been in Winchester family for nearly a century.
Academy, Baltimore County, (Manchester) trustees announce they have hired
    Nathaniel H. THAYER as Principal. Jacob SHOWER, Prst. Bd. Trust., Jacob
    GEIGER, Secretary. Rev. Jacob ALBERT, Sol. MYERLY, George MATTER, P.
    GARNER, Levi MAXFIELD, Jacob KERLINGER, George SHOWER & Peter SAUBLE,
    Trustees. In Westminster refer to: W. VAN BIBBER, Esq., A. F. SHRIVER,
    Esq., William WILLIS, M.D., David UHLER, Esq., Samuel FORRY, M.D. & Jacob
    REESE, Esq.
Baltimore County opponents of Van Buren & Johnson held meeting at John R.
    GWYNN's, Brooklandville. Sol. HOOK & J. Robert COCKEY, Esq., Chairmen; G.
    W. HOWARD & Jesse RITTER, Secretaries. Invite Elias BROWN, Dr. Thomas
    RISTEAU, Samuel TAGART & John H. CARROLL to become candidates for the
    Legislature. Dr. RISTEAU declines. A meeting will take place in
    Baltimore County at "Kelly's Old Fields."
Meeting of Democratic Republicans friendly to present administration at
    Mrs. BISHOP's tavern on Bel-air Rd. Gen. Tobias E. STANSBURY, chair; E.
    T. J. WOODWARD, secretary. Delegates: 1st District, John MARTIN, Francis
    FEELYNIER, Felix HERBERT, Abner KEYS, Jr. & John C. DESHON. 2nd
    District, Dr. James B. PRICE, Col. William CROOKS, Capt. Ephraim WHITE,
    Thomas ELY, S. HARTLEY. 3rd District: Capt. Benjamin BENNET & Nicholas
    KELLY. 4th District: Daniel STULL, John MALEHORN & George BRAMWELL. 5th
    District: William FRESH, John WILLIAMS, James THOMAS, John T. WORTHING-
    TON, George E. WEAVER. 6th District: William MURRAY, Francis SHRIVER,
    Frederick RITTER. 7th District: Marcus R. HOOK, Isaac KIRTZ, John BAKER,
    Capt. N. H. WARE & Thomas STARR. 8th District: Walter WORTHINGTON, E. J.
    MOSHER, Samuel WALDERSON, Augustus CLARK & Benjamin DAVIS. 9th District:
    Capt. Joseph WALKER, Charles G. HICKS, Nicholas STILTS. 10th District:
    Joshua HUTCHINS, Walter PERDUE, A. B. ANDERSON, John B. HOLMES & Thomas
    POWELL. 11th District: John Hillen JENKINS, Maj. Charles W. HOWARD, Maj.
    Joseph G. JOHNSON, Henry GUYTON & John LEWIS. 12th District: Gen. Tobias
    STANSBERRY, E. T. J. WOODWARD, Nicholas GRIMES, Esq. & Booth DORSEY.
    Nominated on 1st ballot for Assembly, E. T. J. WOODWARD, John M. WYSE,
    Victor HOLMES & John C. DESHON; for Commissioner George ELLICOTT.
For Convention, letters signed by John M. WISE of Deer Park & John C.
    ORRICK of Orrickton, Baltimore County.
Whig Delegates, 5th Congressional District convention at New Market: Suratt
    D. WARFIELD, chair; Jacob MATHIAS & Evan MC KINSTRY, assistants;
    Singleton WOOTTON & Joseph BAUGHER, secretaries. William C. JOHNSON
    nominated by unanimous vote of all 10 districts. Committee of
    Correspondence: Dr. J. MANRO, Dr. J. SHIELDS, John DELAPLANE, A. F.
    SHRIVER, R. C. WILSON, W. BURGESS, William P. JONES, Mason PARSONS, John
    ROBERTS & Sebastian RAMSBURG.

19 September 1835
WELTY, H. C., on Friday night his barn with the entire crop of small grain
    burned in the lower part of this county (Hagerstown). On Monday night
    the barn on the farm occupied by Mr. Isaac RIDENOUR, near this place, was
    also burned with his harvest. There is no doubt that these fires are the
    work of incendiaries.

3 October 1835
Elkton thrown into violent commotion on Sunday because of a report that
    murder had been committed by a party of Irish laborers on the Rail Road.
    The Sheriff arrested 3 of the supposed murderers, MC CABE, MC GENNISS &
    MC GLINN. No traces of the body have been discovered up to print time.
Frederick County Jackson Republican Ticket: House of Delegates, Henry
    KEEFER, Isaac SHRIVER, John KINZER & Daniel S. BISER. Whig Ticket:
    Daniel DUVALL, Robert ANNAN, William WILLIS & William S. MC PHERSON. 5th

CARROLLTONIAN

3 October 1835
Congressional District for Congress: William Cost JOHNSON, George C.
WASHINGTON & Richard WOOTTEN, Sr.
Republican Central Committee meeting, Frederick County; chair appointed
Peter H. BROWN, Jacob MARKELL, Caspar QUYNN, John RIGNEY & Matthias E.
BARTGIS to correspondence committee. Henry NIXDORFF, chair; P. H. BROWN,
secretary.
Baltimore County Van Buren Republican Delegate Ticket: Charles S. SEWALL
for Congress; for Assembly, Hugh ELY, George BRAMWELL, Victor HOLMES &
John C. DESHON; for Commissioner, George ELLICOTT, George E. WEAVER &
William JACKSON. Anti-Van Buren, Elias BROWN, Samuel TAGART, John H.
CARROLL & William S. WINDER; for Congress, James TURNER. Independent
Van Buren Candidates for Assembly, J.T.H. WORTHINGTON & Nathan H. WARE.
Democratic Republican Convention at BROOKHARTS in Baltimore County, Walter
WORTHINGTON, chair; John B. HOLMES, Esq., secretary. George BRAMWELL,
Esq. nominated to fill vacancy of John M. WYSE, resigned.

24 October 1835
CROUTE, Hezekiah, seeks journeyman tinner, Westminster.
DERN, Zacheus, seeks to employ man for fulling & dyeing business. Apply
Double Pipe Creek, Frederick County.
ESTEP, John & HOPPE, J. Henry, mercantile business partnership dissolved by
mutual consent. John ESTEP will continue business.
HAWK, Abraham, died near Taneytown at the residence of his father, Mr.
Abraham HAWK in the 19th year of his age, on Wednesday 7 October 1835. A
member in full communion in the German Reformed Church.
HEBBARD, E. B., renting house formerly occupied by himself. Apply to
Joshua SMITH, Jr., Esq. or Mr. Francis HENRY.
HESSON, John married Thursday the 14th instant by Rev'd. Jacob GEIGER to
Miss Catharine YINGLING, d/o Mr. Frederick YINGLING, both of Frederick
County.
JONES, Philip, selling house & lot he presently occupies in central &
business part of Westminster. Two-story brick house, 1 room has been
occupied as a store.
KEISER, Eckard, now in the Almshouse near Frederick city, desires to live
with his family & is seeking Frederick STOCK, his son-in-law or Ann M.
KEISER, his wife. Inform M. Henry STEINER, keeper of the Almshouse.
MC ILHENNY, Elizabeth, selling farm of 283 acres on Meadow Branch, within a
mile of Union-town; adjoins lands of Peter BABYLON, G. WARNER, & heirs of
W. DEVILBISS, deceased. Includes house & barn.
MARTIN, John F. married by Rev. Mr. DEBART to Miss Elizabeth ADELSPARGER,
both of Baltimore City, Thursday the 14th instant.
MILLER, John, Jr., selling 300 acres of land in Frederick County about 2
miles southerly from the Union Mills, late in his occupancy & conveyed to
him by John MILLER, Sr. by deed dated 29 July 1825. Sale to take place
at place formerly known as RINEHART's Tavern near the road from Westminster to the Union Mills. Noah PHILLIPS, Trustee.
REESE, John F., purchased store formerly owned by Jacob REESE, Esq. of this
place; will carry dry goods, groceries, hardware, etc.
REESE, John F., ran an assortment of ads for sale of salt & coffee, cloths
& cassimers, fruit, linseed oil, white lead in kegs & window glass &
compound syrup of Iceland Moss for the cure of colds, asthma, whooping-
cough, spitting of blood & consumption.
SHUNK, Benjamin, Sheriff selling for cash at his residence near Joseph
ECK's mill in Taney-town District, 108 acres of land & buildings, seized
& taken at the suit of Isaac & Joseph BAUGHER. For Mahlon TALBOTT,
Sheriff, Thomas GURLEY.
SUNDERGILL, Joshua, has taken store house formerly occupied by Mr. F.
HENRY, opening cheap new store in Westminster. Dry goods, groceries, etc.

28

24 October 1835
SWOPE, John & Daniel H., dissolving partnership of Mercantile business by
  mutual consent. New firm will be SWOPE & CRAPSTER, (Mr. William L.
  CRAPSTER) Taney-town.
WAMPLER, Abraham, renting brick tavern stand in Westminster, kept by him
  for many years.
WEBSTER, C. W., taken charge of the Union School, latey under Mr. THAYER.
WHITE, George W. Dr., married on the 10th instant by the Rev. Mr. RAHAUSER
  to Miss Elizabeth MYERS, both of Bedford County, PA.
WOODBRIDGE, Rev. Mr., will preach in the Union Church Sunday next.
List of Letters remaining in the Post Office at Westminster 1 October 1835:
  John ARBAUGH or David HILTEBRIDLE, Abraham ALBAUGH, Mr. C. BIRNIE, James
  ROGAN, Thomas CRADDICK, Rezin COOK, David CROUL, John FORMWALT, Nimrod
  FRIZELLE, Thomas GIBSON, William B. GIST, Elias HOLMES, Elizabeth KEYS,
  Henry KNOTE Sr., John LOCKARD, Mrs. Ann LIGHTNER, Thomas LONGMORE,
  Michael MORELOCK Jr., Michael MORELOCK, Stephen & Greenbury OURSLER, Miss
  Rebeca PUDDER, Mrs. Magdalina RINEHART, Jeremiah ROBERTSON, Milton
  RIDGELY, Hunter ROBERTSON, John RISTOR, George ROBERTSON, Jacob STONE
  Jr., Heinrich SPARENBERG, John SHAMER, John B. SNOWDEN, Michael SULLIVAN,
  John SHEAN, Hannah SMITH, Mrs. TAWNEY, Miss Ellen TOOP, P. YINGLING,
  Frederick YINGLING, John ZITE & G. ZELL. E. CRUMBACKER, Post Master.
List of Letters remaining in the Post Office at Taney-town on 1 Oct. 1835:
  George ABLE, Michael BOBLINE, John BAUMGARTNER, John CRAPSTER, Jesse
  DAVIDSON, Rev. Samuel FINCKLE, Joseph FOGGLE, Rev. Mr. GRAVES, Mrs. Mary
  E. HICKSON, John HEAD, John KOONS, Abraham LIEHTENWALTER, William MC
  KALEB, Basil & William SPALDING, Ruban WALLS to the care of Charles
  BLACK & Jacob YINGLING. Hugh SHAW, Postmaster.

12 March 1836
AVEY, Christopher, married on Thursday week, by Rev. Amon RICHARDS, to Miss
  Diana, fifth daughter of the late John MURRY, Esq. of Hampstead.
BROWN, Peter, dividend made on assets in his hands to be paid to his
  creditors. David B. EARHART, Trustee.
COLEGATE, Georgiana Parker, died 24th ult. in Baltimore, in 14th year of
  her age, daughter of the late Dr. George COLEGATE of Frederick County.
CRADDICK, C. & T.W., having declined farming, will offer for sale at their
  residence, 3 miles south of Westminster on Washington Rd. & near George
  WARFIELD's store, all of their stock & 40 acres of grain in the ground, a
  patent cider mill & press complete.
DAHOOF, Peter, late of Baltimore County, dec'd., all real estate of said
  dec'd, for sale; 1 1/2 miles below Manchester on turnpike leading to
  Reisterstown. #1- 87 acre farm, 1 1/2 story log house; cellar & kitchen
  attached. #2- 6 acre lot adjoining said road & farm. #3- 11 acres, one
  mile from said farm & adjoins public road. #4- 12 1/4 acres about 1/4
  mile from turnpike & 2 miles from Lot #1, adjoins lands of John BROWN &
  John FOWBLE. Michael RITTER, Trustee.
DURBIN, Nicholas, selling 5 acre lot with 2-story log house & wash-house;
  near Westminster, adjoins lands of Joseph ORENDORFF, William & John
  ROBERTS & subscriber's farm.
ERB, Peter, late of Frederick County, dec'd, sale at his late residence,
  near public road from Jacob MAUS' Mill to Westminster Turnpike road,
  about 1 mile from said mill on Big Pipe Creek & same distance to Francis
  GROFF's mill on said stream - 6 work horses, 3 colts, 2 bulls, 17 milch
  cows, & other livestock, apple brandy, cider oil, furniture, etc. Jacob
  ERB, Trustee.
ERB, Peter Sr.: late of Frederick County, dec'd, John ERB & Jacob HAHN,
  Jr., Executors.
MAXWELL, Rev. Mr.: meeting at general meeting house in Westminster.
MOUER, Henry: selling 2-story brick house & lot, which he presently
  occupies, near junction of the turnpike in Westminster.

12 March 1836

ORENDORF, Joseph: renting 2-story brick house & lot at the "Forks" of
Westminster, lately owned & occupied as a story & dwelling by Francis
HENRY.

REESE, Jacob: all indebted to him requested to pay.

SHAW, Moses: agent, selling brick house & lot in Union-town, formerly
property of Dr. Thomas BOYER, dec'd. This property is so well known
through the neighborhood, as to render a description unnecessary.

Legislature at Annapolis: Bill reported by Mr. DUVALL entitled, an act to
authorize & empower Joseph L. SMITH of Frederick County to convey to
proper owners, all the lots in town of Berlin in said County, which were
sold by his grandfather, Leonard SMITH, & his father, Joseph SMITH.

Also, on motion of Mr. ANNAN, the bill reported by him, entitled an act to
make valid a deed from Solomon SHEPHERD & Susanna SHEPHERD to William
SHEPHERD, was taken up for consideration.

9 April 1836

Titles of Acts: An act to divorce Mary BESORE, of Frederick county, from
her husband, Jacob BESORE.

An act to authorize the sale of the real & personal estate of Elisha J.
HALL.

An act to authorise Samuel JORDON, former collector of taxes in 2d
collection district (Baltimore County) to complete his collections.

An act to authorize Levy Court of Frederick county to erect a bridge
over Catoctin creek at or near John KEAFAUVER's mill on the road leading
from Middletown by said mill to Berlin.

An act to divorce Abraham REEVER of Frederick County from his wife
Catharine REEVER.

An act authorising Judges of Levy Court of Frederick to levy money to
build a bridge over Catoctin creek on the public road from Middletown, by
the late John SHAFFER's mill, now David RAMSBURG's mill.

Whig Meetings: Meeting at Liberty District at Joseph WAGNER's Tavern,
Abraham JONES, Esq., chair & Thomas CARR, secretary. To represent
district in New Windsor to designate elector for President & Vice
President of the U.S.: Dr. Richard DORSEY, John CLEMSON, William
DUDDERAR, Richard SIMPSON, William A. ALBAUGH, Christopher OWINGS,
William H. POOLE, A. H. OWINGS, Thomas CARR, Anthony KIMMELL, Surrat D.
WARFIELD.

Meeting at house of Enos SCHELL, New Market, to appoint delegates to
Convention for 5th Congressional District. Abel RUSSELL, chair & Thomas
C. BRASHAER, secretary. Delegates: Singleton WOOTON, Plummer IJAMS Sr.,
Washington BURGESS, Abraham JOHNS, John CLAY, Thomas C. BRASHEAR, John
HOUCK, Henry NICHOLS, Nathan HAMMOND of V., William NORRIS, John LOWE,
George P. BUCKEY, John LEASE, Nicholas BRENGLE, Pradby JAMES, Henry
NELSON, Dr. George HUGHES, George PHELPS, Warfield TODD, Jesse RUSSEL,
Zachariah MC ELFRESH, Enos SCHELL & Hamilton STIER.

Meeting of Buckey's town district at tavern of Allen SAIN in Buckey's
town, Charles JOHNSON, Esq., chair & Dr. J. MANRO, secretary. Convention
committee, New Market: J.H.F. COCKEY, Charles JOHNSON, John LEATHER, B.A.
CUNNINGHAM, Maj. James SIMMONS, Dr. J. MAURO, Thomas J. DAVIS.

16 April 1836

DAYHOFF, Peter: late of Baltimore County, dec'd., sale at BECKER's Tavern
on turnpike leading from Hanover to Baltimore, between Manchester &
Hampstead; 12 1/4 acres about 1/4 mile from said turnpike & 2 1/2 miles
from Manchester; adjoins lands of John BURN & John FOWBLE. Michael
RITTER, Trustee.

QUIGLLEY, Joanna, ran away from John ORENDORF, near Westminster; indented
apprentice, 17 years of age. (6 1/4 cents reward offered.)

16 April 1836
WINCHESTER E. & L. caution persons from harboring their coloured servants, Abraham & Sarah without a written order from them.
Hagerstown: Meeting of delegates of 6 congressional districts; Dr. M. A. FINLEY, chair & Henry FIERY & Elias DAVIS, secretaries. William SCHLEY, Esq. of Frederick made motion to appoint committee to recommend a candidate, viz. William SCHLEY, R. M. TIDBALL, William VANLEAR, William MURPHY, Joseph WEST, Isaac NESBITT, Edward A. LYNCH, G. W. STUBBLEFIELD & Joseph GABBY.
Republican Voters of Woodsborough District: meeting at house of David F. YANTIS, secretary, John SMITH, Esq., (of M) chair. On motion of John E.H. LEGGET a committee was appointed to draft resolutions, viz. Mr. LEGGET, James L. MASLIN, Brooks BAKER, Samuel TALLEY & James W. HARLEN.
3d Congressional Convention: met at Watkins' Tavern (Long Green). On motion of John PHILPOT, Esq., Maj. Nicholas DORSEY (3d district Baltimore County), chair & Joshua TRIMBLE (1st district), secretary.

23 April 1836
COHEN, Mendez J., of Baltimore, & James MOORES of Harford County, appointed aids to his Excellency, Gov. VEAZY, with the rank of Colonel.
FISHER, John, renting tavern stand in Westminster, lately occupied by J. COCKEY.
LOCKERMAN, Theodore, nominated by Whigs as Elector on the Eastern Shore, declined serving.
ROBERTS, William & John: have entered into co-partnership in mercantile business & will continue at store formerly occupied by W. ROBERTS.
Appointments of the Baltimore Annual Conference of Methodist Protestant Church: President - Isaac WEBSTER; Baltimore - Thomas H. STOCKTON & Asha SHINN; East Baltimore - Dr. Thomas DUN (of Philadelphia); Pipe Creek - Dr. John S. REESE & John W. PORTER; Baltimore Circuit - George D. HAMILTON & John NICHOLS; Deer Creek - Daniel E. REESE, Jr.; New Market - William SEXSMITH.
Western Bank of Baltimore, Commissioners: William HARDEN, Lewis KEMP, Chauncy BROOKS, Alonzo LILLY, William WOODWARD, George CAREY, A. G. COLE, William SWAN, Thomas E. HAMBLETON, Lot ENSEY, George CARSON, Edward GREEN, C. G. PETERS, David MARTIN, E. P. BARROWS, Eli SCOTT, Robert TAYLOR, Francis BURNS.

13 May 1836
Democratic Republican of Western District meeting at house of Joseph TOPPER, Westminster. Nicholas Hall BROWN, chair & Michael SULLIVAN, secretary. Others attending, Michael BARNITZ, John FISHER, Jacob SCHAEFFER, Dr. George SHRIVER & Isaac SHRIVER.
4th District meeting of Jackson Republicans of Baltimore County held at Mrs. WOOLERY's. William FANNING, chair & George BRAMWELL secretary. Delegates to Convention: George BRAMWELL, David STULL, Edmund GARDNER, Murray SHILLING & John MALEHORN.
Delegation to state convention: Israel RAMSBURG & Somerset R. WATERS of Middleton; George THOMAS & Daniel KEMP of Buckeystown; Benedict BOONE & Dr. GARROT of Petersville; Daniel S. BISER & Capt. John THOMAS of Jefferson; George P. FOX & George FLAUT of Hauver's; David AGNEW & John HARRITT of Emmitsburg; George WARFIELD & John FISHER of Westminster; Thomas ANDERSON & William WERTENBAKER of New Market; John R. CURTIS & William TODD of Cregerstown; Capt. Joseph WOOD & Brook BAKER of Woodsborough; Nicholas HOLTZ, John RIGNEY, Peter H. BROWN, William H. DAINGERFIELD, William P. MAULSBY, Edward B. MC PHERSON, George W. EN?, Madison NELSON, Edward SHRIVER & Matthias E. BARTGIS, of Frederick.

31

27 May 1836
Internal Improvement Convention, Frederick: Outerbridge HORSEY, chairman;
Dr. George SHRIVER, secretary. John H. SIMMONS & Gideon BANTZ, asst.
chairmen; Peter H. BROWN & John K. LONGWELL, secretaries. Edward A.
LYNCH, Esq., offered report. M. NELSON, Esq. submitted resolutions. H.
R. WARFIELD, Esq., gave a speech of several hours.

10 June 1836
BOYLE, J. B., having declined the mercantile business, asks debtors to pay,
& in his absence to pay to A. LICHTENWALTER, Esq.
EVERHART, James, by writ of court of Frederick County, sale to all right,
title, interest & claim of his to 113 acres with all improvements; seized
& taken at suit of David B. EARHART. For Mahlon TALBOTT, Sheriff, Thomas
GURLEY.
HUNT, Elias, has taken hotel in Westminster lately occupied by J. SHRIVER,
Esq.
JENIFER, Mr., of MD has challenged Mr. BYNUM of N.C. to duel in consequence
of some impertinent remarks of the latter.
LIND, John, dec'd of Frederick County, sale at tavern of Jacob GLAZIER in
Uniontown of his estate, to wit: lot & improvements formerly occupied as
a tavern by Moses SHAW consisting of a large dwelling house, brick
stable, ware-house, etc.; also all that piece of land called "Brown's
Inheritance," 11 1/2 acres in Uniontown on corner of the Alley leading in
the direction of Daniel ZOLLICKOFFER's farm, in and near Uniontown.
Abraham LICHTENWALTER, Trustee.
MC PHERSON, Horatio, died at Williamsport Friday evening at 7; cashier at
Washington County Bank, after illness of 2 months, in 35th year.
MAXWELL, Rev. Mr., will preach by divine permission in the Westminster
Meeting House on the 16th.
NULL, John, Taney-town, sale of brick house & lot, late his property,
seized & taken at the suits of John OTT & Michael REEVER, executors of
George OTT, Hugh SHAW, John THOMPSON & Israel HITESHUE.
ORENDORF, Samuel, selling new & cheap goods, cloths of silk, satin,
gingham, calicoes, etc. & groceries, hardware, etc.
REESE, John F., selling nails & grass & cradling scythes.
SHRIVER, George, Dr., located at turnpike Forks in Westminster. He may be
found at the residence of his father or at his office, nearly opposite.
YINGLING, John, dec'd, late of Frederick County, Jacob YINGLING & David B.
EARHART, Executors.
Westminster English & Mathematical Academy, run by C. W. WEBSTER.
References: Nathaniel H. THAYER of Westminster, John J. HARROD of
Baltimore; Stevenson ARCHER of Belair; Dr. William WILLIS, Dr. S. FORRY,
Jacob MATHIAS, Joshua SMITH, Isaac SHRIVER, Dr. John ROSE, Jacob
YINGLING, Jacob POWDER Jr., Elias HUNT, E. CRUMBACKER & J. K. LONGWELL.
Candidates for Sheriff for Frederick County: John BAUMGARTNER, Abner
CAMPBELL, Thomas GURLEY, James HARDING, John HARRITT, Henry HOUCK, Mason
PARSONS, Somerset R. WATERS
Constables appointed by Levy Court of Frederick County for 1836 by
District: No. 1- James S. SIMMONS, John CAREY, Samuel H. HOUSER. No. 2-
James M. DAYHOFF, Daniel HALLER, John BENDER, John M. LOWE, James
WALLING, Joshua DILL, James CARLIN, Robert G. RUSSELL & Joseph S. MC
GARY. No. 3-James WILLIAMSON, John ALEXANDER, Jacob YOUNG of D., John H.
YOUNG of H., Peter YOUNG & Adam RENNER. No. 4- George KUHN, Cyrus
WALKER, Arnold R. FAHS, Warner T. GRIMES & Joseph LIDEY. No. 5- Samuel
DUPHOUR, John MARTIN & Isaac WILSON. No. 6- Henry WANTZ, David KEPHART
Jr. & John CLABAUGH. No. 7- Jacob FRINGER, William CRUMBINE, Frederick
YINGLING & Jacob H. KEMP. No. 8- Daniel SWEADNER, Daniel ROOT, Owen
BURGESS, John WOOD, Aaron GOSNELL & Joel WOOD. No. 9- Frederick COVELL,
Thomas INGMAN, William HOWARD, Levi VANFOSSEN & Jonathan BROWNING. No.
10- Henry NEED. No. 11- John BARRICK & Frederick GRIMES. No. 12- Adam

10 June 1836
  CUSTARD, John D. DABLESTINE & Henry BOTELER of Edward. No. 13- Tobias
  COVER & Isaac PEARCE. No. 14- Jacob B. HALLER, William B. TABLER &
  Jessie M. LITTLE.

17 June 1836
  DALLAM, Henrietta, died at New Ark, Del. Friday 10th inst. after a short
  illness, at the residence of her son-in-law, Thomas BLANDY; aged 70
  years, relict of the late Josias W. DALLAM of Harford County & d/o the
  late Judge JONES of Baltimore County.
  SHEPHERD, William, resuming his former business of manufacturing wool on
  Little Pipe Creek.
  TODD, James, selling small farm of 86 1/2 acres 1/4 of a mile from
  Middleburg; Big Pike Creek runs through; has 2-story stone dwelling &
  stone kitchen, stone stable sufficient for 8 head of horses & log
  building with threshing floor. Also selling a variety of house furniture
  & livestock.
  The Washington County Bank, appointments: John R. DALL president. John
  VAN LEAR, Jr. appointed cashier in place of Horatio MC PHERSON, dec'd.

24 June 1836
  Meeting in Manchester at house of William CRUMRINE to arrange 4th of July
  celebration: Capt. Solomon MYERLY, Chairman, Joseph M. PARKE, Secretary.
  Jacob LINWEAVER & Samuel B. FUHRMAN, Clergy Committee. Celebration to be
  held on land of Jarret GARNER, contiguous to Manchester. Henry BRINKMAN,
  Samuel B. FUHRMAN, Adam SHOWER, Committee.

1 July 1836
  BENNETT, Charles W., sells seed wheat, near Ely's mill or 1 mile from Falls
  Bridge on Westminster & Reisterstown turnpike.
  SMITH, Robert, through Court of Equity of Frederick County, Isaac POUDER,
  Trustee is selling real estate of SMITH called "the re-survey of
  Bedford," on the plat of town of Westminster as 1/2 of Lot No. 10 & 1/2
  of Lot No. 11 (1/4 acre), adjoins lots of William SHRIEVES & Levi EVANS
  and opposite the Catholic Church; 2-story frame dwelling house 35x20',
  log stable, large blacksmith shop.
  STANSBURY, Tobias E. Gen., Commander of 4th Division of MD Militia
  (Alleghany, Washington, Frederick & Baltimore Cos.) requested to meet at
  Gowan's Town, 4 miles from Baltimore on York Road. E. T. J. WOODWARD,
  J. T. H. WORTHINGTON.
  Lottery for property in Village of Funkstown in Washington County, on
  National Turnpike from Baltimore to Wheeling, 2 miles from Hagerstown.
  Mills are up on waters of the Antietam. Lots are situated in & adjoin-
  ing Funkstown; also mansion house. Anyone disposed to risk the small sum
  of $10 may venture without scruples. This is not a scheme of
  speculation, but to relieve the proprietors of the late Antietam Woolen
  factory, which was destroyed by fire. Tickets can be bought at stores
  of: Samuel ORENDORFF, Westminster; William & John ROBERTS, Union-town;
  Hugh SHAW, Taney-town; & John MILLER, Mechanicstown. George SHAFER, Agt.
  Medical & Chirurgical Faculty of MD met at Baltimore. Elected censors for
  Frederick County: William WILLIS, M.D., James L. BILLINGSLEA, M.D., &
  Jefferson SHIELDS, M.D.
  Candidates for General Assembly of Baltimore County: Dr. John C. ORRICK,
  Dixon STANSBURY & Nathan H. WARE.

22 July 1836
  BEST, Rev. Mr., will address the Sunday Schools of Westminster.
  ERB, Peter, dec'd, late of Frederick County, sale of real estate now in the
  occupancy of Isaac MYERS, farm with 119 acres on Big Pipe Creek, near

22 July 1836

Francis GROFF's mill. 2-story log dwelling house & log barn. Jacob
ERB, Executor.

POOL, Albinus, selling lot in town of Westminster (on plat No. 15), nearly
opposite residence of Isaac SHRIVER, Esq.; with 1 1/2 story dwelling
house & kitchen & log stable.

SHAFER, H., G. & Henry I., selling tickets for Lottery of property in
Funkstown.

WARNER, George, sheriff's sale of 18 acres called "Molly's Fancy," adjoins
lands of Michael MORELOCK, John LEISTER, & others. Seized & taken at the
suit of Magdalena RINEHARD. For Mahlon TALBOTT, Sheriff, Thomas GURLEY.

List of Letters remaining in the Post Office at Wesminster 1 July 1836:
Reuben BUCKINGHAM; Nicholas COLEMAN, Joseph C. COCKEY, Frederick DAHMER,
George W. LITZINGER, Jaby MERREY, Joseph MYERS, Miss Mary MYERLY (of
David), George W. M'CLELLAN, Rev. James NICHOLS, Samuel PETERS, Josias
PENTON, Jacob RIGHTER, John SLERS(?), Mrs. Elizabeth TRACY, & John ZILE.
E. CRUMBACKER, Post Master.

List of Letters remaining in the Post Office at Taney-town 1 July 1836:
Samuel ANGLE, C. BIRNIE, Smith CORNELL, George FARQUHAR, Joseph HAYS,
Henry HESS, Samuel HAHN, John M'KALEB, William M'KALEB, Michael NULL,
Henry ORNDORF, Michael REEVER, George SIX (of Philip), Mary STARR, WISE
& HARRITT. Hugh SHAW, Post Master.

Methodist Camp Meeting held by Ministers & Members on Pipe Creek Circuit:
Will be grounds of Burges NELSON, Jr., 5 miles east of Liberty town, on
the old Liberty road. Signed, John S. REESE, John W. PORTER, Thomas SIM,
John WOOD, John NICODEMUS, Robert NELSON, Isaac SHRIVER, J. L. BILLINGS-
LEA, John SMITH, James CLEMSON & Peter BOYER.

Frederick County Whig Meeting: Daniel KOLB, Esq. (Mayor of the City),
chair & Col. James M. SHELMAN, secretary. Gen. Thomas WORTHINGTON
submitted resolutions. Nominating Committee: Thomas C. WORTHINGTON,
Moses WORMAN, William SCHLEY, Charles H. BURKHART, George WACHTER, Lewis
BIRELY, Jacob FAUBEL, Philip ROHR, William WHITE, Francis BRENGLE,
Charles A. GAMBRILL, William S. MC PHERSON, George Adam EBERT, Daniel
GETZENDANNER, Patrick O'NEAL, Frederick NUSZ, Jacob LITTLE, James
RAYMOND, William J. ROSS, George GITTINGER, Gideon BANTZ, James M.
SHELMAN, John H. WILLIAMS, William DURBIN, & Dr. William WATERS.

Union-town District voters friendly to election of Martin Van BUREN &
Richard M. JOHNSON, met at Jacob GLAZIER's in Uniontown. On motion of
Basil ROOT, Esq., Joseph WEAVER was called to chair & Jacob GILEM
appointed secretary. Convention Committee: Isaac APPLER, George B.
SHRINER, John ROOP, Joseph SWIGART, John LOLTZ, George SMELTZER, William
POOLE, Joseph WEAVER, Nimrod FRIZZLE, Jacob GLAZIER, John BILLMYER, John
WEAVER, Isaac PIERCE, Daniel SULLIVAN, John SMELTZER, George LANTZ,
Philip WEAVER, George EARHART, Martin WHITE, Joshua STANSBERRY, David
WARNER, Joseph COOKSON, William HAINES, Elijah BOND, Jacob LANDIS, Jacob
GLEIM, William SEGAFOOSE, J.W. SWANSBAUGH, Solomon FORMWAIT, Tobias
COVER, George HESSE, David SMELTZER, Ludwick ENGLEMAN, Abraham LAMBERT &
John LAMBERT.

Westminster District meeting of Democratic-Republican voters held at house
of Jacob HARTZELL. Nicholas H. BROWN, Esq., chair; Michael SULLIVAN,
secretary. Committee: Michael SULLIVAN, Dr. George SHRIVER & Jacob
HARTZELL. Delegation: Nicholas H. BROWN, Esq., Jacob SCHAEFFER, Issac
SHRIVER, Michael MORELOCK, John A. BYERS, Jacob GROVE, Michael
SULLIVAN, J. Henry HOPPE, Jacob HARTZELL, Michael SAUBLE, James HEARD,
William SHRIVER, John S. MURRAY, David KEEFER, Joseph ORNDORF, David
OUSLER, Joseph SCHAEFFER, John MC COLLUM, J. F. REESE, John FISHER,
Michael BARNITZ, George RINEHART, William SHIPLEY, Jr., Adam FEASER,
David KUHN, David GIEMAN & Hezekiah CROUTE.

22 July 1836
Baltimore County: Gen. Tobias E. STANSBERY candidate for Elector of Senate;
Dr. RESTEAU (11th District) candidate in House of Delegates; George
ELLICOTT, Esq. & Dr. Ephraim BELL, Senatorial Electors.

29 July 1836
Taneytown District Republican Meeting: John JONES, chair, Capt. George
CRABBS, vice president, John B. BOYLE & William B. GWYNN, secretaries.
Convention Delegates: Dr. GWINN, John B. BOYLE, John JONES, William SHAW,
Capt. George CRABBS, Dr. Joseph W. BIGGS, David HAPE, John ADELSPERGER,
Thomas HICKLEY, Samuel DIFFENDALL, Thomas JONES, Samuel NAILL, Lewis
PETERS, Anthony ARNOLD, Andrew HAUGH, Nelson NORRIS, D. GROFF, Johnson
JAMESON, Michael NUSBAUM, Jacob FEEZER, John DUDDERER, Abraham NULL, Jr.,
Daniel MERRING, David GOLLY, John NULL, John KING, Amos MENSER, Peter
HULL, Daniel MC KENZIE & William FISHER.
Baltimore County Candidates: Gen. Tobias E. STANSBERY-Senate; Dr. RESTEAU
(11th District)-House of Delegates; George ELLICOTT, Dr. Ephraim BELL,
Samuel H. TAGART, George HARRYMAN-Senate.
Whig, Liberty District (Frederick County) Committee to attend convention:
John CLEMSON, Jr., David DUDDERER, Thomas J. WORTHINGTON, David W. NAILL,
Nathan H. OWINGS, James DOUTY, William TURNBULL, Thornton POOLE, George
DEVILBISS, Christopher OWINGS, William JONES, Abraham NUSBAUM, Jacob FOX,
Daniel ALBAUGH, Surratt D. WARFIELD, Nicholas NORRIS, John STRAUSBAUGH,
Dr. William COALE, Richard SIMPSON, Dr. Henry BAKER, Daniel ROOT of
Daniel, Maj. Thomas HAMMOND, William ALBAUGH, Abraham JONES & Thomas
CARR.
Whig Meeting was held at Joseph L. WAGNER's tavern in Libertytown. David
DUDDERER, chair; Thornton POOLE & Thomas CARR, secretaries. Attended by:
Abraham JONES, William JONES, Dr. William COALE, Maj. Thomas HAMMOND,
Jacob FOX, Daniel & William A. ALBAUGH. Corresponding Committee: Dr.
Richard DORSEY, Thomas HAMMOND, Dr. William COALE, Dr. Henry BAKER &
Joseph POOLE.
Whig Meeting held in 6th election district at house of Samuel HEAGY in
Taney-town. Dr. William B. HEBBARD, chair & Elias GRIMES, Esq. asst.
chair; Daniel H. SWOPE & Josiah BAUMGARDNER, secretaries. Nominating
Committee: James SMITH, Sterling GALT, Jacob HAHN, Jr., Isaac DERN, Dr.
Samuel SWOPE, John THOMPSON, Henry WANTZ, John COVER, Elias GRIMES,
Samuel GALT, Daniel I. POOLE, David KEPHART, Jr., John CLABAUGH, John
NANKIVEL, George WILT, Thomas RUDISELL, John DELAPLANE, Josiah BAUM-
GARTNER, James M'ALLISTER, George LANDERS, Dr. William B. HEBBARD, Jacob
ZUMBRUN, James CORNELL, Alexander HUTSON & Benjamin SHUNK.
Correspondence Committee: D. H. SWOPE, James SMITH, Isaac DERN, John
DELAPLANE, Dr. William ZOLLICKOFFER. Committee of Vigilance: Alexander
M'ALLISTER, William CORNELL, Abraham NULL, George & David REIFSNIDER, John
CORNELL, William CRABSTER, Upton SCOTT, Benjamin SHUNK, Samuel HEAGY,
Peter, Abraham, Henry & William (of William) KOONS, Jacob BAUMGARDNER,
John N. STARR, John REINDOLLAR, William MEHRING, George G. GRIMES, Robert
MORRISON, William NAILL, William RUDISELL, William HARRIS, Jacob CORNELL,
Abraham FORNEY.

12 August 1836
BEALE, W. M., nominated as Electoral Candidate, declined to run.
BRENGLE, Francis, Esq. married at Pleasant Valley, Frederick County, on the
morning of the 2d of August, by Rev. L. R. REESE, to Miss Maria DOWNEY,
both of Frederick County.
COOPER, Samuel, has opened school for instruction of youth of both sexes,
in room over Mr. SUNDERGILL's store. References: Michael POWER,
Principal of Asbury College, Baltimore, Isaac SHRIVER, Jacob MATHIAS,
William SHRIVER, J. H. HOPPE, Frederick BACHMAN, Nicholas DURBIN, Joseph
ORNDORFF, Elias HUNT & John ERB.

35

12 August 1836

FOWBLE, Frederick, of Baltimore County, has taken up stray iron grey horse, found on Hanover & Reisterstown Turnpike, at the 4th gate. John LAMMOT, Justice of the Peace.

FOWLER, Richard, of Baltimore County, married on Sunday last, by the Rev. N. ZOCCHI, to Miss Mary DURBIN, of Frederick County.

GEYER, John W., candidate for Legislature.

HOOK, Thomas, Colonel, 2d Regt., 1st Regimental Cavalry District, notifies Commissioned Officers MD Militia to meet at YANTIS' tavern in Woods-borough.

MARKS, James, died Friday morning last, at his residence near Taney-town, an aged & highly respectable member of the Society of Friends.

MYERS, Abraham, dec'd, of Frederick, J. Henry HOPPE, Ex'r.

ROBERTSON, John, notifies that Peter ARBAUGH has circulated a slander against a member of my family, which I pronounce to be a malicious lie. He has neither children nor character to protect, & would deceive his best friend, or injure his neighbor for filthy lucre.

SHRIVER, Abraham Ferree, commenced practice of Law in Frederick, MD; may be found at the office of F. BRENGLE, Esq. near the Court-House.

SLINGLUFF, Jesse, dec'd, of Frederick County, sale of estate at his late residence, 1 mile east of New-Windsor, 7 miles south-west of Westminster-all personal property consisting of livestock, farm implements, 18 acres of corn in the field, household furniture. Charles D., George W., & Isaac SLINGLUFF.

WINTERS, Magdalena Mrs., died Monday 8 August, 80 years old. Her afflictions were great--for 28 years she had been an invalid, 14 of which she has been confined to her bed. She died in full communion with the Roman Catholic Church.

WOOLERY, Christopher, dec'd, sale of his farm in Baltimore County, binding on the Westminster Turnpike, about 24 miles from City of Baltimore, 54 3/4 acres, log dwelling, barn, &c. T. Parktin SCOTT, St. Paul's Lane.

Western Bank of Baltimore: Taking subscriptions to stock at REESE's Store, Westminster; W. & J. ROBERTS' Store, Union-town; Isaac BAUGHER's Store, Emmitsburg; Joseph POOLE's Store, Libertytown. Isaac SHRIVER & Dr. William WILLIS, Commissioners for Westminster. William ROBERTS & Dr. J. L. BILLINGSLEA, Comm. for Union-town. Robert ANNAN & Isaac BAUGHER, Comm. for Emmitsburg; Thomas HAMMOND & Joseph POOLE, Comm. for Liberty-town. Commissioners: William HARDEN, Lewis KEMP, Chauncy BROOKS, Alonzo LILLY, William WOODWARD, George CAREY, A. G. COLE, William SWAN, Thomas E. HAMBLETON, Lot ENSEY, George CARSON, Edward GREEN, C. G. PETERS, David MARTIN, Francis BURNS, E. P. BARROWS, Eli SCOTT & Robert TAYLOR.

Methodist Camp Meeting: Church on Pipe Creek Circuit, to be held on grounds of Burges NELSON, Jr., about 5 miles east of Liberty-town, on old Liberty road. John S. REESE, John W. PORTER, Thomas SIM, John WOOD, John NICODEMUS, Robert NELSON, Peter BOYER, Isaac SHRIVER, J. L. BILLINGSLEA, John SMITH, James CLEMSON.

Democratic Republican Convention, Frederick County: John KINZER, Esq., chair, Thomas ANDERSON & William SHAW, Esqs., ass't. chair; William Henry DAINGERFIELD & Dr. George W. MARIS, secretaries. David SCHLEY, Esq., Dr. John Wesley GEYER of New Market, William J. BEALL of Frederick County, John FISHER of Westminster & Dr. George MARIS participated. Elected for General Assembly: Henry KEEFER, Frederick; Isaac SHRIVER, Westminster; John SIFFORD, Middletown; Dr. J. W. GEYER, New Market.

Frederick County Harrison Ticket for Senatorial Electors: Evan M'KINSTRY, Uniontown & Gideon BANTZ, Frederick. For the Assembly: Jacob MATHIAS, Westminster; George BOWLUS, Middle-town; Francis BRENGLE, Frederick; Joshua DOUB, Woodsborough. Van Buren Ticket, Senatorial Electors: John FISHER, Westminster & Casper QUYNN, Frederick. For General Assembly: Henry KEEFER, Frederick; Isaac SHRIVER, Westminster; John SIFFORD, Middletown; Dr. J. W. GEYER, New Market.

19 August 1836
Whig Convention of Frederick County: Elias CRUTCHLEY of Woodsborough,
President; Gen. Thomas C. WORTHINGTON of Frederick & Adam KELLER of
Middletown, Vice Presidents; J. K. LONGWELL & William J. ROSS,
Secretaries. On motion of William J. ROSS, Esq. a committee was
appointed to report resolutions for consideration: Abel RUSSELL, New
Market; Martin EICHELBERGER, Creagerstown; William J. ROSS, Frederick;
Jacob MATHIAS, Westminster; Dr. Thomas SPRINGER, Middletown; William J.
THOMSON, Woodsborough; Sterling GALT, Taneytown; Griffin TYLOR,
Buckeystown; Dr. Joshua JONES, Uniontown; Sebastian RAMSBURG, Jefferson;
Wilson HAYS, Hauvers; William A. ALBAUGH, Liberty; J. N. HOSKINSON,
Petersville. Central Whig Committee for Frederick County: George
BALTZELL, Thomas C. WORTHINGTON, Richard POTTS, Daniel KOLB, Jacob
FAUBEL, Lewis BIRELY, William DURBIN, Edward A. LYNCH, James M. SHELMAN,
Gideon BANTZ, Mountjoy B. LUCKETT, Cyrus MANTZ, Benjamin RUTHERFORD,
Valentine J. BRUNNER, John H. BEALL, James W. PRYOR, William C. SMALL-
WOOD, Jacob LITTLE, William WATERS, Patrick O'NEILL, G. M. EICHELBERGER,
John H. WILLIAMS, William R. SANDERSON, William COOKERLY, Israel MYERS,
Moses WORMAN, George GITTINGER, David KEMP, William Bradley TYLER, James
RAYMOND, William SCHLEY, Greenbury FOUT, William S. MC PHERSON, John
HANSHEW, William J. ROSS, John MILLER, James M. COALE, Daniel GETZEN-
DANNER, Philip ROHR, George KOONTZ, Lewis A. BRENGLE, Eli MOBBERLY,
Abraham KEMP, Nicholas H. PITTS, Jona. GETZENDANNER, Francis BRENGLE,
Ezekiel HUGHES, Henry SMITH, David B. DEVIT, Jonathan BRUNNER. Evan MC
KINSTRY & Gideon BANTZ nominated & approved as 2 Electors of Senate.
Baltimore County Electors for Senate: George ELLICOTT & Dr. Ephraim BELL.
For Assembly: Col. Hugh ELY, John T. H. WORTHINGTON, Dr. Jacob SHOWER,
Dr. Thomas RISTEAU. Democratic-Republican Convention: met at DAVIS's
Hotel, York Road. Richard FRISBY, chair, George BRAMWELL & James J.
MURPHY, secretaries.

26 August 1836
TALBOTT, Mahlon, running for Sheriff of Frederick County.
Frederick County Harrison Ticket for Senatorial Electors: Evan M'KINSTRY,
Union-town & Gideon BANTZ, Frederick. For Assembly: Jacob MATHIAS,
Westminster; George BOWLUS, Middletown; Francis BRENGLE, Frederick;
Joshua DOUB, Woodsborough.
Frederick County Van Buren Ticket for Senatorial Electors: John FISHER,
Westminster & Caspar QUYNN, Frederick. For Assembly: Henry KEEFER,
Frederick; Isaac SHRIVER, Westminster; John SIFFORD, Middletown; Dr. J.
W. GEYER, New-Market.
Baltimore County Jackson Van Buren Ticket Senatorial Electors: George
ELLICOTT & Dr. Ephraim BELL. Same for Assembly: Col. Hugh ELY, John T.H.
WORTHINGTON, Dr. Jacob SHOWER, & Dr. Thomas RISTEAU.
Baltimore County Harrison Ticket for Senate Electors: George HARRYMAN &
Samuel H. TAGART.

9 September 1836
UTZ, Barbara, dec'd, late of Frederick County, J. Henry HOPPE, Admr.

7 October 1836
AIKEN, George P., Dr., late of Baltimore, offers services to citizens of
New-Windsor; at former residence of the late Dr. DODS.
BOND, Elijah, renting 2-story dwelling-house & Wheel-wright Shop in New
Windsor.
ERB, Peter, dec'd, late of Frederick County, Jacob ERB, Executor.
HENRY, Francis, trustee's sale by Court of Equity, Frederick County, at
tavern of Jacob HARTZELL, Westminster, of 2 lots in said county, being
part of a tract called "Fanny's Meadow," being lot #7, conveyed by
William OURSLER to Frances HENRY by deed dated 8 January 1834. Said lots

7 October 1836
   are at the Turnpike Forks in said town, adjoining lots of Dr. HEBBARD &
   William OURSLER & contains a large tavern house (2-stories, part brick &
   part frame), large bank building & barn, log stable. Also selling
   contingent Right of Dower which Elizabeth HENRY, wife of said Francis may
   have in or to lot #5, on north-east side of turnpike road from Westmin-
   ster to Taney-town, being the lot conveyed by Nicholas OGG to said
   Francis HENRY.
REESE, John S. Rev., to deliver address at General Meeting House sponsored
   by the Scholars of The Westminster Sabbath School. C. W. WEBSTER, Secty.
SCHAEFFER, Joseph, married to Miss Susannah ZACCHARIAS, d/o the late
   George ZACCHARIAS, both of Westminster District, on Thursday 29th ult.
   Service performed by the Rev. Jacob ALBERT.
SCHULER, Jacob, dec'd, of Frederick County, Samuel MESSINGER, Admr.
SHIPLEY, William Jr., renting or selling his farm, 2 1/2 miles south of
   Westminster.
SMITH, Joshua Jr., selling lot on the Littlestown Turnpike, adjoins town of
   Westminster, 1 1/2 acres, 2-story brick dwelling.
STONESIFER, Abraham, selling lot on Westminster & Littlestown Turnpike,
   about 8 miles from former place, adjoins lands of John Henry HOPPE, Esq.
   & Michael SNYDER; 7 3/4 acres, 2-story log dwelling house with shop
   attached, log stable & spring-house.
TALBOTT, Mahlon, candidate for sheriff of Frederick County.
WILLIS, Dr., may be found at the office next door to his dwelling.
List of Letters Remaining in the Westminster Post Office 1 October 1836:
   Daniel BATSON, John BIGGS, John BEGGS, George CROWL, Asa COLLINS, Thomas
   COOK, William COCHRAN, Elizabeth DORSEY, Benjamin DAVIS, Thomas DEMESS,
   John EVANS, George EBAUGH, George FOWLER, Henry GEATY, Jacob HORMON,
   James HARDEN, James KENNAN, George W. LITSINGER, Ludwick LONG, Evey
   LOWDENSLAGER, George MATHIAS Jr., Esq., Harriett OBRION, Josiah
   PENNINGTON, John SHAMER, Heim SPARENBERG, David SULLIVAN, James SMITH,
   Lydia SULLIVAN, Prudence WILLIAMS. E. CRUMBACKER, Post Master.
List of Letters Remaining in the Taney-town Post Office 1 October 1836:
   George ABLE, Barbara BOWERS, John DELAPLANE, Joseph GOYVLE, Peter GALLEY,
   William C. HICKSON, Jacob HYTER, Clem JOHNSON, George WILT, W. A.
   MONTGOMERY, Margaret M'KINZIE, Harriet A. & Henry ORNDORFF, Benjamin
   SHUNK, Ann STORM, Philip SIX & Dr. SWOPE. Hugh SHAW, Post Master.
Meeting of Citizens of Westminster regarding Electoral Board: Dr. William
   WILLIS, chair; Jonathan NORRIS, ass't. chair; Horatio PRICE & Elias
   YINGLING, secretaries. Committee: J. K. LONGWELL, C. W. WEBSTER, John T.
   MATHIAS, Samuel COOPER, David UHLER, Jacob FRINGER & Henry WAMPLER.

14 October 1836
SHAW, Moses, of Baltimore Co., married in Baltimore, Thursday evening the
   6th inst., by the Rev. Mr. BACKUS, to Miss Ann, eldest d/o William
   SHEPHERD, Esq. of Frederick County.
Voters of Westminster District of Frederick County met at house of Mr.
   HARTZELL. Isaac SHRIVER, Esq., chair; Michael BARNITZ, asst. chair;
   William SHIPLEY, Jr. & Dr. George SHRIVER, secretaries. Committee
   appointed: Jacob GROVE, Dr. John ROSE, James KEEFER, Michael SULLIVAN,
   Michael MORELOCK, David K. OURSLER, John S. MURRAY, Joseph SHAEFFER, John
   A. BYERS & John BEGGS.
Candidates to represent Frederick County in Reform Convention: Francis
   THOMAS & John H. MC ELFRESH of Frederick; Thomas A. JOHNSON of Jefferson;
   Benedict I. BOONE of Middletown; John FISHER of Westminster; Dr. James
   LIGGETT of Woodsboro.
A public barbecue, sponsored by VAN BUREN men at Rockville. Richard I.
   BOWIE opened political discussion; Henry R. WARFIELD of Frederick,
   Benjamin S. FORREST, Francis THOMAS & Dr. John WOOTTON spoke.

14 October 1836
Uniontown District Reform meeting: Tobias COVER & Daniel SULLIVAN, Sr.,
chair; John SMELTZER & Jacob GLEIM, secretaries. Convention Committee:
Jacob LANDIS, Nimrod FRIZZLE, Daniel SULLIVAN, Jr., Elisha BOND, Basil
ROOT, Joseph SWIGART, Jacob GLEIM, Joseph WEAVER, Lewis SHUEE, Isaiah
PEARCE, John ROOP, William HAINES, John LOUTS, Tobias COVER, William
SEGAFOOSE, Jacob GLAZIER, Joshua STANSBERRY, Isaac SLINGLUFF, George
EARHART, Peter NANCE, Henry ROUTSONG & George B. SHRINER.
Frederick County Meeting, Uniontown District, held at home of Jacob
GLAZIER. Evan MC KINSTRY, chair; William ECKER, secretary. Attended:
Col. Thomas HOOK, J. L. WARFIELD, William SHEPHERD, John MATHIAS, Daniel
SHUNK.
Taney-town District Meeting of MD Constitution Reform: Capt. George CRABBS,
President; William SHAW & John B. BOYLE, Vice Presidents; Dr. GWINN &
David HAPE, Secretaries. Dr. GWINN, J. B. BOYLE, Daniel MC KENZIE, John
JONES & John ADLESPURGER drafted resolutions. Delegates: Dr. GWINN,
William SHAW, Capt. George CRABBS, David HAPE, William FISHER, J. NULL,
Daniel MC KENZIE, John ADLESPERGER, Peter HULL, William WORLEY, James
ROGERS, Nelson NORRIS, John NANKEVILLE, John NAILL, John BURK, Jr., John
B. BOYLE, Jacob OCKER, Daniel MEHRING, David BUFFINGTON, John HILTER-
BREAK, Thomas HICKLEY, Jacob HAPE, Lewis PETERS, John MEHRING, Jacob
MOUSE, Doras GROFF, Thomas JONES, Joseph WIVEL & Peter ORNDORF.
Washington County meeting of friends of State Reform held in Hagerstown.
Attendees: Col. William H. FITZHUGH, late sheriff of Washington County,
Dr. Charles MACGILL & Robert WATSON, Esq., Electors.

28 October 1836
FOWLER, Richard, warns persons against trusting his wife Mary. He will pay
no debts for her.
GERNAND, Emanuel, wants a Journeyman carpet weaver.
JONES, Levi Capt. married on Sunday 24th inst. by the Rev. Mr. GARVER, to
Miss Elizabeth BLACK d/o Mr. John BLACK of Frederick County.
MYLES, Peter, dec'd, of Frederick County, sale of his farm in the Pipe
Creek settlement, 5 miles from Westminster & 3 miles from New Windsor;
adjoins lands formerly owned by Peter MYERS, dec'd., 1/4 of a mile from
Philip NICODEMUS' mill, 150 acres, 2-story white weatherboarded dwelling
house, with 2-story brick kitchen, bank barn & 2 wagon sheds, corn house,
smoke house, & spring house in yard, 2 1/2 stories high with 1-story in
the ground. Apply to Philip NICODEMUS. Valentine NICODEMUS.
RECK, Abraham, selling farm of 100 acres on Pipe Creek, apply near
Middlesburg to above or David MARTIN, 9 Howard St., Baltimore.
TOPPER, Joseph, has purchased patentee & makes & sells the Patent Sausage
Chopper.
YINGLING, John, dec'd, late of Frederick County, sale of tract in Big Pipe
Creek Valley, about 2 miles from the Union Mills & 1 mile from the
turnpike leading from Westminster to Littlestown; adjoins lands of John
ERB & Michael FRACK; 153 acres, 1-story log dwelling, log barn & spring
house. Also selling wheat, rye, corn, oats & buckwheat by the bushel.
Jacob YINGLING & David B. EARHART, Executors.
Allegany County Court: Patrick FRAZER- convicted of petit larceny; Daniel
MC BRIDE convicted of perjury; William MC BRIDE & Isaac PASSMORE
convicted of grand & petit larceny.
Allegany County public meeting at the Courthouse in Cumberland: William MC
MAHON, chair; Meshack FROST & Joseph DILLEY, assistants; John M.
BUCHANAN, secretary; Singleton TOWNSHEND, asst. secretary. Attendees: B.
S. PIGMAN & James DIXON of Frederick; William PRICE of Hagerstown;
Michael C. SPRIGG, Daniel BLOCHER, John J. SELMAN.
Electors, by the Grand Jury of Allegany County: Persons presented by the
Grand Jury as "unfaithful Public agents & disturbers of the Public
Peace": Charles MAGILL, Robert WATSON, Casper QUYAN, John FISHER, George

WESTMINSTER CARROLLTONIAN

28 October 1836
ELLICOTT, Ephriam BELL, Joshua VANSANT, John EVANS, George A. THOMAS,
Samuel SUTTON, Washington DUVALL, Robert T. KEENE, M. FOUNTAIN, Enoch
GEORGE, John B. THOMAS, Sprigg HARWOOD, Thomas HOPE, Wesley LINTHICUM.
Taxes for 1836 to be collected by Joseph SCHELL at following locations:
Woodsborough, Mrs. YANTIS' tavern; Liberty, Mr. WAGNER's tavern; Mr.
FRANKLIN's tavern; Sam's Creek, Mr. ENGLE's store; New Windsor, Mr.
ZIMMERMAN's store; Middleburg, Mr. KOONTZ's tavern; Union Bridge, Mr.
SWISHER's store; Union Town, Mr. GLAZIER's tavern; Union Mills, Mr.
Andrew SHRIVER's; Westminster, Mr. SHRIVER's tavern; Taney-town, Mr.
CRAPSTER's tavern; Emmittsburg, AGNEW's tavern; Mechanicstown,
FUNDENBURG's tavern; Creagerstown, BECKENBAUGH's tavern; New-Market,
SCHELL's tavern; Middletown, RICHMOND's tavern.
At public meeting in Westminster, John KUHN, Sen., Michael MORELOCK, Sen.,
& Jacob SCHAEFFER were appointed judges. William SHIPLEY, Jr., & Charles
STEVENSON, clerks.
Meeting of Friends of Gen. HARRISON & John TYLER held at Owings Mills,
Baltimore County. Elisha S. JOHNSON, chair; William TAGART, assistant;
James E. LYON & A. J. FORTT, secretaries.
Candidates for Sheriff: Ezra DADISMAN, George BECKENBAUGH, Henry HOUCK,
George RICE, Mahlon TALBOTT & Abm. FERREE.
Frederick County Reform Meeting: Gideon BANTZ, Esq., & Col. John H.
SIMMONS, chair; Mahlon TALBOTT (late Sheriff Frederick County) & John
SIFFORD, Esqrs., secretaries; Hon. Henry R. WARFIELD, Hon. William C.
JOHNSON, Hon. Francis THOMAS & Col. H. MC FRESH gave speeches. Committee
to draft resolutions: William C. JOHNSON, Washington BURGESS, Dr. Robert
C. CUMMINGS, Mahlon TALBOTT, W.L. & P.W. BALCH, W. Jacob MARKELL, Madison
NELSON, John RIGNEY, John BONNER, John B. BOYLE, Christian GETZENDANNER,
Col. John MC PHERSON, Dennis DORSEY.
Baltimore County Reform Meeting at Greenspring Hotel. Richard FRISBY,
chair; Robert WELSH, Sr. & William HOUCK, vice presidents; George BRAM-
WELL & John S. TYSON, secretaries. Tobias E. STANSBURY, chair.
Candidates: Ephraim BELL, George ELLICOTT, John S. TYSON, Samuel
WORTHINGTON, Joshua HUTCHINS & Charles W. HOWARD.

4 November 1836
WILLET, Miss, of Frederick County brought suit against a Mr. SMITH for
breach of marriage promise, &c. She was awarded damages in the amount
of $820.
Reform Meeting of 6th Election District, Baltimore County, held at house of
William CRUMBINE in Manchester. President - Philip GORE; Vice President-
Frederick RITTER; Secretaries - Joshua KOPP & Jacob KERLINGER.
Attending: Dr. Jacob SHOWER, Joseph M. PARKE, Jacob GETT, George EVERHART
& Capt. Solomon MYERLY.
Election for Conventional Delegate ticket for Frederick District: Judges
appointed are: John KUNKLE, Henry KAUFFMAN, Sr.; John HOUCK. Daniel
SHAWEN, Jr. & Dr. W. W. KOLB, as Clerks. In same election in Union-town
District, Judges are: Nimrod FRIZZLE, Joseph WEAVER & Lewis SHUEE.

11 November 1836
FISHER, John, Cashier, Bank of Westminster, declares dividend of 3%.
JONES, John, (of Charles), Baltimore County, married Tuesday evening last,
at the residence of Maj. Nicholas DORSEY, by the Rev. Eli HINCKLE, to
Miss Eliza C. NORRIS, d/o Jonathan NORRIS, Esq. of Frederick County.
YINGLING, Joshua, of New-Market District married Thursday evening, the 10th
inst., by the Rev. John S. REESE, to Miss Margaret, d/o Isaac SHRIVER,
Esq. of Westminster.

11 November 1836
Protracted meeting to be held in the Union Church, Westminster, by the
ministers of the Church of God, viz: Rev. Messrs. WINEBRENNER, ROSS,
MC FADDEN & MAXWELL.

18 November 1836
LUGENBEEL, Mr. married Thursday, 10th inst. to Miss Louisa NAILL, both of
Westminster District.
WEAVER, George, married Thursday, 10th inst. by the Rev. Mr. MERRIMAN, to
Miss Sophia COPPERSMITH, both of Westminster.
WHITE, Mr. married Thursday, 10th inst., to Miss Charlotte PEDICORD, d/o
Mr. Humphrey PEDICORD of Baltimore County.
Appointed by the Governor & Council of MD: Abraham WAMPLER, Justice of Levy
Court for Frederick County - vice, Jacob MATHIAS resigned. 15th Reg. of
Baltimore County - Daniel HOOVER, Adjutant; vice JOHNSON resigned. Rifle
Co. of Finksburg - George BRAMWELL, Capt.; Israel LEISTER, 1st Lt. &
Levin WILLIAMS, 2d Lt.

2 December 1836
BRUCE & FISHER vs. Perry G. ENSEY, Joshua SMITH & others, in Frederick
County Court of Equity, October Term 1836. Ordered that the sale made &
reported by Joshua SMITH, Trustee be ratified & confirmed. Henry SCHLEY,
Clerk.
HENRY, Francis, in Frederick County Court of Equity, October Term, 1836:
Ordered that the sale of the mortgaged esstate of Francis HENRY & Eliza-
beth his wife made & reported by Joseph ORENDORF, trustee, be ratified.

23 December 1836
Primary School Convention: Chairman - Jacob CRONISE, Esq. of New Market;
Secretary - William P. MAULSBY of Frederick; Attendance: Nicholas H.
PITTS, William J. ROSS, Richard H. MARSHALL, Francis BRENGLE, Richard
POTTS, L.P.W. BALCH, Madison NELSON, Frederick A. SCHLEY & Dr. William
Bradley TYLER.

14 April 1837
The only known existing issue was found in a time capsule opened the summer
of 1987 in Westminster during the 150th anniversary celebration of the
formation of Carroll County from Frederick and Baltimore Counties in
1837. The issue was obviously saved because it gives information
regarding the first office holders for the county, as well as other
information pertaining to its formation. The following information was
abstracted. The issue has since been replaced in the sealed time capsule
which is not to be opened again until 2037.
BLIZZARD, James, going into mercantile business in partnership with Michael
BABYLON at his old stand.
BOND, Benjamin, offers for sale property whereon he now resides in Mt.
Vernon (formerly Jewsburg) & for many years well known as a tavern stand.
Improvements are dwelling with kitchen, good cellar, hog & smoke house
&c. Also 60 acres adjoining above with dwelling, good cellar, barn,
stabling, &c.
BOYLE, John B., renting storehouse in Taney Town, lately occupied by J.
REIFSNIDER. Has been store for number of years. Also, last notice for
persons indebted to him to pay up.
BROWN, Nicholas, for sale or rent a house & lot in the "Forks" of Westminster, fronts on the Main street; 2-story log house with stable &
garden. Nearly opposite residence of Isaac SHRIVER, Esq. Also 6 building
lots for sale, 5 on the Main street & 1 on Pennsylvania Avenue.
BUCHANAN, James M., will attend Courts of Law & Equity in Carroll County;
office in Baltimore.
BUSBY, A. H., selling large quantity of bacon & lard. (Westminster)

41

14 April 1837
ECKER, Jonas, thanks friends & customers; is going into business with his
    brother & new name of firm to be S. & J. ECKER at old stand in New
    Windsor.
GARNER, Lemuel, married Sunday last by the Rev. J. BERNARD, to Mary Ann
    MILLER, both of Baltimore County.
GARNER, Wesley W., authorized to receive Prospectises for the "Democoratic
    Messenger" of Manchester.
GARRETSON, J. & Co., thankful for favours received & continues lumber
    business at corner of Main & Penn streets, York, PA.
GEIMAN, Daniel J., selling property at "the Forks" in Westminster. A lot
    fronting on the Main street, presently occupied by David MYERLY; adjoins
    lots of Isaac SHRIVER; contains 2-story log dwelling with good cellar
    under the whole house.
GERNAND, Emanuel, has on hand 200 yards of carpeting, both Rag and Girthing
    also selling water oak posts, chestnut rails & pails at moderate prices.
HALL, E. J., Principal, Brookeville Academy, Montgomery County, to resume
    his duties.
HARTZELL, Jacob, has taken Shriver's Hotel, Westminster, lately occupied by
    Elias HUNT. The Mail Stage for Baltimore & Pittsburg arrives at &
    departs from this house daily. Emmitsburg Mail Stage also stops, where
    passengers can at all times be accommodated.
JONES, Philips: Decree in Chancery, J. Mason CAMPBELL, Trustee, offer in
    front of the premises the house & Lot in Westminster, late dwelling place
    of Mr. JONES. Two-story brick house with necessary appendages.
MC KINNEY, John, notifies creditors that he has applied to Judges of Court
    of Common Pleas of Adams County, PA for the benefit of insolvent laws.
    Hearing at Courthouse in borough of Gettysburg.
M'MEAL, Dr., located in Westminster at offices of late Dr. COLEGATE.
MATHIAS, Jacob (of George), intending to remove to the west, selling 30
    acres adjoining lands of Christian ROYER, John BIXLER & Daniel
    STONESIFER. Log House & Kitchen, log barn, blacksmith shop &c. Four
    miles from Westminster & 2 miles from BACHMAN's mill.
MICHAEL, Samuel, has removed his hat manufacturing establishment to frame
    dwelling on the Main street, near the Bank.
MITTEN, William, married Tuesday last, by the Rev. Daniel ZACHARIAS, to
    Miss Mary Ann H. SMELSER, both of Carroll County.
MURRAY, John S., selling 2-story brick house & lot in town of Westminster;
    upon the Main street, opposite the entrance of the Liberty road. Also 2-
    story log house & lot, fronting on the Main street adjoining above; also
    unimproved corner lot with stable in rear thereof, completely enclosed.
NORRIS, John, late of Frederick County, dec'd., sale on premises of farm in
    Little Pipe creek in Carroll County. Adjoins lands of Ephraim HARTSOCK &
    Daniel SAILOR, of 137 acres. House, part Log & part stone, a new stone
    Dairy & a new stone Smoke-house, &c. Nelson & Nimrod NORRIS, Executors.
ORENDORF, S., wants old castings; selling wheat flour.
REED, Enos B., has been doing business in this place (Frederick) as a
    Hatter for several years. When friendless & pennyless he was received by
    people here with kindness. He was lately amerced in the sum of $1500 for
    slandering his neighbor & as soon as he could get his goods in a
    portable condition, decamped for the West, leaving this & other small
    debts & a few cumbersome articles in the hands of a trustee. He is a
    small man; a doctor & occasionally a minister. Upon leaving he assumed
    the name of Enos BACON.
SHIPLEY, George, S.D., Dr., has located in Westminster; can be found at
    office now occupied by Dr. SHRIVER & formerly by Dr. WILLIS.
SHIPLEY, Otho, clerk, Commissioners of Tax for Carroll County.
SHIPLEY, William, Jr., to deliver an essay to the Tammany Society of
    Carroll County at HARTZELL's Tavern in Westminster.

14 April 1837
SHIPLEY, William, Jr., offers services as Conveyancer & Agent for purchase
& sale of real estate, stocks Annuities, Loans on Mortgages & all other
business connected with that of a Broker. Office next door to his
dwelling in that of Dr. George S.D. SHIPLEY, main street, Westminster.
Also has for sale a few lots about 3/4 of a mile from Westminster; 3
Farms of about 300 acres 2 1/2 miles south of Westminster; & a well
secured Ground Rent or Annuity of $50 per year in Baltimore City.
SHRIVER, Charles, second son of Hon. Abraham SHRIVER of Frederick on
Tuesday morning last, married Miss Ann Eliza, only d/o Samuel THOMAS,
late of Frederick County; by the Rev. Daniel ZACHARIAS.
TAWNY, Elizabeth Mrs., dec'd., sale at her late residence about 2 1/2 miles
from Westminster on the road leading to Union-town; selling personal
property to wit: 6 horses, 5 cows, 1 bull, 5 sheep, 9 hogs, 2 wagons, 1
Wheat-Fan, & other farm implements. Also Household & Kitchen furniture;
also rye & wheat in the ground. Jacob SHRIVER, Executor.
WAMPLER, Abraham, selling 2 lots in Westminster, fronting on the main
street & Church street on the west, on which is a tavern house presently
occupied by Abraham KUNS; has stable &c.
WEBSTER, C. W., running the Westminster English & Mathamatical Academy.
References: Hon. Judge ARCHER of Bellair; John J. HARROD, Book Agent in
Baltimore; Dr. William WILLIS; Dr. John ROSE; Dr. S. FORRY; Jacob YING-
LING; Jacob MATHIAS; Jacob POWDER, Jr.; Joshua SMITH; James? J. WEBSTER;
Isaac SHRIVER; E. CRUMBACKER; J. K. LONGWELL; & William SHIPLEY, Jr.
WENTZ, Rachel, selling lot of 4 acres on Pittsburg turnpike, adjoining
Westminster with 2-story brick house, large 2-story brick back building,
log stable, all recently erected.
YINGLING, J., has received & is selling raisens, figs & pruens; soda water
& sugar crackers; also a few barrels of wheat flour & wine, brandy & gin.
ZIMMERMAN, John, his partnership at New Windsor with Jonas ECKER has been
dissolved by mutual consent. (See ECKER above)
From the "Messenger," printed at Manchester: On the Sabbath morning, 26
November, the tavern house in that town formerly owned by Dennis DAVIS
was destroyed by fire, leaving nothing remaining but the walls of the
brick part of the building. Mr. Frederick HAMBURG, who occupied a part
of the building has a hat manufactory, sustained a slight loss; & the
personal effects of Mrs. SWAIM, who occupied another part, were consumed.
Bank of Westminster Newly-Elected Directors: Isaac SHRIVER, Washington VAN
BIBBER, Jacob REESE, Jacob MATHIAS, Abraham WAMPLER, Andrew POWDER,
Richard WARD, Joshua SMITH Jr., John F. REESE, Jacob POWDER Jr. & David
GEIMAN.
List of Letters remaining in the Post-Office at Westminster 1 April 1837:
Stephen BLIZZARD, Mrs. Mary BERRETT, Dinah BOON, Levi T. BENET; David
CROWL, Jacob CAPLE, Mrs. Catharine DIFFENBAUGH, Mrs. Naomi DELL, Thomas
FRANKLIN, James FORD, Richard FRIZZEL, Nimrod FRIZZELL of R., Henry
GETTY, Henry HILSCOMP, Herculus KING, John KEY, Lewis KROH, John KROUSE,
Abraham LAMMOTT, Jesse LOGUE, Miss Susan LITTLE, Joshua LOGUE, Martin
LEYER, George W. LITSINGER, Basel LUCAS, Miss Barbary MARTIN, Jacob
MANTS(?), William NOTT, Mrs. Susannah POWEL, Rev. Daniel R. REESE, David,
Samuel or Charles RODINSON, Peter SHUMAKER, Reason STEPHENS, George
STORMS, Sarah SULLIVAN & William WORD.   E. CRUMBACKER, Post Master.
List of Letters remaining in the Post-Office at Taney-town as of 1 April
1837: John B. BOYLE, Mrs. E. BLACK, Joseph R. BOYLE, Joseph CLUTZ, Daniel
CROUSE, William L. CRAPSTER, John FURGUSON, John FORNEY, Thomas FINGAN,
Alexander FRAZIER, Jonathan GAUGH, Mrs. Sally MORRISON, Henry HANN,
Abraham OLER, Jacob PETERS, William RAMSBURG, David REIFSNIDER, D. H.
SWOPE, H. SWOPE, Dr. W. SWOPE, Clarissa SWOPE, Joanna SHRINER, James C.
WILSON, George WHITMAN & Jacob WYMERT. Hugh SHAW, Post Master.
Candidates for Sheriff for Carroll County: Basil ROOT, Isaac DERN &
Benjamin YINGLING.

14 April 1837
Advertisements for Lawyers: A. F. SHRIVER, William W. THOMPSON, James
RAYMOND, & William P. MAULSBY.
Montgomery County Whig Nominations: Henry HARDING & Ephraim GAITHER for
Electors of the Senate.
Whig Party Candidates nominated for Frederick County: For Senate Evan
M'KINSTRY of Uniontown & Gideon BANTZ of Frederick County; for Assembly:
Jacob MATHIAS of Westminster; George BOWLUS of Middletown; Francis
BRENGLE of Frederick County & Joshua DOUB of Woodsborough.
Organization of Carroll County - - - County Court: _____ B. DORSEY, Chief
Justice; _____ KILGOUR & _____ WILKINSON, Associates; William WILLIS,
Clerk; Nicholas KELLY, Sheriff; William P. MAULSBY, States Attorney.
Orphans' Court: Abraham WAMPLER, Chief Justice; William JAMESON & Robert
HUDSON, Associates; John BAUMGARTNER, Register. Levy Court: William
SHEPHERD, President; Sterling GALT, Henry N. BRENKMAN, John ERB, Jacob
REESE, Nimrod GARDNER, John LAMOTT, Joseph STEEL, Joshua C. GIST; Otho
SHIPLEY, Clerk. Assessors: Isaac DERN, Taneytown; William HUGHES, Union-
town; Peter E. MYERS, Union Mills; George W. GORSUCH, Woolery's; John
WILSON, Freedom; Jacob GITT, Manchester; Jonathan NORRIS, Westminster;
Peter NANCE, Hampstead; Thomas CONDON, Franklin's. Collector of Taxes:
Col. Thomas HOOK. Constables: 1st District--John CLABAUGH, David
KEPHART, George WILDT. 2nd--William SHAW, John FERGUSON. 3rd--Frederick
YINGLING, Jacob H. KEMP. 4th--George OGG Jr., William STANSBURY, John
SHOCKNEY. 5th--Warren L. LITTLE, Evan BLACK. 6th--John KRENTZ, Jacob
FRANKFORTER, Henry BIXLER. 7th--Emanuel GERNAND, William GRUMBINE.
8th--Thomas BROMWELL, Samuel LAMOTT. 9th--Andrew T. BARNES, Abraham
ENGLAND. Magistrates' Courts: 1st District--Elias GRIMES, Benjamin
SHUNK, John THOMPSON. 2nd--Thomas HOOK, John SMITH (of Joshua), Charles
DEVILBISS. 3rd--William CONGHLAN, Peter BANKER, David B. EARHART. 4th--
William JAMESON, Mordecai G. COCKEY, William JORDAN. 5th--Joseph STEEL,
Nicholas DORSEY, Warner W. WARFIELD. 6th--Henry BREAKMAN, Jacob
KERLINGER, John SHAFER. 7th--Joshua SMITH, Jr. (one vacancy), Jonathan
NORRIS. 8th--William M'ILVAIN, George RICHARDS, Jacob TRINE. 9th--
Stephen GORSUCH, Th. E. D. POOLE, Benjamin W. BENNETT.

1 December 1837
Whig Meeting at Shadrach BULL's tavern, Westminster. Jacob MATHIAS, Chair
& Abraham WAMPLER & Dr. William WILLIS, Asst. Chairs & Jacob FRINGER &
Otho SHIPLEY, Secretaries. Col. James M. SHELMAN & James RAYMOND, Esq.
gave addresses.
                                    ---•@•---
12 January 1838
APPLER, Isaac, respectfully begs to inform that he has taken the Store
lately occupied by Basil ROOT in Union-Town, opposite the tavern formerly
occupied by David STEM, 2 doors east of the Post Office, where he is now
opening an extensive assortment of seasonable goods consisting of broadcloths, cassimeres, cassinetts; flannels, silks, &c.; together with
groceries, hardware & Queensware, fur & seal caps, linseed oil, &c.
BENNETT, Robert, a black cow with a white face, who shews age & has a
blemish in one eye strayed from his farm, near Sams Creek Post Office.
BIRNIE, C., will sell any quantity of Land, from 50 to 2000 acres; land
situated on Big Pipe Creek & Bear Branch in Carroll county, about 9 miles
from Westminster, on the Taneytown road; 37 miles from Baltimore.
CROUTE, Hezekiah, having entered the Salting business, will sell during
the winter season pork, bacon & offall. Lard can be had at any time.
DODS, Margaret, for sale or rent a large 2-story brick house & lot in
Union-Town now occupied by Mr. ROOT; situated in business part of town,
has wing suitable for store, stable &c. Apply to John ROBERTS at
Uniontown or to Margaret DODS in New Windsor.

12 January 1838

ECKER, John, dec'd., his executors selling on the premises lot of 12 acres about 1 mile southwest of New Windsor, adjoining road leading to Liberty-town. Improvement is 2-story dwelling house weather-boarded & painted; stables; spring house. Also at same sale a lot of wood-land on the Old Liberty Road, 3 miles below DENNING's post office, 13 acres. William & Jacob ECKER, Executors.

FOWBLE, Andrew C., sale to take place at Charles STEVENSON's tavern a farm about 4 miles from Westminster, near the Baltimore turnpike, adjoining lands of Daniel BATSON & Kinsey TAYLOR; 100 acres, a log house & barn.

GARNER, Evan, dec'd., Maria GARNER, Adm'x.

GROVE, Lewis J. P.M., Warfieldsburgh, Agent for Dr. RALPH of N.Y. to sell his medicine for billisus Remittent Fever, ague & Rheumatism.

HAHN, Jacob, Jr., dec'd., late of Carroll County, administrators selling at his late residence on Silver Run, near MAUS' mill, personal property consisting in part of: 11 head of horses; 25 head of Horned Cattle; 8 Sheep; 27 Hogs; 1 boar & sow of the Lancaster breed; farm impliments; a windmill; grain by the bushel; household & kitchen furniture such as beds, bedsteads & bedding; bureaus, chests & drawers; cupboards, tables & chairs; 2 stoves & pipe, &c. Also 1 set of Blacksmith's Tools.

HAYDEN, Catharine, dec'd, late of Carroll County, Basil HAYDEN, Adm'r.

HOOK, Thomas, Collector of Taxes, in his absence Otho SHIPLEY & Joshua SMITH, Jr., Esq. authorized to receive tax.

HOWARD, Elizabeth, dec'd., of Frederick County, Jesse L. WARFIELD, Adm'r.

KING, Nicholas, dec'd., late of Carroll County, sale by administrator, Samuel KING, containing 17 1/2 acres on Sams creek, adjoining lands of Isaac SAUM & John ROOP. Improved by log dwelling, stable, spring house & other necessary buildings. Title indisputable.

NEIDIG, Benjamin, contemplating to remove to the west, selling mill property about 4 1/2 miles north of Frederick City, on east side of the Monocacy River. Mill House is of brick 38x40' & 3 stories high, with 3 run of Burs. Also 24 acres of land on which there is an orchard.

ORENDORF, Samuel, has just returned from the City with fresh & extensive supply of fall & winter goods consisting of: broadcloths, flannels, shawls, cotton yarn, calicoes; also carries groceries, hardware, hats, boots & shoes, tools, raisens, almonds, filberts, figs, walnuts, &c.

REIFSNIDER, J., has opened a new & cheap store at "the Forks", with large & well-selected stock of goods.

REIFSNIDER, Jesse, will constantly keep on hand Miller's (of York county), celebrated broad axes, drawing knives, axes, &c.

ROSE, John, Botanic Physician, now has office & dwelling at building attached to the frame Store House, at the Avenues, Westminster, where he practices medicine, midwifery & surgery. Also selling cloths, hats & caps, boots & shoes, etc. Has determined to quit the Crockery-ware business, he will dispose of present stock for cash.

ROSE, John, having just received a supply of winter goods, invites the public to pay him a call & examine his Stock. Selling dry goods (muslins from 6 1/4 cents up), groceries & hardware, oils, paints, & Thomsonian Patent Medicines; Paper hangings, hats, boots & shoes &c.

ROSE & ZEPP, new lumber yard, at the Avenue, Westminster. Intend keeping on hand a general assortment of seasonable stuff; have presently 25 to 30,000 feet of Cherry boards & 5 to 50,000 prime Shingles.

SELLMAN, Beal married on the 28th ult. by the Rev. J. GEIGER, to Miss Mary Barbara, d/o John WEAVER, dec'd., both of Carroll County.

SHELMAN, James M., has formed connexion with Joseph M. PALMER, Esq., of Frederick, as Attornies at Law & Solicitors in Changery. Office near the tavern of Jacob HARTDELL in Westminster.

SHEPARD, Solomon, dec'd., sale of farm now occupied by John HAPE as tenant. Within a half-mile of SWITZER's Mill, (Union Bridge), adjoining land of

45

12 January 1838
John HESS & Job C. HAINES; 200 acres with house & Switzer Barn; lime kiln
now in operation. William & Thomas SHEPHERD, Execs.
SPALDING, Basil, wishing to go to the west, selling farm of 140 acres in
Carroll County, 4 miles west of Taneytown, the bulfrog road divides it.
Also the store house & lot of 1/2 acre where he now dwells at Monocacy
Bridge, Frederick County & a mountain lot of 24 acres in Adams co. PA,
about 4 miles from Emmitsburg, near M'DIVITT's Mill.
STONER, John, of Carroll county, married 7 December, by the Rev. David
PLOUTZ, to Miss Polly BOSSERMAN of Liberty township, PA.
SWIGART, Joseph, designing to move to the west, selling his property in New
Windsor (Sulphur Springs) consisting of 2 lots with 2-story house &
kitchen. Also 1 lot with 2-story frame house & large brick shop
attached. Also an out-lot of 1 acre. Will sell low.
TANEY, Elizabeth, dec'd., last notice calling in notes given at sale of her
personal estate. Jacob SHRIVER, Ex'r.
TRYNE, Jacob, renting his farm.
VALENTINE, John, of New Jersey, married on Thursday the 4th inst. to Miss
Sophia HARTZELL, of this place.
WARNER, George, dec'd., sale of farm of 144 1/2 acres, 1 mile east of Union
town, opposite farm of John SMITH & adjoining turnpike road. Improve-
ments: 2-story log dwelling house with cellar, large Switzer barn, Lime-
kiln, &c. Also near the above farm & adjoining turnpike a timber lot of 7
1/4 acres; & another 10-acre timber lot about 3 miles from said farm.
Andrew BABYLON, Executor.
WILLIAMS, Robert, married on Sunday the 31st Dec. by the Rev'd. James
PEARRE, to Miss Ann WAPPING, all of Sams Creek, Carroll County.
YINGLING, Joshua, selling Howard's Tonic Mixture for cure of fever & ague.
Also selling Floardo Howard's crystal cement, for mending broken glass,
china fancy articles, &c. & F. Howard's improved compound fluid extract
of sarsaparilla for the cure of Scrofula or King's Evil; Chronic
Rheumatism; Syphilitic & Mercurial diseases, etc. He also sells hats &
caps, boots & shoes, & Howard's improved chemical chloride soap.
Candidates for Sheriffalty: Henry GEATTY, David HAPE.
Lawyers Advertising Services: Francis BRENGLE & A. Ferree SHRIVER; Samuel
D. LE COMPTE; Madison NELSON.
The Post-Office at "Bridgeport," Frederick County has been discontinued.
The people of upper Anne Arundel county have petitioned to be erected into
a new county to be called Howard, the county seat to be Ellicott's Mills.
PETITIONS for the benefit of the act for insolvent debtors. All must have
resided in Maryland for 2 years preceding date of petition & be confined
for no other cause than debt. Francis ANCHERS, Henry BOMGARTNER, Robert
COMINGS, John EBAUGH, Thomas GIBSON, William B. GIST, William JAMES, &
Thomas JAMES. All signed by Abraham WAMPLER & William WILLIS, Clerk.
List of Letters remaining in the Post-Office at Taneytown, Jan. 1, 1838.
Jacob BAUMGARDNER, Peter BABYLON, F. S. BAUMGARTNER, Daniel CROUSE,
Samuel HESS, Adam KING, John KING, Elizabeth LATHAM, Daniel MC KENZIE,
Cathern RECK, Dr. Samuel SWOPE, David GRABS, Bernard SHOMAKER & John
WAREHEIM. Hugh SHAW, Post Master.
List of Letters remaining in the Post-Office at Westminster, Jan. 1, 1838.
David APPLE, Joseph ARNOLD, William BISH, John BOOM, John BAUGHER, James
BRION, Rachel BUCKINGHAM, J. E. BROMWELL, Jacob BEAVER, Jesse BROWN, Mrs.
Mary Ann BOND, Mrs. Lucy COOK, David CROWL, Mrs. J. CAMPBELL, Thomas W.
DURBIN, Adam DELL, George EHRHART, John FOWBLE, William FANNING, Larkin
HOUCK, Mrs. C. HAYDEN, Samuel HILLMAN, James HERD, Henry HAYNES, John S.
JAMES, Mrs. Elizabeth KEYS, Jacob KNIGHT, Peter KNIGHT, David LEISTER,
Zebulon LOVEALL, George LITTLE, Samuel MATTINGLY, Jacob MORELOCK, Miss J.
MC COMB, James B. MORGAN, Mrs. Ann MALEHORN, Mrs. M. MACKELFRESH, Mr.
MORTON, Mrs. S. OURSLER, William PARROTT, Henry PETREY sen., Miss Mary
Ann POOL, Jehu RANDALL, Susannah STARY, George SHEETS, Peter SLAGLE,

12 January 1838
Micajah STANSBURY, & Cornelius SHIPLEY. The following names were omitted
last week: Greenberry WILSON, Mrs. M. B. WEAVER, Onom WILLIAMS, Jacob
WAGONER, James WILLIAMS, Miss Mary M. WEVER & George WARFIELD.

26 January 1838
The citizens of Emmittsburg in Frederick County held a meeting when
informed of a rumor regarding their fellow-citizen John CRAPSTER being
circulated in Springfield, Ohio, wherein he is charged with having been
concerned with a gang of counterfeiters & was arrested. The group met at
the home of David AGNEW in Emmittsburg; Col. Robert ANNAN chair & Joshua
MOTTER, Esq. secretary. The chair appointed Joseph DANNER, George
GROVER, Maj. John HARRITT, Dr. Jefferson SHIELDS & Joseph WELTY as a
committee to send testimonial of Mr. CRAPSTER's good character to the
Editors of the Springfield Pioneer & Ohio Statesman for publication.

16 February 1838
FINCKLE, Rev. Mr., formerly of Taneytown & latterly of Middletown, PA has
accepted a call from the Lutheran churches near Greencastle.
The Harford Negro Case: The Sheriff of York County, PA has delivered to the
Sheriff of Harford County, MD warrants for the arrest of Messrs. BEMIS,
FORWOOD & PRIGG.

2 March 1838
WORMAN, Moses, new barn, near Frederick, burnt on Saturday. Loss $6000.
ZOLLICKOEFER, William, M.D., in letter to Editor informs that smallpox has
made an appearance in Liberty-town.
Washington's Birthday celebration held in Taney-Town began with the ringing
of bells, discharge of 13 rounds of cannon & military music. A parade of
the Guards took place under direction of Col. Thomas HOOK, as Marshal.
They marched to the Union Church where Washington's Farewell Address was
read by Daniel H. SWOPE, followed by an address from Senary LEADER. They
then retired to the Hotel of Jesse CRAPSTER for supper. After the cloth
was removed Col. Thomas HOOK was appointed President, James SMITH &
Sterling GALT, Esq., Vice Presidents, Daniel H. SWOPE & John K. LONGWELL,
secretaries. Many toasts were drunk. Volunteer toasts were proposed by
Lt. WRIGHT to the Taney Town Guards; by Senary LEADER, Israel HITESHUE,
William C. HICKSON, David S. GOLLY, William W. NAILL, Joseph SHUNK, Jr.,
William RUDISEL, William BURK, Ephraim HITESHUE, George MILLER, Henry
SWOPE, Alexander FRAZIER, Jeremiah SHUNK, William FISHER, T. W. RUDISEL,
Michael NULL & Hugh SHAW.

23 March 1838
DITTERT, Charles, a German, about 24 years old, stabbed himself to the
heart in consequence of being rejected by the parent of young girl whose
hand he had solicited in marriage. He had recently been to the house of
the lady, in Comet street, Baltimore City.

5 April 1838
Carroll County Court: Present Judges DORSEY, WILKINSON & BREWER. Grand
Jury: Isaac SHRIVER, Foreman; William FANNING, Joshua SWITZER, Abel
SCRIBNER, Nimrod STEVENSON, David LEISTER, J. J. BERRETT, Michael
BARNITZ, Larkin BUCKINGHAM, John BEAVER, John SHAFFER, William CRUMRINE,
George RICHARDS Jr., Isaac SLINGLUFF, James HEIRD, James SMITH, Loveless
GORSUCH, Richard A. KIRKWOOD, John MILLER, Peter HULL, David FOUTZ,
Joseph KEEFER, William SHRIVER.
Petit Jury: Nicholas ALGIRE, George BRAMWELL, David BUZZARD, Thomas
CARTER, Thomas W. DURBIN, Joseph EBAUGH, Jacob FARVER, Ignatius GORE,
Joseph GONDER, William GRUMBINE, David HAPE, William HOUCK, John C.
KELLY, John KUHN Jr., Jacob GLAZIER, Jesse MANNING, Joshua PLOWMAN,

5 April 1838
Joseph M. PARKE, Thomas S. POLE, James ROGERS, Daniel SULLIVAN, S.
STOCKSDALE, Jacob FRINGER, Samuel NAIL, B. W. BENNETT.
Taney-town District, a corporation election of officers: Burgess, George
MILLER; Commissioners: James M'KILLIP, Israel HITESHUE & Patrick BURK;
High Constable, Alexander FRAZIER.

20 April 1838
ROOP, John Sr., fire destroyed his dwelling-house attached to his mill
property near Union-town on Wednesday the 11th instant. The fire was
communicated to the roof by sparks from the chimney. The mill sustained
no damage because of the efforts of his neighbors.
List of Constables appointed by Commissioners of Tax: Taneytown District--
John CLABAUGH, David KEPHART & William FISHER. Uniontown--Joseph SMITH &
Jacob MYERS. Myers'--Jacob H. KEMP. Woolery's--William STANSBURY, George
OGG, Jr., & John SHOCKNEY. Freedom--Warren R. LITTLE, Evan BLACK & John
CARTER. Manchester--Jacob FRANKFORTER & John KRANTZ. Westminster--
William GRUMBINE & Emanuel GERNAND. Hampstead--Samuel LAMMOTT & Thomas
BROMWELL. Franklin's--Andrew P. BARNES & Abraham ENGLAND.
Appointment by the Governor of Officers of 4th Division of Maryland Militia
under command of Maj. Gen. JAMESON: Col. Thomas HOOK & Col. James M.
SHELLMAN, Aids de Camp. William Fell JOHNSON, Esq., Division Inspector
& Mordecai G. COCKEY, Esq., Division Quarter Master.

27 April 1838
Titles of Laws: An act for the benefit of the heirs of William BROWN, late
of Carroll county, deceased. An act to levy money for the support of
Catharine HIPSLEY, indigent lunatic, wife of John HIPSLEY.
Convention of farmers of Baltimore County called to establish an
Agricultural Society. David LOWE, Esq., chair; Luther COLE, Esq., ass't.
chair; Christopher C. LOVE & William P. SMITH, secretaries.
Public meeting held at Jacob HARTZELL's Hotel the 21st to prepare for
ceremony for laying of the corner stone for new Court House. Nicholas
KELLEY, Esq., chair & James M. SHELMAN, secretary. Committee of Arrange-
ments: Nicholas KELLEY, James M. SHELMAN, John FISHER, Dr. William
WILLIS, Jacob POWDER, Jr., James RAYMOND, Samuel D. LE COMPTE, A. F.
SHRIVER, John F. REESE, Horatio PRICE, Dr. John ROSE, David UHLER, Joseph
SHAFFER, Henry WAMPLER, Dr. George SHRIVER, Jacob MATHIAS, David KUHN,
Jacob REESE, Jacob GROVE, John K. LONGWELL, Benjamin YINGLING, Emanuel
GERNAND, William SHIPLEY, Jr., Thomas HOOK, William P. MAULSBY & Samuel
ORENDORFF.

11 May 1838
An act to incorporate the Manchester Military Bank of Music. Enacted by
General Assembly of MD that Jacob FRANKFORTER, Joshua F. KOPP, David G.
FRANKFORTER, John KRANTZ, Joseph GANTER, Wesley W. GARNER, George
MASAMORE, Amos BROADBECK, Jarret W. GARNER, Amos GARNER, Jacob W. BORING,
Elias BUCKINGHAM, William BIXLER, Jarret ALMONEY, John KUHN, Henry
KERLINGER, Jacob HOUCK & others are incorporated & made a body politic
for the purpose of extending the knowledge & improving the style of
performance of Martial Music.
Committees appointed at district meetings of the friends of the national
administration: Taneytown District: Hugh SHAW, chairman, John B. BOYLE,
secretary. Delegates to State Convention: F. CRABBS, Hugh SHAW, William
FISHER, Dr. W. B. GWINN, William SHAW, David HAPE, Lewis PETERS, John B.
BOYLE, George CRABBS & David BUFFINGTON. Delegates to County Convention:
John JONES, Patrick BURK, John HILTERBRECK, M. NULL, F. CRABBS, Jacob
HILTERBRIDLE, John ADELSPERGER, Thomas HICKLY, William HANN, Jr., George
MILLER, William SHAW, John NANKEVILLE, David HAPE, George CRABBS, Hugh
SHAW, William B. GWINN, Robert J. JAMESON, William FISHER, Daniel

11 May 1838
MEHRING, Samuel NAILL, Jacob PETERS, George RODKEY, Jacob COONS,
Frederick BIGGS, John DUDRER, David GALLY, Abraham NULL, Jr., Thomas
JONES, John B. BOYLE, William BEAVER, Thomas FINEGAN, John KESELRING, A.
BUFFINGTON & Daniel HARMAN.
Franklin District: Henry DRACH, chairman, R. A. KIRKWOOD, secretary.
Delegates to County [sic, probably should be State] Convention: Evan L.
CRAWFORD, Jacob FARER, Henry DRACH, Larkin BUCKINGHAM, Richard A. KIRK-
WOOD, Henry BUSSARD, Francis P. DAVIS, Vachel BROWN, John MYERS & J.
YOUNG. Delegates to County Conventon: A. ALBAUGH, H. DRACH, Evan L.
CRAWFORD, L. BUCKINGHAM, Henry BUSSARD, R. A. KIRKWOOD, Jacob FARVER,
John SUMMERS, Adam C. WARNER, Johnzee BARBOUR, Francis P. DAVIS, John
FRANKLIN, Jacob WILT, Benjamin BOND, Jacob CASHOUR, Alpheus SPURRIER,
David BUZZARD, Vachel BROWN, Wilton BURDET, Samuel CARR, Joseph T. F.
HOOPER, Zachariah ALBAUGH, Jacob FRIZZEL & Charles HOBBS.

10 August 1838
ARNOLD, Joseph, dec'd., those who gave notes, they are due. Joshua SMITH,
   Jr., Ex'r.
CHAPMAN, Mary Calwell, died Friday 3 August, infant d/o Nimrod & Ruth
   CHAPMAN of Reisterstown, aged 1 year, 4 months & 22 days.
EVERLY, George, will sell at EVERLY's mill, 2 miles north east from
   Westminster, 1 cow & calf, 4 loads of hay, 11 hogs, farm implements &
   household goods.
GERNARD, Emanuel, in business as auctioneer.
GLAZIER, Jacob, removing to the West this fall, renting tavern he presently
   occupies in Union-town.
GREEN, R. R., General Agent for B. BRANDRETH, M.D., selling Brandreth
   Vegetable Universal Pills. Agents selling: John F. REESE, merchant,
   Westminster; S. & J. ECKER, New Windsor; W. W. WATKINS, Sykesville;
   BLIZZARD & BABYLOR, Wakefield; W. H. POOLE & Brother, Planeville, Carroll
   County; W. & J. ROBERTS, merchants, Uniontown; Hugh SHAW, post-master,
   Taneytown.
HAMBLETON, John, dec'd, sale of a black girl, aged about   12 years to
   serve until 25, late the property of dec'd. Sale to be held at tavern of
   Jacob HARTZELL, Esq. in Westminster. Thomas E. HAMBLETON, Exe'r. Also
   selling 20 shares of Westminster Bank Stock for cash.
HARDEN, Joseph, selling 2 tracts of land near Freedom. Lot No. 29,
   "Colross", 106 acres on Little Morgan Run, 1 mile from Liberty Road,
   adjoining lands of John WILSON; with large tobacco house. This land is
   famous for fine Yellow Tobacco. Tract No. 2: 73 acres adjoining lands of
   David PRUGH.
HEISSER, George, dec'd., late of Carroll County, David B. EARHART, Adm.
HESSON, Baltzer, dec'd., of Carroll County, Peter HESSON & John
   BAUMGARTNER, Exe'r.
HOOKER, Jacob, late of Baltimore, but now of Carroll county, dec'd., for
   the benefit of his heirs, in the case of Amos & Lloyd HOOKER vs. Humphrey
   PEDICORD & Elizabeth his wife. Bill introduced to Carroll County Court
   of Equity to obtain a decree for the sale of real estate of dec'd. who
   departed this life having left a will wherein he bequeathed to his
   wife Mary, the dwelling house during her life & maintanance from
   produce of the place. He also appointed that after the death of his
   wife Mary HOOKER, an equal division of lands between Jesse HOOKER, Amos
   HOOKER, Lloyd HOOKER, John HOOKER, Susannah HOOKER, Elizabeth PEDICORD &
   Charlotte BROWN. At the time of his death, Jacob HOOKER owned 3 tracts
   contained in a deed from John MERRYMAN, Nicholas SLUBY & James WIGNAL
   dated 19 July 1806; also a part of a tract contained in a deed from Darby
   SUX to Jacob HOOKER dated 17 October 1778; also parts of 2 tracts
   contained in a deed from Richard HOOKER to Jacob HOOKER dated 9 July
   1774. The Bill states that Jacob HOOKER left the following named

10 August 1838

children & heirs at law, to wit: Jesse HOOKER, since dec'd., & left 1 son
named James S. HOOKER his heir at law; Amos HOOKER, Lloyd HOOKER,
Susannah HOOKER, who is since dec'd., & by her last will has willed all
her interest in said estate of her father to said Lloyd HOOKER; John
HOOKER, since dec'd., has left 1 son named Amos HOOKER, his heir at law,
who is a minor under age 21; Elizabeth PEDICORD, wife of Humphrey
PEDICORD, and Charlotte BROWN, wife of Joel BROWN, the said Charlotte is
dec'd., leaving the following children her heirs at law, to wit: Hester
Ann BROWN, Margaret BROWN, Joel BROWN & Rachel BROWN, all minors under
age 21. The Bill further states that Mary HOOKER, wife of said Jacob,
hath since departed this life & that said lands and tenements are not
susceptible of a division among the said heirs at law without great
detriment, injury & loss; & that it would be for the advantage & interest
of all parties concerned to have the lands sold & proceeds divided
amongst parties entitled thereto. Bill further states that the BROWNs,
Joel, Hester Ann, Margaret & Joel Jr. all reside in the state of Ohio.
The real estate is to be sold by Nicholas BREWER, Jr., associate Judge of
Carroll County Court.

HULL, Abraham & wife, by virtue of deed of trust executed to Jacob GROVE,
selling on the premises, real & personal property of said HULL, a farm
formerly the property of Abraham HULL, sen., 1 mile west of the Westminster & Littlestown turnpike, on Silver Run, contains 155 acres, a 2-story
dwelling house 45x27', with Spring & Dairy in cellar of the house; a
large Brick Switzer barn 82x50' & out-buildings. In a pleasant neighbor
hood, near GROVE's Mill & Silver Run Church, adjoining tan-yard property
of Peter HULL, Esq. Also at same time & place selling personal property
of livestock & farm impliments, a windmill & Cutting-box; grains & household & kitchen furniture.

KERLINGER, Jacob, Secretary of Manchaster Academy, advertising courses.

MURRAY, John S., selling 16 acres to be divided into lots of 1, 2 & 3
acres; adjoins the East end of Westminster on the Manchester Road &
within 200 yards of the public buildings.

OGG, William (of George), John SHOCKNEY, Constable has seized & taken all
right, title, claim & interest of OGG's in the following Tracts of land
in Carroll County, viz: "Riders Industry", 9 acres; a House & Lot on the
Deer Park Road; a tract called "Curgaforgas" of 200 acres & 30 acres
being a part of "Caledonia" adjoining "Curgaforgas". Property to be sold
at George TENNER's Inn (Sandy Mount) by virtue of a writ issued by
Mordecai G. COCKEY, at the suit of William JORDAN against OGG.

POWEL, Barbara, dec'd, of Carroll County, David WENTZ, Adm.

POWELL, William, dec'd., sale of real estate containing 50 acres with a
house & stable thereon, 3 miles from Westminster & 1 1/2 from David
ROOP's mills, adjoining lands of Frederick COLTRIDER & George FITTS.
Frederick WENTZ, Ex'r.

REIFSNIDER, J., calls attention to his new & splendid stock of goods.

ROSE, John, removing to Eutaw street, a few doors from Hill Market,
Baltimore, where he will continue the sale & practice of Thomsonian
Medicine; will also board & nurse the sick.

ROSS, WIlliam J., trustee, selling at the public square in Taney-town a
farm 1 1/2 miles from Taney-town & same distance from CRABB's &
BUFFINGTON's Mills, adjoins lands of Joseph TANEY & Jacob MATHIAS;
formerly conveyed by Raphael BROOK to Henrietta WILSON; 301 acres, a log
dwelling of 2-stories, stone dairy, meat-house & out houses for servants;
a barn with stabling at each end & threshing floor in middle. This
property formerly divided into 2 tracts & will be sold divided or entire.
Now under rent to William SCHRINER, whose term will expire 1 April 1839.

ROYER, Jacob & Co., has opened shop in Uniontown where he is to manufacture
machines & horse powers for speedy & clean threshing with ease to the
horses. William SEGAFOOSE & Emanuel ROYER, Agents.

10 August 1838

RUDISEL, John, selling farm lately occupied by George RUDISEL, adjoining Taney-town & on the Frederick road; 212 acres, 2-story log dwelling house, weatherboarded; log barn, stone spring-house. Also signed by Ludwick RUDISEL.

STEVENSON, H., selling farm 21 miles from Baltimore on the Reisterstown Turnpike; 352 acres, stone dwelling 40x82', rough cast; log barn 65x25' & other out-buildings. To view farm call on John KELLY, on the premises; for terms apply to H. STEVENSON near Rocklandville, Baltimore & Susquehanna Rail Road.

THOMPSON, Lloyd, trustee's sale at his house of 1 mantle clock, 6 chairs, 1 table, 1 kettle, 1 oven, cups & saucers, etc. E. GERNAND, Trustee.

WARFIELD, George, for the benefit of his creditors his trustee, Archibald DORSEY is holding a sale at Warfieldsburg for cash 1 Wheat Fan; 1 Rotery Screen; 1 Cutting Board, 1 Ten Plate Stove. Also selling 1 September next, in Lisbon, Anne Arundel county, 4 improved lots in said town, 1/4 acre each & 1 improved lot in Lewistown, Frederick county, MD.

WEAVER, Daniel, dec'd., sale at tavern of David KEEFER in Westminster, all of WEAVER's real estate; 5 acres adjoining Westminster, divided into 3 separate unimproved parcels & 1 lot fronting the main street, 1/8 acre on which is a small log tenement. Lots are contiguous to property of David KEEFER & William SHREEV. Also selling 2 woods lots, 2 miles from town; 11 acres on the east side of the turnpike, adjoining lands of Andrew POUDER & the other 13 or 14 acres on the west side adjoining lands of Jacob POWDER. Henry W. DELL, Trustee.

WENTZ, Rachel, dec'd, sale of her house & lot. Jacob REESE, Ex'r.

YINGLING, Joshua, has removed his Store to the house lately occupied as the Post-Office & opposite Mr. HARTZELL's tavern.

ZOLLICKOFFER, William Dr., selling ZOLLICKOFFER's patent improved process for bating all kinds of hides & skins. Testimonials by: John COVER of Carroll County; David W. ECKER of Frederick County; Henry CURTIS of Liberty-town, Frederick County; Henry ROUZER of Mechanics town, Frederick County; & Jacob YINGLING of Westminster.

A commission has been appointed to determine a public road should be opened commencing where Double Pipe Creek road intersects the Bruceville & Emmittsburg road, thence to intersect a lane between John WILLIAMS & Phillip TOY, & thence with said lane to intersect the lane between William MERING & Daniel HARMAN, thence to intersect lane between Conrad SHORB & John FOUTZ, thence on line between FOUTZ & MERRING & William SHAW & Joseph HAYS, thence with bed of road to intersect the York & Frederick road. John SWOPE, Philip HANN & Elias GRIMES, Commissioners.

Methodist P. CHurch to hold camp meeting 7 September on grounds of William MYERS, 1/2 mile from Union-town turnpike, 3 1/2 miles above Westminster. Eli HINKLE & Josiah VARDEN.

Judges of Election in Carroll County for 1838: 1st District--Samuel GALT, John COVER & Jacob ZUMBRUN. 2d--John MATHIAS, Michael BABYLON & William ECKER. 3d--Frederick SCHULER, Isaac BANKERT & John FLICKINGER. 4th--Elias BUCKINGHAM, George JACOBS & Edward E. HALL. 5th--Nicholas HARDEN, Nathan BROWN & Eli BENNETT. 6th--Frederick BACHMAN, Frederick BIXLER & Mathias BOLLINGER. 7th--A. H. BUSBY, Lewis WAMPLER & Thomas W. DURBIN. 8th--Jonas DEAL, Jetson L. GILL & Nathaniel SYKES. 9th--Benjamin DUDDERAR, Thomas DAVIS Sen. & Philip SNADER.

The following have petitioned for the benefit of relief of insolvent debtors. All must have resided in MD for two years & be detained for no other reason than debt. William CHAMBERLAIN, Michael CLAPSADDLE, Robert COLLINS, James P. FISHER, James HAHN (colored man), Daniel MYERS, Joshua S. PORTER, Philip SIX & Lloyd THOMPSON. Signed Abraham WAMPLER, witnessed by William WILLIS, Clerk.

51

17 August 1838
BABYLON, Michael, notifies that notes & accounts of the late firm of
   BLIZZARD & BABYLON have been transferred to him & are due now.
CROUTE, Hezekiah, has commenced new Mercantile business at the store-room
   at the "Forks" Westminster, recently occupied by Messrs. ROSE &
   SWORMSTEAD & opposite Mr. TOPPER's tavern; selling dry goods, groceries &
   hardware, &c.
HAINES, Samuel, near New-Market, Frederick County, during the storm of the
   9th instant, barn struck by lightning, barn & grain totally consumed.
HARDEN, Nicholas, President of Oakland Academy near Freedom, seeks to
   employ a Classical Teacher to toake charge of the institution.
GROVE, Jacob, announces as candidate for Sheriff.
JONES, Philip, died in Bangor, Maine on the 6th instant, after a short
   illness. Eldest son of the late Judge JONES of Baltimore County, MD, in
   the 58th year of his age. He was for many years a resident of this place
   & highly esteemed in this community.
OGBURN, John W., (merchant) married on Tuesday last, by the Rev. Daniel
   ZOLLICKOFFER to Miss Eliza POLE, all of this county.
SAPPINGTON, Francis Brown Dr., died Thursday the 9th instant, aged about 85
   years.
SHRINER, Peter, died on Sunday last at his residence near the Union Bridge,
   in the 90th year of his age.
A camp meeting will be held 17 August on ground of Mr. POUDER, on road from
   Westminster to Taney-town, 3 1/2 miles from former & 1 mile from Mr.
   ROOP's mill, 1 1/2 miles from Frizzelburg. John ADAMS.
The Whigs of old mother Frederick (County) have nominated: Senator--Richard
   POTTS; Delegates--Jacob THOMAS (of J), George BECKENBAUGH, Suratt D.
   WARFIELD, George SCHLEY & Grafton HAMMOND.

7 September 1838
TAYLOR, John Rev., of Pittsburg, killed by lightning on the 10th inst.,
   while on a visit to his relatives in Mercer County, PA. Was well known
   in the western country as the calculator of Taylor's Almanac.

5 October 1838
ARNOLD, George, has established a Foundry in Gettysburg, Adams co., PA to
   make castings of every kind.
BAUMGARTNER, Peter, 4 miles west of Taney-town, brought before James SMITH,
   clerk of Carroll co. Court, a stray filly trespassing on his enclosures.
BIRNIE, C., selling 2700 acres in Carroll County, on the great Western Road
   from Baltimore to Pittsburg; between Westminster & Taney-town, 8 miles
   from former & 3 from latter. Big Pipe Creek & Bear Branch running
   through land. Apply at Thorndale, near Taneytown.
CARTER, Rov. Mr., to preach here on Sunday night, the 14th instant.
CROMWELL, Richard C., dec'd., late of Carroll County, William JAMESON, Adm.
DANNER, Daniel, married in Taneytown on 27 September by the Rev. Daniel
   FEETE to Miss Debora ECKER, all of this county.
FOUTZ, Davis, selling farm & Mills where he resides known as the "Centre
   Mills." Farm of 315 acres first quality Red Land, improved by grist
   mill, fulling mill, carding machines & saw mill; situated on Meadow
   Branch, 2 miles northwest from Union-town & 9 miles from Westminster.
   Also selling farm of 122 1/2 acres with log buildings, formerly owned by
   Jacob BISHOP, dec'd.
FOWLER, George, took in stray sow in September (near Westminster).
GARNER, Jarret & Wesley W., have on hand goods from Baltimore &
   Philadelphia & operating as J. GARNER & Son.
HAPE, Mrs., died 30 September, near Middleburg, consort of Jacob HAPE, age
   47.
HULL, Abraham, Jacob GROVE, Trustee asks persons having claims to present.

52

5 October 1838
KEPHART, David, dec'd., late of Frederick (now Carroll County), sale of
real estate of said dec'd., consisting of 3 farms between Taney-town &
Union town, on road from Taneytown (through Uniontown) to Westminster.
Lot No. 1: Part of a tract called the "Brick Mills," 160 acres adjoining
the Brick Mills, Pipe creek runs through; has 2 houses, one stone, the
other log, log barn, hog house, corn crib, waggon shed & spring house.
Lot No. 2: Part of a tract called the "Brick Mills," 115 acres on said
creek, has stone house & stable. Also selling farm of 200 acres
adjoining lands of Henry SHRINER & John N. STARR, with stone house,
rough casted & lately built & log barn. George & Margaret KEPHART, Exs.
MATHIAS, John T., of this place, married 25 September by the Rev. Mr. RILEY
to Miss Mary E. SHORE of Pittsburg.
REED, Margaret Mrs., died Monday last, at her residence in Taneytown, at a
very advanced age.
SHIPLEY, Otho, Clerk, announces adjournment of Commissioners of Tax.
SLIDER, John, of this county, married on Tueday week, by the Rev. Mr.
HARPEL to Miss Catharine WENTZ of Baltimore County.
STARR, John N., removing to the West, selling 104 3/4 acre farm where
resides on Big Pipe creek, Carroll County, adjoins lands of James CROUSE,
Abraham HITESHUE & David KEPHART's heirs, 1/2 a mile from KEPHART's mill;
is improved by log dwelling house (rough cast) front 20x25', & a back
building 20x15' with cellar under front & kitchen under the back building
used for washing, etc.; log barn 54x27', with wagon shed & corn crib at
one end & shed of 16' at other.
YINGLING, Joshua, opening new Store house, which he has erected on the
location of the old stand, at the north corner of Main & Court sts,
Westminster.
List of Letters remaining in the Post Office in Westminster 1 Oct. 1838.
John ARBAUGH, James B. ARNOLD, Jesse BROWN, Nicholas BUCKINGHAM, Mrs.
Mary BISH, Adam BISH, William BEVER, Jacob CLUNK, George CAIN, David
CROWL, Mrs. Catharine CORBIN, Joshua CORBIN, Moses DEVENPORT, Miss
Margaret DURBIN, Ann DAVIS, N. FRIZZLE, Gabriel HENNIMAN, J. W. HOUSE,
Thomas HOOK, John HESSON, David HAEN, Jacob KING, Elizabeth KEYS, Samuel
KELLY, Henry KELLER, George LACHER, Miss Margret LOWDENSLEAGER, George W.
LITSINGER, Ludwick LONG, William LEHR, Casper LAWYER, Lewis LINDSEY,
Cyrus R. MUMMA, J. W. MC GINNIS, Rubin MATHIAS, Jesse MANNING, Jabez
MURRAY, John ORENDORFF, Joseph ORNDORFF, Joshua PLOWMAN, Miss Mary Ann
POOL, Mrs. Susannah POWELL, John RINEHART, J.L.B. ROBBINS, Mrs. Margret
SHREAV, Murry SHILLIN, John SHAEFFER, Miss Mary STEPHENS, James SMITH,
Andrew SHAFFER, Michael SMITH, Elizabeth TAYLOR, Isabelah WHESKLEY,
Thomas WELLS, Andrew WALTER Jr., William WOLF & Charles ZENTZ.
List of Letters remaining at the Post Office in Taneytown 5 Oct. 1838.
George ANGLE, Henry BLACK, John CREGLOW, Alson COVER, James CLABAUGH,
William DURBIN, Jacob KOONS, Samuel KEEFER, Miss LONGWELL, Henry
ORNDORFF, John PATTERSON, B. SPALDING & Peter GALLY.
Lawyers Advertising: Joseph BRECK, James M. SHELMAN & Joseph M. PALMER.
The following have petitioned for benefit of insolvent debtors. Must have
resided in MD for two years & must be detained for no other reason than
debt. Daniel CROUSE, Frederick ENGLAR, & Thomas LONGMORE.
A committee has been appointed to determine whether the public convenience
requires a public road commencing at the Piney Falls, where the present
road crosses said Falls, running thence past DEVRIES' mills, taking bed
of present road between lands of George F. WARFIELD, George PATTERSON &
John HIPSLEY, then nearly southwest to the public road near Sykesville.
John LITTLE, Nicholas DORSEY & William WHALEN, Commissioners.
Taxes for 1838 collected: Franklin District, No. 9: Mr. BOND's tavern in
Mount Vernon; Mr. FRANKLIN's tavern; Mr. TODD's tavern in Ridgeville; Mr.
Peter GOSNELL's. Freedom District, No. 5: Mr. Reuben WARFIELD's store;
Mr. Henry CARTER's tavern; Mr. BARTHELO's tavern near Hood's mill; Mr.

5 October 1838
WATKIN's tavern in Sykesville; Mr. Thomas CARTER's tavern; Mr. John
LITTLE's tavern in Freedom. Finksburg District, No. 4: Mr. HOLMES'
smithshop, near G. W. GORSUCH; Mr. MALLALIEU's factory; Mr. HORNER's
tavern in Finksburg; Mr. ALGIRE's tavern; Mrs. WOOLERY's tavern.
Hampstead District, No. 8: Mr. George RICHARD's mill; Mr. John LAMMOTT's
tavern in Hampstead. Manchester District, No. 6: Mr. CRUMRINE's tavern
in Manchester; Mrs. FREED's tavern; Mr. Frederick BAUGHMAN's mill; Mr.
Michael MILLER's; Mr. SHAUCH's mill & Mr. Martin KROH's mill. Myers'
District, No. 3: Mr. MYERS' tavern & Mr. WARNER's tavern. Taney Town
District, No. 1: Mr. Lewis PETERS' tavern; Mr. LEADER's tavern in Taney-
town; Mr. MARTIN's tavern in Middleburg; Mr. George LANDER's store,
Double Pipe Creek. Union Town District, No. 2: Mr. LANDER's store at
Union Bridge; Mr. ECKER's store in New Windsor; Mr. BLIZZARD's store in
Wakefield; Mr. David STOUFFER's tavern in Uniontown; Mr. FRIZZEL's tavern
in Frizzelsburg. Thomas HOOK, Collector. During his absence tax payers
of Westminster District can pay Otho SHIPLEY or Joshua SMITH.

26 October 1838
OLIVER, Thomas, "Oakland" his estate of 587 acres was sold yesterday on
change by Messrs. GRUNDY & Co., to George R. GAITHER, Esq., merchant of
Baltimore City, at $84 per acre. Property situated on Elk Ridge in Anne
Arundel County, about 15 miles from Baltimore City.

2 November 1838
ARMISTEAD, R.L., offering reward for negro man named Jerry; 40 years of age,
5'7-8" high, color approaching yellow or tawny, remarkably high forehead,
bald on the hind part of his head, very shrewd in his manner of express-
ing himself & much given to intemperance. Deliver to R. L. ARMISTEAD
near UPPERVILLE or to his master, residing near Martinsburg, VA. He was
accompanied by a negro man, Abraham, belonging to John P. DULANY. He was
taken up & put in the Fredericktown Jail & escaped 6 October between
Frederick & the Point of Rocks. It is that he went towards Westminster.
FOUTZ, David, his mill property on Meadow Branch recently purchased by Mr.
BAER of York county, PA for $16,000!
LYNCH, Thomas, renting tavern stand on Littlestown turnpike, 6 miles from
Westminster, formerly occupied for many years by James HEIRD, at present
occupied by Mrs. GARNER as a store. 30 acres of land attached to the
house & good stabling & sheds.
MATHIAS, Joseph married on the 25th inst. by the Rev. Mr. HARPEL to Miss
Sarah SELLERS, both of Manchester District.
SHIPLEY, Larkin, offers reward for strayed cow, near Liberty Road.
SHUNK, Joseph Jr., hat manufactory in Taney-town.
STEWART, William, on trial for the alleged murder of his father, Benjamin
in Baltimore County. George R. RICHARDSON, Esq., State's Attorney. On
22 June the body was discovered within the limits of the city, very
mangled. After being shot Benjamin STEWART had been hacked by a hatchet,
then stabbed in the back (presumably such mutilation would reduce chances
for identification). Two pistols belonging to William were found at the
home of his uncle, Thomas STEWART (recently fired). Dr. DURKEE who
examined the body after exhumation & found in the body a ball that
corresponded precisely. A hatchet was found 100 yards from the deceased,
a similar hatchet had been purchased by the prisoner at the store of Mr.
DRAKE the day previous to the night of the murder & state's attorney
expected to prove that no hatchet precisely similar can be purchased
elsewhere in the city of Baltimore. When asked what the prisoner did
with the hatchet he purchased, he said he had left it at Mr. WHITELY's
auction store to be sold. William P. PRESTON, Esq., senior, counsel for
the prisoner. Mrs. STEWART attends her husband every day with apparent
devotion. Verdict rendered was guilty of murder in the second degree;

2 November 1838
   punishment is confinement in the Penitentiary for not more than 18 years
   nor less than 10. Motion for a new trial was asked for & overruled 9
   November.

9 November 1838
GIST, Joshua, selling 60 barrels of prime yellow corn, near Westminster.
HARMAN, Joseph, the Washington Blues to meet for parade at Bachman Mill.
KEEFER, Samuel, warns all persons from trusting his wife, Catharine, who
   has been purchasing goods on his credit; also forewarns persons from
   removing any goods now in his possession as he is determined to enforce
   the law against all who disregard his notice.
OTTER, William, of Emmitsburg, married in Taneytwon on the 1st inst., by
   the Rev. Daniel FEETE to Miss Elizabeth LATHEM, of Taneytown.
THAYER, Nathaniel H., invites citizens to assemble with patrons of school
   he intends to open in the General Church.

25 January 1839
ARNOLD, Joseph, of Ohio, dec'd., Joshua SMITH, Jr., Trustee, selling farm
   recently owned & occupied by dec'd., in Carroll county, 2 miles northeast
   of Westminster, 1/4 of a mile from EVERLY's mill & adjoining mill
   property of Abraham WAMPLER & farms of David LEISTER & Abraham SHAFER.
   Contains 170 acres; is watered on 2 sides by Patapsco Falls & Cranberry
   Branch. Two-story stone house, log barn, stables, barrick, smoke house,
   stone spring house.
BEAM, Robert M., has taken that well known House, the Globe Inn, corner of
   Baltimore & Howard Sts. in Baltimore. Formerly kept by Mr. George
   BELTZHOOVER, but more recently by Joshua W. OWINGS. It has long been a
   favorite stopping place for country merchants.
CRAPSTER, John, selling farm of 155 acres & tavern stand, between Westmin-
   ster & Taneytown, now occupied by Cornelius BAUST. Has brick house,
   brick Switzer barn, & spring house. Apply to Mr. C. in Emmittsburg or to
   Sterling GALT, living near Taneytown.
CROUSE, Mary, died, William B. GWINN, Trustee, selling by decree of Court
   of Equity, Carroll County, land seized. 200 acre farm in neighborhood of
   Taney Town on the main roads from Emmitsburg & Gettysburg. Contains log
   dwelling with Brick Back Building & Piazza, good barn & stables with
   sheds attached. Also for sale well-secured Ground Rents, being the rents
   arising from the land upon which Taney Town is built.
FROUFELTER, Jacob, sale of farm on which he resides of 233 acres, on Bear
   Branch, Carroll County, 1 1/2 miles from Westminster & Taneytown & 2
   miles from the Littlestown Turnpike Roads, & 8 miles from Westminster.
   Good log house & barn. Being sold by C. BIRNIE.
HAINES, Nathan of William, selling his Pipe Creek farm of 182 1/2 acres,
   in Carroll county, lying on waters of Pipe Creek, 4 1/2 miles southwest
   from Westminster & 2 1/2 east from New-Windsor; adjoining lands of Reuben
   HAINES, Abraham BAILE, John NICODEMUS, Joseph CASSELL, Louis SHUE & Isaac
   HAINES. Has 2-story weatherboarded house with 62' front with brick
   addition back, large bank barn 56x24'; another barn nearly new 30x57';
   Granary, Smoke & Wash houses, 2 grain Sheds & Spring-house. Also 2
   tenant houses on the place.
HEBBARD, W. B., by virtue of a deed of trust from him to E.E. HALL of
   Reisterstown (MD) & E. J. HALL of Brookville (MD), they are selling the
   farm on which HEBBARD resides, on the road from Taneytown to Frederick, 3
   miles from former & 20 from latter, improved by 2-story brick house with
   extensive back buildings, large barn 60' long, wagon shed with corn crib
   on each side, outbuildings & Overseers House. Contains 225 acres.
   Another farm adjoining above with 244 acres, a log dwelling, stable & log
   barn and lime kiln in an unfinished condition. Also selling 2 lots in
   the western part of Westminster. One contains a 2-story house part brick

WESTMINSTER CARROLLTONIAN

25 January 1839
& remainder frame. Also 2 young servants, 1 a boy 10 years old, another
female about 8 years old--both healthy & of remarkably fine family.
HOOKER, Jacob, dec'd., of Carroll County, his farm of 125 acres being sold
by decree of Court of Equity; on both sides of Baltimore & Westminster
Turnpike Road, immediately above 21st milestone & adjoining farms of
Edward STOCKSDALE, of John, & the late Joseph KELLEY's. Improved by 2-
story log dwelling house, barn & other outhouses. Also selling a wood &
meadow lot of 75 acres, detached about 30 perches distant from above
farm, lying on both sides of Beaver Run. William JAMESON, Trustee.
JORDAN, William, selling 100-acre lot in Carroll county, within 5 1/2 miles
of Westminster & 1 1/4 from the Deerpark road. Mr. JORDAN lives within
one mile from said land.
MANNING, Richard, dec'd., of Carroll County; Nancy MANNING, Exec'r.
MARTIN, John, dec'd., of Carroll County; Michael GARBER, Adm'r.
MONTELL, HYAH?, intending to remove to Baltimore, will sell his 135 1/2
acre farm on which he resides. Formerly owned by Capt. CAMPBELL & known
as his "Dublin Farm," more recently by Peter KEMP, about 5 1/2 miles from
Frederick. Includes dwelling house, new wagon shed 30x27', corn houses
on each side with Granary above, new carriage house 20x15', Ice & Meat
house, Blacksmith Shop. The Monocacy at distance where Stock can at all
times have free access to water. A lime kiln has been erected.
PLAINE, Beniah E., of Carroll County, married Tuesday the 13th, by the
Rev'd. M. WILES, to Miss Hannah M., second d/o John MYERS of Adams
county, PA.
RICHARDS, John, married Sunday the 13th inst. by the Rev. J. ALBERT, to
Miss Margaret Ann HORCH, both of this county.
SHOEMAKER, Peter, late of Carroll County, dec'd., selling one farm, called
the "Home Place" being the mansion farm of the dec'd., on road from
Westminster to Taneytown, about midway between the two. Contains 204 1/4
acres, large 2-story house & log barn & number of out houses. Has been
occupied as tavern stand for many years. Also, selling another farm
called "Barnhart's Place," adjoining first farm, containing 122 3/4 acres
of limestone land. Buildings are of Logs. Also selling another small
farm of 36 1/2 acres called "Foutz's Place," adjoins above-named farms.
Has 2-story log house, log barn & other buildings. Also another farm of
148 1/2 acres called "Stonesifer's Place," adjoins 1st named place.
Improvements are part stone & part log. Also selling another farm of 173
1/4 acres called "Sell's Place," adjoining the last named farm.
Improvements are of log. Another farm of 137 acres called "Burgoon's
Farm," adjoining last-named farm. Improvements of Log. Also selling lot
of 1/4 acre in the town of Westminster, contains 2-story log house
weatherboarded & painted, kitchen attached, good stable, now in possession of Baltzer ARBAUGH. Also selling a number of building & out-lots
adjoining last-named lot. Jacob MATHIAS & Joshua SMITH, Jr., Executors
of Peter SHOEMAKER, dec'd.
UHLER, David, persons indebted to him are notified the notes have been
given to Samuel Jackson DELL for collection.
UHLER, David Jr., died in Illinois the last week in December. Son of David
UHLER Sen., late of Westminster, in the 17th year of his age. Came to
his untimely death by a fall from a wagon loaded with wood, which horses
bolted & threw him off.
WELCH, Mary, late of Carroll County, dec'd., her property seized & for sale
by James RAYMOND, Trustee. Farm of 218 1/2 acres 1 mile from Eldersburg
& 19 miles from Baltimore, north of the Liberty Road, now occupied by G.
CAMPBELL, Esq. Tract called "Arabia Petra Enlarged". Has dwelling
house, barn & out-houses.
YOUNG, George, late of Carroll County, dec'd., his heirs at law selling his
real estate of 104 1/2 acres, 2-story dwelling 30x20' with kitchen
attached, stone dairy & log barn. Property lies on head waters of Sams

25 January 1839
Creek & adjoining lands of Robert BENNETT, Stephen GORSUCH & Nathan
FRANKLIN. Call on Michael ZEPP who will shew same. John & George YOUNG,
& Elizabeth FRIZZEL, Sarah LAMBERT, Juliet STEM, Mary Ann ZEPP, Ann &
David YOUNG, heirs at law.
ZENTS, Asa, died the 14th inst., of Carroll County, aged 35 years.
Road Notice: Commissioners have been appointed to open a Public Road,
beginning at the Hanover road near the mill of Andrew SHRIVER; thence to
or near David E. EARHART's saw-mill & through his land. Thence on a line
of said EARHART & Philip ORTER, through the land of Joshua WISNER, near a
corner-stone at the end of the first line of "Empty Bottle," thence to
intersect the PA-MD line west on said line from a corner-stone on said
line between Philip WENTZ & John RINEMAN.
The Misses BIRNIE's school for young Ladies is located 37 miles from
Baltimore, on road from Westminster to Emmitsburg, near Taney Town in
Thorndale. References: Rev. Dr. JOHNS, Rev. J. G. HAMNER, Rev. R.J.
BRECKENRIDGE, Rev. J.C. BACKUS of Baltimore, F. S. KEY, Esq. of Washing-
ton, D.C., Dr. J. RIDOUT of Annapolis, R. POTTS, Esq. of Frederick, Rev.
J.P. CARTER of New-Windsor.
Candidates for Sheriff of Carroll County: Isaac DERN, Henry GEATTY, David
HAPE, Basil ROOT, Jacob GROVE & Benjamin YINGLING.
Attorneys advertising: James M. SHELMAN & Joseph M. PALMER of Frederick
County. Office adjoins tavern of Jacob HARTZELL in Westminster. Madison
NELSON, West Church St. in Frederick Town, nest door to Tannery of Gideon
BANTZ & opposite the Methodist Episcopal Church. James RAYMOND has
removed to Westminster from Frederick. Francis BRENGLE & A. Ferree
SHRIVER in Westminster. Samuel D. LE COMPTE located 3 doors below the
residence of Dr. WILLIS in Westminster, & Joseph BRECK of Hampstead.

8 February 1839
HAINES, Henry, of Uniontown District, his dwelling house robbed & $70 in
silver taken from a bureau drawer.
QUYNN, Caspar, nominated for Orphans' Court of Frederick County, expected
to be rejected.

22 February 1839
The Westminster Academy has been incorporated by an act of legislature.
The following persons are incorporated members: Jacob REESE, Isaac
SHRIVER, Nicholas KELLY, Jesse REIFSNIDER, John M'COLLUM, J. S. MURRAY,
Joshua SMITH Jr., J. K. LONGWELL, Levi EVANS, Francis SHRIVER, Hezekiah
CROUT, Basil HAYDEN, James RAYMOND, William P. MAULSBY, John FORMWALT,
William SHIPLEY Jr., John F. REESE, David KEEFER, George SHRIVER,
Nathaniel H. THAYER, Henry GEATTY, Benjamin F. FORRESTER, Nimrod BECK,
Mordecai PRICE, Joseph SHAFER, Jacob HAASE, William SHREEV, Emanuel
GERNAND, John KELLER, Jacob GROVE, Lawrence ZEPP, E. CRUMBACKER, Jesse
MANNING, James M. SHELMAN, John BAUMGARTNER, S. J. DELL, David BURNS,
George SHEETS, William GRUMBINE, John FISHER, John BAURGELT, Samuel
ORENDORF, Solomon ZEPP, A. H. BUSBY, Otho SHIPLEY, Conrad MOUL, J.P.H.
SHIPLEY, J.S. SHIPLEY, C. W. WEBSTER, M. BARNITZ, Covington D. BARNITZ,
S.D. LECOMPTE, John SWIGART, William ZEPP, Amos LIGHTNER, James KEEFER,
N. MANNING, John A. KELLEY, Joshua YINGLING, G. WIVEL, E. YINGLING, Jacob
POWDER Jr., J. D. POWDER, B. YINGLING, Jacob HARTZELL, L.W. HARTZELL,
J.F. HARTZELL, J.M. YINGLING, George RAMBY, William YINGLING, David
HILTEBRIDLE & all others who may have subscribed previous to passage of
this act or who hereafter shall subscribe to the amount of not less than
$5.

1 March 1839
ARNOLD, Joseph, late, his farm sold to Levi EVERLY for $4200.

1 March 1839
BRENDEL, Henry G. of Hagerstown, married Thursday the 14th ult., by the
Rev. Daniel FEETE, to Miss Mary A. FEETE, of Middletown, Frederick Co.
DEER, Israel, married in Taneytown by the Rev. Daniel FEETE to Miss
Elizabeth CRISE, all of Taneytown, on Thursday the 7th ult.
HAINES, Nathan, his farm on Little Pipe Creek was sold lately to Philip
ENGLER for $14,620, being at the rate of $80 per acre.
HEINER, Levi, married on Thursday week by the Rev. Mr. ZOLLICKOFFER, to
Miss Mary, d/o Thomas MEDCALFE, both of the Union-town District.
KELLY, John Somerfield, died Friday the 22d ult., aged 2 years, s/o John
Greenbury KELLY & Rachel MORRIS.
SCHLEIGH, John Mrs., of Hagerstown, has for some months past been in
delicate health & at times gave evidence that she was laboring under
hallucinations. On Tuesday morning it was discovered that she had left
her room & a search was made without success. Several hundred citizens
turned out to search the neighborhood until night, but she was not found.
The next two days hundreds of persons re-searched the town, equally
unsuccessful. She is tall & slender & when she disappeared had an old
sun bonnet, a calico dress & large black & white cross-barred over shaw.
[Mrs. S. has since been found dead in MIDDLEKAUFF's woods, near
Hagerstown.]
SNOWDEN, Henry Col., formerly of this county, married Thursday, 17th of
January last, at Green Lawn, Oldham county, KY, to Mrs. Elizabeth
FREDERICK of the former place.

8 March 1839
TODD, Joshua Jr., petitions for relief under insolvency laws.
Nominations for Carroll County by the Governor to the Senate. Justices
Orphans' Court--Nimrod FRIZZLE, Michael SULLIVAN & Michael BARNITZ.
District Justices--1st District--George CRABBS, John NANKIVILLE, John
THOMPSON. 2d District--Jacob LANDIS, Bazil ROOT & Nelson NORRIS.
3d District--James HEIRD, Adam FEISER, Robert CRAWFORD. 4th District--
William FANNING, Abraham LAMMOTT & John C. KELLEY. 5th District--
Jonathan DORSEY, Edward DORSEY of Eli, William WHALAN. 6th District--
Jacob GITT, Philip GOSE & Thomas SATER. 7th District--John Henry HOPPE,
Hezekiah CROUT & John BEAVER. 8th District--Henry LAMMOTT, George
RICHARDS & David FOWBLE. 9th District--Thomas B. OWINGS, Henry DRACH, &
Larkin BUCKINGHAM. Jacob KERLINGER, Surveyor. Coroners--Wilton BURDITT,
William EWING, David HAPE & Elijah WOOLERY. Notary Public to reside at
Westminster, Jacob REESE.
Commissioners: 1st District--William SHAW; 2d--John ROOP of Joseph; 3d--
Peter HULL; 4th--Daniel STULL; 5th--Eli HEWITT; 6th--Frederick RITTER;
7th--Jacob SHAFFER; 8th--William HOUCK; 9th--Johnza BARBER.
Justices of the Peace: George MILLER, Alpheus SPURRIER, John A. BYERS,
Henry BUZZARD, Daniel GEIMAN, Jacob FARVER, John F. REESE, Charles
DENNING, Thomas WELLS, John FRANKLIN, Jesse MANNING, Jacob CASHOUR, John
MALEHORN, William JOHN, Nicholas H. BROWN, Adam C. WARNER, David LEISTER,
Cornelius GRIMES, John FISHER, Vachel BROWN, Sr., James KEEFER, Richard
A. KIRKWOOD, Nicholas ALGIER, Jacob WILT, George FOSTER, Thomas INGELS,
John FOWBLE of F., Loveless GORSUCH, Henry NEFF, Michael FARE, Jacob
MEIXELL, David Z. BUCHEN, Benjamin YINGLING, David DEAL, Jacob GROVE,
James KELLEY, Jacob WICKARD, John MYERS, Willton BURDETT, Joshua YOUNG,
J.T.F. HOPPER, Michael SAWBLE, Josiah SHILLING, Samuel NAILE, Denton
SHIPLEY, David HAPE, Thomas WARD, David BUFFINGTON, Nimrod WOOLERY, John
JONES, Joseph STANSBURY, John DUDDERAR, Joseph POOLE, Michael NULL, Sr.,
Israel LEISTER, Johnson JAMISON, Daniel BUSH, Elijah BOND, Charles
STEVENSON, Isaac SLINGLUFF, John LOCKARD, John WEAVER, James MORGAN,
Melpher CRAMER, Jacob HILTEBRIDLE, William POLE, Benjamin BENNETT, Peter
CHRIST, Thomas J. CARTER, Lewis SHUE, George W. MANRO, David SMELSER,
Samuel W. MYERS, Isaac APPLER, George WEAVER of H., Jacob NICODEMUS, John

WESTMINSTER CARROLLTONIAN

8 March 1839
WERTZ, Andrew SHRIVER, Martin KROH, Daniel DEAL, Henry SHAUCK, Michael
LYNCH, Henry FAIR, George RINEHART, John HOFOCKER, Jacob MAUSE sen.,
Henry MILLER, John JONES of Jno., Solomon MYERLY, Peter BECKTEL, George
EVERHART, Samuel MESSINGER, Andrew GRAMMER, Adam BOWERS, Michael RITTER,
Benjamin STONESIFER, John BROWN, George FLEEGLE, Samuel JORDAN, John
FEISER, Isaac SHRIVER, Peter HESSON, David KUHN, John FLITTER, John
M'COLUM, & John MILLER.

22 March 1839
BROWN, Peter H., has retired from Editorial Management of the "Republican
Citizen," purchased by Messrs. RIGNEY & MC LANAHAN of Frederick.

5 April 1839
GRAMMER, Andrew, the Commissioners of Tax has elected him as Clerk in place
of Otho SHIPLEY, Clerk to the former board--the latter is retiring.
The citizens of Hagerstown met to discuss raising money for the extension
of the Franklin railroad to the town. R. M. TIDBALL, John SWARTZWELDER,
George L. HARRY, George FECHTIG & Charles WILSON, Esq., to be committee
to procure authorization from the General Assembly.
Grand Jury of Carroll County for April Term: Mordecai G. COCKEY (foreman),
States L. GIST, Jacob FARVER, Nicholas PLOWMAN, Emanuel LINN, John C.
KELLY, George SHOWER, Abel SCRIVENOR, Loveless GORSUCH, Ignatius GORE,
Charles DEVILBISS, Daniel BUSH, John JONES of John, John ROBERTSON, Dr.
John SWOPE, Joseph BRUMWELL, Benjamin BENNETT, John NICODEMUS, David
WOLF, William T. HAMMOND, Abraham H. BUSBY, Andrew POUDER & John LANTZ.
Petit Jury for April Term: Thomas JONES, Upton SCOTT, William FISHER,
Michael NULL, William SHAW, Basil ROOT, Joseph WEAVER, Andrew K. SHRIVER,
Henry HAINES, Elijah WOOLERY, Archibald DORSEY, Johnza SELBY, Reuben
CONOWAY, Philip GORE, Michael RITTER, Jacob GROVE, Benjamin YINGLING,
William S. BROWN, Isaac SHRIVER, Patrick KELLY, Thomas B. BUCKINGHAM,
Richard BRASHERS, Jacob NICODEMUS, Richard A. KIRKWOOD & Nathaniel H.
THAYER.
Constables appointed by the Commissioners of Tax: Taney-Town District--
William FISHER, Washington GWINN & John CLABAUGH. Union-Town--William
SEGAFOOSE. Myers'--Jacob CRAWFORD, Jacob H. KEMP, Jacob STONESIFER &
David HULL. Finksburg--Nimrod WOOLERY, Benjamin WILLIAMS, Nathan GORSUCH
& John C. COLEHOUR. Freedom--Johnza SELBY & Ferdinand DORSEY.
Manchester--John KRANIZ, James MARSHALL & James DAVIS. Westminster--
Henry OURSLER, William B. GIST, Isaac POUDER & Francis FRANKLIN.
Hampstead--Joseph ARMAGOST & Richard HARRIS. Franklin--Benjamin SPURRIER
& Joseph T. F. HOPPER.

12 April 1839
BUCKINGHAM, Obadiah, died at his residence in this county on Wednesday the
3d instant, aged 81 years. Among the many who stood around his grave
were 27 or 28 lineal descendants; extending to the 4th generation.
COVER, Tobias, elected Tax Collector for the Union town District.
FOWLER, John, (of George), of this county, married Tuesday last, by the
Rev. Mr. LAIQUE to Miss Lydia CLUNK of Adams county, PA.
HARDEN, Joseph & wife vs. Robert WELCH, in Carroll County Court of Equity,
the sale made in this case by James RAYMOND, Trustee, is confirmed &
amounted to $2,403.50. Nicholas BREWER, Jr.
KELLEY, Nicholas, Sheriff, gives notice regarding licenses to traders &
keepers of ordinaries.
LOOKINGBEAL, William, married Sunday last by the Rev. N. ZOCCHI to Miss
Sarah ROACH, both of this county.
NICODEMUS, Henry & Andrew, have retired from the Mercantile business & are
looking to close their books as speedily as possible.

59

12 April 1839
SULLIVAN, David, married Sunday evenlast by the Rev. J. GEIGER to Miss
    Julian, d/o Lewis REAGLE, all of Manchester District.
WEISER, Charles & Emanuel ZIEGLER, have opened new lumber yard on North
    George St., near the Stone Bridge in York, PA.
WILLIS, William, renting large room lately occupied as the Clerk's Office.
Bank of Westminster, Directors elected for this year: Washington VAN
    BIBBER, Abraham WAMPLER, John F. REESE, William ROBERTS, Joshua SMITH,
    Jr., Jacob REESE, Andrew POUDER, James RAYMOND, Jacob POWDER, Jr. &
    Richard WARD. Isaac SHRIVER, Esq. was re-elected President.
There was an accidental fire two weeks ago in a large body of Wood about 3
    miles east of Westminster, belonging to David ROOP & Jacob TRYNE & before
    subdued it had spread over 60 or 70 acres. On Tuesday last, fire was
    communicated by the burning of brush to the timber on the adjoining lands
    of Isaac SHRIVER, Esq. & George CASSELL near the town (John SHAFER
    occupies the latter property).
Bill in MD Legislature to divorce Leah & Frederick HOPPE was rejected by
    the Senate.
Announce Col. Anthony KIMMEL as a candidate to the House of Representatives
    & Abraham Ferree SHRIVER as a candidate for House of Representatives.
Additional appointments for Carroll County: Notary Public--John F. REESE
    in place of Jacob REESE, resigned. Justices of the Peace--Michael SMITH,
    Henry W. DELL, Richard MERCER, Peter MARTIN & John SMELSER.

26 April 1839
BUCKINGHAM, Owen F., selling 100 acre farm on which he resides, fronting on
    Westminster Turnpike, 22 miles from Baltimore City & 6 miles from
    Westminster, adjoining lands of the late Joseph KELLEY & William CAPLE,
    Esq. Improved by a large 2-story log house with adjacent store room &
    kitchen, barn & out buildings, &c.
LANTZ, John, intending to quit the Mercantile business selling a variety of
    cloths, shoes, &c. at his residence, 2 miles from Union-town & same
    distance from New-Windsor.
LAUDER, Samuel A., married in Frederick City on Tuesday last, by the Rev.
    Mr. MC ELROY to Mrs. Fanny MARTIN, d/o Moses SHAW, Esq., all of Union-
    town District.
SHOEY, Rosanna Mrs., died at residence of Mr. John GREENWOOD, near New-
    Windsor on 12th of April, relict of Daniel SHOEY, dec'd., aged 82 years 9
    months & 19 days.
SHOEY, Rosanna, late of Carroll County, John GREENWOOD, Ex'r.
SMITH, Samuel Gen., died at his residence in Baltimore Monday afternoon
    last, in his 87th year. He was a Revolutionary War officer & a veteran
    statesman. He was believed to be born in Lancaster County, PA, but
    resided 79 years in Baltimore. Although he had reached a great age, his
    death was sudden & unexpected. He had been riding in his carriage, after
    dinner & upon returning to his home, laid himself down upon a sofa to
    repose. His servant found him dead.

3 May 1839
CARLYLE, Margaret, died near Union-town on Friday last, in the 54th year of
    her age, after a lingering illness. Consort of Ebenezer CARLYLE, she
    died as she lived, an exemplary Christian, a worthy member of the German
    Baptists (or Tunker) Society. She has left a husband & 4 children.
DUNLIN, A.F. (M.D.) married on Tuesday, 23rd ult. by the Rev. Daniel ZOL-
    LICKOFFER to Caroline Susan, eldest d/o David KEENER, Esq. of Baltimore.
GOSNELL, William S., died near Union-town 25 April of Scarlet Fever; d/o
    William & Matilda GOSNELL, aged 9 years 5 months & 25 days.
HAINE, Sarah Jane, died on Sunday last, youngest d/o Joseph & Margaret
    HAINES, aged 9 years & 24 days.

3 May 1839
HANN, William of Sams Creek, some evil-disposed persons having put in
circulation a report prejudical to my character, which I pronounce a
malicious falsehood, & can establish my innocence if necessary--this is
to notify those persons making use of my name improperly that I will
prosecute to the fullest rigour of the law.
HOOD, James (of John), died at his late residence in Freedom District, in
the 64th year of his age; a highly esteemed & worthy citizen.
MAGEE, Isaac, married on the 4th ultimo, by Rev. Daniel FEETE to Miss
Margaret DEAHOFF, both of Union-town District.
POLE, Thompsey Mrs., died in New-Windsor on Friday, 26 April, in her 52nd
year after a severe & painful illness of 4 days. Consort of Capt.
William POLE, leaving him & a large family of children & friends.
POLE, William Jr., having taken the New-Windsor Hotel, formerly occupied by
John D. WOODS, has opened same as House of Entertainment & solicits
patronage. The Sulphur Springs are only a few rods from the door.
SALTZGIVER, Henry, informs that he has commenced the manufacture of hats in
the frame dwelling opposite store of John F. REESE, Esq.
SHRINER, Samuel, married 21 March by Rev. Isiah KELLER to Miss Margaret
MARING, both of Taneytown District.

10 May 1839
CLOSE, Elijah, married on 1st inst. by Rev. Samuel R. FISHER of Frederick
County to Miss Susan d/o Frederick BIGGS of Carroll County.
CULP, Peter, his barn struck by lightning Thursday evening last at borough
of Gettysburg and entirely consumed.
ENGLAR, Philip, of this county, living within 2 miles of Westminster,
Michael SMITH, Justice of the Peace, certified that he is keeping a stray
bright Bay mare; rides tolerable well.
EVANS, Levi, acknowledges liberal patronage, which he has received for his
carpentry business; solicits manufacture to order furniture, coffins, &c.
GERNAND, Emanuel, has taken that old & established Tavern stand in
Westminster known as KEEFER's Tavern. Wagoners & Travelers welcome.
STANSBURY, Rebecca, Mrs., died 2 May near Emmitsburg, consort of Abraham
STANSBURY & d/o the late Charles STEVENSON (formerly of this county) in
the 64th year of her age.
SWORMSTED, S. L., (at "Forks" in Westminster), agent for Joseph TOPPER,
late of Westminster, requests those indebted to said TOPPER pay.
Petitioners of relief for insolvent debtors. Must reside in MD for 2 years
& be imprisoned for no other reason than debt. Abraham BUFFUSS, Joseph
LANTZ & Joshua TODD, Jr.

17 May 1839
Town Council (Westminster) met Monday last & elected Mr. Jacob YINGLING
President & Otho SHIPLEY Clerk.
Taney-Town District Magistrates, George CRABBS, John THOMPSON & John
JONES, Esquires.

24 May 1839
Candidates: Abraham BIXLER, Esq., of Manchester District, Evan L. CRAWFORD
of Franklin District; & John MC COLLUM of Westminster for House of
Delegates.

14 June 1839
Vacancies in Magistrates' Court for Westminster District have been filled
by the Governor as follows: John Henry HOPPE, John MALEHORN & John
MILLER. John J. BERRETT, Esq. to be Judge of Freedom Election District
Court in place of William WHALEN, Esq., resigned.
Whig Convention assembled at Ellicott's Mills Saturday last, nominated John
P. KENNEDY & Charles H. PITTS, Esq's. as candidates to represent the

14 June 1839
District composed of the City of Baltimore & Anne Arundel County in next congress.
Candidates: Francis THOMAS for Congress; William H. FITZHUGH, of Washington County, independent Van Buren candidate for same station.

21 June 1839
BITTLE, Barbara Mrs., died on the 1st inst., in the 79th year of her age, wife of Thomas BITTLE of Germany twp, Adams County, PA.
MAULSBY, Israel D., died on the 14th inst., at Bel-Air, late a member of the Legislature from Harford County.

5 July 1839
A Post Office has been established at New London, Frederick County, MD & Benjamin F. NORRIS has been appointed Post-Master.
Thomas CONN has been appointed Post-Master at Sabillisville, Frederick Co.

12 July 1839
4th of July Celebration at Manchester: There was the Village Bell & the frequent loud discharge of Musketry by the members of the new company, the Manchester Greys under Lt. Wesley W. GARNER, at an early hour. Between 9 & 10 the Greys assembled for drill & a procession was formed under the chief Marshal, Capt. Solomon MYERLY, in the following order: In front was Samuel DEWEESE, a soldier of the revolution, the Chaplain, the Orator of the day J. M. PARKE & the Hon. John T.H. WORTHINGTON. Procession moved to an adjoining grove (formerly belonging to Jarret GARNER, Esq., now the property of Samuel B. FUHRMAN), where an ample dinner had been spread by William CRUMRINE. After dinner toasts were announced & saluted with occasional discharges of the cannon under the direction of Henry N. BRINKMAN, Esq., assisted [by] J. Whitfield GARNER. The Manchester Military Band under Capt. Wesley W. GARNER performed. 13 toasts were drunk & then volunteer toasts were made by: Samuel W. MYERS, Esq.; Amos GAUMER; Samuel D. LECOMPTE; Nicholas KELLY; Henry N. BRINKMAN, Esq.; George E. WEAVER, Col. Thomas HOOK; Henry H. SULLIVAN, Jacob GROVE, Esq.; Jacob CAMPBELL; William SHIPLEY, Jr.; George WENTS; J. Henry HOPPE, Esq.; John R. BOON; Uriah B. SULLIVAN; Lt. Wesley W. GARNER; John RIGNEY; Henry LIPPY, Jr.; John KUHN; Jacob LINEAWEAVER; William GETTINGER; John SWARTSBAUGH; Daniel GARRET; Adam SHOWERS; Frederick RITTER; William CRUMRINE; Paoli SULLIVAN; David SHULTS; Dr. Jacob MYERLY; Henry REIGLE; Anthony HINES; Elias MYERLY; John C. PRICE; J. M. PARKE; Levi MAXFIELD; George WEAVER, of H.; Jacob SELLERS, Jacob KERLINGER, Esq.; Michael SULLIVAN, Esq.; John EVERHART; Henry BELTZ; Capt. S. MYERLY; Michael RITTER; & David SULLIVAN.

19 July 1839
We have received, as a present from Mrs. George SPALDING of Monocacy, 2 very fine Beets, which we challenge all creation to beet! Also From Mr. John MYERS, a head of Timothy which measures 13 1/4"! Also, Mr. Washington NICODEMUS has presented us with an Onion measuring 11 1/4" in circumference.
Mr. James ROGERS, of Taneytown, has been appointed by the Governor as a Justice of the Peace.
Tuesday night last, the Van Buren Convention nominated the following as candidates to represent the City of Baltimore in the House of Delegates: John C. LEGRAND, William Fell GILES, John J. GRAVES, J.G. SEIDENSTRICKER & Francis GALLAGHER.

26 July 1839
COALE, Richard, Capt., (near Liberty), a copper mine was recently
    discovered on his lands. Extensive examinations have been made & has
    been pronounced inexhaustable.
WINE, Jacob, near Bachman's Mill in this county, his large Switzer Barn
    was struck by lightning & totally destroyed.

2 August 1839
BACHMAN, Frederick, of this county, has sent our office a large bunch of
    Oats, longest stalk measuring 7'6".

9 August 1839
KELLER, Samuel, s/o Mr. Samuel KELLER, residing near this place, met with
    an accident on 26th ult., which terminated in his death on Sunday last.
    He was on his way home from a blacksmith shop when his horse took fright
    and threw him. He unfortunately fell on a dung-hook, one of the prongs
    of which entered his head, injuring him so much that all hope of his
    recovery vanished. He was 6 years 10 months 23 days. (Hanover Herald)
PRICE, Jacob, died Monday the 22nd inst., an aged & respected farmer of
    Washington twp, in that county. He dropped dead whilst in the act of
    sowing some turnip seed; & Mrs. M. GUSH, an aged lady of the same twp.,
    suddenly fell dead whilst viewing the funeral of Mr. PRICE passing by her
    dwelling. (Chambersburg PA Repository)
Methodist Protestant Church has determined on building a Meeting-House in
    Westminster & contracted with Conrad MOUL for its erection. It is to be
    located on a lot near centre of town, belonging to estate of the late
    Jacob SHERMAN, dec'd.
We have been shewn a stalk of corn, which grew in a lot of the Rev. Mr.
    FEETE in Taneytown which measured 15'8" in length. Also a stalk of oats
    grown on farm of John B. BOYLE, Esq., measured 8' lacking 1". Also Mr.
    Jesse YINGLING, who resides on a farm of Mr. Frederick WARBLE near town,
    presents us an Onion measuring 13 1/4" in circumference & weighs 14 oz.
    Another we have received is an onion from Daniel ENGLE, Esq., of Sams
    Creek, in cumference 13 1/2" & 12 oz. in weight.

16 August 1839
PRICE, William Esq., of Washington County, candidate for Congress in the
    upper district, in opposition to Francis THOMAS.
At a Convention held at Towsontown (Baltimore Co.) the Van Buren Party
    nominated the following ticket for Delegates, viz: Dr. T. C. RISTEAU,
    Dixon B. STANDBURY, Philip POULTNEY, John B. HOLMES & Robert WELCH, Jr.
    James TURNER declined being a candidate.
Washington County--The Vanites have nominated John T. MASON, Michael
    NEWCOMER, Dr. Frederick BYER & William MC K. KEPPLER, as candidates for
    next House of Delegates.
This is the most prolific season we have ever known. Every day we hear
    accounts of extraordinary productions. Our jovial friend C. DEVILBISS,
    Esq., has forwarded a large mess of very large Mercer Potatoes, raised
    from a patch 90'x27', which produced 27 bushels of potatoes. He has also
    sent us a Hen's Egg measuring 8" in circumference. To cap the climax we
    learned that a lady of Old Freedom District (where the Whigs are as thick
    as blackberries) has given birth to 4 children at one birth. Also have
    been shewn a Tomato raised by John ADLESPERGER of Taneytown District, that
    measures 19" & weighs 2 pounds! A turnip is growing on the farm of our
    old friend, Michael NULL, Esq., 30" in circumference.

23 August 1839
ADAMS, Joseph, announces camp meeting, 2 miles east from Taney-town on or
    near the road from that place to Westminster, in the woods below the
    stone bridge crossing the Pipe Creek on said road, land owned by James

23 August 1839
 CROUSE. Held under direction of the Churches of God at Frizzelburg &
 Uniontown. All hucksters & traffickers advised to stay at home, or at
 least to leave their trafic[sic] at home.
 BARTHOLOW, J., of New Windsor, selling new stock of seasonable goods
 including clothes, silk & Pongee Handkerchiefs, calocoes, etc.; Berlin
 gloves, Stray & Tuscan Bonnets; Groceries, drugs, paints, &c.
 BARTHOLOW, Thomas (of Thomas), petitions for relief of insolvent debtors.
 BECK, Nimrod, house caprenter, has removed his shop to the house occupied
 by Mr. Nimrod STEVENSON at the "Forks" in Westminster. He will build
 houses to order; also makes coffins to order & has a Hearse to convey the
 dead to a place of burial, without any extra charge.
 BOWMAN, William H. & Samuel M. BODEN, inform the citizens of Wakefield &
 vicinity that they have taken the shop adjoining the Store of James
 BLIZZARD, where they intend carrying on a tailoring business.
 CONDON, Richard, late of Carroll County, dec'd., his property of 2 Negro
 men, Amos (ran away on 4 May last; dark Mulatto, 5'7" high; full mouth'd;
 has scars on arms occasioned by a scale) & Abraham (dark Mulatto, 5'7-8"
 high; has mark on his neck similar to warts & rather a down look when
 spoken to). Runaways are about 30 & 32 years old; brothers & used to
 call themselves SAPPINGTON. Thomas CONDON, Adm'r. offering reward.
 CRUMBACKER, David, of this county, married on Thursday the 8th inst., in
 Union-town, by the Rev. Philip BOYLE, to Miss Elizabeth KINSEY, of
 Frederick County.
 DILL, Nicholas, by reason of his advanced age & increasing bodily
 infirmities, feels desirous to lessen his worldly cares & troubles, & as
 a means to attain that end, he will sell the following real estate in
 the valley of Silver Run. His farm & tavern stand on the turnpike road
 from Westminster to Littlestown, 9 miles from former, 5 from latter,
 which has been occupied for several years by Joseph WERNER, containing 63
 acres with a 2-story tavern house, part of logs & weatherboarded & part
 of bricks with a porch in front & kitchen attached to rear. A log barn
 with sheds, log stable, spring-house. Also all that farm on the said
 turnpike, adjoining the former & occupied by David BIEHL, containing 224
 acres with log dwelling house & large back building of stone; 2 log
 barns, one on each side of the turnpike, wash house &c. Silver Run flows
 through this farm; & in 1 field limestone rock project over the surface,
 promising an extensive, if not an inexhaustible quarry of lime-stone.
 Also selling a lot of 12 3/4 acres situated on the Stone Road, about 1
 mile from Peter HULL's tannery & 4 miles from Littlestown; adjoining
 lands of George MORTER & Henry CRINER.
 FRANKLIN, John, died on last Saturday week, of Franklin District.
 GARNER, J. & Son, of Manchester, having determined upon removing West in
 September, request all persons to present claims for payment.
 GARNER, Jarret, removing West, selling at his residence in Manchester, MD 1
 cow; a first-rate one-horse Sleigh; household goods; imported & domestic
 Carpet. Also 3 lots adjoining the lot owned by the Methodist Episcopal
 Church & another lot in front of the Academy, owned by Wesley W. GARNER.
 GERNAND, Emanuel, has taken old Tavern Stand in Westminster known as
 KEEFER's Tavern. Good beds, excellent Table & Liquors, Stabling, &c.
 GRIFFITH, Alfred P.E. & Oliver EGE, announce Camp Meeting 1 1/2 mile south
 west of Hampstead & 9 miles from Westminster, near Capt. W. HOUCK's, on
 lands of Richard RICHARDS & Capt. HOUCK.
 HAINES, Nathan (of William), notifying that notes from sale due & payable
 at house of Samuel HAINES near Wakefield.
 HALL, Edward E., Bank of Westminster & John MC KALEB vs., No. 44, Equity
 Docket, the object of which is to obtain a decree to vacate & set aside
 as fraudulent, as against creditors a deed of trust, executed by William
 B. HEBBARD, now dec'd., & Susan J. HEBBARD, his wife, to Edward E. HALL &
 Elisha J. HALL, dated 30 October 1838, of all the personal estate of said

23 August 1839
   William B. HEBBARD & of certain real estate in said deed specified,
   consisting of tract in Carroll County conveyed by B. S. PIGMAN & Frederick
A. SCHLEY to said HEBBARD by deed of 28 March 1836, recorded in Frederick
County & consisting of 225 acres; a tract conveyed by said SCHLEY &
PIGMAN to William KNOX & the said Wm. B. HEBBARD as stated. Said KNOX by
deed of 24 December 1828 & recorded, having released his interest to said
HEBBARD; (245 1/2 acres); also tract conveyed by Joseph PEDDICORD & wife
to Wm. B. HEBBARD & Ebenezer B. HEBBARD by deed of 24 March 1834 &
recorded; the interest of said Ebenezer B. HEBBARD & Wife by deed of 29
April 1837 & recorded having been conveyed to said HEBBARD; and also to
obtain decree to sell for the benefit of creditors the property & payment
applied to debts of said HEBBARD. William B. HEBBARD left a will by
which Susan J. HEBBARD, his wife, and his children, William A., Ann R.,
Moses B., HEBBARD & Mary R. PATTERSON (wife of John R. PATERSON), Lydia
and John Marshall HEBBARD are the only persons intended in the estate
after payment of debts. The bill alleges that at the time HEBBARD the
deed to Edward E. HALL & Elisha J. HALL, that he was insolvent & indebted
to the complainants in large sums & that said deed was a conveyance for
the use & benefit of his wife at a time when he was insolvent & in fraud
of & to defraud his creditors & to hinder, disturb & delay complaiants as
creditors from collection of their debts.
HARTSTOCK, Ephraim, by virtue of deed of trust, Upton SCOTT & Nimrod
   NORRIS, Trustees, selling 3 tracts in Frederick county, called "Come by
   Chance," "Mill Right's Design" & "Black Flint," 140 acres of excellent
   land with dwelling house, barn & out buildings. Also a merchant mill, a
   clover mill & a saw mill, all at the junction of Beaver Dam & Little Pipe
   Creek.
HAYDEN, William, late of Baltimore (now Carroll) county, dec'd., died,
   seized, one farm of 134 acres, on road from Westminster to Washington
   city, about 3/4 mile from Westminser. Improvements consist of a log
   dwelling-house, 1 1/2 stories high, barn & out-houses. Also a small farm
   of 80 acres, a short distance below, being 3 miles from Westminster & 1
   from the Baltimore & Reisterstown Turnpike, with no improvements thereon.
   Basil HAYDEN, Trustee.
HINER, Henry, about to remove to the West, selling farm on which he lives
   of 127 acres in Frederick county, on the public road from Emmitsburg to
   Woodsborough, near EICHELBERGER's mill, with 2-story weatherboarded log
   house & kitchen.
MC ILVAIN, William, removing to the West, selling old & well-established
   Tavern Stand known by the name of WHITE HALL, in Carroll County, on
   turnpike from Baltimore to Hanover & Carlisle, 3 miles from Manchester &
   1 from Hampstead with 27 acres, improved by large 2-story stone house &
   Kitchen, brick store, all shelved complete, attached to the house, stone
   stabling, smoke-house, &c. Also selling 75 acres adjoining above with
   large 2-story log house & Kitchen, log barn with sheds.
MOUL, Conrad, has taken establishment recently occupied by Jacob HARTZELL,
   Esq., & opened same as a House of Entertainment, solicits patronage at
   Moul's Hotel & Stage Office in Westminster.
MURRAY, John S., great bargains for cash! Intending to decline the Dry
   Good business selling stock. Will continue grocery business & selling
   boots and shoes, which he manufactures.
MYERS, John, selling the farm on which he now resides, on waters of Little
   Pipe Creek in Carroll county, 6 miles from Westminster & near New-
   Windsor, adjoining lands of Thomas TOWNSEND & Abraham BAILE, 200 acres,
   brick 2-story house, brick barn, brick granary, wagon-shed &c.
ORENDORF, S., fresh stock from the City, cloths, groceries, hardware, etc.
PRICE, Horatio & Alfred TROXEL, new firm at old stand (of H. PRICE), a few
   doors above the "Forks", will manufacture made to order wagons, ploughs,
   harrows, cultivators, hay rakes &c.

23 August 1839
REESE, John F., agent in Westminster selling Phelp's Compound Tomato Pills.
REIFSNIDER, Jesse, selling spring & summer goods, Groceries, Carpenters
Tools, Queens & Glassware & Earthenware. (Westminster)
ROYER, Jacob, selling complete portable threshing machines. (Uniontown)
SHAUCK John, Esq., of Manchester District, died 14 July in the 85th year
of his age. Legal notice Henry SHAUCK, Exe'r.
SNADER, Jacob, of Sams Creek, has sent to this office a Timothy Stalk
measuring 7'.
YINGLING, Joshua, Westminster, selling dry goods, groceries, hardware, etc.
Also selling "The Life of the Rev. Charles W. JACOBS of the Methodist
Protestant Church," by the Rev. A. A. LIPSCOMB.
Candidates for House of Delegates, Thomas HOOK; John MC COLLUM, Esq., of
Westminster District; Evan L. CRAWFORD, Esq., of Franklin District;
Abraham BIXLER, Esq. of Manchester.
Public Meetings: Whig voters of Baltimore & Carroll counties embraced in
the 3d Congressional District to meet & appoint 5 delegates each to meet
in Convention at Baltimore 31 August to appoint Delegate to National
Convention. Carroll County meetings: MARTIN's Hotel in Middleburg, S.
LEADER's Hotel in Taneytown, POLE's Hotel in New Windsor, Peter E. MYERS'
tavern, near the Union Mills, in Union-town at Mr. SEGAFOOSE's tavern &
in Finksburg at Mr. HORNER's tavern.
Van Buren Convention of Frederick County has nominated Casper QUYNN, John
MC PHERSON, John H. SIMMONS, Daniel S. BISER & Jacob FIROR for Legisla-
ture & Abner CAMPBELL for Sheriff.
Misses BIRNIE's Seminary for young ladies, 37 miles from Baltimore on road
from Westminster to Emmitsburg near Taney-town, MD. References: Rev. Dr.
JOHNS; Rev. J. G. HAMNER, Rev. J. C. BACHUS, Rev. J. R. BRECKINRIDGE of
Baltimore, Rev. J. P. CARTER of New Windsor, F. S. KEY, Esq., of
Washington DC, R. POTTS, Esq., of Frederick, Dr. J. RIDOUT of Annapolis.
Corner stone of the new Methodist Episcopal Church at Manchester, MD to be
laid 24 August. Address to be delivered by the Rev. THORTON of Carlisle,
PA. One of the Trustees being about to remove to the West, is anxious to
have the business closed.
Commission to examine requirements of public road to commence at a poplar
tree, on the road from Bruceville to Little Pipe Creek bridge & thence to
a road from Middleburg to Mechanicstown. Lewis HAINES, John WHITE & John
DUTTERAR, Commissioners.

13 September 1839
HILTERBRICK, William, a very promising & able boy aged 11 years (s/o John
HILTERBRICK), 2 miles from Taneytown, Wednesday 21 ultimo, in company
with another brother while taking horses to a pasture field some distance
from the house, was thrown with considerable violence across a fence-rail
& injuried so badly as to cause death the following day.
Pipe Creek Bridge: Messrs. Benjamin FORRESTER & Henry ORENDORFF have
contracted for repair of above by 1 November for $565.

20 September 1839
CHRIST, Jacob, of Lancaster, PA, married Thursday last by the Rev. Daniel
ZOLLICKOFFER to Miss Ann, d/o Capt. Charles DEVILBISS, of this county.
MAY, Henry & Robert BEALE, the latter the assailant, his weapon an iron
poker attacked Mr. MAY in the street in Washington. BEALE fired a pistol
& missed. MAY also drew a pistol, put it up again, telling BEALE he
spared him for the sake of his family.
OWINGS, John, died at Kaskaskia, Illinois, aged upwards of 60 years. He
had quite recently left this state to visit & reside with his son in that
place. He had just reached there when he was attacked by disease, which,
in 9 days, terminated his existence. He was born in PA, but early in
life removed to Baltimore, where he became a successful merchant.

20 September 1839
SHUEE, John Capt., his creditors to participate in the final Dividend to be
made by Paul MAURER, Trustee, are to present their claims to David W.
NAILL, Sams creek.
Public Meetings: Woolery's District--KELLY's tavern; Hampstead District--
DUNCAN's tavern; Myers District--MYRES' Tavern.

11 October 1839
GARBER, John, died after a protracted illness, at his residence near Union-
town Friday the 4th inst., in the 78th year of his age. Member of the
German Baptist [or Tunker] society; has left a wife & 6 children.
KILER, Simon, of Union-town District, died Tuesday the 1st inst.

18 October 1839
RIFFLE & THOMAS, 2 robbers who escaped from our Jail, have not been heard
from since they made off. (Westminster)
SHAFER, Nicholas, of this town has presnted us with a Beet measuring 21" in
circumference.

22 November 1839
BLOOM, __am, of this county, married at MOUL's tavern in Westminster on
Thursday the 14th inst. by the Rev. Isaac WEBSTER, to Miss Mary DUDDERAR,
d/o William DUDDERAR, Frederick County.
ROOP, Jesse, of Westminster, married in Hanover the 14th inst., to Urith
GOSNELL, youngest d/o Mr. V. GOSNELL, late of Union-town District, dec'd.
STULLER, John, married on Sunday the 1st inst., to Miss Lydia RO__SON, both
of this county.

17 January 1840
BREWSTER, James, Thursday the 2nd instant his dwelling & storehouse in
Shirleysville, Huntingdon County (PA) destroyed by fire. Mrs. Margaret
BREWSTER the mother, a young woman named Margaret MITCHELL & a boy (son
of Henry BREWSTER) perished in the flames.
DAVIS, John A., public house occupied by him in Littlestown (PA) took fire
on the night of Wednesday last; some furniture destroyed, building
partially injured.
Schuykill Bank: Indictments have been found against the following for
alleged participation in the late fraudelent election of directors of the
bank: Peter WAGNER, Daniel SAINT, J. CROSBY & Ishi CRAVEN.

24 January 1840
HEART, Jacob, of Frederick, slaughtered a few days since 2 hogs, the
aggregate weight of which was 1018 lbs. & Messrs. CANBY & DUER
slaughtered two which weighed 979.

31 January 1840
CONTEE, John, late from 6 miles near Upper Marlboro, land sold for $60.25
per acre, 416 acres purchased by Thomas E. BERRY, Jr.
WORTH/WROTH, James P., victim on 4th instant from Georgetown Cross Roads,
Kent Co. The perpetrator of the foul deed was Edgar NEWMAN, s/o a widow
lady now residing in Philadelphia. NEWMAN became acquainted with a young
lady by the name of Lavinia PINER d/o the late B. PINER of Kent County &
fell in love. She did not return his affections. She loved WROTH.
NEWMAN fired a gun through the window where WROTH was sitting with the
PINER family "with deliberate aim fired & literally blowed the head of
the unfortunate victim to atoms--the brains were scattered all over the
room & those who were sitting around." Was taken to Chestertown jail.
Carroll County Temperance Convention: John M'COLLUM, President, Daniel
FEETE, Secretary. New election results: Isaac SHRIVER, President, J. K.
LONGWELL, Secretary.

7 February 1840
RINEHART, Israel, a large gray eagle was shot whilst flying over his farm
on Sams Creek 29 January by Richard ADAMS. It measures 7' from the
extremity of one wing to that of the other.

14 February 1840
BAILE, John, has taken in on his plantation between Westminster & New
Windsor 6 head of stray sheep.
BRENGLE, Francis & A. Ferree SHRIVER, attorneys & soliciters in chancery.
Office in Westminster near store of S. ORENDORF.
CHAFFEE, Nicholas U., corn & rye wanted. Deliver to his distillery on the
Hooks' Town Road, Baltimore.
CRAPSTER, W. L., positively the last notice for persons who know themselves
indebted to him requested to make immediate payment as he intends
leaving the county by the 12th of March.
CRAWFORD, Evan L., selling 180 acre farm on which he resides in Carroll
County immediately at the head of Sams Creek. Improved by 2-story log
dwelling house, with piazza at the south side, log barn & stables with
sheds attached. Is eligibly situated for public business as the junction
of the Sams Creek & Crawford Roads is directly at the dwelling of said
farm. Farm is known as the Waterloo P. O. & has a large Blacksmith Shop
on the Sams Creek Road near the dwelling, and the subscriber is now
erecting a large store house.
CRUMBINE, William, has purchased the Tinning Establishment of John BAURGELT
& is prepared to continue the tinning business as formerly.
FISHER, William, Secretary. Taneytown Guards to meet at the usual parade
ground in full winter uniform with 18 rounds of blank cartridge.
GERNAND, Emanuel, resumed old business of sellilng beef, veal, mutton,
pork, etc. Also continues his business as auctionerr.
GIST, Joshua Col., late of Carroll County, dec'd., executor's sale at his
late residence near Westminster selling personal property of livestock,
crops, farm utensils & household burniture. Joshua GIST, Samuel D.
LECOMPTE & James RAYMOND, Executors.
GOLDSBOROUGH, L. W. Dr., formerly of Frederick County, offers professional
services to citizens of Westminster. His office is near Mr. MOUL's
tavern & nearly opposite residence of James RAYMOND, Esq.
HAINES, Job, intending to remove to the West, selling 142 acre farm on road
from Union Bridge to Union-town; adjoins lands of Joel HAINES, Joseph
ENGLER & A. H. SENSENEY. Improved by large frame dwelling & kitchen,
frame & stone Switzer Barn, spring house, smoke house &c.
HAWK, Samuel, dec'd., late of Carroll County, George HAWK, Adm'r.
KELLY, John C., meeting of persons favorable to the establishment of free
schools in Carroll County in the 4th District at his tavern.
KUHN, George, wants to hire a Miller. Inquire at the Pamano Mills, 2 miles
north east of Creagerstown, Frederick County.
MILLER, John, having rented all his land, will sell at his residence near
Westminster livestock, grain, wagons & carts. Also selling his farm of
200 acres.
NELSON, Madison, attorney, office W. Church Street in Frederick-town, next
door to the tannery of Gideon BANTZ, Esq. & opposite the Methodist
Episcopal Church.
PALMER, Joseph M., attorney, has business connection with Charles W.
WEBSTER, Esq. Office adjoins tavern of Mr. MOUL.
POOLE, Albinus & wife, by virtue of their Deed of Trust, Horatio PRICE,
Trustee, selling at Benjamin DAVIS' tavern at the forks of Westminster
the house & lot in which POOLE now resides on the Littlestown Road in the
town of Westminser. 1/4 acre lot with 2-story log dwelling nearly new.
POOLE, Daniel J., finding it impossible to attend to all his business &
farm his lands to profit to the extent to which he has been accustomed,
has determined to sell his personal property & rent his farm. Farm

14 February 1840
   situated near Monocacy, directly on the public road from Middleburg to
   Mechanics-town. Selling livestock, grains, farm utensils, household &
   kitchen furniture. Also renting 450 acres farm.
REED, Mary, dec'd., late of Carroll County, George REED, Adm'r.
REIFSNIDER, Jesse, has been appointed agent for the sale of G. SHETER's
   Augers, manufactured in York, PA.
SHELMAN, James M., attorney, office at Court & Main Streets, admoins hotel
   of Mr. Conrad MOUL in Westminster.
SHRIVER, George Dr., dec'd., late of Carroll County, Joshua YINGLING, Admr.
SMITH, James, being very anxious to remove from Carroll County, selling or
   will exchange for property in Baltimore County, the farm whereon he now
   resides of 370 acres, 1 1/2 miles from Thomas WELLS' mill.
STEELE, Joseph, Esq., married Tuesday evening by the Rev. Dr. JOHNS to Miss
   Catherine Ann, eldest d/o John LITTLE, Esq. both of Freedom District.
STONESIFER, Adam, petitions the Justice of Orphans Court for relief under
   insolvent debtors' act.
STULTZ, Conrad, late of Carroll County, dec'd., sale of his 200 acre farm
   on which he formerly resided on the road from Westminster to Hagerstown &
   3 miles from Uniontown. Has dwelling, Switzer barn of stone & out
   buildings. To view call on Mr. Philip LEASE, who resides on it. Thomas
   HOOK & David STULTZ, Executors.
TODD, James, selling property on which he now resides in Carroll County
   containing 50 acres on the road from Westminster to Frederick-town,
   Mechanics-town & Bruceville at the Forks of the road leading to either of
   the 3 latter places. Has large 2-story stone house nearly new & Stone
   Stable.
WELLS, Thomas, seeks Miller, sober, honest.
YINGLING, Jacob, has taken that well known stand at Union-bridge lately
   occupied by Mr. J. LANDIS where hs is now selling dry goods, groceries,
   liquors, hardware, boots, hats, school books medicines &c. He also
   operates a store in Westminster at the corner of Court & Main.
Carroll County Lyceum: Newly elected officers: President--Samuel D.
   LECOMPTE; Vice President--John K. LONGWELL; Treasurer--Samuel ORENDORFF;
   Secretary--William REESE.

28 February
WHITE, Eliza Ann Miss, at West Chester, PA recovered $1500 damages from a
   fickle swain named Albert HINAMEN for violation of a marriage promise.
Meeting of New-Windsor Temperance Society called, J. C. ATLEE, President &
   J. L. WARFIELD, M.D., Sec. pro tem.

3 April 1840
The following appointments were made by the Baltimore Annual Conference of
   the Methodist Episcopal Church: N. Baltimore District--Alfred GRIFFITH,
   P.E. N. Baltimore--David STEELE, John A. GERE, John M. JONES, sup. E.
   Baltimore--Samuel KEPPLER, Gerald MORGAN. Seamen's Bethel--John SMITH.
   Great Falls--Thomas B. SEARGEANT, Aquilla A. REESE, T. A. MORGAN, sup.
   Harford--William PRETTYMAN, Robert EMOTY. Shrewsbury--Isaac COLLINS,
   Penfield DOLL. York--John POISAL. Carlisle Circuit--Thomas MC GEE,
   Thompson MITCHELL. Gettysburg--Josiah FORREST, Wesley HOWE. Liberty--
   T. H. W. MONROE, Basil BARRY. Frederick City--James H. BROWN. Frederick
   Circuit--H. G. DILL, R. W. H. BRENT. Montgomery--Richard BROWN, J. W.
   CRONIN. Codorus Mission--Oliver EGE.
Delegates from Freedom to the 3rd Congressional District Convention, which
   assembles in city of Baltimore Thursday next, to nominate an elector of
   President & Vice President. Elias BROWN, Micajah ROGERS, Maj. Nicholas
   DORSEY, Weslley BENNETT, Able SCHIVENOR, Joseph STEELE, Joshua C. GIST,
   Warren L. LITTLE, Thomas BARTHOLOW, Peregine GOSNELL, Beal BUCKINGHAM,
   Dr. Nathan BROWN, Warner W. WARFIELD, William H. WARFIELD, Christian

3 April 1840
DEVRIES, Joseph COX, John DEVRIES, Cornelius SHIPLEY, Henry CARTER,
Robert T. SHIPLEY, Ignatius GORE, Greenbury SHIPLEY.

10 April 1840
GINTLING, Mr., a German of Franklin township (PA) on Thursday last, after
eating a hearty breakfast, went out into his field to sow oats. He was
later found dead sitting in a corner of the fence, with the seed bag on
his shoulder!
Titles of Acts passed at the last session of the Legislature of Maryland:
An act for the relief of Henry BUSSARD. An act to divorce Nancy COOK of
Carroll County from her husband Rezin COOK. An act to empower Sarah
MURRAY, widow & administratrix of John MURRAY late of Baltimore county,
dec'd., to execute a conveyance therein mentioned. Supplement to
previous act for relief of heirs of Dr. Elisha J. HALL, late of Balti-
more, dec'd. Act to incorporate trustees of Wolf Bottom Academy, in
Carroll County.
Spring term of Carroll County Court, Judges DORSEY & WILKINSON on the
bench. Grand Jury: Elias BROWN, foreman, Jacob MAUS, Caleb BORING,
Jacob STONESIFER, Michael LYNCH, Joseph KEEFER, Thomas CONDON, Joshua F.
C. ALGIER, Abraham ALBAUGH, Peter HESSON, George W. GORSUCH, James KELLY,
John DIFFENDALL, Samuel FUHRMAN, Josiah ADELSPERGER, Michael MORELOCK,
Jahael GRIMES, Edward DORSEY, George WEAVER, Daniel STONESIFER, John
SHULTZ, John LAMMOTT, John FOWBLE.
Petit Jury: Jacob ZUMBRUN, Thomas JONES, Henry SHRINER, Andrew NICODEMUS,
John KOONZ, Abraham BAILE, Helpher CRAMER, Lewis SHUEE, George RICHARDS
Jr., John B. CHENOWETH, John LOCKARD, Stephen OUSLER, Denton SHIPLEY,
John K. LONGWELL, David CASSELL, Benjamin BENNETT, Philip SNADER, Wilton
BURDETT, Greenbery SHIPLEY, Warren R. LITTLE, MIchael MILLER, Frederick
BACHMAN, Frederick BIXLER, John BAUGHER, Thomas FRANKLIN.
Delegates from the 5th Congressional District of MD assembled at the house
of Hamilton STIER in New Market 28 March; meeting called to order by W.
BURGESS, Esq. On motion of Dr. T. W. JOHNSON, A. JONES & Henry HARDING
called to Chair & on motion of T. SAPPINGTON, Dr. T. W. JOHNSON (of
Frederick) & George W. DAWSON (of Montgomery) appointed Secretaries.
Committee appointed to consult & recommend candidates: Thomas SAPPINGTON
from Liberty District, Washington BURGESS from New Market, Wm. P. JONES
from Creagerstown, Col. Rovter ANNAN from Emmitsburg, T. W. JOHNSON from
Woodsborough, J. H. T. COCKEY from Budkeystown. From Montgomery County,
1st District--H. C. GAITHER, 2d District--William T. GLAZE, 3d District--
John GRASSAWAY, 4th District--F. C. CLOPPER, 5th District--R. Y. BRENT.
Westminster District--John SMITH of J. Richard I. BOWIE of Montgomery
County was chosen as a suitable person for the office of Elector. Col.
A. KIMMEL, George W. DAWSON & John SMITH of James appointed to inform Mr.
BOWIE.
Maryland Law Books: Recent acquisition of the Maryland Bar are "Digested
Chancery cases" by James RAYMOND, Esq. of Westminster & "Maryland
Chancery Practice" by Thomas S. ALEXANDER, Esq. of Annapolis.
Carroll County Petitioners for relief of insolvent debtors act: Anthony
BEARD, George DIXSON & Rezin MULLINIX.

17 April 1840
BENNETT, Benjamin of Frederick County, dec'd., 11 of his heirs are entitled
to a dividend of $2.85 each as final settlement. The money can be had at
any time by calling on Robert BENNETT, Exec.
BRAMWELL, George has been again appointed Postmaster at Finksburg in the
place of M. G. COCKEY, resigned.
CARTER, Rev. M., to deliver address at Temperance meeting in Taney-town.
FIRST, Michael, persons owing on their notes given at sale of his personal
property can pay at D. & D. ENGLE's Store or Richard H. BURGESS' tavern.

17 April 1840
GARRET, John E., has been appointed Postmaster at Sykesville in place of W.
W. WATKINS, resigned.
GERNAND, Emanuel & James O. HEDINGTON, have formed a co-partnership in the
butchering business in Westminster.
GREEN, Diff, publishing a new daily newspaper in Baltimore, "The Pilot".
HAHN, James, a coloured man, was found guilty of stealing a half-bushel bag
of clover seed & convicted by a Carroll County court to serve 7 years in
the Penitentiary!
LAMBRECHT, Michael, wishes to employ 10 first-rate millwrights for the
season. Apply at his residence in Frederick City.
MC KINSTRY, Samuel, of MC KINSTRY's Mills, wishes to employ a first-rate
cooper; also a good stand can be had for a shoemaker, single man.
MOUL, Conrad, of Westminster, killed a hog raised about his tavern which
weighed 459 pounds. Beat that who can!
POOLE, William, died, his lands seized by Carroll county for payment of his
debts. Court of Equity Ann ROBERTS vs. William POOLE, Jr., Adm'r of
William POOLE, dec'd., Thomas POOLE, Ann ZIMMERMAN, Mary NEFF, Francis
POOLE, Thompsey DANNER, John DANNER, Ellen POOLE, Margaret POOLE & Dennis
POOLE. The object of the bill to to obtain a decree for sale of such
lands. The said Ann ROBERTS had obtained a judgement in Frederick County
Court in her favor against William POOLE for a large sum of money & that
same is still due. William POOLE died intestate in October 1839, his
estate greatly insufficient to pay his debts. William POOLE, Jr. Thomas
POOLE, John POOLE, Ann ZIMMERMAN, widow of Jacob ZIMMERMAN, Mary NEFF,
widow of Samuel NEFF, Francis POOLE, Thomsey DANNER, wife of John DANNER,
Ellen POOLE, Margaret POOLE & Dennis POOLE are the children & only heirs
at law of said William POOLE, dec'd. & that all heirs reside in Carroll
County, except said John POOLE, who was beyond the limits of the State of
Maryland & that said Thompsey, Margaret & Dennis are infants under the
age of 21 years.
PORTER, Gustavus, all persons who gave their notes at his sale last fall,
they are due & to be left with Joshua C. GIST.
VAN PATTEN, Charles H. M.D., married at Gettysburg on the 7th inst. by the
Rev. James C. WATSON to Miss Amelia Caroline d/o R. G. HARPER, Esq.,
Editor of the "Sentinel."
WAGNER, Michael, dec'd., late of Carroll County, Jacob WAGNER & Andrew
BABYLON, Executors, sale of 34 acres with grist & saw mill came to gross
sum of $5000.00. John BAUMGARTNER, Register of Orphans' Court.
WEAVER, George, tax collector for the Borough of Westminster, 1839.
An election for a Burgess & Fire Commissioner to conduct the affairs of the
corporation of Westminster for the ensuing year, to be held at KING's
Tavern, in Westminster 4 May. James M. SHELMAN, Burgess.
The following appointments were made at the 12th annual conference of the
Methodist Protestant Church, President Dr. J. S. REESE. Baltimore--Isaac
WEBSTER, Dr. S. K. JENNINGS. East Baltimore--Josiah VARDEN. Washington-
-Augustus WEBSTER. Georgetown--Levi R. REESE. Alexandria--A. A.
LIPSCOMB. Philadelphia--Filbert St.--- [sic] T. H. STOCKTON. Kensington-
-J. G. WILSON. Anne Arundel Circuit--William COLLIER, J. ELDERDICE.
Pipe Creek Circuit--G. D. HAMILTON, B. APPLEBY. Williamsport Circuit--
Frederick STIER, Washington ROBY. Harper's Ferry Circuit--John W.
EVERIST. Deer Creek Circuit--William HUNT. Concord Circuit--J.
ROLLISON, H. MILLER. Trough Creek--Daniel COLLIER. Baltimore Circuit--
Eli HENKLE, James ELDERDICE. Cumberland Circuit--Joshua RUTLEDGE. New
Market Circuit--John KELLER. Prince William Circuit--Timothy REMICK.
New Leeds Circuit--W. W. MADDOX. Queen Anne's and Talbot--S. L.
RAWLEIGH. Snowhill & Princess Anne Circuit--Avery MELVIN, L. A. COLLINS.
Dorchester Circuit--Daniel F. EWELL. Sussex Circuit--L. A. COLLINS.
Kent Circuit--William KESLEY, James K. NICHOLS. Northampton & Accomac
Mission--John R. NICHOLS. Dr. DAVIES without an appointment at his own

17 April 1840

request. R. H. BULL without an appointment on account of ill health on his own request. J. W. PORTER, R. WILSON, N. DORSEY & Dr. WATERS transferred to the unstationed districts, at their own request.

Bank of Westminster newly elected officers: Isaac SHRIVER, President; Directors: Washington VANBIBBER, Abraham WAMPLER, William ROBERTS, Andrew POUDER, Jacob FISHER, Richard WARD, John F. REESE, Jacob POWDER Jr., James RAYMOND & Joshua SMITH Jr.

List of Constables for Carroll County: Taneytown District--Jacob HAPE, Washington GWINN, William BURKE. Union-trown--William SEGAFOOSE, William POLE. Myers'--David HULL, Jacob CRAWFORD. Woolery's--Nimrod WOOLERY, Nathan GORSUCH. Freedom--Loveless GORSUCH. Manchester--John KRANTZ, James DAVIS, Jacob FRANKFORTER. Westminster--Henry ORSLER, Francis FRANKLIN, Joseph ARTHUR, William B. GIST. Hampstead--David WOLF. Franklinville--Bennet SPURRIER, Jacob CASHOUR.

24 April 1840

Delegates appointed to the Young Men's County Convention assembled in Westminster. Dr. Nathan BROWN appointed President, William BACHMAN, Vice President, Tobias W. RUDISEL appointed Secretary. Committee appointed to report Resolutions for consideration: John K. LONGWELL, Dr. Samuel SWOPE, A. F. SHRIVER, Dr. Thomas WELLS & Ignatius GORE. William REESE made resolutions that were unanimously adopted. Delegates appointed to represent each district: Taneytown--Dr. Samuel SWOPE, Tobias W. RUDISEL, Norman SCOTT, David KEPHART & Hanson CLABAUGH. Uniontown--William ECKER, William HUGHES, Thomas SHEPHERD Jr., John SHRINER (of Abraham), William ENGLAR. Myers'--Daniel BANKERT, David EARHART, David STONESIFER, William BAUGHMAN, David BANKERT. Woolery's--Mordecai G. COCKEY, E. E. HALL, Perry JORDAN, Solomon STOCKSDALE, John KNIGHT. Freedom--Ignatius GORE, W. H. WARFIELD, Christian DEVRIES Jr., John WADLOW, William GORSUCH. Manchester--Jacob FRANKFORTER, George TRUMP, David BAUGHMAN, Reuben MATHIAS, Jacob BOURING. Westminster--Dr. Thomas WELLS, Abraham MILLER, Jonas DEAL, Jacob MILLER, Jetson L. GILL. Franklin--Henry S. DAVIS, John GOSNELL, Abraham ENGLAND, Dr. Gasaway S. GRIMES, John BALL. The following persons form a Harrison Central Committee: Maj. Jacob MATHIAS, Col. Thomas HOOK, Col. J. M. SHELMAN, Isaac VAN BIBBER, Dr. William WILLIS, Abraham WAMPLER, John K. LONGWELL, Jacob REESE, A. F. SHRIVER, William REESE, Joshua SMITH Jr., Dr. John SWOPE, Evan MC KINSTRY, Daniel BANKERT, Henry N. BRINKMAN, Dr. Thomas WELLS, William MALLALINE, Joseph STEELE, Col. Joshua C. GIST.

15 May 1840

DAVIS, ?, near the Point of Rocks on the 6th inst., a woman named DAVIS & her child, living in the family of her brother at one lock of the Canal were murdered in their bed room in the dead of night; the woman was left insensible & it was supposed would not recover, & the 11 year old boy was clubbed to death & the club left standing in the room. The fiend who is supposed to have committed this midnight murder has been arrested & committed to the Frederick County Jail.

LAUGHLIN, Thomas H., died of a blow on the back of the head in Baltimore while walking in a platoon destroying an effigy, which was being carried down the pavement by a number of half grown boys. Dr. N. R. SMITH examined the body & determined that death was caused by a blow to the back of the head with a club. John HORN swore he knew nothing of the affray; thinks the effigy came from Marion street; saw it come that way. Another witness, Mr. LINGENFELTER, testified that the effigy was made in the New Market Engine yard. Andrew WAYSON saw HORN in high glee with the youngsters carrying the effigy. They are unable to determine who struck the deadly blow.

72

22 May 1840

BEAN, Samuel, married Thursday the 14th inst. by Rev. Mr. BOYLE to Miss Cevilla FORMWALT, both of this county.

BUXTEND, George, a miller in the employ of Joseph CARTZENDAFFER residing in the Middletown Valley attempted to commit suicide on Wednesday last. The shot however did not prove immediately fatal, but there are small hopes of his recovery. He had been married but a few weeks. We also understand that a young man, name of WORTHINGTON, residing somewhere about New Market, shot himself a few days ago, cause unknown.

CAMPBELL, Jacob, married Thursday the 14th inst. by the Rev. J. GEIGER to Miss Elizabeth SHOWER, all of Manchester.

CHRIST, Jacob, cabinet maker in Uniontown; manufactures all kinds of furniture viz: bureaus, tables, bookcases, bedsteads, chairs.

DORSEY, Benjamin, at the suits of Samuel STEVENSON & Peggy DORSEY, Jacob GROVE, Sheriff has seized & taken all right, title &c. of said Benjamin DORSEY in & to those tracts called "Part of Dorsey's Thicket" & "Part of Kendall's Delight" & "Part of John's Chance," being the same lands devised to said Benjamin DORSEY in & to that part of a tract called "Brother's Discovery," of 45 acres. Also another tract called "Dorsey's Pleasant Meadows" or "Bagdad" containing 135 acres. Above property to be offered at public sale to the highest bidder for cash.

DORSEY, Edward H., wishes to dispose of his 650 acre farm in Carroll County, which has been laid off into Lots. Adjoins farms of Elil HEWITT & Jonathan DORSEY, Esq.

FETTERLING, Jacob, dec'd., late of Carroll County, Jacob FRINGER & Hezekiah CROUT, Administrators.

FISHER, John, Cashier of Bank of Westminster accounces 4% dividend.

FORSYTHE, Jacob James, his creditors notified that he will meet them at his residence at HILBERT's (formerly BACHMAN's) Mill for the purpose of receiving claims. Frederick BACHMAN, Adm'r.

FOWBLE, Melchor, dec'd., late of Baltimore County, the undersigned commissioners to meet to value & divide his Real Estate. Richard HOOKER, John MAY & Jonathan TRACY.

GARNER, Ephraim, married Tuesday the 12th inst. by the Rev. Mr. BOYLE to Miss Margaret BEAN, both of this county.

GRAMMER, Andrew, all persons indebted to him are notified that he has left his papers in the hands of Andrew REESE for collection.

HAYWEISER, Mr., of Adams County (PA), on Monday last was deprived of life in a mournful manner. He was engaged in digging sand when a bank fell upon him & crushed him to death instantly. He was a German & somewhat advanced in years.

KEYS, Stephen & William SULIVAN vs. David KEYS & Others, Carroll County Court of Equity. Ordered that the sale made & reported by Abraham STONESIFER, Trustee. Report states sales of $510.00.

MILLER, John, formerly of Gettysburg & bother of Gen. MILLER. The body found in Jones' Falls near the City Block has been identified as that of Mr. MILLER (brother of Prof. J. H. MILLER of this city, Baltimore) who resides in Anne Arundel County on the B&O Railroad. He had come to Baltimore to attend the celebration on the 4th inst. & not returning his family became uneasy at his absence. His sister arrived in the city & went with Professor MILLER to the house of the coroner & identified his clothing. In the afternoon his body was disinterred & placed in the vault of the First Presbyterian Church. He leaves a wife and 7 children.

PEDDICORD, Humphrey, died Wednesday last at his residence in Woolery's District, aged about 63 years.

REIFSNIDER, David, married the 7th inst. by the Rev. Mr. KELLER to Miss Susanna SHOEMAKER, both of Taney-town District.

SHRIVER, Francis, strayed away from his place near Westminster, a black bull of the Durham breed, weighs between 400 & 500 pounds.

22 May 1840
STONER, Daniel, died aged 22 years, s/o Daniel STONER residing near Union
Bridge, by suicide. He had been in bad health for some time past & left
his father's residence Saturday last in a state of mental alienation. No
tidings were had of him until Sunday morning when he was found suspended
by a rope from a limb of a tree at a considerable elevation from the
ground. We deeply sympathize with the highly respectable relations.
THOMPSON, Nancy W., living 3 miles north of Ridgeville, Frederick County,
offers reward for runaway Negro woman named Hannah or Hannah RIDGELEY.
Said woman is a mulatto, 5'3-4" high, has a scar on one arm & a large
scar on her thigh, both from a burn when she was young; about 26 years
old, speaks quick. She took two calico dresses & a red linsey dress;
shoes much worn at the toe.
TYSON, Nathan, his flouring mill 3 miles from Baltimore destroyed by fire
on Sunday morning last. It is supposed the fire was from a drying kiln.
WARNER, David, married on the 7th inst. by the Rev. Daniel FEETE to Miss
Catharine HAPENER, both of this county.
WOODALL, James, died in an encounter with John SCHWATKA in New Market
Wednesday last. The parties had not been on friendly terms for some time
& when they met that day a fight ensued. Mr. WOODALL was struck over the
head with a stick, which terminated his life in the course of 8 or 9
hours. Mr. SCHWATKA is now in confinement in this town.
The officers & members of the "New-Windsor Guards" take pleasure in
acknowledging the kind welcome they received from the Taney-town Guards &
citizens of Taney-town. Signed Jonas ECKER, James EREHARD, Elias WOODS,
& J. H. T. WEBB.

5 June 1840
WHITINGHAM, Rev. Dr., professor of Theology in New York Episcopal Seminary
has been elected Bishop of the Diocese of MD by the Episcopal Convention
now in session in Baltimore.

12 June 1840
Tippecanoe Club has formed in the Freedom District. 86 persons became
members & elected the following: Robert HUDSON, President; Christian
DEVRIES Sr., John WILSON & Thomas BARTHOLOW, Vice Presidents; Moses SHAW
& William H. WARFIELD, Secretaries; John WADDOW, Treasurer.
The Mayor of the City of Baltimore offers reward for arrest & conviction of
the murderer of T. H. LAUGHLIN, Whig Marshall, who was murdered in the
procession 4 May. Jefferson GRIFFITH alias John ALEXANDER has been
arrested & committed for trial at present at the City Court.

19 June 1840
A meeting was held at the house of Aaron MANAHAN in New Windsor to for a
Democratic Tippacanoe Club. Michael BARTHOLOW, Jr. called to the Chair &
Capt. William ECKER appointed Secretary. A committee was appointed of
Samuel ECKER, John SMITH & James BLIZZARD, to draw up preambles &
resolutions. The meeting was addressed by Col. HOOK, Col. SHELMAN, C. W.
WEBSTER & O.H.P. YINGLING. Committee to draft constitution: Capt.
William ECKER, Dr. William BARTHOLOW & John SMITH (of James). Committee
of Correspondence: Jonas ECKER, Ephriam EGGLAR, Isaac BLIZZARD, Dr. W.
BARTHOLOW, G. W. WILLSON &. J.T.H. WEBB.
Carroll County Temperance Convention met in Uniontown. President Isaac
SHRIVER in the Chair. Rev. M. KELLER addressed the meeting. The Secretary
being absent, James C. ATLEE was appointed. The following representa-
tives were called for & appeared: Taney-town--John N. STARR, Phillip
HANN, Jacob ANGEL & Henry RINEDOLLER. Westminster--Isaac SHRIVER, John
MC COLLUM, Nicholas H. BROWN & Horatio PRICE. New Windsor--James C.
ATLEE. Union-town--Moses SHAW, Daniel SULLIVAN & Henry H. HETBAUGH.
Clergymen--Rev. Ezra KELLER, Rev. Daniel ZOLLICKEFFER & Rev. Daniel FEETE.

26 June 1840
BROWN, William, of Cromwell township, Huntingdon County (PA), his wife &
all of his children with the exception of his eldest daughter, Mrs. MC
CONAHY who was not at home that day, were murdered brutally. Mr. BROWN
barely escaped being murdered himself. His son-in-law, Mr. MC CONAHY is
being held awaiting his trial for murder in August. (See 20 Nov. 1840)

3 July 1840
FINCKLE, S. D. Rev., formerly of Taneytown has accepted a call from the
Lutheran Congregation in Germantown (PA), lately under the charge of Rev.
William SHOLL.

10 July 1840
BENNETT, Eli, dec'd., late of Carroll County, Rachel BENNETT, Executrix.
CHALMERS, George W., M.D., treats rheumatism, & deafness. Testimonials by
Adam MYERS of Unionville, Frederick County & Michael FIRST of Carroll
County. Office next to Mr. BROWN's Store, Forks of the main street,
Westminster.
GEIMAN, Daniel J., intending to quit farming selling all his real estate in
Carroll County consisting of 195 acre farm in the valley 3 miles north of
Westminster, adjoining lands of John MYERS, David GEIMAN, & Christian
ROYER, lying on the county road from town to BACHMAN's Mill.
Improvements are a very large 3-story brick house, Switzer barn of stone
71x45', built within 3 years, having 3 threshing floors & stabling,
double wagon shed, carriage house, 2 corn cribs, hog house, smoke house,
spring house, work shop, cider press. Head waters of the Patapsco Falls
runs through farm. Also overseer's house, 2 stories high, frame
stabling, brick spring house, &c. Also 6 acres of woodland adjoining
lands of Michael SULLIVAN & Abraham SHAFER. Also 12 1/2 acres of woodland near the Westminster & Manchester Road, adjoining lands of Henry
SALTZGIVER. Also a lot in Westminster of 1 1/4 acres on which is a
double 2-story log dwelling house with cellar under whole & a lot in
Westminster, adjoining Isaac SHRIVER's property at the Forks containing
1/4 acre on which is a 2-story dwelling house.
GOOD, Henry L., has opened a barber & hair dresser's shop in a room next
door to David BURNS' & 2 doors from Dr. WILLIS' dwelling. Will prepare &
make curls & frizets &c. for the ornamental dresses of the Ladies, will
also employ servants for families, will scour, clean & dress up woolen or
silk clothes by removing dirt or grease, so they will appear almost as
new. Second-hand clothing bought & sold.
GROVE, Jacob, Sheriff, offering reward for Michael HERSH alias David
RODFELTZ who escaped from his custory. He is 5'5" high, and tolerably
good looking. He is a German by birth & followed the occupation of a
Pedlar. He speaks the English language very broken.
HESSON, Baltzer, dec'd., Executors Peter HESSON & John BAUMGARTNER notify
legatees that they have settled their final account in relation to the
dec'd's estate.
JACOBS, Geroge, offering reward for runaway mulatto woman named Matilda.
25 years of age, 4'10-11" high; well made in proportion; much freckled in
the face; looks sulky; free on the tongue when crossed. (Westminster)
M'ALLISTER, John W., having purchased a tract of Land from John A. HARTSOCK
of Carroll County, said HARTSOCK has failed to comply with the article of
agreement, M'ALLISTER cautions persons against purchasing notes given in
payment.
MATHIAS, Mrs. Capt. John, of this county has sent us a few heads of
extraordinary growth of cabbage.
MITTEN, Henry G., has commenced the saddle & harness making business in the
shop adjoining Mr. HAUSE's dwelling & next to Dr. CHALMER's office at the
Forks of the Main street.

10 July 1840
NICODEMUS, John (of H.) has opened a new store at Jacob NICODEMUS' Mill
selling dry goods, groceries, hats, boots & shoes, &c.
RECK, John, dec'd., late of Carroll County, Thomas METCALF, Adm'r.
RODGER, John has petitioned the Orphan's Court for benefit of insolvent
debtors.
SCOTT, Thomas Parkin, had an unfortunate accident yesterday afternoon. He
was riding in a carriage on the Belvidere road, near Madison street
(Baltimore City) owing to the carelessness of the driver, Mr. SCOTT was
thrown out & badly bruised, the wheels of the vehicle passing over his
legs. He is in a very critical situation.
SLYDER, William, Executor of Peter SLYDER dec'd., reports the sale of a
small farm of 68 acres in Carroll County for the price of $36.15 per acre
making the gross som of $2458.20; also one other small farm of 66 acres
in same county for price of $16.50 per acre.
SNIDER, Jacob, living near John GRASS' Tavern on the Westminster &
Littlestown turnpike has taken in a stray sorrel mare colt.
WAMPLER, Lewis, selling 10,000 chestnut rails 1/2 mile east of Westminster.
The Fourth of July celebrated as usual at Manchester. The Rev. Mr. HARPEL
acted as Chaplain, J. K. KINNEY read the Declaration of Independence &
Joseph M. PARKE pronounced an Oration on the occasion.
Road Notice: A commission appointed to open a public road in Carroll
County commencing at or near the Piney Falls, where the present public
road crosses said Falls & running past DEVRIES Mills, taking the bed of
the presnt road between the lands of George F. WARFIELD & wife & those of
George PATTERSON, & through the lands of John HIPSLEY, then a south-west
direction to the public road near Sykesville.

24 July 1840
SNEADER, Jacob of Sams Creek sent in a head of wheat measuring 7" long.
Tippecanoe Club founded at Middleburg. Elected: John DELAPHANE, President;
George H. WAESCHE & John COVER, Vice Presidents; Isaac DERN & Nimrod
NORRIS, Secretaries.

7 August 1840
BURNS, Jacob, dec'd., during the storm of Tuesday afternoon last, one of
the barns beloning to his heirs, occupied by John GEIMAN, 1 1/2 miles
west of Manchester was struck & lightning & destroyed by fire.
From 150 to 200 friends of the Farmer of North Bend assembled at NULL's
Mill on the banks of the Monocacy Saturday last to raise a Tippecanoe
Flag. A meeting was held & Abraham NULL & Elias GRIMES were appointed
Presidents, William & James CORNELL Vice Presidents, & Dr. John SWOPE &
Benjamin SHUNK appointed Secretaries. Dr. Jefferson SHEILDS of Emmits-
burg & Col. HOOK, our late Delegate in the legislature, delivered an
address.

21 August 1840
BENNETT, Eli, dec'd., late of Carroll County, sale of tract of land called
"Searborough" situated in Freedom District, adjoins lands of Columbus
O'DONNEL, Thomas BARNES, Adam SHIPLEY & adjoining home place of dec'd.
containing 102 1/4 acres. Also personal property of dec'd. consisting of
5 milch cows, 22 head of sheep, farming utensils &c. Rachel BENNETT, Ex.
CARUANA, Dr., Dentist, office at MOUL's Hotel, Westminster.
CURRY, Mary, dec'd., late of Carroll County, John HESS, Adm'r.
ENGLE, Daniel, offers himself as Independent Candidate for Legislature.
FRANKLIN, Charles, dec'd., late of Carroll County, Joshua FRANKLIN & Rezin
FRANKLIN, Ex'rs.
FREEZE, Mr. Rev., Pastor of German Reformed Church of Emmitsburg to preach
at St. Benjamin Church (Kriders) & in Union Church in Westminster.

21 August 1840
FRINGER, Nicholas, dec'd., late of Carroll County. George FRINGER of
    Carroll County & Jacob FRINGER of Franklin County, PA, Ex'rs.
FUSS, Mary, dec'd., late of Carroll County, Abraham BUFFINGTON, Adm.
GARNER, Jarret & Wesley W., late of Manchester, their accounts in hands of
    Philip GORE & Jacob FRANKFORTER of Manchester for collection and have
    been there since they removed to the west. Do not delay payment. Late
    the firm of J. GARNER & Son. Jarrett resides in Springfield, Clark
    County, Illinois & W. W. resides in Winchester, Preble County, Ohio.
HAHN, Jacob, dec'd., late of Carroll County, Jacob ERB, Admr.
HINKLE, George, his wife Barbara having left his bed & board without
    provocation, warns people from trusting her on his account. He is
    willing to receive her again & maintain her if she acts as a good wife he
    will treat her with kindness & affection. If however she persists in not
    returning & will not remain with him he will not pay her debts.
HOOK, Thomas, candidate for House of Delegates.
LEISTER, John, has taken in stray sheep on his farm between Uniontown &
    Westminster.
MATHIAS & MYERS, boots & shoes manufactured in Westminster.
MILLER, Henry, dec'd., late of Carroll County, George BUSHMAN of Adams
    County (PA) Admr.
NORRIS, Jonathan, candidate for sheriff.
OGG, Mary, dec'd., late of Carroll County, John OGG Ex'r.
SANTZ, Andrew & Salone his wife, Jacob RENOUL & Mary his wife, Frederick
    ZIMMERMAN & Catharine his wife, George SANTZ & Mary his wife, Henry
    MILLER & Margaret his wife, John R. SHAFFER & Susannah his wife against
    Adam SANTZ & Mary his wife & John SANTZ & Mary his wife, David SANTZ &
    Elizabeth his wife, & George WINK & Susan his wife. The object is to
    obtain a decree to sell the real estate of Peter SANTZ, died, seized,
    lying in Carroll County 158 acres consisting of tracts "Irons Intention,"
    "Windfaw," "Molly's Delight" & "Christopher's Lot." The children & heirs
    at law of said Peter are Andrew SANTZ, his wife is Salone; Mary RENOULL,
    her husband is Jacob RENOUEL; Catharine ZIMMERMAN, her husband is
    Frederick ZIMMERMAN; George SANTZ his wife is Mary; Margaret MILLER, her
    husband is Henry MILLER; Susannah SHAFFER, her husband is John R.
    SHAFFER; Adam SANTZ, his wife is Mary & both reside in Ohio; John SANTZ,
    whose wife is Mary & both reside in Ohio; David SANTZ whose wife is
    Elizabeth, both reside in Ohio; and Susanna WINK, whose husband is George
    W. WINK, both reside in Carroll County. It would be to the advantage &
    interest of all involved if the land were sold & money divided.
SHELMAN, James M. Col., Independent candidate for Legislature.
SHOEMAKER, William, of this county married on Thursday week by the Rev. S.
    GETELIUS to Miss Maria Rebecca BENNER of Adams County (PA).
STEELE, Joseph, of Freedom District is a candidate for General Assembly.
STOCKSDALE, Edmund H., died, his property seized, 202 acre farm in Freedom
    District called "Caledonia" better known as the residence of the late
    Nathan STOCKSDALE, dec'd., improved by a dwelling, barn, tobacco house
    &c. Near the public road from Westminster to Washington, 26 miles from
    Baltimore & 8 from Westminster. Also another farm, "Edingburg" with a
    small tenement thereon, 1 mile from former, 70 acres lying on the
    Washington Road. Mordecai G. COCKEY, Trustee.
WORMAN, Andrew, mill feed, has off-alls, brown stuff, shorts and shipstuff,
    1 mile east of Uniontown, New Liberty Road, Frederick County.
ZENTZ, Charles, took in a stray white male hog, 2 miles from Westminster.
ZOLLICKOFFER, Daniel, selling Rock Wheat seed.
Camp Meetings: 2 1/4 miles south of Uniontown on old Father APPLER's Farm
    Church of God. Also The Methodist Episcopal Church, Codorus Mission
    meeting 1 mile sw of Hampstead on lands of Richard RICHARDS & Capt.
    William HOUCK. Also meeting of the Methodist Episcopal Church on Liberty
    Circuit, on land of Mr. DANNER, well known as Pearre's old camp ground.

21 August 1840
Petitioners for relief under insolvent debtors act: Jesse LOOGUE, William
ROACH & John RODGER.

18 September 1840
BRELY, William, married on the 6th inst. by Rev. Daniel FEETE to Miss
Elizabeth MORNINGSTAR, both of Frederick County.
STONER, Augustus, married the 13th inst. by Rev. Daniel FEETE to Miss
Hannah STONER, all of Frederick County.
WELSH, Mary, dec'd., James M. SHELMAN, Auditor. In the case of Rosannah
PHILLIPS vs. Ferdinand WELSH, creditors are ordered to file their claims.
By divine permission there will be a Protracted Meeting held by the German
Reform Church of Taneytown. The Rev. Jacob HEIFENSTEIN will assist.
The Undersigned, a committee appointed by the stockholders of the Western
Mechanics' Saving Institution to investigate their affairs: Robert MILLS,
Folger POPE, William H. ROLOSON, William H. WALKER.
There will be a political public Barbacue held on the land of Abraham
BAILE, near Jacob FRIZZLE's in Franklinville District. By order, Richard
A. KIRKWOOD

25 September 1840
ENGLE, Daniel, independent candidate for the Legislature.
HAHN, Benjamin, married Tuesday last by the Rev. Dr. ZOLLICOFFER to Miss
Mary Ann STONEBRAKER, both of Union Town District.
HOOK, Thomas, candidate for General Assembly.
KNAPP, Frederick H. & Eber F. COOK, ex-presidents of broken institutions
for the issue of small notes, released from prison having given bail.
(Baltimore)
NORRIS, Jonathan, candidate for sheriff.
SHELMAN, James M., candidate for Legislature.
STEELE, Joseph, of Freedom District, candidate for General Assembly.
Grand Rally of the Whigs of Young Carroll will be long remembered by all
who participated in the festivities. Early in the morning the Tippecanoe
Club of Westminster District & raised the Liberty Pole in the center of
town. James RAYMOND gave a speech. The procession was then formed under
the direction of Maj. Jacob MATHIAS as Chief Marshal, supported by A. F.
SHRIVER & J. K. LONGWELL as Aids, & by Assistant Marshals, viz: O.H.P.
YINGLING, Henry H. WAMPLER, William REESE, George WEBSTER, Augustus
SHRIVER, A. W. HUGHES, Emanuel GERNAND, William MITTEN & G. W. GIST.
There was a miniature Log Cabin from Franklinville District, drawn by 110
boys, under direction of Maj. Benjamin GORSUCH. Then followed the
Franklin Club on horseback under direction of Col. J. C. GIST as Chief
Marshal. Next followed the Taneytown Club with 120 delegates under the
direction of Col. Samuel GALT assisted by Dr. Samuel SWOPE, John
THOMPSONS, Rogers BIRNIE, Benjamin SHUNK, Augustin ARNOLD. The Union
Bridge Club followed under the direction of Thomas SHEPHERD, then the
Union Town Club under the direction of Samuel MYERS. The New Windsor
delegation led by Capt. William ECKER & Israel NORRIS. The Wakefield
Club; John SMITH Chief Marshal. The Finksburg Club, Mordecai G. COCKEY,
Marshal. The Hampstead Whigs under direction of Dr. Thomas WELLS. The
procession formed & proceeded in best order up Main Street marching to
martial music & the shouts of the crowds. Speeches were delivered by
Col. SHELMAN, James RAYMOND and J. Erskine STEWART & George R. RICHARDSON
of the City of Baltimore, who spoke for 1 1/2 hours.
Public Meetings at the following places to wit: Charles STEVENSON's on the
Turnpike 3 miles below Westminster. At Uniontown at SEGAFOOSE's Tavern.
At HORNER's Tavern in Woolery's District. At DUNCAN's Tavern in
Hampstead. At CRUMRINE's Tavern in Manchester. Candidates will address
the people.

25 September 1840
The Taney-town Tippecanoe Club will meet. Josiah BAUMGARTNER & Josiah WOODS, Secretaries.

2 October 1840
The Whigs of Sams Creek raised a Liberty Pole at the Forks of the Road near John STONER's Mills, 100 feet tall. Jacob SHRINER managed the raising. Dr. William ZOLLICKOFFER gave an address of more than 1 hour

16 October 1840
ZOLLICKOFFER, William Dr., has been elected a corresponding member of the Royal Medico-Botanical Society of London.

30 October 1840
Meeting of Whigs at Union town. Procession was led by John HARTZELL.

13 November 1840
CRAWFORD, E. L., having rented his farm is selling his entire stock of horses, cattle, cows, hogs, shoats, sheep, & grains, household furniture. Also selling timber lot of 5 acres adjoining said farm & several 1/2 acre lots in the town of Waterloo.
ECKMAN, William, has petitioned the court for benefit of the act of relief for insolvent debtors.
HALL, Elisha J., dec'd., sale of his estate consisting of 800 acres of land in Carroll County, 5 miles from Reisterstown & 8 from Westminster, within 2 miles of the Turnpike from Baltimore to Westminster. Also selling a number of negroes & livestock, farm implements & household goods. Edward E. HALL (residing on premises) & Elisha J. HALL, Trustees.
HESS, Samuel, wishing to dispose of his property selling 9 acres of land which formerly belonged to John GRIFFITH, being south of the main street in Waynesboro, Franklin County (PA). Has a tolerable good log barn & dwelling house of brick & frame, also stable. Apply to William FULTON living on the premises.
KILER, David, Trustee, selling on the premises of Jacob GREENHOLTZ 50 acres of land 4 miles south of Westminster, on the head waters of Little Pipe Creek, improved by a log house, barn, stabling &c.
MIDDLETON, R. W., Editor of the Lancaster (PA) Examiner was attacked at the polls by James CAMERON's bloodhounds & injured very badly.
MURRY, Thomas B., living on the turnpike from Baltimore to Carlisle, PA, about 2 miles below Hampstead & 22 miles from Baltimore, offering reward for runaway Negro man named Henry, but called himself Henry FRANLIN, about 21 years old, very black, 5'8-9" high, slender built, is a tolerably sharp looking fellow.
NEFF, Susanna, dec'd., John NICODEMUS, Executor. 58 1/4 acres were sold at the estate sale at $9.25 per acre; also 330 acres at $3.50 1/2.
NORRIS, Nimrod, selling house & lot where he now resides in Middleburg. There is 3 acres of land, a 2-story house of stone, with back building & shed room attached.
SHAFER, George, has taken in a stray heifer on his farm 3 miles from Westminster near Crider's Church.
SHAUCK, John, dec'd., late of Carroll County, sale of his plantation & mill property, lying in Carroll County, 2 miles from Martin KROH's (formerly KERLINGER's) Mill, 3 miles from STICK's (formerly HETRICK's) Tavern, on the public road from Said STICK's to Manchester, adjoining the PA-MD line & lands of Valentine B. WENTZ, John BRODBECK, Henry JAMES, George FAIR & John FAIR Jr. Contains 272 acres, a large grist mill, 1 story of stone & 2 of brick, a saw mill on a good stream of water & a large brick dwelling house with cellar & 2 large brick kitchens, brick Switzer barn 81x37', a still house, stone dairy, smoke house &c. Henry SHAUCK, Ex't.

13 November 1840
SULLIVAN, David s/o Michael SULLIVAN died Tuesday last at his residence in
Manchester, about 24 years of age.
SULLIVAN, Hannah Mrs., wife of Michael SULLIVAN died Thursday last. The
mother & 3 of her sons have, within a few days of each other, died while
her husband & daughter are yet confined to bed by a dangerous illness.

20 November 1840
M'CONACHY, Robert in Huntington (PA) was executed on the 6th instant for
the murder of the entire BROWN family (see 26 June 1840). Upon first
being hanged the rope broke & when he was led to the gallows again he
confessed & made a full confession to the clergy present, Mr. BROWN & Mr.
PEEBLES, whereupon he was hanged.

4 December 1840
BARNHART, John, of this county, married Wednesday the 18th inst. by the
Rev. James BUNTING to Miss Susan, eldest d/o William CARMACK of Frederick
County.
BAUMGARTNER, Jacob Sr., dec'd., late of Carroll County, Jacob BAUMGARTNER
Jr. Executor.
BILLINGSLEA, James L., selling his tavern property in Union Town, for many
years occupied by the late David STEM, now by John HAPE. Tavern has 4
rooms above & 3 below, new kitchen attached, stable for 10 horses.
BLINSINGER, Samuel, of Adams County (PA), committed suicide by hanging
himself on the 28th ult. He had been mentally deranged.
DERN, George, married Thursday evening the 19th by Rev. James BUNTING to
Mrs. Juliann SNOOK, all of this county.
DORSEY, Nicholas, Major of the Extra Battalion of MD Militia in Carroll
County, notifies all persons formerly under Capt. Ephraim COOK's Rifle
Company are to deliver their arms to Capt. COOK forthwith.
ECKER, Samuel, Chairman of the New Windsor Library Company.
FRINGER, Nicholas, dec'c., George & Jacob FRINGER, Executors report the
sale of land in Carroll County, a farm of 93 acres, a farm of 70 acres
with a grist & saw mill, gross sum $3000.00.
GORSUCH, Nathan, died recently after a lingering illness, of Freedom
District.
KEPHART, David, dec'd., late of Frederick county, now part of Carroll
county, sale of his property at Charles STEVENSON's public house on the
turnpike from Westminster to Baltimore, selling 45 1/4 acre wood lot
situated 1/2 mile left of said turnpike, 3 1/2 miles below Westminster,
adjoining lands of Elijah WOOLERY, Thomas TAYLOR & Acquilla MC GEE.
George & Margaret KEPHART, Executors.
NAILL, D. W., of Sams Creek, letter to the editor recommending a pruning
process for the preservation of the Morrallo Cherry Tree. Also, the
editor regrets to learn that D. W. NAILL, a delegate elect to the
Legislature received a kick in the stomach from his horse the Saturday
before the Presidential election, when he was riding home from the Beaver
Dams. It is supposed he has suffered permanent injury.
OURSLER, William, wishing to leave town, selling house & lot where he now
resides at the Forks of Westminster (adjoins DAVIS' Tavern) with 2-story
log dwelling, weatherboarded, a good brick shop attached, log stable,
corn house, hog house, garden &c.
SPENCE, Carroll, attorney will attend Carroll & Baltimore counties &
Baltimore city courts, office in St. Paul Street over G. DULANEY's.

11 December 1840
GITTINGER, Daniel, a few miles north of Frederick, his barn damaged by fire
a few nights ago, the work of an arson.
KELLY, Patrick, Trustee selling at the Widow SLACK's White-hall tavern a 50
acre tract of land in Hampstead District, 1 mile from town of Hampstead &

11 December 1840
3/4 mile from the Baltimore turnpike, adjoins lands of Frederick FRANK-FORTER, Peter B. SMITH & George GRUMBLE.
SCHWARTZ, John married Thursday the 26th ult. by Rev. Jacob ALBERT to Miss Sarah HEISER, both of Carroll County.
TURNER, Thomas, tried last week in Hagerstown & convicted of attempting to poison a family! and only sentenced to pay a fine of $1.
WORTHINGTON, Mary T., wife of the Hon. John T. H. WORTHINGTON, Member of Congress from Baltimore County, died suddenly on the 1st instant.
The "Herald" published at Hanover, PA has changed owners & is now conducted by John GRUMBINE & William BART.

25 December 1840
BEGGS, Mrs. died Wednesday evening week, mother of John BEGGS of this District.
BIXLER, Barbara, dec'd., late of Carroll County, Frederick BIXLER, Admin.
GORSUCH, Nathan, dec'd., sale of property to be held at the late residence of said dec'd., on the B&O Rail Road near Sykesville. Selling livestock, farm implements, grain, & household goods. Pelatiah GORSUCH, Admin.
HARPEL, Rev. Mr. will preach in the Union Church Christmas Day.
HARRIS, David married on Sunday week last to Miss _____ FOREMAN, both of Uniontown District by the Rev. Philip BOYLE.
HILTERBRICK, John, seeks blacksmith to rent his shop on the York Road, 2 1/2 miles from Taney town.
HOUCK, George, died on the 3d instant, at his residence in Manchester, in the 52d year of his age.
KIRKWOOD, R. A., Secretary Franklinville Tippecanoe Club.
LOGUE, Emanuel Rev., formerly of New Windsor, married on Tuesday week last by Rev. Mr. ROSS to Miss Tabitha FORMWALT of Uniontown.
MERING, William, Secretary Taney Town Temperance Society.
MILLER, Henry, dec'd., late of Carroll County, bill in the Court of Equity to obtain a decree for the sale of his real estate. Magdelena BUSHMAN vs. Adam TAILOR & Elizabeth his wife, Mary BUSHMAN &c. Henry MILLER died intestate, seized of part of a tract in Carroll County called "Ohio" & part of a tract called "Shriver's Bottom" & "Addition to Shriver's Bottom" containing in the whole 160 acres. Said Henry MILLER at the time of his death left no child, wife, or brothers & the complainant, Magdalena BUSHMAN, a sister of the dec'd., & the descendants of another dec'd. sister by the name of Catharine BUSHMAN, who left at the time of her death the following children as her heris: Elizabeth TAILOR, who married Adam TAILOR residing in Bedford Co., PA; Mary BUSHMAN, living in Ohio; Henry BUSHMAN, residing in Adams Co., PA; Susan TAILOR who married Jacob TAILOR & reside in Bedford Co., PA; John BUSHMAN, residing in Allegany Co., PA; Rachel BARKELY, who married Frederick BARKELY & reside in Adams Co., PA; Jacob BUSHMAN, who resides in Ohio; Fanny KAUFFMAN who married David KAUFFMAN & reside in Franklin Co., PA; & Margaret BUSHMAN residing in Ohio.
SMITH, Henry of Manchester District married in Baltimore on the 25th ultimo to Mrs. Mary LEMMON, formerly of Uniontown District.
SUNDERGILL, Joshua, received a letter from a person with a little authority, admonishing him that he is not treating a certain person under his charge as I ought to do, &c. He pronounces the author a false & malicious calumniator & dares him to substantiate charges.

1 January 1841
CARLETON, William, Esq., Register of the Corporation of Frederick, died while running with an engine company on an alarm of fire, on Tuesday week, fell & expired almost immediately, supposedly from the rupture of a blood vessel.

1 January 1841
POTTS, Richard, of Frederick is proposed by the Frederick Herald as a
suitable person to fill the Gubernatorial Chair of this state.

15 January 1841
BABYLON, Jacob, deceased, Peter BABYLON, Administrator.
BANKER, Peter, deceased, estate sale of tavern house & lot in Myers'
District, on Westminster & Littlestown turnpike, about 6 miles from
Westminster; 1 acre, 2-story log house, occupied for many years as a
Tavern, a log stable. Daniel BANKER, Trustee.
BILLINGSLEA, James L., of Uniontown, will rent farm on Sams Creek, 2 miles
from MC KINSTRY's mills; adjoins farms of John ROOP & Upton STONER, &
lately occupied by Nathaniel BOONSOCK.
BOWER, Samuel married on the 27th ult. to Miss Rachel PANNEBECKER, both of
this county by the Rev. Mr. GEIGER.
BULLER, Cyrus Jr., has removed his shop & chair making business to the west
end of town, a few doors from Benjamin DAVIS's Hotel.
COVER, Tobias, Tax Collector, giving taxpayers last notice to pay back
taxes of 1839, as well as 1840, will collect at the following locations:
Myers' District--Peter LIPPY's tavern & MAUS' Mills. Taneytown-- Mrs.
HEAGY's & MARTIN's Tavern. Uniontown--ECKER's store & SEGAFOOSE's
tavern. Manchester--CRUMRINE's tavern & Joshua STANSBURY's store.
Hampstead--Henry LAMMOTT's tavern. Finksburg--HORNER's Tavern & Charles
STEVENSON's tavern. Franklin--HAUSER's tavern, Ridgeville & FRANKLIN's
tavern. Freedom--Henry CARTER's tavern, John LITTLE's tavern Freedom, &
Thomas CARTER's tavern.
CROUT, Hezekiah & NICODEMUS, John of H., have entered into a partnership in
the Mercantile business near Warfieldsburg, Carroll County.
DORSEY, Edward H., selling 600 acres in Carroll County, adjoins land of Eli
HEWIT & Jonathan DORSEY, Esq.
ECKMAN, William has applied to Michael BARNITZ, Justice of Orphan's Court
of Carroll County, for benefit of the Act for relief of insolvent
debtors.   Mr. ECKMAN has resided in the county for over 2 years &
Francis FRANKLIN, Constable, has testified that he is under arrest for
debt and no other cause.
ENGEL, Daniel, Esq. has been appointed Post Master at Sams Creek in place
of D. W. NAILL, Esq., resigned.
GERNAND, Emanuel & HEDINGTON, James O., Partnership in butchering buisness.
GERNAND, Emanuel continues the business of auctioneer.
GORSUCH, Nathan, late of Carroll County, Pelatiah GORSUCH, Administrator.
KNOX, Margaret Miss, died at Emmitsburg on Wednesday morning 7th inst.,
aged about 70 years.
LEE, T. Sim, selling tract of land, "Never Die," 900 acres, 5 miles from
HOOD's Mills & same from Sykesville; 23 miles from Baltimore City & 9
from Westminster. 4 dwelling houses, 2 tobacco houses, a grist mill on
Fall's Creek, which runs nearly through the centre of the farm. Also
connected with it a saw mill. Also a residence for the Miller's near
the mill. A lime kiln has been built & rail road cars come within 3
miles of the farm. Direct inquiries to Knoxville Post Office.
MATHIAS & MYERS, just returned from Philadelphia & Baltimore and are
opening at the stand formerly occupied by Mr. John S. MURRAY, opposite
KEEFER's Tavern, in Westminster, a stock of seasonable goods; cloths,
shaws, handkerchiefs, groceries, hardware, hats, boots, paints, etc.
MILLER, Conrad W. married to Miss Sarah Matilda COOK by Rev. Eli HINKLE,
both of Baltimore City, Tuesday evening last.
ORENDORFF, Samuel, wants old castings and flax seed. Also ad for fall &
winter goods; yard goods, groceries, hardware, shoes, hats, etc.
OURSLER, William, wishing to leave town, selling house & lot where he now
resides at the Forks of Westminster. Lot is 70' front & 196' deep;

15 January 1841
  adjoins DAVIS' tavern. 2-story log dwelling, weatherboarded, brick shop
  attached, log stable, corn-house, hog-house, etc.
PALMER, Joseph M., Attorney at Law, has formed a business connexion with
  Charles W. WEBSTER, Esq., Attorney. Office at Court & Main, Westminster.
RAYMOND, James, Esq., will deliver a lecture to the Westminster Lyceum.
  William REESE, Secretary.
REESE, John F., selling Moffat's Life Pills & Phoenix Bitters. Also Drs.
  KUHN, DRESBACH & PRYOR's Dyspeptic Cordial, also sold at C. HERSTON's,
  Frederick City, Md.
REIFSNIDER, Jesse, at the Forks, has large stock & fall & winter goods.
ROOT, Basil, Clerk, notice of meeting of Commissioners of Tax.
ROYER, Jacob, continues to manufacture shaker & threshing machines based on
  T. D. BURRAL's patent. Union-town.
SCHLEY, Frederick, selling farm called "Spring Garden," 213 acres 6 1/2
  miles north of Frederick, adjoining village of Walkersville. 2-story
  dwelling & back building with outhouses, barn, corn house, carriage
  house, wagon shed, blacksmith's shop, &c. Also selling 115 acres of
  woodland, part of "Mackey's Luck," 1 mile from above farm. Shown by
  Mr. DEAN, residing thereon.
SLINGLUFF, Isaac, President of the New Windsor Library, which is now open.
SLYDER, Peter, deceased, notes given at the sale of his personal property
  are due & are being collected by John THOMPSON, Esq. William SLYDER, Ex.
SPENCE, Carroll, attorney practices in the Courts of Carroll & Baltimore
  Counties and Baltimore City. Office St. Paul St., over G. DULANY's, Esq.
SUNDERGILL, Joshua, 15 stray sheep came to his plantation.
SUNDERGILL, Joshua, has received a letter admonishing him that he is not
  treating a certain person under his charge as he ought to. He dares the
  author to substantiate the charges brought against him.
WARFIELD, J. L., M.D. of New-Windsor, recommends Dr. ZOLLICKOFFER's
  Vegetable Purgative & Alterative Pills, which can be purchased wholesale
  & retail from John F. REESE, merchant. Also recommended by William
  WILLIS, M.D., John SWOPE, M.D., George B. AIKEN, M.D., Samuel SWOPE,
  M.D., John E. A. LIGGET, M.D., Joseph W. BIGGS, M.D., John W. DORSEY,
  M.D., & William H. POOLE, M.D.
WEBER, Henry, died on the 29th ultimo, in this county, aged 69 years, 10
  months & 1 day.
YINGLING, J., will take Franklin Bank Notes at par in exchange for goods at
  his store. Several ads appear for medicines he sells as well as dry
  goods, china & groceries.
The Mail between Baltimore & Wheeling having been robbed frequently of
  late, a driver on the route near Uniontown named CORMAN, on being
  arrested made a voluntary confession, implicating 3 persons in Uniontown,
  viz: Dr. BRADDEE, a quack physician, PURNELL, his clerk, & STRAYER, an
  associate.
State Armory & Town Hall Lottery, to be drawn. Samuel LUCAS, William
  GWYNN, George Gordon BELT, Charles F. MAYER, Charles G. RIDGELY & William
  J. WIGHT, Commissioners. James H. COX, General Agent, Baltimore.

5 February 1841
MATHIAS, George Jr. & Benjamin, executors of Joseph MATHIAS, deceased.
POLE, William, O.S., the New Windsor Guards will meet in full uniform.
State Appointments by the Governor: James MURRAY, Secretary of State. David
  RIDGELY, State Librarian. Julius T. DUCATEL, State Geologist. John H.
  ALEXANDER, Topographical Engineer. Thomas KARNEY, Examiner General,
  Western Shore. John S. GITTINGS, Commissioner of Loans. Aaron DUVALL,
  Armorer at the City of Annapolis.
 Insolvent Commissioners: Henry STUMP, Richard FRISBY, Edward PALMER.
  Jacob BEAM, Inspector General of Flour; David RICKETS, John WITMER of J.
  Henry J. WILLIAMS to be Assistant Inspectors of Flour in Baltimore.

5 February 1841
Leonard KERNAN & Alexander DAYHUFF, Inspectors of Sole Leather. Nathaniel
B. KEENE, Inspector of Green Hides & Skins in City of Baltimore. John MC
PHERSON, Luther RATCLIFFE, Daniel HOOVER, Dinwood H. BARROW, William
RONEY, Emanuel STANSBURY, to be Gaugers of casks & inspector of Domestic
distilled spirits for Baltimore City. James COALE, State Wharfinger in
Baltimore. John DUTTON & William W. AMOS, Inspectors of Lime in
Baltimore. Michael LAMB, Inspector of Plaster of Paris in Baltimore.
Daniel ORRICK, Inspector of Ground Black Oak Bark in Baltimore. Peter
STORM, Inspector of Hay & Straw for the Eastern Scales in Baltimore &
John BURKE for Western Scales.
Auctioneers: Robert LEMMON, S. HOFFMAN, Robert A. TAYLOR, William G.
HARRISON, Nicholas W. GOLDSBOROUGH, Hugh DOWLING, Anthony WHITELY, John
H. NEFF, Columbus E. COOK, Henry W. BOOL, John I. GROSS, William H.
ROBINSON, Samuel H. GOVER, John WHITBECK, James S. WEVER, Henry BEEKLY,
John R. WRIGHT.
William BOULTON, Warden; Jacob WHITE, Purveyor; H. R. LAUDERMAN & Lemuel
W. GOSNELL, Directors; all of the Penitentiary.
Charles HOWARD, William R. STUART & Franklin ANDERSON, Managers for
removing free people of color.
Nicholas KELLY, Weigher of Live Stock.

12 February 1841
BRANDRETH's Pills, agents: John F. REESE, Westminster; D. HOUCK & Co.,
Manchester; W. & J. ROBERTS, Uniontown; BLIZZARD & CASSEL, Wakefield; S.
& J. ECKER, New Windsor; J. EBAUGH, Hampstead; Hugh SHAW, Taneytown; W.
W. WATKINS, Sykesville; Solomon CHOATE, Reisterstown; W. H. POLE &
Brothers, Planeville.

26 February 1841
HOGG, William, of Brownsville, PA, died lately at age 86.
Baltimore Annual Conference of the Methodist Episcopal Church appointments:
Liberty circuit--John A. GERE, J. W. CRONIN, T. A. MORGAN, Sup.
Patapsco--T. H. W. MONROE. Great Falls--Basil BARRY. Luzerne--Ephraim
MC COLLUM. Lancaster--Hezekiah BEST.

2 April 1841
GORDON, John M., Esq., elected President of the Union Bank of Maryland in
place of H. W. EVANS, Esq., resigned.
M'PHERSON, John Col. withdraws as candidate for Governor.
NEWMAN, Jesse D., of Adams County, Pa., owner of wagon & horse which had
been borrowed from him has had them returned; the wagoner has
mysteriously disappeared and it is assumed that he has absconded.
PRESTON, Jacob A. Dr., of Harford County, candidate for Congress in 3rd
District; Harford, Baltimore county & part of Carroll. Opposition
candidates: James W. WILLIAMS & Thomas HOPE of Harford & Dr. John C.
ORRICK of Baltimore County.
SHIPLEY, William G., Esq., Postmaster, announces a new Post Office
established at Woodbine on the B&O Rail Road.
THOMAS, Francis Hon., declines re-election to Congress.
WEED, Alonzo F., ex President of the Bank of Millington, Maryland has been
arrested in New York on charges of embezzlement.
Official Appointments by the President: (MD only) William COAD, St. Mary's
collector. William FLOYD, Town Creek, MD, Surveyor. Nathaniel F.
WILLIAMS to be Collector of the port of Baltimore. Tench RINGGOLD,
George W. P. CUSTIS, John W. MINOR, Edgar SNOWDEN & Reuben JOHNSTON, all
Justices of the Peace for the county of Alexandria, in the District of
Columbia.

WESTMINSTER CARROLLTONIAN

9 April 1841
BARTHOLOW, Wesley Dr., located in New-Windsor, in room recently occupied by
DANNER & WEBB.
BOWMAN, William H., has purchased store stand at Ladysburg of John A.
HARTSOCK.
BOYD, William, Esq., Superintendent of the Susquehanna & Tide Water Canal,
died by drowning at the canal. His son Dr. J. J. BOYD. (Havre De-Grace)
CORRELL, Jacob of Uniontown District, died 23d ultimo, aged 84 years, 5
months & 27 days. Jacob YON, Executor of his estate.
COX, Ephraim G. Dr., located in Uniontown, practices medicine & surgery;
at house of Mr. William COLLUM, opposite Mr. SEGAFOOSE's hotel.
CRUMBACKER, E., Secretary of the Westminster Temperance Society.
DEVILBISS, Harriet Mrs., died 28 March, at her son-in-law's, John G.
SHAW's, New Bethel, Indiana, after a severe affliction of 3 weeks. She
was formerly of this county.
EVANS, Levi, continues cabinet making business in Westminster.
FORREST, Moreau Dr., located in Finksburg in dwelling formerly occupied by
Mr. George BRAMWELL, offers services to Carroll & Baltimore Counties.
FRITZ, Frederick, indictment for murder removed from Frederick County Court
to Carroll County Wednesday last. Jury selected: Henry BUZZARD, Philip
WEAVER, David LEISTER, Martin KROH, John SWIGART, Joseph BRUMWELLS,
Peter MARTIN, Jacob MORELOCK & William SULLIVAN; John FLETTER, John
MALEHORN & Samuel YOUNG, Talismen. Fritz is charged with the murder of
Eleanor DAVIS, who resided on the banks of the C&O Canal in Frederick
County. A verdict of "guilty of Murder in the first degree, & not
insane," was reached. Council for the State: James RAYMOND, Esq.; for
the Prisoner: Carroll SPENCE, C. W. WEBSTER, S. D. LE COMPTE & L. W.
BALCH, Esqs. Court ordered him to be hung by the neck until dead.
GRAMMER, Henry, deceased, Andrew GRAMMER, Administrator.
GRIFFIN, C. Wesly, married on the 7th to Miss Mary WAGONER by the Rev. Mr.
FORREST, both of Carroll County.
HENKLE, E. Rev., to deliver address at Temperance meeting in Uniontown.
HUGHES, A. W., petitions as insolvent debtor; Joseph ARTHUR, Constable.
KERR, Francis T., Secretary of the Carroll County Lyceum.
KEEFER, Widow, indictments against Isaac THOMAS & Joseph RIFFLE for a
robbery against her came up. THOMAS was acquitted & RIFFLE's case
removed to Baltimore County Court.
KEEFER, Lewis, wants stone & brick masons; he lives near D. & D. ENGEL's
Store, Sams Creek.
KILER, Simon, his Executor David KILER vs. Jacob GREENHOLTZ, case in Court
of Equity in April 1841 term regarding ratification of a note.
KIMMEL, Anthony, candidate for Congress, Fifth Congressional District.
NULL, Jacob, renting Tan-Yard 1/2 mile north of Taneytown on main road to
York, Pa.; has been occupied by Andrew WELTY for several years.
POOLE, Daniel J., selling 1000 seasoned cogs, lives on road from Middleburg
to Mechanics town.
RAITT, Nathan & Contee H., intending to remove westward, selling farm of
130 acres on which they reside; on Public Road to Frederick 1 1/2 miles
south of Taneytown. Log dwelling, brick barn, granary, wagon shed, stone
smoke-house &c.
REESE, John F., married Thursday evening last to Miss Mary FISHER by the
Rev. Mr. CRONIN, all of this town.
SHUNK, Joseph & Jeremiah brothers in partnership in Taneytown where they
intend to manufacture hats.
SIX, George, petitions for relief of insolvent debtors. Mr. SIX has
resided in Maryland for at least 2 years & William BURK, Constable
attests that he is under arrest for debt & for no other cause. Michael
BARNITZ, Justice of the Peace, William WILLIS, Clerk.
STONER, John, deceased of Carroll County, John STONER, Philip ENGLAR &
Jacob SHRINER, Executors.

9 April 1841
VAN BIBBER, I., selling 3 work horses & mercer potatoes.
WEAKLEY, Thomas petitions relief under insolvent debtors act.
YINGLING, J. selling celebrated compound horehound candy.
YINGLING, Jacob E., appointed Post Master at Union Bridge Post Office in
    place of Jacob CORRELL, resigned.
Chesapeake & Ohio Canal Company, Michael C. SPRIGG, President. Directors:
    Frisby TILGHMAN, John R. DALL, John O. WHARTON, Daniel BURKHART, James M.
    COALE, John O. WHARTON & John P. INGLE. Met at Frederick Thursday last.
Carroll County Court commenced Monday last: Grand Jury: Sterling GALT,
    foreman, Vachel HUMMOND, Jacob SHEETZ, John KERLINGER, Hanson T. WEBB,
    John HOUCK, Cyrus BULLER, John DRONEBERGER, Jacob WOLFGANG, John DOTERO,
    Francis HAINES, Benjamin HESSON, Horatio PRICE, Isaac APPLER, Joseph T.
    F. HOOPER, John KOONTZ, David BUCHEN, James CROUSE, Levi MAXFIELD, John
    ABBOTT, Abraham KOONTZ, Charles DEVILBISS & Benjamin WILLIAMS.
Petit Jury: Samuel NAILL, Martin KROH, Philip WEAVER, Loveless GARDNER,
    Daniel LEPPO, Joseph BRUMWELL, Joseph SHAFFER, William SULLIVAN, Jacob
    MORELOCK, John SWIGART, Peter MARTIN, David LEISTER, David GEIMAN, John
    SMITH, William WARD, Thomas CARTER, George W. MANRO, James C. ATLEE,
    Jacob H. KEMP, Isaac JONES, Daniel BUSH, Beal BUCKINGHAM, Henry BUZZARD,
    Jacob FARVER & Augustin ARNOLD.
Election in Taneytown on Monday 8th April for borough officers: David S.
    GOLLY, Elected Burgess. Senary LEADER, Israel HITESHUE & Charles FAIR
    Elected Commissioners.
Whig County Convention assembled at MOUL's Hotel. Sterling GALT, Esq.,
    chair & Thomas F. SHEPHERD, Secretary. Primary Meetings set to choose
    delegates to County Convention, said meetings to be held at: 1st
    District at LEADER's tavern in Taney town; 2d District at SEGAFOOSE's
    tavern in Uniontown; 3d District at MYERS' tavern; 4th District at
    Charles STEVENSON's tavern; 5th District at LITTLE's tavern in Freedom;
    6th District at Manchester; 7th district at BULL's tavern, Westminster;
    8th District at DUNCAN's tavern, Hampstead; 9th District at FRANKLIN's
    tavern in Franklinville.
Appointments by Commissioners of Carroll County: Constables: District #1-
    Washington GWINN, William BURKE & Jacob HAPE. #2-William SEGAFOOSE &
    William POLE. #3-David HULL, Jacob CRAWFORD & Samuel BOWERS. #4-George
    WILLIAMS & Nathan GORSUCH. #5-Lovelace GORSUCH. #6-John KRANTZ, James
    DAVIS & Jacob FRANKFORTER. #7-Joseph ARTHUR, Joseph SHAFFER, Francis
    FRANKLIN & Benjamin WILLIAMS. #8-David WOLF. #9-Jacob CASHOUR & Bennet
    SPURRIER. Judges of Election: District #1-Thomas JONES, John
    ADDLESPERGER & Samuel NAILL. #2-Elijah BOND, Joseph WEAVER & Cornelius
    BAUST. #3-Jacob MAUS, Daniel YEIZER & Jacob MEIXELL. #4-Abraham
    LAMMOTT, John KELLY of William & Joseph STANSBURY. #5-Benjamin BENNETT,
    James MORGAN & Rhees BROWN. #6-Michael RITTER, John FAIR & George WEAVER
    of Henry. #7-John KUHN, Edward FOWLER & John FORMWAIT. #9-Nicholas
    ALGIER, John FOWBLE of F., Jacob CALTRIDER. #9-Joseph T. F. HOOPER,
    Beal GOSNELL & Frederick RYERS.
New Meeting House for The Methodist Episcopal Church, Westminster,
    dedicated April 18th. Rev. Henry SLICER to speak. Horatio PRICE, John
    MC COLLUM & S. L. SWORMSTED, Building Committee.
The Academy at Freedom seeking teacher. Trustees: Thomas BARTHOLOW, Joseph
    STEELE, Nathan BROWN, R. T. SHIPLEY, Joshua FRIZZEL, John WADLOW & G. W.
    MANRO.
List of Letters remaining in the Post-Office in Westminster, 1 April 1841.
    Mary ARBAUGH, Miss Lucy ALLGITE, John J. BROWN, Francis H. BOYER, L.
    BENNET, Anny BEVARD, John BEAVER, Arthur R. BROWN, Nicholas BUCKINGHAM,
    John BAKER, James CHALMON, George W. COOK, William CAPEL, Henry CROOKS,
    Mrs. M. CHENNEWITH, David FROWNFELTER, Simon FLEGLE, Mr. J. FRIZZLE,
    Henry GEATY, Joseph HYLE, Mrs. Jane HARR, William HAINES, Ludwig HELWIG,
    Stephen KEYS, Miss Elizabeth KRISHER, Miss Margaret LEISTER, Lewis LONG,

9 April 1841
Vincent LEVEY, Henry MOUREY, Henry W. MARSHALL, John MICHAIL, Miss MATEN,
Thomas B. OWINGS, Miss Mahala POOL, Henry ROBINSON or Miss ESTHRA, David
RINEHART, Miss Caroline RECK, Miss Isal SHRIVER, John SAWERWALD, John
SHOCKNEY, John SWAIM, Esq., Miss Sarah SMITH, Mr. SNIDER, Miss Mary
STEPHENS, George SHAFFER, George THOMAS, J. W. WHITTLE, David DANIZ,
William WAGERS & Mrs. Elizabeth YOUNG. Joshua YINGLING, Post Master.
New High School Organized at New-Windsor. Rev. J. P. CARTER appointed
Principal. Trustees: Dr. J. L. WARFIELD, Samuel ECKER, Isaac SLINGLOFF,
James C. ATLEE, Jacob LANDIS, William SHEPHERD, Samuel MC KINSTRY, D. W.
NAILL. References: C. BIRNIE, Esq. of Taney-town, Rev. G. W. MUSGRAVE,
Rev. J. C. BACKUS, Rev. Dr. R. J. BRECKENRIDGE, Dr. M. S. BAER of
Baltimore and Rev. J. B. SPOTSWOOD of Randallstown, MD.
Testimonials for Drs. DRESBACH KUHN & PRYOR's Dyspeptic Cordial by Thomas
H. W. CONROE of Liberty Town, William WILSON of John of Clarksburg,
Montgomery County, Phillemon TOWSON of S. Liberty St., Baltimore, Henry
C. BRISH & Benjamin PITTENGER formerly of Frederick town, Md.

16 April 1841
Bank of Westminster: New Directors Elected: Abraham WAMPLER, James RAYMOND,
Andrew POUDER, John ROOP, John F. REESE, William WARD, Jacob FISHER,
Jacob POWDER, Jr., Jacob GROVE, D. J. GEIMAN & Isaac SHRIVER, President.

23 April 1841
SLICER, Henry Rev., of the Methodist Episcopal Church, formerly chaplain to
Congress, preached a Funeral sermon on the demise of the late President.
Congressional Candidates: 6th District-Edward A. LYNCH, Whig in Frank
THOMAS' district; John Thompson MASON of Washington County, the Van Buren
candidate.

30 April 1841
Meeting of citizens of Manchester regarding the death of President
Harrison, passed resolutions regarding the wearing of black armbands, the
tolling of bells, etc. Jacob KERLINGER, chairman & H. F. BARDWELL,
secretary.

21 May 1841
ATLEE, James C. Col. his Bull Calf was weighed at the public scales at 1
year, drawing full 945 pounds.
BRINGMAN, Jacob, who mysteriously disappeared & supposed murdered on the
Reisterstown turnpike last winter, returned home one day last week. (as
stated in the Hanover Pa. Gazette).
DOWLING, George F., a young man of Baltimore was engaged to be married on
Tuesday morning. When the groom-man went to his boarding house, he found
him absent & found a letter addressed to a relative intimating a design
to destroy himself. Other than this, nothing has been heard of him.
TAWNEY, Frederick, his farm sold lately for $11,000, an example of how real
property has risen in value in this region.
Third Congressional District: James W. WILLIAMS elected by very large
majority over Dr. ORRICK, independent. Fifth District: Hon. William Cost
JOHNSON elected over Col. KIMMEL by large majority. Sixth District: John
Thompson MASON has beaten Mr. LYNCH.

28 May 1841
DICKINSON, Samuel S. Dr., Lottery Commissioner, found dead last evening
near the Shot Tower in Eutaw Street. (Baltimore) He was a native of
Talbot County.
FRITZ, Frederick, alias John Jacob BRUKER, convicted murderer has been
granted a second stay of execution by the governor of Maryland.

28 May 1841
THOMSON, John P., President of the Frederick County Bank, offers $10,000
reward for recovery of money taken in robbery. ($135,976.54)
Whigs of Old Frederick held County Convention & nominated candidates for
Legislature: Sebastian RAMSBURG, Ezra DOUB, William JOHNSON, James
SIMMONS & Dr. E. HUGHES.   Delegation to State Convention: Richard COLE
of Liberty, William J. ROSS of Frederick, Robert ANNAN of Emmitsburg;
Grafton HAMMOND of New Market, Dr. Jacob BAER of Middletown & Joshua DOUR
of Woodsborough.

4 June 1841
Frederick Bank Robbery: Mr. DOYLE, cashier, has sworn in a statement made
to Judge SHRIVER, the manner in which he always kept the keys.

11 June 1841
Whig State Gubernatorial Convention Delegates: Washington County: Col. J.
HOLLINGSWORTH, J. Dixon ROMAN, H. W. DILLINGER, Lewis ZEIGLER & Jon
WEIST. Montgomery County: H. C. GAITHER, G. C. PATTERSON, George W.
DAWSON, William M. STEWART & R. Y. BRENT. Baltimore County: Horatio
HOLLINGSWORTH, William MATTHEWS, William HUTCHINGS, E. G. KILBURN, C. D.
GOODWIN, W. Govan HOWARD & H. HOLLINGSWORTH. Allegany County: Alpheus
BEALE, Hanson B. PIGMAN, Thomas SHRIVER & William PITTS. Frederick
County: Richard COALE, William J. ROSS, Robert ANNAN, Dr. J. BAER, Joshua
DOUB, Benjamin NEIDIG & Thomas SAPPINGTON. Carroll County: John
MATTHEWS, John G. CHAPMAN, P. W. CRAIN & George BRENT. A. F. SHRIVER of
Carroll was appointed delegate to nominate officers, who nominated
William Cost JOHNSON for Governor. Gen. CHAPMAN of Charles County
nominated the Hon. Richard POTTS of Frederick. Mr. RICAUD of Kent County
nominated John LEE, Esq. of Frederick County. William Cost JOHNSON won
the nomination.

25 June 1841
Convention of the friends of Frank THOMAS met & chose Isaac SHRIVER, Esq.
President; Elias BROWN, Esq. & Capt. William HOUCK as Vice Presidents,
William B. NELSON, Thomas J. CARTER & Basil ROOT as Secretaries.
Candidates nominated: Jacob POWDER, Jr., Francis T. DAVIS, John B. BOYLE
& Daniel STULL. G. W. MANRO received 2 votes & Nelson NORRIS 1. Dr.
SHOWER & Mr. LECOMPTE declined being candidates.

2 July 1841
Frederick County Bank Robbery: money stolen has been recovered in New York.
Dr. William Bradley TYLER, a director of the bank, & William M. BEALL,
Esq., Cashier of the Farmers' & Mechanics' Bank of Frederick county,
repaired to New York & recovered the whole amount, less $30,000.

9 July 1841
BENNETT, Rachel, executrix of Eli BENNETT deceased, of Carroll County.
C. BIRNIE, Jr., Attorney, has removed his residence from Baltimore to
Westminster.
COCKEY, J., during the re-building of the tavern house on Howard Street
(Baltimore), entrance to the Wheatfield Inn will be on Market.
CRIST, Conrad C., murdered at his house in Berks County, PA some time ago;
the Hagerstown Torchlight states that John RHINEHEART & John F. FLOSHMAN,
arrested in Miami County, Ohio are on their way to Reading, PA to stand
trial.
DANNER, Joseph, dec'd. of Frederick County, sale of store & residence in
estate. House fronts on Main street 80', in Emmitsburg, brick. Also
woodhouse, house to keep iron, a milk & a ice house. Also 4 acres
separated by an alley from this property with brick barn. Property sold

9 July 1841
  all together & clear of the widow's right of dower.   Joseph BAUGHER &
  Joseph WELTY, Executors.
DAVIS, Ureth, infant d/o Benjamin & Mary DAVIS of this place, died aged 17
  months, Saturday last.
DORSEY, Presley W., selling 741 acres in Carroll County within 3 1/4 to 6
  miles of the B&O Rail Road; adjoins lands of David DUDDERAR, Esq. In-
  cludes small building. Apply to Mr. DORSEY at Poplar Springs, Anne
  Arundel Co.
DUDDERAR, William, selling his farm of 156 acres on the head waters of
  Linganore; adjoins lands of John CLEMSON. 2-story log dwelling, log
  barn. Shown by Daniel ENGEL, Sams Creek.
FRANKLIN, Charles, dec'd., Joshua & Rezin FRANKLIN, Executors.
GROSS, John, Trustee in case No. 46 Equity. William WILLIS, Clerk.
HAFLEIGH, George, died on the 1st inst. near Frizzlesburg.
HARMON, Jacob, died on the 24th ult. near Frizzlesburg; aged 93 years, 6
  months & 3 days.
MAULSBY, William P., his dwelling house was struck by lightning during a
  storm Monday night last, as was the house of the Miss COCKEYS, across the
  street.
RAYMOND, James, Esq., candidate for Congress, 5th District, to fill vacancy
  of Hon. William C. JOHNSON.
SHRIVER, A. F., intends to be absent from the County for some time, has
  placed his accounts in the hands of Joshua SMITH, Esq.
SHRIVER, Jacob Col. of Pipe Creek has raised a remarkably fine specimen of
  the celebrated Rock Wheat.
STULTZ & CORRELL dissolving partnership.
THOMAS, James, his wife Catharine having left bed & board, he will pay no
  debts of her contracting. (Ridgeville)
WAMPLER, Lewis, selling 3 acres of woodland 1/2 mile from Westminster,
  adjoins lands of John FISHER & Miles MITTAN. Also selling 37 3/4 acres 1
  1/4 miles from Westminster.
WATERS, Zadock M., living near Hood's Mill, offers reward for 2 negro men;
  the elder, Henry, is 5'6-8" high, sturdy made & has a scar on the crown
  of his head, about 26 years old. Other called Otho, an inch or 2 higher,
  more slender & about 23 years old. Being brothers will no doubt keep
  together.
Washington County Whig Candidates for Legislature: David ZELLERS, Charles
  H. OHR, Samuel CLAGETT, & Charles A. FLETCHER.
New Windsor Temperance Celebration of the 4th of July: Rev. Mr. RITCHIE &
  Rev. Mr. GERE made addresses.
List of Letters remaining in the Post-Office at Westminster, July 1, 1841.
  Miss Eliza ANGLE, Norman BRUCE Esq., David BRIEN, David BALDWIN, Jesse
  BROWN, Nicholas BUCKINGHAM, Mrs. Sarah BAILE, George BECKLEY, William
  BURGOON, Tobias COVER, Israel COOK, Resin COOK, Peter FORNEY Jr., Richard
  FRIZZEL, John GALLION, James GILBERT, Isaac GREEN, William HOSTLER,
  Daniel HOOVER, Isaac HORNER, Miss B. HINES, Andrew HAWK, David HOUCK, H.
  W. HUGHES, Ellxis HARRIS, John H. HULSKANS, Mrs. Amelia JAMES, Christian
  KEGEL, Col. A. KIMMEL, Jeremiah KEY, Mrs. Elizabeth LOWE, Barbara LIPPY,
  Rev. P. D. LISCOMB, John T. MATHIAS, John S. MARTIN, Micajah MARTIN,
  Nicholas OGG, John Leonard OFF, Henry ORNDORF, David PUGH, Thomas PUSEY,
  Mrs. Susannah POWELL, Miss Caroline RECK, Jeremiah ROBINSON, Jacob
  RIGHTER, Henry RAUL, John SHAFFER, Robert STEPPHENSON, Mrs. Mary SHAUCK,
  John SHEAN, William TAWNEY & C. WITHERODE. Joshua YINGLING, Post Master.
H. HAMMOND's Window Sash Springs sold by Samuel ORENDORFF, J. F. REESE &
  Joshua YINGLING in Westminster; D. HOUCK & Co. in Manchester; H. SHRIVER
  in Littlestown (PA); S. & J. ECKER in New-Windsor; W. & J. ROBERTS in
  Union-town. C. MOUL of Wesminster, reference.
Candidates for Sheriff: William GRUMBINE, Lewis TRUMBO, J. Henry HOPPE,
  & Jonathan NORRIS.

WESTMINSTER CARROLLTONIAN

16 July 1841
EMMERT, Margaret Miss, drowned in the C&O Canal, 3 miles below Harper's
Ferry on the 20th ult. She was 17 years old & to be married in a few
days subsequent. (Hagerstown Mail)
KONIG, Bos (alias Frederick) & HANNA, William were arrested in York, PA
charged with being participators in the riot in Franklin St. on 5 July.
Committed to prison by Justice BARNARD.
WISE, John, celebrated Aerial Navigator made his 28th balloon trip. He set
sail at 2 p.m. & passing over Barry township, Schuylkill County near
Peter CLINE's Hotel; was seen 5 miles west of Pottsville at 3 & again 3
miles east of Reading about 4 & landed at Morgantown, Berks County (PA)
at 4 & 25 minutes, making a distance of 87 miles in 145 minutes! At that
rate he could travel from Philadelphia to Liverpool in the short space of
3 1/2 days!

30 July 1841
Heavy storms struck the area on Saturday & Sunday last. The barn of James
WILLIAMS on the Deer Park Road was struck & entirely consumed; 2 cows of
Edmund GARDNER & a bull of Edward STOCKSDALE's were also killed. John
MARSHALL on his way from Reisterstown to his home near St. John's Church
in Baltimore carrying a scythe on his shoulder was killed by lightning.

6 August 1841
Independent Candidates for the Legislature: Jacob REESE, John THOMSON,
William ECKER & John MC COLLUM.
Frederick County Van Buren nomination for the House of Delegates: John H.
SIMMONS, John W. GEYER, James SCHLEY, Daniel S. BISER & Cornelius STALEY.
"Catoctin Enterprise & Middle Town Valley Gazette," printed by Jacob T. C.
MILLER & Joseph W. WALKER at Middletown, MD, is neutral in its politics.

13 August 1841
BOWIE, Richard J., Esq. of Montgomery County will be supported by Whigs.
GREER, Robert S. Rev. married Miss Sarah Jane ANNAN, both of Emmittsburg,
MD; married by Rev. James C. WATSON in Gettysburg.
JONES, Mary Mrs., wife of the late Philip JONES, Esq., formerly of this
place, died at her residence in Bangor, Maine on Wednesday the 4th inst.
in the 56th year of her age.
M'ELFRESH, John H., died on the 4th inst. near New Market.
MARKER, Mrs. ---, wife of David MARKER of Westminster District died
Thursday the 5th inst.
SAPPINGTON, Thomas Col., candidate for 5th Congressional District.
SHAW, John G., died 30 July last at New-Bethel, Marion County, Indiana; son
of Moses SHAW Esq. of Union-town. In the autumn of 1838 Mr. SHAW with
his Mother-in-law, his Brother-in-law & wife left this county to make
their home in a Western state.
SHOEMAKER, William Henry Harrison, died 6 August near Taney-town; only son
of Barney & Mary SHOEMAKER, aged 4 weeks & 5 days.
WELLS, Thomas Esq., died Sunday morning last at his residence near
Westminster, aged 74 years & 11 months.
Baltimore County Opposition Convention assembled at Green Springs
nominating Thomas C. RISTEAU, Joseph WALKER, Philip POULTNEY, T.B.W.
RANDALL & Marcus R. HOOK.
Carroll County Lyceum meeting, officers elected: President, Col. Thomas
HOOK, Vice President, William B. NELSON, Treasurer, Solomon ZEPP &
Secretary, F. Thomas KERR.

21 August 1841
RAYMOND, Thompson, s/o James RAYMOND, Esq., died 13th inst. after a short
illness, aged 2 years & 9 months.

21 August 1841
Whig Candidates in Montgomery County: Thomas GITTINGS, John C. GOTT, John W. DARBY & John BRADDOCK.

10 September 1841
ATLEE, James C., New-Windsor, sale of short-horned Durham cattle & Berkshire hogs & Gaudy, roan heifer calf; owned by William MC CLELLAN, Esq. Gettysburg, PA. & many others.
BEALL, William M., Esq., has resigned the Cashiership of the Farmers' & Merchants' Bank of Frederick County to devote his time to the estate of the late Col. MC ELFRESH.
BOWIE, Richard J. Esq., of Montgomery County, if he will consent to represent the 5th District he will be supported by many Whigs.
CLAPSADLE, Margaret Ann Miss, died 4 September in Taney-town of a severe attack of Dysentery, aged 21 years, 6 months & 24 days.
CLEMSON, James, deceased, H. T. CLEMSON, Administrator.
CORRELL, Jacob, late of Carroll County, dec'd, sale of 20 acres on the north side of the farm on which he resided, adjoins lands of John WISE & C. BIRNIE.
CRUMBACKER, E., Secretary of Westminster Temperance Society.
ECKER, William is an Independent candidate for House of Delegates.
GREEN, Shadrack, deceased, sale of 66 1/2 acres in Carroll County, 2 miles south of Manchester, log house & stable; adjoins lands of Joshua BOSLEY, John STANSBURY & others; shown by Shadrack BOSLY. Joshua GREEN, Trustee.
HEWITT, Eli, near Carter's X Roads, Carroll County, offers reward negro man who absconded, calls himself Ben HOLLAND, the property of Richard HOLMES, Esq. of Montgomery County. 25 years old, 5'9" high, very straight & well made, etc.; is said to have a wife in Washington, D.C.
HUDSON, John, of Carroll County, applying for insolvent debtors act, Lovelace GORSUCH, constable testifies that he is under arrest for debt & no other cause.
KELLER, John, Minister in Charge, announces Camp Meeting on ground of Mr. GRIFFY, near the Providence meeting House.
KIMMEL, Anthony Col. candidate to Congress for the 5th District.
LONGWELL, Joseph M. Col., died 21 August of congestive fever at Sommerville, TN, an only brother of the editor of this paper, age 29.
M'COLLUM, John, candidate as Delegate in General Assembly.
MATHIAS, Jacob, selling tan yard in Westminster; 2-story house with all buildings & vats necessary to carry on business.
MOUL, Conrad, warns the public to be on the lookout for a traveling sportsman who has been imposing upon the good nature of keepers of taverns, hotels, etc. & decamping without paying the bill.
NAILL, William W. has applied for benefit of act for insolvent debtors.
PENN, Stephen, near Franklinville, Carroll County, offers reward for negro man calling himself John H. HARDY, 5'9-10" high, scar on forehead, left hand much disfigured.
POOLE, William Capt., dec'd, of Carroll County, sale in New-Windsor: Lot No. 1: 1/2 acre corner lot, No. 22 on plan of said town with large house, store-room & warehouse now occupied by Mr. J. BARTHOLOW. Also large barn & stabling. Adjoining this property are 2 unimproved lots, #23 & #24. Lot No. 2: lot opposite to 23 & 24 & #6 on town plan with a large log house, weatherboarded & painted; has been occupied as a tavern for many years; good stable & outbuildings. Lot No. 3: 1/2 acre lot with 2-story brick house & good back buildings. Adjoins store & residence of Messrs. ECKER's; 1/2 acre adjoins this with small stable. Lot No. 4: 1/2 acre lot adjoins last described with 2-story brick house & kitchen. Lot No. 5: 1/2 acre unimproved; adjoins property of G. AIRHART. Lot No. 6: 1 acre, about 1/2 mile from town with dwelling house & blacksmith shop; adjoins lands of Mr. Isaac SLINGLUFF. Lot No. 7: 8 1/2 acres on County Road from New Windsor to Westminster; adjoins land of Mr. Henry FULKERTH.

10 September 1841
Lot No. 8: 4 acres; short distance from No. 7. Lot No. 9: 4 acres;
adjoins farms of Messrs. M. BARTHOLOW, Joseph ENGLAR & L. SHUE. Lot
No. 10: 117 acres. Lot No. 11: 123 acres. The last two lots a short
distance west of the town, adjoins farm of Col. James C. ATLEE & others.
Call on Mr. William POLE to show property. William ROBERTS, Trustee.
REINDOLLER, Henry of Taney-town married to Miss Mary Ann BUFFINGTON of
Carroll County on the 7th inst. by the Rev. S. SENTMAN.
REESE, Jacob is a candidate for House of Delegates.
RITSCHHART, Elizabeth, dec'd. of Carroll County, John ALBAUGH & John R.
SHEFFER, Administrators.
ROOP, John Sr., selling mill property on Meadow Branch, 1 1/2 miles from
Union-town; adjoins lands of Jacob BAER, Jacob YON & Jacob ECKARD; 45
acres, a grist mill (part stone & part log), a new 2-story dwelling &
barn & other outbuildings. Shown by Emanuel ROYER at the Mill.
SCOTT, Norman, Secretary pro. tem. of the Middleburg Tippecanoe Club to
meet at MARTIN's Hotel in Middleburg.
STEVENS, Thomas H., dec'd. of Carroll County, Otho SHIPLEY, Administrator.
STONER, John, deceased, John STONER, Philip ENGLAR & Jacob SHRINER, Exec.
THOMSON, John of Taney-town District is candidate of House of Delegates.
VAN BIBBER, Isaac, selling a kiln of lime just burnt; also renting a quarry
of most excellent limestone 200 yards from the County Road between his
house & Westminster.
WARREN, Thomas & Co. of Gettysburg has purchased from S. H. LITTLE his
Patent for 2-horse Portable Threshing Machine & Horse-Power & is making
at his steam foundry a large quantity. Also signed by George ARNOLD.
Offering testimonials: George SMYSER, David ZIEGLER, C. N. BERLUCCHY,
John BARRETT, William M'CLELLAN, A. B. KURTZ, W. TAUGHINBAUGH, Jesse
ASHBAUGH, J. B. M'PHERSON, Daniel CULP, John HAMILTON, C. STOUT, D.
HORNER, J. WHITE, D. TROXELL Jr., Amos MAGINLY, David M'MURDIE, D.
ARMSTRONG, J. F. MACFARLANE, William N. IRVINE, William SETTLE, Robert
KING, J. B. DANNER, S. R. RUSSELL, John GILBERT, Michael ROOP, James C.
WATSON, G. STRICKENHOUSER, S. S. KING, J. M. STEVENSON, B. LEFEVER, H.
AUGHINBAUGH, Joseph LITTLE, James D. PAXTON, John SCOTT & B. GILBERT.
WEBSTER, George, O.S., orders guards parade in full uniform on the Chappel
Ground.
WILLSON, Mary Mrs., died Tuesday morning last at the residence of the late
Thomas WELLS near Westminster in the 93d year of her age.
Fall term of Carroll County Court, Grand Jury: Mordecai G. COCKEY, Foreman;
John GRASS, Henry HAINES, David BRILHARD, Jesse BROWN, William LOCKARD,
Jacob NULL, Thomas SATER, Jacob CLUNK, David B. EARHART, Adam FEISER,
David FOWBLE, Samuel BARE, John LEGORE, Robert T. SHIPLEY, D. C.
FRANKFORTER, Abraham LEISTER, Ephraim ENGLAR, John WHITE, Erasmus FOWBLE,
Peter PANABAKER, John MEARING, Henry SWOPE.
Petit Jury: Thomas B. OWINGS, Wilton BURDET, Jacob NICODEMUS, David
EVANS, Henry FLEEGLE, John WEAVER, Johnzee SELBY, William FRIZZEL, Henry
KELLER, Samuel W. MYERS, Daniel YEISER, Micajah ROGERS, Reuben WARFIELD,
Daniel DIEHL, Elias JORDAN, John BEAVER, Jacob SHOWER, Joshua SELLMAN,
Joshua STANSBURY, George FOSTER, Jona. DORSEY, Andrew BABYLON, Noah
WOOLERY, Joseph EBAUGH.
Reticule lost containing gold spectacles, money & other articles somewhere
on the turnpike between Westminster & Mrs. ARBAUGH's tavern.

24 September 1841
CLEMSON, James, dec'd., H. T. CLEMSON, Administrator.
CONDON, Richard & Arey, late of Carroll County, dec'd, Thomas CONDON, Admr.
DAVIS, Craig, a negro of dark complexion, 5'10" high, committed to jail as
a runaway; says he is free & lives in Mercersburg, PA when at home.
Jacob GROVE, Sheriff.

24 September 1841
DORSEY, Archibald, selling 1000-acre tract in Freedom District, about 2 1/2 miles from rail road, 12 from Westminster & 22 from Baltimore, includes 5 tenements, a stone grist & saw mill. Apply 4 miles south of Westminster.
ECKER, William, independent candidate House of Delegates.
GORSUCH, Nathan, dec'd, sale of farm in Freedom District, near to B&O Rail Road, 2 miles east of Sykesville, adjoins lands of William F. WARFIELD, Mrs. Susan BROWN, &c. 162 acres, 2-story house & large double log barn. William P. GORSUCH, Trustee.
GREEN, Shadrack, dec'd, sale of 66 1/2 acres, 2 miles south of Manchester; log house & stable, adjoins lands of Joshua BOSLEY, John STANSBURY. Sale to held at tavern of Mr. BRILHART near the premises. Shadrack BOSLEY lives on property & will show. Joshua GREEN, Trustee.
IRELAND, Edward wants farm manager, apply 17 miles on the Liberty-town Rd.
M'COLLUM, John, candidate as a Delegate in General Assembly.
REESE, Jacob, candidate House of Delegates.
SHAEFFER, John, Hamiltonban township, Adams County (PA), wife Barbara has left bed & board without just cause; he shall pay none of her debts.
SHIPLEY, Aramintea, selling land on the Sams Creek road, 4 miles from the rail road; adjoins lands of Mrs. POLTNEY, Richard U. CONDON &c; 114 acres; owner may be seen in Baltimore at corner of Green & German Sts.
SHUNK, Jer., Secretary, Guards ordered to meet in full winter uniform & with 13 rounds of blank cartridge for each day.
THOMSON, John, of Taney-town, candidate House of Delegates.
WEBSTER, C. W., Attorney in partnership with Joseph M. PALMER, occupy room joining tavern of Mr. MOUL in Westminster.
WOOD, John, late of Frederick County, sale of 270 1/2 acre farm about 3 miles northeast of New Market; adjoins lands of Basil DOWNEY & Dr. HAYS. Has brick dwelling house, log barn, 2 tobacco houses, &c. Also farm 3 1/2 miles east of Liberty, on the Liberty road to Baltimore, adjoins lands of Cornelius SHRINER, Basil LUGENBELL & the mills & farm of the late Andrew WORMAN; 200 acres, log dwelling & other outbuildings. Also 1 mile from the last 27 acres of woodland on road from Liberty to Baltimore. Thomas HAMMOND, Trustee.
Meeting of the friends of William Cost JOHNSON at the hotel of S. LEANDER in Taneytown.
Road Notice: to locate public road to commence near the Middletown road intersects the Hanover turnpike, thence to near Henry Z. BUCHER's Mill, thence to intersect road leading from Manchester to Westminster. Joseph ARMACOST, George FOSTER & David BRILHARD, Commissioners.
Statement of charges of Expenditures & Receipts in county for present year including: James RAYMOND, S. Dexter LECOMPT, James M. SHELMAN, & Madison NELSON fees for State business; Henry HOUCK's bill--Sheriff of Frederick County; Levi EVANS bill for coffin for pauper & hauling; Jacob POUDER, Jr. 4 cords of hickory wood; Philip GORE's bill for state business; James M. GORSUCH's bill for opening road; Nelson NORRIS' bill for maintainance of pauper; Peter BABYLON's bill for maintaining Mrs. JOHNSON; H. ORENDORFF use P. ORENDORFF repairing P. C. Bridge; Samuel NAILL's bill for coffin for pauper; Henry REINDOLLER's bill for 2 coffins for paupers; John MALEHORN's bill for finger boards; Michael SHOLL's bill for repairing bridge, Union mills; John B. SUMMERS for coffin for pauper; Joseph M. PARKE's & John K. LONGWELL's bills for printing; Joshua YINGLING's bill for stationaries; Mathias GEESERD's bill for burying Paul HOOK; William N. DORSEY to repairing bridge at Sykesville; Jacob OCHER to repairing bridge at Bruceville; Vachel BUCKINGHAM to attendance on G. W. BOCKER; John CLABAUGH, Constable, Joseph ARTHUR, William BURK, David HULL, Lewelass CONGUCH, Daniel WOLF, William SEOAFOOSE, all for state business; David HAPE & Edward DORSEY acting as Coroner & Jury; Basil ROOT as Clerk to Commissioners; William P. MAULSBY as Commissioners council; George KEPHART for building bridge at KEPHART's mills.

8 October 1841
ARNOLD, George, small notes signed by him & payable at his store at
  Gettybsurg, PA are a fraud. He has never issued any notes of this
  description & the public is cautioned against receiving them.

15 October 1841
ARMSTRONG, Thomas, inquest of his suicide held yesterday at Barnum's City
  Hotel, where he was found dead on the floor of his room of a gunshot
  wound (Baltimore City). William T. RICE, Esq., coroner. He was in good
  circumstances, left a will with a letter to a relative in this city. He
  was a native of this city; booked at Barnum's on arriving from Phila-
  delphia. He had been in the interior of New York, & returned to this
  city to terminate his existence, cause not known.
SHRIVER, Agustus of Pipe Creek, raises Rohan Potatoe, some weighing 2
  pounds each.
Meeting of the Westminster Guard: Capt. WILLIS, A. SHRIVER, J. S. MURRAY,
  William REESE & O. H. P. YINGLING delegation to Frederick convention.
Grand Jury for City of Baltimore have found true bills against Jefferson
  GRIFFITH, Alex. CURRAN, Jacob GETTIER, Peter MC COLLUM, Frederick KONIG,
  William HANNA & Patrick MC DIVITT for the willful murder of John BIGHAM
  5 July last.

22 October 1841
BARTHOLOW, Michael Sen., his farm in Little Pipe Creek valley, of 150
  acres, recently sold to Mr. BOWLEY for the sum of $90 per acre!
NICODEMUS, John of Little Pipe Creek Valley, has placed on our desk, a
  Rohan Potatoe weighing nearly 3 1/2 pounds!
STEWART, John, of Union Bridge neighborhood, suddenly killed by falling in
  a well last week.
WEAVER, Greenbury, of Manchester, was stopped by 2 men Friday night last on
  the road from Hampstead to Manchester inquiring of the way to Baltimore.
  He was struck by a club, dragged out of the wagon, tied hand & feet & his
  pockets rifled, $110 taken in Rail Road notes.

29 October 1841
BURGESS, Richard, of New Windsor, reports that a lame man who professes to
  be a varnisher named Vincent GRIBBLE came to his house & ran up bills and
  left without paying; is anxious to give the "gentleman" his just deserts.
COALE, James, trustee, reports sale to Court of Equity #35.
CURRAN, Alexander, charged with the murder of John BIGHAM. G. R. RICHARD-
  SON, Esq. attorney for the state; William P. PRESTON, Esq. counsel for
  the defence. Verdict of guilty of murder in the 2d degree rendered.
  Jefferson GRIFFITH also convicted same day. William HANNA's trial for
  participating in the murder of John BIGHAM ended also with verdict of
  guilty. (Baltimore)
DORSEY, Archibald, selling 1000 acre tract in Freedom District, 2 1/2 miles
  from the Railroad, 12 from Westminster & 22 from Baltimore. 5 tenements,
  grist & saw mill.
HASSE, Sarah, died on Friday last, d/o Jacob & Sarah HASSE, aged 4 years.
KERR, F. T., Secretary of the Carroll County Lyceum.
KRILLEY, Michael, well known to people of Hanover, came from Gettysburg to
  visit his aunt (Mrs. CROSS) in Hanover. The aunt found herself minus
  about $100 and had him arrested in Gettysbuug. He immediately confessed.
  He stole the money on Saturday--on Sunday evening he was married at
  Gettysburg--on Monday he was in jail.
REIFSNIDER, David, dec'd., late of Carroll County, sale of his 156 acre
  farm in Taney-town District, 30 miles from Frederick, 30 from York & 4
  from Taneytown on the roaad to Littlestown & adjoining lands of Lewis &
  Jacob PETERS & Jacob BAUMGARDNER. Has 2-story brick dwelling with back

29 October 1841
   building attached, log barn, 4 sheds, grainery. Apply to George
   REIFSNIDER 3 miles south of Taneytown, Agent for Heirs.
RITSCHHART, John, dec'd., late of Baltimore now Carroll County, sale of 250
   acre farm in Manchester District, 2 miles southwest from Manchester &
   about 3 miles from Hampstead; adjoins lands of William ALBAUGH, Joshua
   BOSLEY & Peter SELLERS. Improved by a log dwelling house, log barn,
   spring house. John R. SHEFFER & John ALBAUGH, Trustees.
SOWERS, Eli, near Taneytown, has taken in 14 head of stray sheep.
STALEY, Abram, who resided a few miles from Frederick on the mountain,
   buried Wednesday last week, disinterred under suspicion that he had been
   poisoned by his wife. Analysis shows arsenic; woman has been arrested.
STEWART, John, dec'd., late of Carroll County, Sarah STEWART, Admn.
WEYGANDT, William, has purchased from S. H. LITTLE rights to the portable,
   2-horse threshing machine. Gettysburg PA.
Military Convention: Col. J. M. COALE of Frederick, chair; Adjutant DUNHAM
   of Baltimore, secretary. Gen. George H. STEUART, President; Gen. T. C.
   WORTHINGTON, Col. J. M. COALE, Col. Charles CARROLL, Col. N. PHILLIPS,
   Lieut. Col. EICHELBERGER, Col. E. H. HUNTER, Lieut. Col. Z. S. WINDSOR,
   Maj. Richard COALE, Adj. George HOSKINS & Capt. BUCKLINGHAM, Vice
   Presidents. Lieut. P. W. LOWRY, Capt. L. J. BENGLE, Lieut. P. H. BROOK &
   Capt. G. R. LONG, Secretaries.

5 November 1841
DEVILBISS, Charles Jr., married Tuesday last in Frederick City to Miss
   Louisa SMITH d/o John SMITH of Uniontown.
GRABILL, Peter of Frederick County, married on the 26th ult. by the Rev. S.
   SENTMAN to Miss Sarah RUDISEL of Taney-town.
HOLLENBERG, Peter Jr., married Thursday evening last by the Rev. Philip
   BOYLE to Miss Susan STEM d/o Reuben STEM, both of Uniontown District.
KONIG, Frederick, alias Boss, found guilty in the murder of John BINGHAM.
   The prisoner though but 19 years of age, & when his broken-hearted mother
   was at his side with her eyes filled with tears, stepped from the prison
   bar laughing with cold indifference.
MC COLLUM, Peter, last of the party charged with the murder of John
   BINGHAM 5 July last, was discharged with an admonition from his Honor
   Judge BRICE to avoid bad company & behave himself in the future. Since
   his acquittal he threatened to assault a witness who had testified
   against him & was again committed to prison.
WARNER, Emanuel married on the 7th ult. by Rev. S. SENTMAN to Miss Margaret
   MORT, both of Carroll County.

12 November 1841
BILMYER, John, married on Thursday week by the Rev. ZOLLICKOFFER to Miss
   Margaret BLACKSON, both of Uniontown District.
BROWN, Nicholas H., dec'd., sale of his late residence of 150 acres, 1 1/2
   miles from Westminster at head waters of Little Pipe Creek; weatherboarded 2-story house, bank barn, wagon shed, corn crib & granery. Also
   small farm 3 miles north of Westminster between Littlestown & Taneytown
   roads adjoining lands of George FITES & Esther POWELL, of between 40 & 50
   acres with log dwelling house. Also lot at "Forks" in Westminster with
   2-story log dwelling house & stable, nearly opposite residence of Isaac
   SHRIVER & now occupied by Dr. CHALMERS. Shown by Nicholas H. BROWN,
   residing on premises or William S. BROWN in Westminster, Trustees.
BULLER, M. Mrs., at her residence at the west end of Wesminster, selling
   assortment of straw, braid & silk bonnets.
CLAY, George married Tuesday last by the Rev. Mr. CRONIN to Miss Martha M.
   KING d/o William KING, both of this place.
JORDAN, William Col. of Woolery's District, his house consumed by fire
   Saturday last.

95

12 November 1841
KEEFER, David, living in Westminster, has taken in a stray hog.
KREIDER, Jeremiah of Emmitsburg, married the 4th inst. in Gettysburg by the
Rev. FORREST to Miss Elmira CLAPSADDLE of Taneytown.
LELGORE, Ezra married on the 21st ult. by the Rev. Jacob GEIGER to Miss
Elizabeth FROCK, both of Silver Run, Carroll County.
ROHRBAUGH, Joseph married Thursday last by the Rev. Jacob GEIGER to Miss
Maria E. BANKERD, both of Silver Run District, Carroll County.
SHIPLEY, Lewis, renting mansion house of late John M'ELFRESH of
Reisterstown.
SNIDER, Mrs. _____, died Saturday last at her residence in Myers District,
consort of Jacob SNIDER, aged about 60 years.
WARFIELD, Thomas, dec'd., Sarah WARFIELD, his widow, selling 132 1/2 acre
farm, 2 miles west of Westminster on county road to Warfieldsburg.
Adjoins lands of Larkin HOUCK & David CASSELL; log dwelling house with
attached kitchen, log barn & spring house.
Petitioners for benefit of insolvent debtors act: Robert DUNCAN, John
HUDSON & William W. NAILL.

19 November 1841
BOWMAN, James L. of Brownsville, PA, published result of an experiment he
has found successful to prevent the decay of roofs.
CONNELLY, Frances Mrs., died Tuesday last at her residence at this place in
the 75th year of her age.
GALLAHER, Barney (Baltimore County) on trial for the murder of his wife
Barbara 4th of August; was found guilty. Attorney for the State J.
Nevett STEELE; for the defence T. Y. WALSH & M. F. TIERNAN.
GARNER, J. Whitfield, of Springfield, OH, late of Manchester, married at
Franklin, Warren County, OH by Rev. M. MALAY to Ann Maria d/o Charles
HOUSEL.
HANN, Philip, of Frederick County, married Monday last in Taneytown by Rev.
N. ZACCHI to Sophia ROBINSON of Westminster District.
HESS, Jacob, of Uniontown District, married Tuesday last by Rev. Mr. GEIGER
to Catharine JONES, only d/o David JONES of York County, PA.

26 November 1841
ALBERTSON, Elias, in employ of Messrs. WHITE & WILLIAMS on Smith's wharf,
Baltimore, attempted suicide yesterday by taking laudanum. He was
closely watched by his friends Dr. DURKEE & WHITRIDGE & was restored.
Love is said to have been the cause.
FORREST, Moreau Dr., Post Master at newly revived Finksburg Post Office.
RIFFLE, Joseph, charged with robbing Mrs. KEEFER of Baltimore County, tried
& found guilty, sentenced to 9 years, 6 months.
WILLARD, O. Rev., late of the Theological Seminary at Gettysburg, has
accepted a call from the Lutheran Church in Manchester.
The Carroll County Lyceum to meet at the M.P. Church. The Quaere: "Is
Dueling more criminal than Suicide in the eye of reason, religion & moral
rectitude?" to be discussed. F. T. KERR, Secretary.

3 December 1841
BOWMAN, John married Tuesday last by the Rev. Jacob HOLMES to Miss Matilda
d/o John LOVEALL, all of this county.
CLABAUGH, Edwin A. married Wednesday the 17th ult. by Rev. M. ZOLLICKOFFER
to Miss Elizabeth M., eldest d/o John DELAPLANE, all of Middleburg in
this county.
CONELLEY, Frances, dec'd., Jacob MATHIAS, Ex'r.
FLEMING, Robert P. Hon., a member of the PA State Senate from Lycoming
county, started for Illinois on business and was expected home about the
1st of October. He has not returned & no word of him has reached his
family.

WESTMINSTER CARROLLTONIAN

3 December 1841
HAPE, Jacob, at suit of Thomas & Philip BALTZELL vs. J. HAPE, Jacob GROVE,
Sheriff has seized all rights & titles to that tract called "Fuss's
Purchase" being part of resurvey on "MacKey's Choise", 90 acres with a
large dwelling, store house, still house & barn, now occupied as a
tavern; at forks of 2 county roads & is well known s a tavern stand. 1/4
mile of Pipe Creek Bridge, adjoins lands of John COVER. Also selling
livestock & household goods.
SHRIVER, Jacob, dec'd., late of Carroll County, A. F. SHRIVER, Adm'r.
TROXELL, Mr., sentenced by Washington County Court to 5 days imprisonment &
fined $15 for voting twice at the last Presidential election.
Coburn's Patent Leather Roller, agents in Washington County: Jonathan
SHEAFER, Boonsboro; Henry LEFEVER & Isaac MOTTER, Williamsport; David
RIDENOUR & Daniel SCHINDEL, Hagerstown; Benjamin WAGONER, Sharpsburg;
David TROUP, Beaver Creek. Frederick County Agents: Lewis M. MOTTER,
Emittsburg; William OU, Lewistown; Richard HARPER, Adamsville; John
HARBAUGH, Harbaugh's Valley; William HAUER, Frederick City. Winchester,
VA Agents (Frederick Co.) L. V. SHEARER & F. A. SHEARER; Corydon K.
MOORE, Strawsburg (Frederick Co.) VA. For rights apply to David
GELWICKS, Boonsboro, MD.

10 December 1841
FROCK, Jacob, s/o William FROCK married Thursday 25th ult. by Rev. Mr.
GEIGER to Catharine FLICKINGER d/o John FLICKINGER, both of Myers Dist.
GALT, Samuel & John THOMPSON, Trustees, seek teacher for "Galt's School
House" near Taneytown.
GREEN, Shadrack, dec'd., Joshua GREEN, Trustee reports sale of real estate
total $465.50.
LOGSDEN, John, dec'd., sale of 2 1/8 acres known as "Bond's Meadow
Enlarged" joining the town of Westminster & lands of Jacob MATHIAS, John
MILLER, Lewi SHREEV & John KUHN. Jacob MATHIAS, Trustee.
RANDALL, Joshua, in Carroll County Jail as runaway, negro, 5'8" high, 27
years of age; says he is from Somerset County.
ROBERTS, Ann vs. William POLE, &c., William ROBERTS, Trustee.
SLINGLUFF, Isaac, President of New Windsor Library Company declares 6%
dividend & election of directors.

17 December 1841
FOWLER, Richard, Petitions the Court for benefit of insolvent debtor act.
GORE, Emily Jane, d/o Jabez & Mary A. GORE, died on the 6th ultimo, age 2
years 4 months & 8 days, of Freedom District.
GRAMMER, Andrew, of Finksburg, selling lot on Baltimore & Hanover Turnpike
2 1/4 miles from Baltimore & 20 from latter. 22 3/4 acres, 2-story log
dwelling house, weatherboarded & painted. To view call on Frederick
FOWBLE living nearby.
GREENWOOD, Joseph B. married Wednesday 15th inst. by Rev. E. KENKE of
Westminster to Adah Zillah DEVILBISS, both of Frederick County.
KELLY, Deborah Miss, of Baltimore, died Monday last d/o the late Joseph
KELLY of this county.
LEAS, John, of this county married on Tuesday week by the Rev. Mr. ALBERT
to Lucia Anna MYERS of Manheim township, York County (PA).
MATHIAS, Elizabeth Mrs., died on the 9th inst. wife of George E. MATHIAS
Sr., 74 years 4 months & 14 days.
MOORE, Jehu, died on the 2nd inst. at his residence near Union Bridge, aged
86 years.
PEREGO, Michael married the 9th instant by the Rev. William MONROE to Mary
Elizabeth FOWBLE, both of Baltimore County.
SMITH, Joshua Sr., died at his residence on Little Pipe Creek on Monday
last, aged 81 years.
SPREADAU, Albert C., dec'd., late of Carroll County, James GILBERT, Adm'r.

97

17 December 1841
TAYLOR, John; married on the 9th inst. by the Rev. William MONROE to
Susannah ES_, both of this county.
WEAVER, John, dec'd., late of Carroll County, sale of 375 acres of his home
farm, 9 miles from Westminster, 2 from Manchester & same from Frederick
BACHMAN's Mill & 3/4 from the mill of the late John BIXLER. County road
from Bachman's Mill to Hanover Turnpike passes through the farm. Contains
2-story dwelling house, bank barn, wagon shed, corn house, blacksmith
shop, still house, spring house, lime kiln, & tenant house with bank barn.
Also selling 2 wood lots of 25 acres, 1 mile from above farm, adjoining
lands of Christian GEIMAN, George HENKLE & Peter PANABAKER. Also 25 acre
farm adjoining lands of George LINEAWEAVER & Frederick BIXLER with log
dwelling house & stable. Also chestnut timber lots of 8 to 12 acres
adjoining the county road from Westminster to Manchester one mile from
above adjoining lands of William CRUMRINE & Solomon MYERLY. Other 4 lots
1 mile from said county road near Henry GLASE's store, adjoining lands of
Jacob GUMMELL & Henry ZIMMERMAN. Also unimproved lot of 1 acre in town
of Manchester. See Jacob MORLOCK, Esq. residing on the home farm. (Name
of Trustee cut off.)

24 December 1841
BENNETT, Robert, will rent the farm occupied by A. P. BARNES for the last 3
years, lying on the head waters of Sams Creek, Carroll County.
BROWN, Nicholas Hall, dec'd., valuable farm one mile from Westminster will
be sold on Saturday next.
ELY, Hugh Col., State Senator of Baltimore County, married Thursday 17th
instant by Rev. H. S. HARRISON to Miss Marietta MC LAUGHLIN of Ellicott
Mills, Howard District, MD.
HEBBARD, Silas, has for sale at his factory 1 mile north of New Windsor a
large assortment of domestic goods.
LANDERS, John, selling small farm of 3 acres, 5 miles south east of Taney-
town near the from from Bruceville to Emmitsburg; adjoins lands of
William MERRING & John SIX. 2-story dwelling house. Apply to subscriber
at Double Pipe Creek.
LAUGHLIN, Thomas H., lost his life during the procession of the Whig
Convention May last year in Baltimore. Mr. J.V.L. MC MAHON, last year's
president of the Convention announces that $3,269 has been collected for
the benefit of his widow & children.
MCKENZIE, Eli, died suddenly Tuesday night last, of this place, aged 45.
SENTZ, Peter, dec'd., late of Baltimore now Carroll Couty, farm for sale of
206 1/2 acres in Manchester District, 3 miles from Manchester on the road
to Westminster, adjoining lands of Frederick RITTER & heirs of Jacob REED,
Christian SNYDER &c. Log dwelling house & barn & springhouse. Abraham
WAMPLER, Trustee.
SHIPLEY, Larkin, will sell 112 acre farm on which he resides, situated on
Gillasses falls, 1 mile southwest of the Sams Creek Road.
SHREEV, Joseph, being so advanced in age that hs is not able to do the
work, is selling his farm in Carroll County on Beaver Run, 23 miles from
Baltimore near the turnpike road to Westminster; 6 miles below Westminster. Large stone mill 3 stories high, also sawmill & 2-story weatherboarded log dwelling with porch on each side, large stone smoke house
with cellar, barn, stable & outhouses. 50 acres of land with mill
property. There is a county road from the Deer Park Road past the mill
to the turnpike road.
STEVENSON, Basil D., his former farm, 2 miles from this place, sold at $40
per acre; Mr. Thomas STEVENSON the purchaser.
THOMAS, Jacob, was committed to Carroll County jail as a runaway Negro man
who says he belongs to Dr. COLE of Liberty, Frederick County. He is
5'8" high, well proportioned, about 30 years old.
VAN BIBBER, Isaac, lime for sale at his kiln.

WESTMINSTER CARROLLTONIAN

24 December 1841
WELLS, Thomas, dec'd., his Home Farm, 1 1/2 miles from this place was sold
Monday last for $19,785.25! Mr. Joseph ORENDORFF purchased 1/2 of the
Home Farm, including Mills & Mr. Joseph SMITH purchased the other half.
WELLS, Thomas, dec'd., selling 400 acre farm of limestone land in Pipe
Creek Valley near head waters of Little Pipe Creek, 1 1/2 miles south of
Westminster, adjoining lands of Messrs. VAN BIBBERs, John ZILE, Jacob
POWDER, Joshua LOGUE & Michael SAWBLE. Improved by large brick merchant
mill at the confluence of 3 branches forming Little Pipe Creek. Also a
saw mill, 2-story dwelling, part brick & part stone, brick Switzer barn,
corn, wagon & hog houses, granery & large spring house, a number of
barracks &c. Several quarries of limestone & a lime kiln. Also 154 acre
farm adjoining above property on the east & lands of the late Col. Joshua
GIST, formerly owned by Basil D. STEVENSON; has 2-story brick house,
Switzer barn, corn, smoke & spring houses & blacksmith shop within two
miles of Westminster. Also selling 3 wood lots of 8, 10 & 13 acres
adjoining lands of Nicholas DURBIN & Jacob POWDER, Jr. Thomas STEVENSON
will show property. Joshua SMITH, Jr., Exec.
WILLIS, William Dr., Clerk of Carroll County Court, died in Baltimore on
Wednesday morning last, where he had been seeking aid of professional
skill--having been in bad health for some months past.
Tax Collectors: Lewis PETERS, Esq. for Taney-town, Union-town & Myers'
Districts; Benjamin YINGLING, Esq., for Westminster, Freedom, Manchester,
Hampstead, Woolery's & Franklin Districts.

31 December 1841
FARQUHAR, Mary R. Mrs., died on the 14th inst. of a protracted illness,
wife of George A. FARQUHAR of Richmond, Indiana (formerly of this county).
SMITH, James Augustus, died on Saturday last, s/o Jacob & Catharine SMITH,
in the 4th year of his age, of this district.
STOUFER, Elizabeth Mrs., Uniontown District, died Saturday last, aged 82.
YON, Jacob of near Uniontown has taken in a stray cow.
Westminster Temperance Society will meet in the Methodist Episcopal Church.
Rev. Mr. PHILLIPS, James RAYMOND, Esq. & John K. DELL are expected to
address the meeting. By order of C. W. WEBSTER, Secretary.

7 January 1842
ATLEE, James C., of New Windsor, selling 100 acre farm in vicinity of New
Windsor, adjoining lands of Messrs. WORMAN, GREENWOOD & PLAINE.
ENGLE, David, dec'd., seized for sale his 167 acre farm 1/2 mile south of
New Windsor, adjoining lands of Isaac ATLEE & Andre NICODEMUS. Stone &
log dwelling house, Switzer barn, spring & smoke houses. Also selling
blacksmith tools & household goods. The Heirs.
HOLLINGSWORTH, John, dec'd., late of Carroll County, Mary Ann R.
HOLLINGSWORTH, Ex'r.
HOOK, Thomas, selling 210 acre farm on Big Pipe Creek 11 miles west of
Westminster, 4 miles west of Uniontown & 1 1/2 east of Middleburg. Large
2-story dwelling house with kitchen adjoins, barn. To view call on
Joseph LINN, who resides on the farm.
KEEFER, James, candidate for Sheriff.
NOEL, Maria, died on Sunday week in this county, aged 93 years.
SHADE, Catharine Mrs., died Tuesday last at Manchester, aged 50 years.
SHADE, George, selling his tavern property on Littlestown Turnpike, 3 miles
from Westminster, 10 acres & dwelling house 35x53', large frame double
barn, smoke & spring houses & blacksmith shop.
SIFFORD, John, Esq., of Frederick County has been appointed Secretary of
State.
SMITH, Joshua Sen., dec'd., late of Carroll County, John SMITH, Ex'r.
UTZ, George, died at his residence in Manchester District on Sunday last,
aged 67 years, 2 months.

99

WESTMINSTER CARROLLTONIAN

7 January 1842
WEAVER, John, dec'd., his farm in Bachman's valley was recently sold for
$11,985.00. It was purchased by a company of persons of Manchester, with
a view of improving their lands by the application of lime, which is
abundant on this farm.
WILEY, Bill, who acted as the negociator[sic] between the robbers of the
Frederick county Bank & the officers of that institution, in restoring a
large portion of the stolen money--has been tried & found guilty of
receiving stolen goods. Messrs. TYLER & BEAL, of Frederick, were the
principal witnesses against WILEY.
County Currency Meeting convened for the purpose of taking into consideration the present deranged state of the Currency & to recommend to the
Legislature measures beneficial to the community. Nicholas DURBIN, Esq.,
appointed President; Augustus SHRIVER & Basil ROOT, Esq., Secretaries.
Col. J. M. SHELMAN explained the object of the meeting. On motion Col.
T. HOOK, John SWIGART, Basil ROOT, Joseph SHAEFFER & John SMITH, Esqrs.,
were appointed a committee to draft resolutions.
List of Letters remaining in the Post Office at Westminster, 1 Jan. 1842:
Betsey ABBOT, John ABBOTT, John ARBAUGH Sen., Henry BANE, John BEAVER,
Frederick FOXLER, Julius B. BERRETT, Jacob CORRELL, David ROWL, Resen
COOK, Frederick DICKENSHEETS Sen., Moses DERENPORT, Mr. HOUSE Esq., A. W.
HUGHES, Jacob HOLMES, Elizabeth HYLL, J. Henry HULS, Stephen KEYS, KIRK &
COROTHERS, Jacob MEYERLY, Joseph T. MARSHALL, John MC ELROY, Miss J. MC
HANNEY, Daniel MC LEMAN, Thomas PRICE, Joseph EIFFLE, George & Andrew
SHAFFER, Micaj STANSBURY, Frederick STIER, Ann P. STEPHEN, William
SHAFER, William T. R. SAFFELL, Jacob STONE, James SMITH, Miss S. & Alex
WARFIELD, H. H. WAMPLER, A. WADLE, David H. WHITE & Henry WILLIAMS.

14 January 1842
SHOWER, Jacob Dr., of Manchester, has been nominated by Gov. THOMAS to fill
the vacancy occasioned by the death of Dr. William WILLIS, late Clerk of
Carroll County Court.
SHRINER, Jacob, of Little Pipe Creek, Uniontown District, raised a large
pig; the length of the pig when slaughtered & hanging was 8'10"; his
weight when cleaned 650 pounds; this pig about 34 months old.
Carroll County Temperance Society met in New-Windsor 25 December, 1841.
Col. James C. ATLEE, President & Chair, John N. STARR, Secretary.
Meeting was opened by singing & prayer by the Rev. J. P. CARTER & Rev. D.
ZOLLICKOFFER. Society was addressed by Mr. Samuel MOFFIT & Rev. J. A.
SIESS. Committees set up, Rev. D. ZOLLICKOFFER, Jacob KING & Jessee
LAMBERT, chairs. Taneytown Total Abstinence Society--Rev. ZOLLICKOFFER &
John SMITH of Uniontown; New-Windsor Society--Rogers BIRNIE & John N.
STARR. Union-town Society--Rev. J. P. CARTER & Col. J. C. ATLEE.
Westminster Society--Rev. J. P. CARTER & Theodore CURRY. Manchester
Society--Rev. J. A. SIESS & Rev. Mr. PHILLIPS. Union Mill's Society--
Rev. J. P. CARTER & John N. STARR. Middleburg Society--Rogers BIRNIE &
Peter KEPHART. Union Bridge Neighborhood--Col. J. C. ATLEE & Rev. D.
ZOLLICKOFFER. Providence & Freedom--Rev. Ely HENKLE & John MC COLLUM.

21 January 1842
BANKER, Peter, dec'd., late of Carroll County, to be sold his 150 acre farm
Myers District, 1/2 mile from turnpike at WARNER's tavern, 1/2 mile from
Silver Run Church; adjoins lands of Dr. STUDY & Jacob MAUS on the Silver
Run. Improved by double log dwelling house 44' long & a log back barn &
spring house. Limestone quarry on place. Daniel BANKER, Trustee.
BEACHTEL, Jacob, of Myers District, died Friday night last aged 25 years, 5
months & 14 days.
CARTER, John, Pastor of the Methodist Episcopal Church in Westminster.
DORSEY, Nicholas renting Temperance Tavern on the Liberty road, 2 miles
below Freedom, now occupied by J. W. BROWN, to be kept as Temperance

100

21 January 1842
house, a store & mechanical business. Also 150 acres of land with small
log dwelling with kitchen, smoke house & dairy near Henry CARTER's tavern
on Liberty, Washington & Westminster roads.
KELLY, James, married Thursdaya the 13th inst. by Rev. Amon RICHARDS to
Caroline CHENOWETH, all of this county.
MORGAN, John, runaway negro jailed. 5'5" high, dark complexion. Has a
certificate of freedom or purporting to be one from Philemon HAWKINS,
Justice of the Peace of Franklin County, NC signed 24 August 1841. Also
has certificate from D. MORSELL, Esq., Justice of the Peace of Washington
D.C. dated 24 December 1841 stating that he was in jail in D.C. for some
time but was released through evidence of a Mr. RAWLEY of NC.
NORRIS, Nelson, selling 100 acre farm on road from Westminster to
Uniontown, 4 miles from former, 3 from latter. Also lot of 20 acres &
another timber lot of 18 acres, both adjoining said farm.
REIFSNIDER, J., renting house occupied by Dr. SWORMSTEADT in Westminster
SHRIVER, Jacob, dec'd., his heirs offer for sale 163 1/2 acre farm 3 miles
from Westminster on the Deer Park road, recently owned by Samuel KELLY.
Consists of log house, log barn, all recently under repair. Presently
occupied by Mr. CARADICK, who will show it. Also selling brick & frame
house & lot in town of Westminster occupied by C. BIRNIE, opposite
residence of Maj. Jacob MATHIAS.
SMITH, James died Monday morning last, gatekeeper on the Littlestown
Turnpike near this place, aged 78 years.
STONER, Jacob Sr., dec'd., heirs selling on premises 134 acre farm, whereon
Isaac LANDIS now resides. Situated in Frederick County on county road
from Uniontown to Liberty, 2 miles south of Union Bridge, adjoins lands
of Noah WORMAN, Israel RINEHART & John NICODEMUS. Has dwelling house,
stone spring house & Sweitzer barn. Also selling 20 acre wood lot 4
miles from above farm. Jesse LANDIS & Israel SWEITZER, Trustees.
WARFIELD, Alexander J., married Tuesday 18th by the Rev. Mr. HENKLE to Ann
M. MARTIN, all of this county.
WILLIAMS, S. Rev. to preach at meeting in New Windsor at Presbyterian Ch.

28 January 1842
CASSELL, Henry, dec'd., late of Carroll County, Joseph CASSELL, Ex'r.
OLER, Andrew of Carroll County, married Tuesday 25th inst. by the Rev. Mr.
ZINCCHI to Miss Mary Ann BUTTY of Adams County (PA).
SHRINER, C., will sell his 113 acre farm, situated 3 miles east of Liberty
Town, nearly adjoining Unionville. Also wood lot 1 1/2 miles from farm.
See Mr. SHRINER in Frederick or William LUGENBELL in Unionville.
SYKES, John, dec'd., late of Carroll County, John SYKES Jr., Adm'r.

18 February 1842
NICHOLSON, Mr., who keeps a Broker's Office near the corner of Market &
Howard Sts., Baltimore, was returning home to Green street, & met 2
persons who knocked him down with a club & robbed him of $10 or
$12,000. $2,000 reward offered for robbers & money.
In Jefferson County, VA, a feud has been pending for some time between
Hicromc L. OPIE & his brother-in-law, Capt. GORDON. The origins of the
quarrel cannot with propriety be printed. GORDON & his young nephew,
MAWLE, appeared at OPIE's house in a threatening attitude with the
purpose of attacking him. GORDON was arrested & released. Then MAWLE,
17 or 18 years old, was passing alone by the house of OPIE on horseback.
Smith CRAIN was in OPIE's house at the time sallied forth, the purpose
being to encounter MAWLE. At which point CRAIN then shot MAWLE, CRAIN
has been arrested & committed to prison in Charlestown. MAWLE, even
though the ball passed through his body, was not killed & it is hoped he
will recover.

11 February 1842

BABYLON, Philip, dec'd., late of Carroll County, John BABYLON, Exr. Sale at his late residence 1 mile north of Uniontown, selling personal belongings, livestock, grain, bee hives, blacksmith tools.

BEAN, George of this county, married on last Tuesday week to Mary SMITH of Bainbridge, Lancaster County, PA.

CAMPBELL, Catharine Mrs., died in Baltimore on the 3d inst. in the 55 year of her age, consort of Benjamin CAMPBELL, dec'd., formerly of this place.

JORDAN, George W., dec'd., late of Carroll County, Esther JORDAN, Ex. Notes are in the hands of Henry H. HERBAUGH, Esq. of Uniontown for collection.

LEISTER, John, intending to move to the west, selling 130 acre farm on which he now resides, situated in Carroll County on the Westminster & Hagerstown turnpike roads, 4 miles from Westminster, 2 1/2 from Uniontown; 2-story log house & kitchen & new Switzer barn, &c. Adjoins lands of Michael WAGNER, Jacob MORELOCK & David ROOP.

SHRIVER, Isaac, selling or renting well-known tavern stand in Westminster, corner of Main & Court Streets.

Carroll County Lyceum Stockholders: Jacob MATHIAS, James M. SHELMAN, Samuel D. LECOMPTE, Isaac VAN BIBBER, Jacob GROVE, John K. LONGWELL, Charles W. WEBSTER, A. Ferree SHRIVER, Levi EVANS, John F. REESE, William REESE, John MC COLLUM, Horatio PRICE, William YINGLING, Augustus SHRIVER, Nelson MANNING & James KEEFER.

18 February 1842

BROWN, Jacob, petitions for benefit of insolvent debtor act.

BULL, Shadrack, having rented in Baltimore will sell at his residence in Westminster livestock, looking glasses, bureaux, &c.

EVERETT, Nathan Rev. Mr., to deliver sermon at meeting house, Westminster.

LAMMOTT, David, will sell house & lot in Frizzlesburg, 5 miles from Westminster & 7 from Taneytown; 2-story house of logs & lot of 1 acre.

SHIPLEY, Otho, candidate for sheriff.

SIESS, Rev. Mr. to preach next Sunday at the Methodist Church, Westminster.

SWOPE, Henry Sr., died in Taneytown Sunday 13th inst. of dysentary in the 75th year of his age, a respectable inhabitant of this borough.

WILLIS, William Dr., dec'd. late of Westminster, selling personal property of 1 colored woman 32 years old & 16 year old colored boy, both slaves for life. Also household & kitchen furniture, books, medical instruments &c. Joshua SMITH, Adm'r.

Tax Reform Meeting, citizens of Warfieldsburg nominated Esau B. RANDALL President, Nelson FORREST Vice President & Francis FRANKLIN, Secretary.

German Reformed Church Meeting under the charge of the Rev. Mr. PHILLIPS with Messrs. Rev. HEINER, WOLFE & FREEZE of Baltimore expected.

Road Notice: To open public road commencing at the Baltimore & Hanover turnpike road, near to David Z. BUCHEN's dwelling & opposite the county road to Middletown in Baltimore County; & running from thence in the most direct direction that the country will admit, to a point near to Henry Z. BUCHEN's Mill. George FOSTER & Abraham WAMPLER, Commissioners.

25 February 1842

(From the Hagerstown Herald of Freedom) The County meeting held to establish a Home League was numerously attended. Messrs. PRICE, WEISEL & ROMAN addressed the meeting.

BOYD, John G., Cashier of the Towanda Bank, became indebted to the Penn Township Bank in a large amount. Mr. SAUNDERS, the Sheriff's officer took him into custody. They went to the office of William L. HIRST, attorney for the Bank & thence to C. CUILLOU, his counsel. BOYD returned to his house, packed his clothes & burnt some papers. He told the officer that he had left something & went back upstairs & shot himself with a pistol. He died yesterday. He was a married man with a family, but he

25 February 1842
  lived with a woman in this city, in violation of the law. (From the
  Philadelphia U.S. Gazette.)

4 March 1842
COCHRAN, Thomas, proprietor of several large ice houses in PA has engaged
  cars of the Balto. & Susquehanna Railroad to carry ice about 37 miles to
  the city.
NICODEMUS, John, his farm on Sams Creek of 104 acres was recently sold for
  the gross sum of $8,000!
Merchants' meeting held in Manchester, the undersigned Traders of Hampstead
  & Manchester, having for a long time past been oppressed by heavy rates
  of discount extracted upon them by the Rail Road Orders, resolve to pay
  80 cents on the dollar & no more. That Jacob CAMPBELL & Daniel L. HOOVER
  wait upon Merchants of Westminster to solicit aid to carry out
  resolutions. George MOTTER, Samuel LAMMOTT, Joseph EBAUGH, HOUCK &
  CAMPBELL, A. L. HOOVER & Co., George EVERHART & Frederick BACHMAN.
Merchants of Carroll County meeting, held at Mr. MOUL's hotel. Eli HENKLE,
  chair, William REESE secretary. William REESE, Hezekiah CROUT & Jesse
  MANNING to present resolutions. John S. MURRAY, Samuel ORENDORF &
  William REESE, Standing Committee to carry out resolutions & support the
  Traders of Hampstead & Manchester. Signed: (in addition to above) Jesse
  REIFSNIDER, James KEEFER & Joshua YINGLING.
A verdict of $5000 damages was rendered in Baltimore County Court on Friday
  in favor of John MORTIMER & wife in a suit against David H. WHITE for
  slander.
Temperance Meeting to be held at the Friends' Meeting House, Pipe Creek,
  near Union-Bridge. Dr. REESE to address the meeting. James C. ATLEE &
  Daniel ZOLLICKOFFER, Committee. Also, the Rev. Messers. William PHILIPS
  & J. A. SIESS to visit Manchester to deliver addresses on Temperance.
  The Westminster Temperance Society to meet in the Methodist Episcopal
  Church, C. BIRNIE, Esq. to address the meeting. C.W. WEBSTER, Sec.

1 April 1842
BUSHMAN, George, Trustee selling farm in Myers' District, Carroll County,
  adjoins lands of Andrew MOTTER, George ARNOLD; 160 acres, includes log
  house, log barn & cooper shop.
DAYHOFF, Mary, her body found dead on land of William BEAVER, a short
  distance from town Wednesday last week. She was believed to be insane,
  seen at different times wandering about the neighborhood. Coroner's
  inquest by James KEFFER, Esq.
MC LAUGHLIN, David B. Dr., from City of Baltimore, has located in
  Westminster in house occupied by Mrs. ADDLESPERGER, next door to John F.
  REESE's store & opposite Joshua YINGLING's store.
STORMS, George, cautions "Whereas my wife Naomi STORMS has left my bed &
  board without any just cause or provocation, taking with her two of my
  sons. This is to forewarn persons from trusting her or them on my
  account."

8 April 1842
BAUGHMAN, Michael married Tuesday evening last by Rev. Eli HENKLE to Miss
  Mahala POOLE, both of this district.
BEAM, Robert M., has repaired Globe Inn, corner of Market & Howard Streets,
  Baltimore.
COALE, William Dr., of Liberty-town Frederick County, died Monday 27th
  ult. of Neuralgia in the 37th year of his age.
DAVIS, John, married Thursday 24th ult. by Rev. HOLMES to Miss Ellen
  PENNINGTON d/o the late William PENNINGTON, both of this county.
DEVRIES, Christian Sen., died on 29th ult., at his residence in Freedom
  District, in the 70th year of his age.

8 April 1842

EHRMANN, C. Dr., homoeopathic physician, Taneytown, tenders his services to those suffering from chronic diseases.

HAPE, David, farmer of Carroll County, filed petition for bankruptcy.

HARRIS, Sarah Miss, d/o William HARRIS, Esq., dec'd., died Monday 21st ult. in York.

HAYDEN, Basil, returns his thanks to those gentlemen who, at the risk of limb & life, so nobly exerted themselves to save his house from ruin on evening of Saturday, 2 April.

KELLY, John C., candidate for sheriff.

POWDER, Jacob Sen., dec'd., late of Carroll County, sale of his furniture, grain, hogs, lot of ground in Westminster adjoining lots of Andrew WERBLE & Andrew POWDER, on which is erected dwelling house occupied by Benjamin YINGLING, Esq.; also 20 acre lot adjoining town of Westminster, with orchard. Polly POWDER, Ex'r.

VAN BIBBER, Isaac & Thomas E., of Avondale, selling cows, hogs, sows, plough, old iron, dairy furniture, cooking stove &c.

WELLS, Thomas, dec'd., persons who gave their notes at the sale of his personal property are informed that they are due. Joshua SMITH, Ex'r.

Fire in Manchester, about 10 o'clock on Friday night last, a fire broke out in a frame house owned by Mr. EVERHART in Manchester. When the fire was discovered, it had made too rapid progress to save the building & it was suffered to burn, whilst efforts of the people of the town were mainly directed to the preservation of other property endangered by a high wind at the time.

A large portion of the city of Frederick was endangered by fire on Thursday week last. During a prevailing strong easterly wind, the handsome dwelling houses of Dr. William TYLER on Record Street, occupied by himself & Mr. KEITH were discovered to be on fire. The Court House, Academy, Farmers' Branch Bank, the Clerk's Office, GILBERT's Tavern & several shops & dwellings were on fire at the same time. Dr. TYLER's houses were insured for $6000, but his loss must still be considerable. The records were removed, through the indefatigable exertions of the Clerk, Mr. Henry SCHLEY, from the Court-house to the fire-proof offices.

The village of Greensborough in Caroline County was destroyed by fire on the same day of the Frederick fire. The fire broke out in a kitchen, from whence it communicated with other buildings. The stores & dwellings of Thomas BURCHENAL, Mr. GOODWIN & Messrs. DOWNES & MASSAY were destroyed, together with a number of other dwellings, shops &c.

Meeting of the citizens of Manchester & vicinity held at the public house of Mr. CRUMRINE to consider offering assistance to those who suffered losses in late fire in this borough. Rev. Ezekiel B. RING, Chairman, H. F. BARDWELL, Clerk. Committee: George E. WEAVER, Jacob CAMPBELL & Joshua F. KOPP.

Appointees of the Baltimore Conference of the Methodist Episcopal CHurch: Patapsco Station--T. H. MONROE. E. Baltimore--H. SLICER, W. PRETTYMAN, E. D. OWEN. Seamen's Bethel--H. BEST. Great Falls--David STEELE, B. BARRY. Liberty--J. A. GERE, T. T. WYSONG. Westminster--J. W. CRONIN, T. SWITZER. Lycoming--George GUYER, E. MC COLLUM. Lexington--E. SMITH, T. A. MORGAN. J. SPRIGG, Sup.

Carroll County Court. Judges DORSEY, WILKINSON & BREWER.

Grand Jury: Elias BROWN (foreman), John WENTZ, Upton SCOTT, Jacob OCKER, Ignatius GORE, John KERLINGER, Abel SCRIVNER, John COLHOUN, John HESSON, Flinn GARNER, Jacob FRINGER, Abraham LAMMOTT, Samuel MYERS, Richard OWINGS, Thomas HICKLEY, Thomas BROWN, Israel LEISTER, George RUDKEY, John JONES, John FLETTER, Joseph MOORE, Vachel BROWN & Jacob WILT.

Petit Jury: Michael GETTINGER, James ROGERS, Joshua LAMMOTT, Andrew K. SHRIVER, Benjamin FOWLER, Charles W. HOOD, Rezin FRANKLIN, Joseph WIVEL, Earhart WINTERS, David FOUTZ, Levi SHREEV, Michael RITTER, Joseph ARMACOST, Samuel MOFFET, John P. GALLION, Daniel SULLIVAN Jr., John F.

8 April 1842
REESE, Israel NORRIS, David Z. BUCHEN, James MORGAN, John SYKES, Joshua
BARNES, Henry ALGIRE, John RUDOLPH & William FROCK.
Letters Remaining at the Post Office, Westminster: John ARNOLD, John
ABBOTT, Margaret ARBAUGH, William BICKLE, John BROWNER, Samuel
BLINTZINGER, Thomas S. BROWN, Samuel BOWERS, John BLANKLY, George BAKER,
James H. BAKER & Co., John BAUGHER, N. Louis CORDAINER, John C. COLEHOUR,
Edward DORSEY, Jacob DELL, David FOUTZ, Jacob FINKBONE, Capt. Joseph
GARRETSON, Perry GREEN, John GIBB, A. W. HUGHES, John HOLMES, Abraham
HITESHUE, Peter HAFLLEIGH, John HIRSH, Stephen KEYS, David KNIPPLE, KIRK
& CROTHERS, Peter KNIGHT, Israel LEISTER, Samuel LILLY, Sophiah LEVELY,
Abraham LAMMOTT, Barbara LIPPE, Daniel M'COOK, Jacob NICODEMUS, Thomas B.
OWINGS, Susannah POWEL, Abraham PROOF, Thomas PRICE, John H. PRICE, Dr.
James PARRY, Samuel ROBINSON, Jesse REIFSNIDER, Jacob RIPLE, Peter
SLAGLE, William & R. M. SEYMAN, John G. SIMMONS, Joseph SHARER, Michael
SAMUEL, William SHREEV, Sarah SMITH, Ann Rebecca TIPTON, Nimrod VELROY,
Dr. W. WILLIS, Nicholas WILLIAMS. Joseph YINGLING, Post Master.
Abingdon Academy, Harford County, MD, to commence his summer session on May
2. Charles S. SEWELL, President, Board of Trustees; Robert BOLTON, Secy.

15 April 1842
BANKER, Daniel, Trustee, conducting Equity Sale.
DEVRIES, Christian Sen., de'd., SAEB (?), Ex'r.
PHILLIPS, William Rev., married Tuesday morning last by Rev. WOLF to Miss
Martha M. WORTHINGTON, eldest d/o Col. Thomas HOOK, both of this place.
PRICE, Horatio & Alfred TROXEL to dissolve co-partnership.
ROOP, John Sen., married Sunday last by Rev. P. BOYLE to Mrs. ___ GEIMAN,
both of Westminster District.
SHAW, Hugh & William L. CRAPSTER, Taney Town, co-partnership opening with
fresh supply of seasonable goods.
SHEW, Henry, of this place, married Thursday evening by Rev. HINKLE to Miss
Sidney Ann CARR, d/o Samuel CARR of the 4th District.
Sentenced: Peter LILLY, a coloured man, to the Penitentiary for 4 years
for stabbing another coloured man with intent to kill. Charles
JEFFERSON, coloured man, sentenced to 2 years for stealing.
Delinquent lands in Carroll County for taxes due in 1839, 40 & 41. Tobias
COVER, Collector.
  District 1: John BOWERS 25 acres; Daniel BOYLE's heirs "Boyle's Retreat,"
  brick house, 195 acres; Henry BIDDLE 6 acres; Abraham FORNEY "Boston" 12
  acres; William KOONS (of H.) "Epping Forest" 50 acres; George LONGSTRAW
  "Brothers Agreement" 41 acres; Francis LEASE 40 acres; Daniel MC KINSEY 1
  lot; George PRICE's heirs "Addition to the Pines" 200 acres; Jacob
  ROUTSONG "Ohio" 50 acres; Jonas SPANGLER "Brooks Discovery" 20 acres;
  Nicholas SNIDER, "Middlesburg"; Peter WEANT "Heads Industry" 4 acres.
  District 2: Paul MOURER "Hills & Valley" 43 acres; David BROWN, 21 acres;
  Eleanora BANKS "Retirement Corrected" 90 acres; Peter BOWENS (col'd)
  "Haines' Inheritance" 3 1/4 acres; Francis KEY (col'd) "Susan's Fancy" 5
  3/4 acres; David MEASLER "Reserved or Amended" 137 1/3 acres; Susan NAILL
  "Forrest in Need"; John SHRINER "Bedford" 2 1/2 acres; Michael SPONGLER's
  heirs, 1 lot; Samuel STULLER "Mollys Fancy" 48 acres; William LLOYD, 1/2
  acre.
  District 3: Henry FELTY "Ohio" 5 1/2 acres; Joseph HOOVER, 101 acres;
  Elisha JONES "Ohio" 162 acres; Hannah LITTLE "Ohio" 60 acres; Adam RIGLE,
  50 acres.
  District 4: William ALEXANDER "Caledonia" 100 acres; Joshua BROTHER's
  heirs, "Glendock & John" 171 acres; Nathan BUCKINGHAM "Caledonia" 160
  acres; Rezin BROWN "Heels Addition" 220 acres; Elias BUCKINGHAM "Buck'ms
  Venture" 53 acres; Francis ELSRODE "Hales Adventure" 5 acres; Ann FULLER
  "Hooker's Meadow" 28 1/2 acres; Joshua GORSUCH "Rochester" & others 396
  acres; Jacob HALL's heirs "Deep Valley" 325 acres; Nathan HAINES "Waber

WESTMINSTER CARROLLTONIAN

15 April 1842
  Hall" 80 acres; Peter G. HUNTER "Mount Pleasant" 263 acres; Edward E.
  HALL, "Green Vale" 1000 acres; Jonathan HOLME's heirs, "Point of
  Rochester" 180 acres; Upton S. HEATH 484 acres; Edward JORDAN
  "Buckingham's Good" 101 acres; Nicholas KELLEY "Hales Adventure" 105
  acres; William & Hy MC KINSTRY 300 acres; Gideon MITCHELL "Peach Brandy
  Forest" 200 acres; John H. MYERS "Success" 141 acres; Letitia MC CREARY
  "Clover Hill" 508 acres, "Kinfawn" 240 acres, "Pith" & others 120 acres;
  James OWINGS "Rochester" 160 acres; William OWINGS' heris "Survey on
  Discovery" 30 acres; Jonathan PARRISH "Flag Meadow" 120 acres; Henry
  SELLMAN 1 lot in Warfieldsburg; Andrew SHRIVER "Wilson's Intent" 66
  acres; John SMITH "Meadows & Hills" 20 acres; Widow WAMPLER "Peter's
  Discovery" 3 acres; Honor WOOLERY "Kitchen" 36 acres; Henry SMITH's heirs
  "Smith's Fancy" 15 acres.
  District 5: Jacob ALBERT "Upper Marlborough" 265 acres; Josiah BORINGs'
  heirs, 100 acres; Margaret BROWN "Sandy Bottom" 275 acres; William
  BAKER's heirs "Edinburg" 100 acres; John BECRAFT's heirs, 10 acres;
  Archibald BROWN's heirs "Pettycoat Hoop" 100 acres; Elizabeth MC CULLEY
  "Adams' Garden" 86 acres; Nicholas COOK, 70 acres; John COAD "Forest
  Levee" 150 acres; Jacob CARTER's heirs "Hunter's Chance" 315 acres;
  Andrew COOK "Longtrusted Resurveyed" 240 acres; Solomon CONOWAY's heirs,
  162 acres; Samuel DORSEY "Meadows" 150 acres; John DAVIS' heirs "Addition
  to Headway's Quarter" 32 acres; Rezin DORSEY "Warfield's Forrest" 25
  acres; James DRIVER "Part Sally's Chance" 100 acres; Hamlet GILLIS' heirs
  "Bachelors Refuge" 550 acres; Nathan GORSUCH "Dorseys Neglect" 162 acres;
  Cornelius HOWARD "John's Chance" 196 acres; Samuel HOWARD "Eldersburg" 4
  acres; Joseph HARDEN "Windsor Forrest" 74 acres & "Colross" 106 acres;
  Nicholas ISRAEL "Chancy Strong Meadows" 34 acres; Thomas JONES "Sewall's
  Belief" 36 acres; Nicholas KELLEY, house in Eldersburg; John R. KEMP 135
  acres; Peter LITTLE's heirs 123 acres; Margaret LUCAS "Lowrys Lot" &
  "Gytsylvania" 175 acres; Andrew MERCER's heirs 13 ac.; Robert T. MERCER's
  heirs 165 acres; Beal OWINGS' heirs 98 acres; Jesse OWINGS' heirs
  "Batchelors Refuge" 400 acres; Eli BENNETT 310 acres; Levin BENNETT's
  heirs 116 acres; John PHILIP's heirs "Wylmonts Wilderness" 125 acres;
  George W. RIGGS "Part of Caledonia" 500 acres; John SHIPLEY (of A.) "Union
  Forest" 191 acres; Seth WARFIELD's heirs 100 acres; John WIER's heris,
  house & lot in Eldersburg; Joseph WILLIS, "Part of Caledonia" 100 acres;
  Samuel WARD 96 acres; Henry WHALEN "Mount Pleasant Enlarged" 230 acres;
  Benjamin YOUNG's heirs 121 acres; Christopher ZEPP 65 acres.
  District 6: Ezekiel BORING Sr. "Stoney Ridge" 102 acres; Daniel BOLINGER
  "Contrivance" 320 acres; Joseph BOWSER's heirs 150 acres; George BECK "Iron
  Intention" 140 acres; Joshua & John CROKER "Boring's Range" 80 acres;
  Philip FUHRMAN "Troy" 71 acres; William HOFFMAN "Ground Oak Hill" 55
  acres; ___r (?) HOFFMAN 140 acres; Conrad KERLINGER's heirs 95 acres;
  John MILLER's heirs 1/4 acre; Thomas MARSHALL's heirs 12 acres; ___anora
  B. MARSH 10 acres; ___es PLOUGHMAN's heirs 58 acres; __ry PETRE "Spring
  Run" 45 acres; ___n REESE 30 acres; Danier SHARER Sen. 12 acres; Henry
  SALTZGIVER "Joshua's Fancy" 40 acres; Henry SHUMAN 5 acres; ___m SHOWER's
  heirs 20 acres; Michael SAUBLE 180 acres; Christian SNIDER "Iron
  Intention" 200 acres; Amon TIPTON "Plowman's Defence" 100 acres; Daniel
  UTZ "Inheritance" 32 acres; John WORTHINGTON & S. COCKEY "Dye's
  Adventure" 60 acres; Prudence WELSH, "Society Hills" 106 acres; John
  LAMMOTT "Society Hills" 106 acres; C. ZIMMERMAN's heirs 165 acres.
  District 7: Eleanora BRIGGS "Rochester" 25 acres; Mary COLEGATE "Bond's
  Meadow Enlarged" 30 acres & house & lot in Westminster; John CROUT's
  heirs; A. H. BUSBY brick & log house; Joseph M. CROMWELL 2 lots; Charles
  W. CARTHOUSE 1 acre; Elizabeth ECKER Old buildings 1 acre; Catharine
  ETTERLING "Caty's Delight" 160 acres & 1 house & Lot in Westminster;
  Benjamin DURGIN's heirs "Iron Intention" 102 acres; Jacob GRAMMER's heirs
  Old buildings & lots; Henry GETTY brick house & lot; David GILBERT

WESTMINSTER CARROLLTONIAN

15 April 1842

"Sherman's Retreat" 12 acres; Eve GROGG "Part of Rochester" 10 1/4 acres; George HOFFMAN's heirs 60 acres; Thomas E. HAMBLETEON 100 acres; Daniel LEISTER 1 lot, 1 1/2 acres; David LAMPTER 40 acres; Henry MOURER house & lot; Henry NEFF's heirs 217 acres; James OWINGS "BC Rochester" 600 acres; Albinus POOL; Henry LOVEALL's heirs "Loveallty" 230 acres; Ludwick RIGLE, lots 4 acres; Charles STEVENSON house & lot, 1/4 acre; George SHEETS brick house & lot, 1/4 acre; Nimrod STEVENSON house & lot; Joseph TOPPER "Lehigh Furnace" 5 acres; David UHLER house & lot; Washington VAN BIBBER "Avondale" 755 acres; George WEBSTER 4 acres; Lovelace WILLIAMS "Warberhill" 72 acres; A. & L. WAMPLER Old buildings 1 1/2 acres; Lud'k WAMPLER's heirs "Traveller's Rest" lots 2; Leonard ZEPP's heirs house & lot & 15 acres; Nicholas H. BROWN's heirs "Rattlesnake" 110 acres, "Brown's Delight" 104 acres, "Lehigh Furnace" 29 acres, "Dry Works" 8 acres, small buildings 5 acres, "Rochester" 20 acres, woodlot 14 & 38 acres.

District 8: Rachel BOSSOM "Cornhill" 28 acres; George W. BROWN "Harriett's Retreat" 14 acres; Ulrich BUCHEN "Canton Bare" 189 acres; Peter BOBLITZ "Peter Claim" 30 acres; John CREIGH "Chenoweth Enlargement" 186 acres; Joshua F. COCKEY "Dyes Chance" 97 acres; A. F. CRAWFORD "Mount Pleasant" 128 acres; James F. SMITH 10 acres; Thomas GIST's heirs 477 acres; David R. GIST 200 acres; William HOFFMAN "Frankford" 132 acres; Jacob HELDEBRAND "Louderman's Chance" 155 acres; John HARE "Foster's Neglect" 210 acres; John T. JOHNS "Frog Forrest" 100 acres; C. KELBAUGH's heirs "Pleasant Spring" 122 acres; Samuel KERLINGER "Merryman's Meadows" 127 acres; John LOUDENSLAGER "Come By Chance" 10 acres; Rebecca MURRAY "Merryman's Meadow" 108 acres; Elizabeth Ann MURRAY "Blizzard" & "Harris" 134 acres; Harriet MURRAY, "Small Meadow", Susanna NEFF 333 acres; Chissilla OWINGS 100 acres; James PEARCE "Petersburg Resurveyed" 2 acres; Elizabeth STANSBURY 150 acres; Micajah STANSBURY "Reignburg" 200 acres; Elizabeth STANSBURY "Rockland" lot; Andrew STEVENS "Hunter's Range" 50 acres; George STEVENS 50 acres; Adam SHOWER's heirs "Foster's Hunting Ground" 179 acres; Greenberry TIPTON "Pleasant Spring" 25 acres; William TOWNEY Jr. "Jacob's Beginning" 81 acres; Amon TIPTON "Hunter's Range" 36 acres; Jacob TROIERO's heirs "Hale's Adventure" 5 acres.

District 9: Lewis BELL (colored) "Baker's Discovery" 4 acres; H. & D. BUSSARD "Tan-yard" 68 acres; William H. BEATTY, house & lot; Jacob CROWL "Rich Meadow" 25 acres, & "Resurveyed on Father's Gift" 152 acres; Grafton DOTTY; Thomas DAVIS "Beggers Discovery" 12 acres; Jacob FRIZZLE "Larrences Industry" 50 acres; Thomas GORSUCH "Baker's Discovery" 150 acres; Joseph GOSNELL's heirs "Batchlers Refuge" 100 acres; Harriett HAMMOND 380 acres; Philip HAMMOND 350 acres; Warfield HALL "Hampton Court" 200 acres; Reubin ISRAEL "Bit Him Softly" 90 acres; Nicholas KELLEY 160 acres; Widow LONG 36 acres; Samuel MOALE "Absalum Chance" 116 acres; Edward MYERS, small house 1 acre; Thomas PHILLIPS "Upper Marlboro" 10 acres; Henry REPP house in Ridgeville 5 acres; _____ SENSENSEY's heirs "John's Industry" 6 acres; Rezin SIMPSON "Dorsey's Industry" 28 acres; Michael SHRINER "Light Castle" 45 acres; Gustavius SAVOY "Log Cabin" 1 acre; George SMITH 5 acres; Samuel SHIPLEY "Blooming Plane" 53 acres; Henry William SHPLEY 100 acres; N. & T. WORTHINGTON "Manclo's Purchase" 800 acres; Airy WALKER 360 acres; Phyllis WILLIAMS 20 acres; Henry WAYMAN "Blooming Plane" 70 acres; J. HOOD & H. WAYMAN "Blooming Plane" 30 acres; Nicholas WARFIELD "Chase's Forest" 154 acres; Christopher ZEPP "Steven's Meadows" 14 acres. Basil ROOT, Clerk to Commissioners of Carroll County.

22 April 1842

DOKINNODD, Samuel W. has purchased the cabinet work shop lately occupied by Levi EVANS in Westminster. Will manufacture sideboards & bureaus, wash-stands, coffins &c.

22 April 1842
HEBBARD, Susan I. Mrs., died in Brookville, Montgomery County, MD, Monday
28th ult., consort of the late Dr. William B. HEBBARD of Taney-town &
eldest d/o the late Dr. Elisha J. HALL of this county.
KROUSE, Jacob, watch-maker wanted, Westminster.
MATTHIAS, George, dec'd., Jacob MATTHIAS, Ex'r.
SHRIVER, Jacob, dec'd., sale of his personal property, household goods,
livestock &c., Augustus SHRIVER, agent for his heirs.
WARFIELD, Suratt D. Jr. of Frederick County married Tuesday 12th ult. by
Rev. John A. GERE to Clarissa Jane 2nd d/o Rev. Samuel GORE of Freedom
District, this county.
New Windsor High School, Carroll County [curricula described] Boarding,
washing, per session of 5 months, $50.00. John P. CARTER, Principal

29 April 1842
CONRADT, George M., executed a deed of trust to Frederick A. SCHLEY &
William J. ROSS, Trustees, who are selling for the benefit of his
creditors a lot on Patrick Street, Frederick, upon which is erected well-
known Carpet Factory with a variety of machinery.
DEFENBAUGH, Mrs., died Wednesday last at her residence near this place,
aged about 75 years.
DORSEY, John, living near Ellicott's Mills, Anne Arundel County, offers
reward for 2 negro men: Ben, light mulatto man, about 28 years of age,
5' 8 1/2", round shouldered & stoops; when spoken to has a rather
pleasing countenance; a smart lively fellow. Ned has a dark complexion,
about 18 years of age; 5'7", slender made, full-eyed. At the same time 5
other negros left with them from the same neighborhood & were seen
together near the PA line.
HOUCK, John, married Thursday last by Rev. WILLARD to Miss Catharine
FORMWALT, all of this county.
LOCKARD, John, married in Taney-town on Tuesday last by Rev. Nicholas
ZOCCHI to Miss Margaret LUCAS, all of the 4th district.
WELLS, Thomas, dec'd., Joshua SMITH, Executor selling 45 acres of wheat &
12 acres of rye in the ground; also 2 lots.

6 May 1842
HAYDEN, Basil, having returned to Westminster for a season, tenders his
prompt services as auctioneer. Being in possession of a safe horse &
carriage, he will convey those to any of the neighboring towns & will
receive 2 or 3 boarders.
LAMPERT, William, married Thursday 28th ult. by Rev. FORREST to Miss
Cadeel Ann GLASS, both of this county.

13 May 1842
CHALMERS, G. W. Dr., has removed his residence from the west end of town to
the dwelling owned by Mrs. FISHER, 1 door above the Methodist Episcopal
Church, opposite dwelling of Major Jacob MATHIAS. His office is in the
building formerly occupied by late Dr. COLEGATE, next door to MOUL's
Hotel.
COX, E. G. M.D., Uniontown, has removed his office & dwelling to the house
formerly occupied by David FOUTZ.
HITESHUE, William, married last Tuesday week by Rev. SECHLER to Miss
Elizabeth HULL, both of this county.
MITTEN, Henry G. married at Hanover on Monday 9th instant by Rev. Martin
LOHR to Miss Catharine EBAUGH, both of this place.
SHAFFER, Susannah & Elizabeth & others, Equity Case, sale made by John R.
SHAFFER & John ALBAUGH as Trustees, case #76, for $1680.53.
WEBB, George, married Monday last at MOUL's Hotel in this place by Rev.
PHILLIPS to Miss Senia M. SWARMLEY, both of Frederick County.

WESTMINSTER CARROLLTONIAN

13 May 1842
Petitioners for relief under insolvent debtors act: Simon GOAL & Jonathan
NORRIS.

20 May 1842
BOWMAN, John D., married Thursday 12th inst. by Rev. Philip BOYLE to Miss
Ann Elizabeth, eldest d/o Isaac DERN, Esq., all of this county.
BRINKMAN, Henry N., clock & watch-maker, Manchester.
CASSELL, Abraham (of David) married Thursday 12th inst. to Miss Mary DIEHL,
d/o Jacob DIEHL, both of Little Pipe Creek Valley.
DEFFENBAUGH, Catherine, dec'd., Adam GILBERT, Executor.
HANNA, Nathan married Thursday 5th inst. by Rev. Eli HENKLE to Miss Joanna
WARNER, all of this county.
KOONTZ, Emanuel L. married Thursday 12th inst. by Rev. Eli HENKLE to Miss
Eliza LOWMAN, both of this place.
KUMP, Andrew, Damask coverlet weaver, continues business in Baltimore
Street, Hanover (PA) in the shop adjoining dwelling of John BEARD, a few
doors down Dr. CULBERTSON's, where he manufacturers the lastest & most
fashionable patterns. Yarn will be received at the following places &
returned finished: Samuel ORENDORFF's store, Westminster; Joshua
YINGLING's & Joseph EBAUGH's in Hampstead.
RIDINGER, Peter, of Taney-town District, died last Tuesday week.
WENTZ, Jacob, Westminser, has taken up a stray cow.
WHITE, Nicholas, living on the Taney-town road, halfway between ROOP's Mill
& Frizzelsburg, has taken up a stray cow.

27 May 1842
GALT, John Dr., of Baltimore, married Tuesday last by Rev. R. S. GRIER to
Miss Nancy d/o Sterling GALT, Esq., of this county.
JONES, Jacob married in Littlestown (PA) Sunday the 15th inst. by Rev. LOHR
to Miss Mary CUSHING, both of this county.
NICHOLAS, Johns, died at his residence in Greensburg, Tuesday morning 10th
instant (formerly of Emmitsburg, MD) in 79th year.
OURSLER, Charles Lewis, died Saturday last, s/o Henry & Mary OURSLER, in
the 4th year of his age, of this district.
Carroll County Temperance Society meeting held in Westminster, Rev. Eli
HENKLE President; C. BIRNIE Jr. Secretary. Committees: Uniontown--S.
SENTMAN & Samuel MOFFETT; New Windsor--Rev. Daniel ZOLLICKOFFER & James
L. BILLINGSLEA; Freedom--J. MC COLLUM & C. BIRNIE Jr.; MIddleburg--R.
BIRNIE & P. KEPHART; Westminster--J. HEISER & William HAIDEN; Union
Mills--J. N. STARR & H. F. ZOLLICKOFFER; Bethesda & Salem--J. MC DOLLUM &
Rev. Eli HENKLE; Wolfs-bottoms & Bethesda--Rev. William PHILLIPS & George
WEAVER; Providence--John K. DELL & Jacob HOLMES; Finksburg--S. D.
LECOMPTE & Rev. S. GORE; Taney-town--T. CURRY & C. W. WEBSTER;
Manchester--Rev. Wm. PHILLIPS & Philip GORE.

10 June 1842
ALBRECHT, George Augustus married Sunday last by Rev. WILLARD to Miss
Catharine ZENTZ, both of this county.
BROWN, Nicholas Hall, dec'd., his heirs holding Equity sale of farm on the
head waters of Little Pipe Creek, about 1 mile northwest from Westmin-
ster, known as the homeplace on which said dec'd. resided--150 acres with
2-story weather-boarded dwelling house, bank barn & lime kiln. William S.
BROWN.
ENGLEMAN, Lewis, cooper, Carroll County, petitioning under bankruptcy law.
FRANCIS, Andrew, left his residence at the corner of Hillen & Potter sts.,
Old Town, Baltimore, Thursday 2d last & has not since been heard of. He
is about 70 years old, 5'6-7", somewhat stooped in the shoulders; scar on
his forehead over his right eye occasioned by a fall. Talks freely on
religious subjects & is supposed to be labouring under mental aberration.

10 June 1842

Direct any information on his whereabouts to Robert FRANCIS, City Hotel, Baltimore.

HOUCK, Catharine Mrs. died 17th of May last, wife of Capt. William HOUCK of Hampstead District, this county, aged 65 years, 1 month.

HUGHES, Elizabeth Mrs., died at the age of 88. Relict of John HUGHES, late of Taneytown.

MITTEN, John, died Monday last at his residence at New-Windsor at an advanced age.

WOLF, William, clock & watch-maker, commencing business in a room attached to Mr. YINGLING's Hotel in Court Street.

Road Notice: To open a public road in Carroll County, commencing at the New Liberty Road at the land on the division line between Thomas CONDON & Joseph TEENER; & running thence to TEENER's saw mill & thence to Ebenezer's Meeting House to intersect a certain road on the public ground of said meeting house. Elijah BOND, Francis T. DAVIS & Daniel ENGEL, Commissioners.

Petitioners for relief under insolvent debtors act: Elijah CRISWELL, Silas HOWARD & Samuel SMITH.

17 June 1842

BACHMAN, Peter, dec'd., David B. EARHART, Executor.

BILLMYER, Jacob, of Union-town, Carroll County, married Thursday the 9th inst. by Rev. Daniel ZOLLICKOFFER to Miss Caroline BLACKSTONE of Sams Creek, of Frederick County.

BLIZZARD, Sarah, has secured a bill of sale of all of the property of her daughter Rachel BLIZZARD on 21 May 1842; she therefore cautions all persons from trusting her daughter on her account as she is determined to pay no bills of her contracting.

BOOS, Josiah, married on the 2d inst by Rev. GEIGER to Miss Catharine FREED d/o Lorentz FREED, dec'd., both of Carroll County.

FUHRMAN, Stephen, of Carroll County married on the 31st ult. by Rev. GEIGER to Miss Margaretta HOFFMAN d/o William HOFFMAN of Baltimore County.

OWINGS, Levi, to rent or lease a woollen factory 12 miles from Baltimore & 1 1/2 miles from Reisterstown turnpike.

PATTERSON, George, married Tuesday evening 31 May by Rev. J. B. SPORTSWOOD to Miss Prudence Ann d/o the late Thomas Cockey BROWN, all of Freedom District, Carroll County.

SAWYER, John, dec'd., John THOMPSON, Executor.

24 June 1842

DELL, Samuel J., tailor, shop nearly opposite Westminster Bank, formerly occupied by David UHLER.

DULANY, G. L., Trustee, conducting Chancery sale of 103 acre farm & tavern stand known as CONN's Tavern on Reisterstown Turnpike, Baltimore County, 14 1/2 miles from Baltimore City, midway between Owings Mills & Reisterstown. Apply to James C. CONN of Owings Mills or Alexander UNDERWOOD who resides on the premises.

KENDALL, Amos, publisher of penny newspaper at Washington, has discontinued same for want of support.

RAITT, Nathan & Contee HANSON, selling 130 acres farm where they reside in Carroll County, lying on the public road from York to Frederick, 1 1/2 miles south of Taney-town; consists of log house rough casted, brick Switzer barn, &c.

WIVEL, George & Joseph ORENDORFF, dissolving partnership in lumber business.

Death by lightning--Alexander W. GOLDSBOROUGH, Joseph FRAZIER Sr., his son Joseph & John HARVEY assembled at St. James' Meeting house in Howard District to attend a temperance meeting. The 3 latter took seats at the root of a large oak, Mr. GOLDSBOROUGH standing 3 feet off, awaiting the

24 June 1842
arrival of the speaker, when the 3 were struck by lightning. Young
FRAZIER was instantly killed. The other 3 recovered.

1 July 1842
DELL, George Washington, formerly of Westminster, married at Quincy, IL on
Sunday 28th ult. by Rev. GEDDINGS to Miss Sarah MILLEKEN that place.
GOODMAN, Ann E. Mrs., died on Monday last at the residence of her husband
in this place, in the 22d year of her age, consort of Rev. James W.
GOODMAN & d/o George & Margaret RICHARDSON of Lynchburg VA.
GORE, Stephen R., of Carroll County, married Tuesday the 28th ult. by Rev.
CARTER to Sarah Jane PAXTON of Frederick County.
HIMES & PURPER, 2 of the persons engaged in robbing NICHOLSON of Baltimroe
have been found guilty.
SHERMAN, Elizabeth Mrs., died Tuesday last at her residence in this place,
relict of the late Jacob SHERMAN, in the 85th year of her age.
ZACHARIAS, Conrad, living 1 mile from Westminster on the Baltimore-
Gettysburg Turnpike, has taken up stray steers.
Two persons named BARRY & DAVIS were killed in the Navy Yard by the
explosion of detonating shells.
The Finksburg Sabbath School Society will celebrate the 4th of July in the
grove near Finksburg on Mr. GARDNER's land.

8 July 1842
COX, E. G. Dr., of Uniontown, married in Huntington Twp., Adams County
(PA) to Miss Mary d/o Charles KETTLEWELL of Petersburg, York Springs, PA.
GORE, Nathan C., died at the residence of his father near Freedom in this
county, in the 25th year of his age, 3rd s/o Samuel & Theresa GORE.
GORSUCH, Peregrine, sheriff's sale of his property, part of "Caledonia" &
part of "Old Deerpark," same land now occupied by Elizabeth GORSUCH,
widow of John GORSUCH; about 10 miles from Westminster, 1 mile from
Providence Meeting House & 2 miles from Deerpark road, lying in Carroll
County & joins land of George W. GORSUCH. Taken by virtue of writs of
Carroll & Baltimore Counties at the suits of Diedrick KLOCKINGATER, use
of Nimrod CHAPMAN, Lowry F. GORSUCH.
SHIPLEY, Otho, clerk, gives notice that the authorities of Westminster,
burgesses & commissioners, will meet at Mr. ARTHUR's tavern, for the
purpose of passing through the town & taking a view of the different
streets for the purpose of making improvement.

15 July 1842
LEE, T. Sim, selling 280 acres tract in Carroll County known as "Berry's
Purchase" on Westminster Road to Washington, 4 miles from B&O Railroad,
with dwelling & new tobacco house; also the mill adjoining the property
known as O'DONNELL's Mill.
ROBERTS, Basil, whereas his wife Hester has left his bed & board without
just cause, notifies persons not to trust her on his account.
RUDISEL, Ludwick, died in Taney-town Tuesday 28 June last, after a severe &
lingering illness of 9 weeks, in the 64th year of his age. He was
engaged more than 35 years in the manufacture of leather in this area &
had accumulated considerable property.
WAMPLER, George E., Secretary, members of Carroll Infantry, meeting to be
held at house of William KING, members to sign constitution.
WARD, William married Tuesday 7th inst. by Rev. FORREST to Miss Mary d/o
John ROBERTSON, all of this county.
WELTY, William, Drover of Carroll County, filed petition of bankruptcy.
Camp Meeting of Methodist Protestant Church to be held on the grounds of
John FLETTER, 5 miles below Westminster & 1 mile of turnpike from
Baltimore. A boarding tent will be kept by Joshua SUNDERGILL.

15 July 1842
Letters Remaining at the Post Office in Westminster: Miss Elizabeth ABBOT,
Mary ARBAUGH, Balser ARBAUGH; N. H. BROWN, Mr. BURTON, BIXLER & Lawyer,
Joseph BROWN, Arthur R. BROWN, Joseph BOWSER, John CROUSE, William
CRUMBINE, Jacob CROUS, James CROCKET, Dr. G. W. CHALMER, Benjamin DAVIS,
Charles DEVILBISS, Samuel ECKENROAD, Miss Ellen FISHER, Joseph FISHER,
Miss M. A. FORREST, John F. FLEMMING, Daniel GEIMAN, Miss M. GOODWIN,
John HAYNES, Mr. E. HARDCASTLE, Mr. HALL, A. W. HUGHES, Mr. KEYS, Wilhelm
KRENSE, Jacob KNIGHT, Jane A. KING, David KILGORE, David KEEFER, Peter
KLINE, John LEGORE, Manah LOIR, George LANDES, Jacob LINN, Israel LEISTER,
Michael LYNCH, Thomas LYNCH, John MICHAEL, Peter MORT, Solomon MIERLY,
Henry NATE, David PFOUTS, Mr. PRISE, Daniel PLAINE, Mrs. RHEINHART,
George SWIGART, Lydia SULIVAN, George SCHAFFER, John STULLER, David
SUTTER, James SMITH, George TALLER, Miss Ann M. TROYER, Catharine WINTER,
Miss R. WERBEL, Margaret WALTER, German - John Henry MYLE. Joshua
YINGLING, Post Master.

22 July 1842
BACHMAN, Frederick, Esq., of this county had a Durham calf of 130 pounds at
the age of 24 hours.
BIXLER, Jacob, died Friday last at his residence in Manchester District,
aged 72 years.
CARTER, J. P., Pastor of New Windsor Presbyterian Church, announces the
Presbytery of Baltimore to hold meeting in Presbyterian Church of New
Windsor.
CROWL, David, has left with us a bunch of volunteer stalks of wheat, number
247, which proceded from one root, probably from one grain.
ECKER, Jacob, at his farm near this place yesterday morning was found a
large swarm of bees, which had formed a considerable comb on the upper
part of a wheat shock.
HAINES, Isaac, left a bunch of timothy which had been pulled from his field
measuring 6'4".
GORE, Nathan Covington, died, Union Hall Dickinson College. (PA)
GROSH, Mrs., wife of Jonathan GROSH, residing on the Conococheague creek,
near the Turnpike Bridge in that county, was killed by lightning on the
evening of the 8th. Her little son was knocked down. (Hagerstown Herald
of Freedom)
SHERMAN, Elizabeth, dec'd., sale at her late residence in Westminster of
colt, cows, heifer, furniture, &c. Isaac SHRIVER, Adm'r.
SHRIVER, Isaac, left at this office a stalk of timothy raised on his farm
adjoining town, which measures 6'2" in length.
SHUEE, Lewis, in his wheat fields in the valley of Wakefield of 18 acres,
on which was cut & shocked this season 1824 dozen of wheat sheaves of
ordinary size.
SHREEVE, Joseph, wants miller, 6 miles below Westminster.
Committee of the Union Philosophical Society: R. R. BATTEE, P. G.
BUCKINGHAM, R. CREERY, B. F. WRIGHT, C. P. WILKINS.
Sacrament of the Lord's supper to be administered at Krider's church; Rev.
D. ZACHARIAS of Frederick City to be present. William PHILIPS.

29 July 1842
CROCKETT, Mr., barn on his farm occupied by John LONGLY on Piney Creek, 1
mile north of Taney-town struck by lightning & destroyed.
DORSEY, Francis Barnum, infant d/o [sic] Daniel & Harriet DORSEY of
Frederick City, died Thursday the 10th inst., at the residence of Edward
DORSEY, Esq., in Carroll County. Age 1 year, 1 month, 11 days.
DURBIN, Elizabeth, consort of Col. William DURBIN formerly of Frederick
County, died in the 49th year of her age.
FLEMING, A. W., of Baltimore City, married on Tuesday 12th inst. by Rev.
BLAKE to Miss Hilia Ann, eldest d/o Joseph TRAINER, Esq., of this county.

29 July 1842
PETERS, Jacob, of Menallen Twp., during the violent store on Tuesday last, his barn was struck by lightning & consumed.
POWDER, J. Sen., late his property for sale, a woodlot, 10-11 acres at west end of town, adjoining farms of Frederick WERBLE, heirs of Nicholas Hall BROWN dec'd. & Albins POOL; fronts on the county road to VAN BIBBER's Mill; also 10 lots in corporation of Westminster on South Church Street.
ROYER, Peter, died at his residence near this place on Friday last after a protracted illness in his 67th year of his age. He was born in Lancaster County, but for the last 42 years, has been living here.
SALTZGIVER, William Cornelius, infant s/o Henry & Magdalena SALTZGIVER died Monday last in this place, age 3 weeks & 1 day.
SAUM, Peter, died Tuesday last at his residence on Sams Creek. He had gone into the fields on his farm in the afternoon for the purpose of grubbing. Not returning, his family supposed he had gone to his brother's on the adjoining farm. Next morning he was found dead in the field with the hoe by his side & one of this shoes off.
SHOWER, G., lightning struck his dwelling near Manchester. Mrs. SHOWER lay insensible for some time.
WOOLERY, Noah, married on Thursday last by Rev. Amon RICHARDS to Miss Sarah d/o George RICHARDS Sen., all of this county.

5 August 1842
COLEHOUSE, W. H., formerly of this place, married Thursday evening week by Rev. Dr. JENNINGS to Miss Susan A. ROSENBERG, both of Baltimore City.
NICODEMUS, John, near the Stone Meeting House has taken up a stray cow.
ZAHN, John married Sunday 24th ult. by Rev. WILLARD to Miss Elizabeth EVERLY, both of this county.
An affray recently occurred at Unionville, Frederick County, between a man named DYEDERHOOVER & Samuel JOHNSON, which resulted in the death of the former. Samuel JOHNSON, residing in Liberty, came on Saturday evening to John I. MULLER's in Unionville, which he had made his boarding place on Sundays during the time he expected to harvest in the neighborhood.

26 August 1842
BOOM, John, of Westminster, whereas his wife Rachel has left his bed & board without any just cause or provocation, he informs the public that he will not pay any debts of her contracting.
CASSELL, Henry, dec'd., of Carroll County, according to his will lots in the City of Baltimore on north Pearce st., between Pine & Chatsworth sts. being sold, Joseph CASSELL, Ex'r.
CASSELL, Jacob, living near CASSELL's Mill, Pipe Creek, has taken up a flock of stray sheep.
ORENDORF, Samuel, of Westminster, gives notice that during the past winter & Spring there has been residing in this place a professional gentleman bearing the name of Henry SWEET, of middle stature, slightly pock marked, & rather prepossing in address & genteel appearance; professes to have been a merchant who failed in business & originally a citizen of western New York. He decamped from this place about 2 months since, prudently forgetting to satisfy several small bills.
POOLE, Bushrod of Double Pipe Creek, John DOTTERER certifies that he has taken up a stray horse.
Road Notice: Commission issued to open a road commencing near the junction of Manchester & Hampstead Road on main stem of said road; to point near Union School House, hence to best route to point near Henry Z. BUCHEN's mill, thence to intersection of Hanover turnpike road near David Z. BUCHEN's house. Abraham WAMPLER, Jacob BEAVER & Joseph SHARRAR, Commissioners.

9 September 1842

BIXLER, Jacob, dec'd., late of Carroll County, Jacob & John BIXLER, Admrs.

HAGERTY, James, cheap boots of fine calf skin ($3.50) & cork sole water
proof boots ($5.50) can be had at John F. REESE, Westminster.

JOHNS, John T., selling parcel of land on Hanover Road, 24 miles from
Baltimore & 8 from Reisterstown known as "Sportsman's Hall" or "Hooker's
Meadows" adjoining lands of Richard HOOKER & George HOUCK.

LOGUE, Joshua, living near ORENDORFF's (WELLS) Mill, has 7 bushels of clean
timothy seed for sale.

LONG, Christian, to sell 2000 chestnut rails & a number of posts, to be
deposited 1/2 mile from Westminster.

REEVER, George, dec'd., late of Carroll County, Samuel REEVER, agent for
his heirs, selling 80 acres owned by dec'd. during his lifetime, 2 1/4
miles from Taney-town, adjoings lands of Michael NULL, Frederick HARNER
&c. To view call on Abraham REEVER, living in Taney-town.

SAWYER, John, dec'd. of Carroll County, sale according to his will of 1
acre on the public road from Taney-town to Littlestown, 1 mile from
former; brick dwelling with kitchen attached &c. John THOMPSON, Ex'r.

WISE, John, by virtue of a deed of trust, selling for the benefit of his
creditors, 154 3/4 acres of land called the "Beautiful Farm" on which
said WISE now resides, situated in Carroll County on road from Taney-town
to Westminster, 4 miles from Taney-town; adjoins lands of C. BIRNIE,
Peter BABYLON & others. Includes brick dwelling occupied for many years
as tavern stand, bank barn, corn house, wagon house &c.

Insolvent debtors: James B. ARNOLD, Lewis ENGLEMAN, David WARNER & James
BRYAN.

Fall Session of Carroll County Court commenced on Monday last; present
Judges: DORSEY, WILKINSON & BREWER.

Grand Jury: Isaac SHRIVER (foreman), John W. GORSUCH, Nicholas H. BROWN,
Michael SHULL, Chas. W. BENNETT, Jesse MANNING, Moses PARRISH, John
BEAVER, Michael NULL, David KUHN, Josiah BARNES, John LOCKARD, John
WILLIAMS, Sr., David FOUTZ, Jacob ROOP, John BEGGS, Henry CARTER, John
SWITZER, Frederick YINGLING, Henry W. DELL, John ADDLESPERGER, Samuel
SWOPE, Elijah BOND.

Petit Jury: John WENTZ, Joshua PLOWMAN, Abraham BIXLER, Henry MILLER,
William CRUMRINE, Christian HENDRICK, Sr., Henry BECHTEL, Adam FEISER,
Israel RINEHART, William STULTZ, Nicholas HARRISON, Samuel LAMMOTT,
Zachariah EBAUGH, John OGG, Mordecai G. COCKEY, Cornelius MERCER, Moses
BARNES, Joseph STULL, Beal GOSNELL, Evan L. CRAWFORD, Francis T. DAVIS,
Resin FRANKLIN, John ORENDORFF, Michael LYNCH, George TRUMBO.

16 September 1842

BEAVER, Miss Nancy, died Tuesday the 6th inst., at her residence near
Westminster, in the 48th year of her age.

BUSHMAN, George, trustee in chancery sale in case of Magdalena BUSHMAN vs.
Adam TAILOR &c. #60.

EDELL, Samuel J., tailor, shop opposite the Westminster Bank & formerly
occupied by David UHLER.

DORSEY, Roderick, Esq. has declined serving o the Opposition ticket.

ENGLEMAN, Lewis, Cooper, of Carroll County, filed for bankruptcy.

FRIZZEL, Washington Lewis, eldest son of Isaac & Anna, died on the 5th
inst. after a short & painful illness, aged 16 years 5 months & 8 days.

GROVE, Jacob, Sheriff, announces election to be held.

HAGERTY, James, selling cheap boots at the store of John F. REESE.

JOHNS, John T., selling land on or near the Hanover road, 24 miles from
Baltimore & 8 from Reisterstown, known by the name of "Sportman's Hall"
or "Hooker's Meadows," adjoining lands of Richard HOOKER & George HOUCK.
Has been laid off in lots from 10 to 40 acres.

LIPPE, Mrs. Elizabeth, wife of John LIPPE, of Myers' District, died Monday
the 5th inst., in the 38th year of her age.

16 September 1842
LONG, Christian, selling chestnut rails & posts.
LOGUE, Joshua, selling timothy seed, near ORENDORFF's WELLS'?? Mill.
MAULSBY, David J. Dr., offers professional services, can be found at Mr.
    YINGLING's Hotel.
MAULSBY, Margaret Howard, departed this transitory life Thursday the 30th
    ult., youngest d/o William P. MAULSBY, Esq., aged 13 months & 27 days.
ORENDORF, Samuel, selling seasonable goods cheap as can be bought in
    Carroll County; all kinds of cloths, ribbons, veils, blankets & yarns &c.
PENSEL, Jacob, of Taney-town District, committed suicide Saturday evening
    last. He was discovered hanging by a rope to a weaving loom, at which he
    had been working during the day, in the 2d story of his dwelling, while
    his family, a wife & several children were on the 1st floor.
RIDDINGER, John married Thursday last in Littlestown by the Rev. B. SPECK,
    to Miss Emma FLEAGLE, both of this county.
SAWYER, John, dec'd., sale of his real estate: a lot of 1 acre on the
    public road from Taney-town to Littlestown, 1 mile from the former, with
    2-story brick dwelling house, with kitchen attached, frame stable. John
    THOMPSON, Ex'r.
SCHAFFER, Mary Jane, died Wednesday the 8th inst., infant d/o Nicholas
    SCHAFFER, aged 21 months & 18 days.
WARNER, David, has applied for benefit of insolvency laws.
WARREN, T. & Son, selling at the Gettysburg Steam Foundary horse powers &
    threshing machines.
WELTY, William, Petitioner for Bankruptcy, date set for court.
WISE, John, for benefit of his creditors, his trustee holding sale of
    right, title & interest to tract of land called the "Beautiful Farm,",
    154 3/4 acres on which WISE now resides, on road from Taney-town to
    Westminster, 4 miles from former & 8 from latter, adjoining lands of C.
    BIRNIE & Peter BABYLON. Large 2-story brick dwelling-house occupied for
    many years as a tavern stand, large brick bank barn, cornhouse, wagon
    shed, springhouse. Sterling GALT, Trustee.
WISE, John, the celebrated Aeronaut, made a splendid ascension in a Balloon
    from Gettysburg Saturday last; nearly 1 hour in the air, he went 3 miles.
WOLF, William, new establishment as clock & watch-maker, in room attached
    to Mr. YINGLING's Hotel in Court Street, Westminster.
YINGLING, Joshua, Proprietor of the Westminster Hotel.
ZEPP, Solomon, selling lot fronting on Court-street, between Main & the
    Court-house on which is a large 2-story dwelling house with 2-story brick
    back building recently built. Also, another lot nearly in the rear of
    the aforementioned property, on which is a large brick brewery, with all
    the kettles, tuns, casks in & about 400 kegs & all appendages. Also for
    sale a wood lot on the ridge at the west end of the town of 10-11 acres;
    adjoins lands of Frederick WERBLE, the heirs of Nicholas Hall BROWN,
    dec'd., & Albinus POOL, fronts on the county road to VAN BIBBER's mill.
    Also 10 lots in the corporation of Westminster on south Church st., late
    property of J. POWDER, sen. Being desirous of removing from the place,
    all above are for sale.
Announcing Samuel D. LECOMPTE, of Westminster & Isaac APPLER, of Union-Town
    as Independent Democratic Candidates for House of Delegates.
The Bedford Gazette (PA?) contains account of the execution of James RICE
    in that county, for the murder of James MC BURNEY.
Ordered by Carroll Co. Court of Equity that the sale made by George
    BUSHMAN, as Trustee in the case of Magdalena BUSHMAN against Adam TAILOR
    & others, be ratified. Amount of sales $2371.16. Jacob SHOWER, Clerk.
New road to be opened commencing near junction of the Manchester & Hump-
    stead road on the main stem of said road leading to Westminster, thence
    to near the Union School House, thence to a point near Henry Z. BUCHEN's
    mill, thence to intersect the Hanover turnpike near David Z. BUCHEN's

16 September 1842
house & opposite the public road from said turnpike to Middletown in
Baltimore County. Abraham WAMPLER, Jacob BEAVER & Joseph SHARRAR, Comm.
Drs. DRESBACH, KUHN & PRYORS' Dyspeptic Cordial for sale by D. & D. ENGLE
of Sams Creek & John F. REESE, Westminster. Recommended by Jacob KESSLER
of Frederick County, Thomas BARTHOLOW of Carroll County, Thomas H.W.
MONROE of Liberty-town, Frederick County, John MONTGOMERY, Jr., of
Frederick County, & John M'COLLUM of Westminster.
Candidates for Sheriff: J. Henry HOPPE, James KEEFER, Jonathan NORRIS,
Thomas GURLEY, Hezekiah CROUT, Lewis TRUMBO, E. L. CRAWFORD, William
GRUMBINE, Otho SHIPLEY, & John KELLY.
The best method for abolition of disease is to cleanse & purify the body
with Wright's Indian Vegetable Pills of the North American College of
Health. The best medicine in the world for the care of every variety of
disease. Sold by Joshua YINGLING, Westminster; Peter CHRIST, Uniontown;
Francis T. DAVIS, Ridgeville; SHAW & HICKSON, Taneytown; Nimrod FRIZZEL,
Frizzelburg & E. A. CLABAUGH, Middleburg.
Applicants for relief under insolvency laws. Must reside in the state for
two years & be detained for no other reason than debt: James B. ARNOLD,
Silas HOWARD, & Joel JOAL.

23 September 1842
BAKER, George Washington, died Thursdaya 15th inst., s/o Samuel & Ruth
BAKER, age 6 years.
BAUBLITZ, Sara, infant d/o Henry BAUBLITZ of this county died 15th inst.
BUCHEN, David Z., of Hampstead died Thursday last, aged 34 years, 5 months
& 4 days.
BURCHENAL, Thomas, of Caroline County, announces himself as an independent
candidate for the MD Legislature.
KRAUZER, Jacob, married on the 16th inst. by Rev. WILLARD to Miss Catharine
STUMP, all of this county.
MARKER, David, infant s/o David MARKER of near C[K]riders Church died, aged
1 year 10 months 26 days.
MARTIN, George, married Tuesday last by the Rev. HENKLE to Miss Elizabeth
NELSON d/o Burgess NELSON, Esq., of Warfieldsburg, Carroll County.
MC KINSTRY, Joanna Mrs., died 24 August, consort of Evan MC KINSTRY in her
55th year, leaving husband & children.
ROHRBACK, Otho W., eldest s/o Col. ROHRBACK, near Sharpsburg (MD), aged 22
years met with an awful accident which occasioned his death in a few
hours. He was engaged in thrashing his father's wheat, with a large
portable machine--himself standing on a peat form in the center of the
horse power to drive the horses. He stopped the horses, intending to
jump off & his foot slipped & falling, his leg being caught between the
arms of the 2 wheels, was instantly shorn off below the knee & the thigh
utterly torn & crushed to the hip. (Adams, PA)
SAUBLE, Samuel married Thursday last by Rev. WILLARD to Miss Mary MYERLY,
all of this county.
SINTCLAIR, William, of Baltimore County, married on the 23rd ult. by Rev.
WILLARD to Elizabeth FUHRMAN of Carroll County.
SMITH, John, of Franklin District, died the 19th August, aged 83 years.
SMITH, John, dec'd., late of Carroll County, George SMITH, Exc'r.
STRICKLAND, Jacob, s/o Joshua STRICKLAND of Hampstead District, died
Saturday last, aged 21 years.
WEBB, Rev. Mr. & Mrs., their School commenced in Westminster MD on a
turnpike road 28 miles north west of Baltimore. A few young ladies may
be received into Mr. WEBB's family, where they shall receive parental
care & kindness, to form their moral as well as their mental character.
The price for such young ladies includes board, washing, lodging, rooms,
fuel, lights, tuition in any branches taught is $150 a year.

23 September 1842
This newspaper is authorized to announce Samuel D. LECOMPTE of Westminster
& Isaac APPLER of Union-town as Independent Democratic Candidates to
represent Carroll County in the next houuse of Delegates.
Expenditures & receipts of Carroll County: James RAYMOND, state case;
Francis BRENGLE, state case; Henry HOUCK, Sheriff of Federick County; W.
D. BALL, Sheriff Baltimore County. Constables: Isaac POUDER, Benjamin
WILLIAMS, Joseph ARTHUR, Bennet SPURRIER, Washington GWINN, John M.
YINGLING. Joseph M. PARKE & John K. LONGWELL printing. Improper
Assessment: J. COOKSON, David ENGLAR, Nathan HAINES, John NICODEMUS, DR.
L. W. GOLDSBOROUGH bill of medicine; Samuel MOFFIT for attending on
pauper; John A. KELLEY, sweeping court house; Patrick KELLEY, Jonathan
DORSEY, Joh B. SUMMERS & Richard FRIZZLE for burying paupers; John F.
REESE, medicine at jail; Rev. John MALEHORN, attending on poor; Levi
EVANS, desk in commissioners office & in clerk's office; Basil ROOT,
postage, etc.; Joshua YINGLING, books & stationary; John BAUGHER,
removing negroes; Nelson NORRIS & John B. SNOWDEN, support of paupers;
Dr. Samuel SWORMSTEADT for medicine &c.; Jacob CHRIST & A. C. WARNER,
coffins for paupers; Henry ORENDORFF, bill for privy; William GRUMBINE,
mending of lightning rod; Dr. G. W. CHALMERS, attending Jail &c.; Lewis
WINTERS, work on Court House; John MATHIAS, clothes for the aged pauper
____ DAVIS; L. BUCKINGHAM, error in mileage; William SHAW, committees
examining bridges &c. Total expenditures $15,695.99 Total taxes:
$16,259.90.

7 October 1842
GERNAND, E., 1st Sgt., notifies Carroll Infantry to meet at the house of
William KING on business of importance.
HOPPE, John Henry, elected Sheriff by a majority of 62 votes.
M'CLELLAN, Col., J.H., of Gettysburg, to make Balloon ascension with Mr.
WISE, Balloonist. Mr. WISE accidently remained on the ground; Mr.
M'CLELLAN returned yesterday & we learn that he descended 5 miles from
York, near EMICH's mill, an hour after he left, returned himself to the
ground without injury after passing over Hunterstown & Berlin.
VAN BIBBER, Isaac, selling a kiln of lime, recently burnt.
WHITTINGHAM, Rev. Dr., Bishop of the Episcopal Church for MD, to preach in
the Union Church the 16th inst. & Rev. Mr. AUSTIN in the afternoon.
WILLIAMS, Mr. at Yingling's Hotel, will make a daguerretype likeness. We
have seen several specimens, which are very correct.
A military meeting held by officers of the Military Companies of Westmin-
ster, viz. the Carroll Artillerists, Carroll Infantry & Westminster
Guards, for purpose of holding a parade on the 19th as the Anniversary of
the surrender of Lord Cornwallis at the battle of Yorktown. On motion of
Capt. William P. MAULSBY it was resolved that the Chair appoint a commit-
tee to make arrangements: Capts. William P. MAULSBY & Benjamin YINGLING,
Lts. Jacob GROVE, Abraham H. BUSBY & George Edward WAMPLER. Capt. John
MC COLLUM, President, Lt. George Edward WAMPLER, Sec.

14 October 1842
BENNETT, Larkin S., dec'd., late of Carroll County, Catharine A. BENNETT,
Administratrix.
BOWERS, Joseph, by virtue of writs issued by William FISHER, Justice of the
1st District Court, at suits of Thomas JONES, John & S. SWOPE, John MC
KALEB &c., against goods chattels, lands &c. of above BOWERS to Washington GWINN, Constable, he has seized & taken all right, claim & title of 1
house & lot in Taneytown, Carroll County; also all personal property viz:
1 horse, 1 cow, stoves, clock &c.
CASSELL, Henry, dec'd., late of Carroll County, sale of his real estate
reported by Joseph CASSELL, Executor; said real estate located in the

117

14 October 1842
  city of Baltimore--one lot on Pearce St. & brick dwelling sold. John
  BAUMGARTNER, Reigster.
CASSELL, Margaret Ann, died Saturday, 17 September, d/o David & Mary
  CASSELL, aged 1 year 7 months & 27 days.
ENGLEMAN, Lewis, property sold to benefit his creditors, William ENGLEMAN,
  trustee.
HAINES, Elizabeth Miss, on Wednesday 5 October was removed from our midst
  [died], eldest d/o Eli HAINES, aged 16 years, 3 months, 17 days.
KEY, F. S. Jr., having rented out his farm, "The Elms", Carroll County,
  offers for sale stock & farming utensils.
MATTHIAS, John George, dec'd., late of Carroll County, Jacob MATTHIAS,
  executor selling 246 acre farm in Big Pipe Creek valley, Carroll County,
  adjoining lands of Frederick BACHMAN, Henry WAREHIME &c., 1/2 mile from
  BACHMAN's Mills, 4 from Manchester & 8 from Westminster; consisting of 2-
  story dwelling with kitchen, large bank barn, wagonsheds, blacksmith shop
  &c. Also 1-story tenant house with stable. Also 22 acre wood lot
  situated 1 mile from said farm, adjoining lands of John SHAFER [farmer] &
  others.
MC LANE, Hon. Louis, President of the Baltimore & Ohio Railroad Company has
  made his annual report. In a few weeks the road will be completed to
  Cumberland, a distance of 12 miles. It is estimated it will cost $20,000
  per mile.
RIDINGER, Peter, dec'd., late of Carroll County, Catharine RIDINGER, Admr.
SHEPHERD, Thomas F., married on Thursday last, 13 October, by Rev. Philip
  BOYLE, to Miss Harriet only d/o Job C. HAINES, all of Uniontown district.
SHRIVER & SCHOLL, selling at Linganore Mills in Frederick County, 5000
  bushels of brown stuff; 4000 bushels shorts & 1000 bushels ship stuff.
STIMMELL, Jacob, dec'd., late of Frederick County, selling 124 acre farm,
  occupied by dec'd. during his lifetime, 1 mile west of Woodsboro; adjoins
  lands of John D. CRUMBAUGH & T. WORTHINGTON. His dwelling, finished in
  superior style inside, stone Sweitzer barn, blacksmith shop, &c. Also: 3
  acre lot midway between Creagerstown & Woodsborough with 2-story house,
  blacksmith shop &c. Also 400 acres of land in Harrison County VA,
  consisting of 2 dwelling houses, about 10 miles from Clarksburg & 3 miles
  from The Monongahela river. Paul CARMACK, Executor.
WILLIAMS, J. T., Daguerreotype operator, to remain in Westminster Hotel a
  few days, where he will execute likenesses buy the novel & interesting
  process. Price of a perfect likeness in a neat morocco case or frame
  from $2.50 to $4.50.
List of Letters remaining in the Post Office in Westminster 1 October 1842:
  Mr. BUCKINGHAM, Miss Ann C. BOND, Miss Diana BROWN, J. BAUMGARDNER,
  William BRADENBURG, Rezin COOK, James Z. CRAY, Thomas DOYLE, John C.
  DORFLER, Reubin HANES, Mrs. H. HILLMAN, Ellxis HARRIS, William HOWELL,
  Joseph HITE, Jacob HOLMES, Nathan HAINES, Jacob HAPE, Peter & Henry
  KLINE, Mary Ann KEMP, Mrs. Betsey LOWE, John & Elizabeth LEGORE, John
  LYNCH, Jacob MARTIN, Micajah MARTIN, Elizabeth MARSHALL, Henry MARSHALL,
  John NICODEMUS, George ORNDORFF, Mrs. E. RILEY, Henry RIALL, John
  SHERMAN, John SHAFFER, Rev. Thomas SWEITZER, Miss Mary Ann STORME, E. H.
  STIMMEL, William STEWART, Elizabeth SLORP, Mathew WRIGHT, Mrs. Jamina
  WARFIELD, Henry WANTZ, William Y. WAGERS, Jesse YINGLING, Peter ZENTZ,
  (German Letter) George Aden SINDLE. Joshua YINGLING, Post Master.

21 October 1842
HENKLE, Eli, notifies the public of connecting the chair-making business
  with his store in the west end of Westminster.
HILLEN, Solomon Col., has been re-elected Mayor of Baltimore City by a
  large majority.
ORNDORFF, Peter, late of Adams County (PA), executors selling 176 acre farm
  in Carroll County, about 2 miles from Jacob MAUS' mill on Big Pipe Creek

21 October 1842
& 1 mile from Joseph ECK's Mill on same stream of water, containing stone
dwelling house, basement story under ground, in which there is a kitchen
& spring of excellent water, log barn, log stable with wagon shed &c.
Joseph ORNDORFF & John BAUMGARDNER, Ex'rs. Also on same day, will be
sold by Joseph ORNDORFF, as adm'r. of Rosina ORNDORFF, dec'd., all
personal property, milch cows, 3 shoats, 3 sheep, carpeting, chaff bags,
comforts &c.
REIFSNIDER, George, agent for heirs of David REIFSNIDER, dec'd., late of
Carroll County, offer at sale 156 acre farm in Taney-town District,
Carroll County; 30 miles from Frederick, 30 miles from York, 4 miles from
Taneytown on road leading to Littlestown; adjoining lands of Lewis &
Jacob PETERS, Jacob BAUMGARDNER & others, containing 2-story brick
dwelling with a back building attached.
RINEHART, David, married Tuesday evening last by Rev. D. JOHNSON to Miss
Hannah ENGLAR, d/o Philip ENGLAR, all of Uniontown District.
To stockholders in Hagerstown & Westminster Turnpike Company, an election
to be held at the house of Parmenio R. HARRY in Graceham, 2nd Monday of
October next for president, 8 managers & treasurer. William BIGGS,
President.
On Saturday night last, the clothing store of George FECHTIG, the Produce
store of Mr. J. S. HAMILTON, the Tailor shop of Mr. S. RIDENOUR & the
Saddler shop of William FIELDS were forcibly entered by some ruffians.
They however failed in procuring anything of value. Unsuccessful
attempts were also made upon the stores of Messrs. J. & W. ROBERTSON, J.
K. HARRY, G. GILLMYRE, A. & D. MIDDLEKAFF & F. FECHTIG, also several
stores in Lettersburg & Chewsville.

30 December 1842
BOYLE, John B., Esq., of Taney-town District, has been appointed by the
Governor, a Justice of the Orphans' Court in place of Nimrod FRIZZLE,
deceased.
ECKER, Samuel, farmer near New-Windsor, had fine crop of sugar beets.
SHRIVER, Abraham Hon., Judge of Judicial District of Frederick, Washington
& Allegany Counties, has resigned his seat on the bench. Gen. T. C.
WORTHINGTON or Richard H. MARSHALL, of Frederick, may succeed him.
SLINGLUFF, Isaac, farmer near New-Windsor, raised crop of 87 1/2 bushels of
corn to the acre. His soil is deep limestone intermixed with blue slate;
it laid 2 years in clover & blue grass, frequently manured, but never
limed.
Carroll County Temperance Convention at Methodist Protestant Church in
Westminster was opened with prayer by the Rev. William HARDEN, Rev. J.
HISER & John Joseph BAUMGARDNER delivered addresses. C. W. WEBSTER, Esq.
made a motion for committee to plan 4th July procession: J. MC COLLUM,
chair, H. CROUT, N. H. BROWN, C. BIRNIE, Jr., & J. J. BAUMGARDNER. Mr.
MOFFIT made motion for committee to select speakers: Isaac SHRIVER, Dr.
SWORMSTEADT, Horatio PRICE, H. CROUT & C. W. WEBSTER. Eli HENKLE, Pres.

—•⊙•—
3 February 1843
GISH, Jacob W., a short-time resident of Frederick who kept a periodical
agency office, was asked to leave town when it was learned that he was
using the alias of James RAFFERTY & ordering the printing of bank notes
in Philadelphia. He left.

10 February 1843
RAYMOND, James Esq., has resigned his office of Prosecuting Attorney for
Frederick County & L.P.W. DALOH, Esq. has been appointed.
In Cumberland on Friday of last week Henry R. ATKINSON & John SWAN, 2 young
men of the town got into an affray on the public street in which the

10 February 1843
   latter was stabbed in the side with a knife or some other sharp
   instrument.
Professor N.R. SMITH, surgeon & Professor R. W. HALL, obstetrican of the
   Medical School at Baltimore, quarrelled in the college on Wednesday
   last. Blows were given & a sword cane drawn. They were parted.
Appointments in Baltimore: James ROACH appointed Flour Inspector in place
   of RICKETTS; Nicholas KELLY, Weigh-Master.

17 February 1843
POWDER, Mr. reported to the MD Senate on an act for the benefit of Jacob
   GROVE, late Sheriff of Carroll County.
1843 Appointments for Carroll County: Orphans' Court: Michael SULLIVAN,
   Jesse MANNING & John B. BOYLE. Commissioners of Tax: John ADDLESPERGER*,
   Lewis SHUEE*, Peter HULL, George BRAMWELL, James MORGAN*, Frederick
   RITTER, Jacob SHAFER, William HOUCK, & Larkin BUCKINGHAM. Coroners:
   Wilton BURDETT, David HAPE, Nelson MANNING*, Joseph ECK*, Nicholas SHIL-
   LING, & William EWING. Jacob KERLINGER, Surveyor. John F. REESE, Notary
   Public. Justices of the District Courts: Taney-town District--George
   CRABBS, William FISHER & Johnson JAMISON. Union-town District--Samuel A.
   LAUVER, Tobias COVER*, Helpher CRAMER*. Myers' District--Adam FEISER,
   Robert CRAWFORD, & John LEGORE*. Woolery's District--Abraham LAMMOTT,
   Josiah SHILLING*, & George WILLIAMS*. Freedom District--Jonathan DORSEY,
   John H. LINSAY*, & Thomas J. CARTER*. Manchester District--George E.
   WEAVER, Thomas SATER, & Jacob KERLINGER*. Westminster District--John
   MALEHORN, N. H. BROWN*, & Thomas GURLEY*. Hampstead District--Henry
   LAMMOTT, George FOSTER, & Jesse BROWN. Franklin District--Thomas B.
   OWINGS, Henry DRACH, & Adam C. WARNER.
Magistrates: Taney town District--Isaac DERN*, Ephraim COVER*, George
   MILLER, David HAPE, David BUFFINGTON, James ROGERS, John DOTERO, John
   MAUS, Dorious GROFF, Caleb SHEELY, Winchester CLINGAN & Jacob
   HILTEBRIDLE. Union-town District--Isaac APPLER*, David ROOP*, John
   RINEHART*, Elijah BOND, John WEAVER, Peter CHRIST, David SMELSER, John
   LANTZ, George RINEHART, George FLEAGLE, Jacob SULLIVAN Jr., Isaac
   SLINGLUFF, Daniel SULLIVAN, William POLE, William BUCKINGHAM & Henry W.
   DELL. Myers' District--Michael LYNCH, Jacob MAUS Sen., John JONES of
   John, Peter BECHTEL, Benjamin STONESIFER, John FIESER, Peter HESSON,
   Abraham STONESIFER, John KOONTZ & David HULL. Woolery's District--Daniel
   STULL*, Joseph STANSBURY, Denton SHIPLEY, Thomas WARD, Israel LEISTER,
   Daniel BUSH, Samuel JORDAN, John FLETTER, Jacob WICKET, James KEEFER,
   Levin WILLIAMS, John C. COLEHOUR, & Thomas BROWN. Freedom District--
   Edward DORSEY (of E.)*, Benjamin BENNETT, George W. MANRO, & William
   WHALEN. Manchester District--Michael FAIR*, Samuel W. MYERS, Levi
   MAXFIELD, Joshua F. KOPP, William B. MEIXSELL. Westminster District--
   Washington VAN BIBBER*, Jacob GROVE*, Jabez GORE*, Daniel J. GEIMAN,
   William S. BROWN, John BEAVER, John MILLER, Hezekiah CROUT, Basil ROOT,
   Samuel MOFFIT, Joseph SHAFER, Jacob NICODEMUS, & John BAUGHER.
   Hampstead District--Benjamin WILLIAMS*, George RICHARDS*, Samuel LAMMOTT,
   David LEISTER, Nicholas ALGIRE & John FOWBLE (of F.). Franklin
   District--Benjamin BOND*, T. B. BUCKINGHAM, Charles DENNING, William
   YOHN, Vachel BROWN Sen., Jacob WILT, Richard A. KIRKWOOD, Thomas INGLIS,
   Wilton BURDETT, J.T.F. HOOPER, & Jacob FARVER. (* new appointments)

24 February 1843
BAILE, John, sold his farm of 90 acres to David NICODEMUS at $58.88 per
   acre.
BROWN, Nicholas Hall, dec'd., his farm sold Saturday last to John BAILE for
   $55.51 per acre, making in gross the sum of $8437.50.
CLUNK, Jacob, of this place, has been appointed by the Governor, Flour
   Inspector for the "City" of Westminster. Verily!

WESTMINSTER CARROLLTONIAN

24 February 1843
NICODEMUS, John, sold his farm of 150 acres, on which he resides, to
Richard SMITH for $85.00 per acre.
STAHL, James, while walking along the road he fell & expired instantly,
without a struggle. A coroner's inquest held by Dr. HORNER Sunday the
12th near Littlestown (PA) ruled 'death by apoplexy.' He has been about
that neighborhood for some time past & we have not heard where his
relatives reside. He was a man of middle age.
The Democrat states that the names of Andrew SHRIVER, John MILLER & Joshua
LAMMOTT were accidently omitted in the list of Magistrates.

24 March 1843
WINTERODE, Levi S., dwelling-house at the tannery on the Hanover turnpike
between Hampstead & Manchester, in his occupancy, & recently purchased by
him from the heirs of Col. Jacob SHRIVER, took fire by accident on Friday
last & was entirely consumed together will all the furniture, &c.

7 April 1843
KELLAR, Jacob, Esq., of Mountjoy Twp. (PA) put an end to his existence by
hanging himself in his mill on Wednesday morning last. He has left a
large family; was the Whig candidate for Sheriff at last election.
PITTS, John L. Rev., was in Washington some days after leaving home, no
trace of him has since been found.
WOODS, Nathan, in Dickinson township (PA), his old barn was entirely
consumed by fire; believed to be the work of some evil disposed person.
Friday afternoon last, the new barn on the same plantation was burnt to
the ground. The wind blew strongly at the time & sparks were
communicated to the house & barn of Samuel GALBRAITH, nearly 1/4 mile
distant. The house was saved with difficulty, but the barn & contents of
livestock, grain &c. were destroyed.
Spring session of Carroll County Court on Monday last--Present: The Hon.
Thomas B. DORSEY, Chief Judge & his Associates the Honorables Nicholas
BREWER & William H. WILKINSON. Grand Jury: Adam C. WARNER, Foreman,
Michael SMITH, Cornelius GRIMES, John SWIGERT, William FISHER, John
JONES, John KUHN Jr., Joshua STRICKLAN, Daniel DIEHL, Thomas SMITH,
Samuel A. LAUVER, George MATHIAS, William JONES, Jacob H. KEMP, Caleb
STANSBURY, Joshua TIPTON, Jonathan DORSEY, Philip CRUMRINE, Daniel BUSH,
Henry ALGIRE, Henry FOWBLE, Benjamin YINGLING & George CROUSE.
Petit Jury: Jacob BAUMGARTNER, Joseph ECK, James SMITH, Abraham BUFFING-
TON, John MATHIAS, Charles DEVILBISS, Daniel STONESIFER, Andrew SHRIVER,
David LEISTER, Daniel STULL, Jacob HOLMES, Thomas J. CARTER, John WADLOW,
Warner GAITHER, Thomas BARTHOLOW, Martin KROH, Joshua F. KOPP, David
BRILHART, George LIPPY, John COLEMAN, Otho SHIPLEY, Thomas FRANKLIN,
Richard RICHARDS, T. B. BUCKINGHAM & Andrew P. BARNES.
Constables appointed by the Commissioners of Carroll County for 1843:
Taneytown--William BURKE, Adam LICHTENWALTER, Washington GWINN & Nicholas
HECK. Uniontown--William SEGAFOOSE & Thomas BARTHOLOW. Myers'--Samuel
BOWERS, David FEEZER (of J.), Henry KUHNS. Woolery's--C. Harr. Samuel
DEVILBISS & George B. SHIPLEY. Freedom--Julius BERRET, Stephen R. GORE.
Manchester--Jacob FRANKFORTER, John KRANTZ, & Samuel SHUE. Westminster--
John M. YINGLING, David KUHN, Isaac POWDER & F. FRANKLIN. Hampstead--
David HOUCK. Franklin--Bennet SPURRIER.
Fire broke out in the village of Dover, York County (PA) Friday last, which
consumed the store of Messrs. WIEST & KLING & a tavern occupied by Mr.
DARRON.

12 May 1843
COLEMAN, Edward, dec'd, his farm of 97 acres, within 3 miles of the city of
Philadelphia, sold at $193 per acre.

12 May 1843

HORN, Adam, alias HELLMAN, on trial in Baltimore County before Justice
SNYDER for supposed murder of his wives. J. N. STEELE, Esq., attorney
for the State, James M. BUCHANAN, Esq., counsel for the defence. Walter
SLICER, Esq., Sheriff of Logan Co., Ohio, met with Gov. THOMAS to make
arrangements to take the accused to Ohio to stand trial there also.

MARTIN, John G., Esq., has been removed from the Post Office (Bedford, PA)
& Capt. James REAMER appointed in his stead.

TAYLOR, Jesse, laborer on the Rail Road against Dr. SMITH of New Market for
maliciously causing the plaintiff to be arrested for perjury. (Frederick
County Court). The jury gave the plantiff $400 damages.

The first issue of a new paper, entitled the "Maryland Gazette," was issued
in Cumberland by Messrs. STECK & SMITH.

19 May 1843

ANDERSON, Isaac C., Esq. (Howard District) was brought before Judge DORSEY
on a warrant issued by James TREAKLE, Esq., charged with assault with
intent to kill, upon Richard INGLEHART, Jr., who lies ill from a pistol
shot wound.

READ, William George, Esq., of Baltimore, delivered an oration at the
Chinese Saloon in Philadelphia on the anniversary of the Colonization of
Maryland.

Additional Constables for Carroll County appointed: Jacob HAPE, Taneytown
District; Lovelace GORSUCH, Freedom District; & William LAMBERT, Westminster District.

16 June 1843

MEHARY, Samuel, of Concord, Lancaster County (PA), a disagreement between
him & a man named HAWK from New Holland, the latter picked up a stone &
struck MEHARY in the head, fracturing his skull in several places. He
died Tuesday evening.

SHRIVER, Thomas Capt. has been elected Mayor of Cumberland.

Suit brought in Baltimore County court last week of R. D. BURNS vs. George
R. VICKERS, the plaintiff sued to recover damages sustained in 1841 when
he broke his leg on a slide board which extended over the footway from
the 2d story of the defendant's warehouse to a wagon standing by the
curb. George M. GILL, G. L. DULANEY & George R. RICHARDSON for the
plaintiff; Reverdy JOHNSON, William SCHLEY, John NELSON, J.V.L. MC MAHON
& William H. COLLINS for the defendant. $20,000 damages were sought.
The plaintiff was awarded $1000.

Temperance Celebration at Frederick: Procession formed in North Market St.
under direction of Col. CARMAC, Chief Marshall & marched to Court-house
square, where there was a prayer by Rev. Mr. HANKEY & a speech from Mr.
LAVINE, a reformed drunkard, of Baltimore.

21 July 1843

BARNS, Thomas, dec'd. of Carroll County, Joshua C. GIST, Executor

BARTHOLOW, Michael, dec'd., late of Carroll County, executors sale of small
farm of 50 acres improved by dwelling house & barn, all new; adjoins
property recently sole to Mr. BOWLEY & the farm of Isaac SLINGLUFF. Also
a wood lot of 10 acres adjoining lands of Mrs. WARFIELD, & John ZILE.
Thomas BARTHOLOW. John BARTHOLOW, Michael BARTHOLOW, Jr. Exec.

CONOWAY, Charles W., 320 acre farm & tavern stand formerly occupied by him,
in Carroll County on the new Liberty Road, 25 miles from Baltimore & 9
from Westminster, to be sold by decree of Equity Court. Adjoining lands
of Col. Joshua C. GIST, Jr. & Greenberry WILSON. Improved by dwelling of
2 1/2 stories, basement story stone, balance frame; with double piazza in
front, kitchen attached, cellar &c; new Switzer barn 50x20'; stable,
granary, smoke house & dairy. Charles W. WEBSTER, Trustee.

WESTMINSTER CARROLLTONIAN

21 July 1843
EVANS, David vs. Joshua FRANKLIN & others, Carroll County Court of
Chancery. Ordered that sales made & reported by Daniel ENGLE, Trustee,
to be ratified & confirmed. Jacob SHOWER, Clerk.
GAITHER, Frederick, of near Unity in Montgomery county, was returning home
from Baltimore riding in a sulky with his son, a youth of 13. The horse
was frightened when Mr. G's hat fell off & galloped off at full speed,
overturning the sulky & throwing out both occupants. Mr. G. was struck
on the head & face with the iron part of the vehicle & had his skull
severely fractured & his face & cheek terribly mutilated; he died on the
spot. An elder son of Mr. G. travelling with them on horseback witnessed
the accident. Mr. G. has left a widow & a numerous family. The younger
son recovered.
GARRETSON, Jerry, committed as a runaway to Carroll County Jail, a negro
man 5'7" high. He says he is free & came from the neighborhood of
Hookstown in Baltimore County. J. Henry HOPPE, Sheriff.
MATHIAS, Jacob, Trustee appointed by Carroll County Court of Equity,
selling a house & lot in Westminster, at the Forks of said town, opposite
residence of Isaac SHRIVER, Esq., fronting on the Main street 60' &
running back to an alley 198'; & 1/4 acre lot on which there is a large
2-story log dwelling house, rough casted, 48' in front by 18 back. Also
stable & garden well enclosed. (The creditors of James O. HEADINGTON are
directed to exhibit their claims with proper vouchers within 2 months
from the day of sale.)
MATHIAS, William A. Dr., tenders professional services; office opposite Mr.
Samuel ORENDORF's Store.
MYERS, Samuel W., dec'd., of Carroll County, sale of farm of 180 acres in
Carroll County, about 1 mile from Frederick BACHMAN's mill, on the head
waters of Big Pipe Creek; adjoining lands of Peter BIXLER & John WEAVER.
Large 2-story log dwelling house, rough casted & plastered, new Switzer
barn, carriage & stone houses, &c. Also a lime kiln. P.H.L. MYERS, Ex.
ORENDORF, S., has lumber for sale consisting of panel stuff; first &
second common; and cullins, also pine shingles.
PALMER, Joseph M., to attend the Carroll County Court for trials; Charles
W. WEBSTER, Esq., will take charge of cases in his absence.
POOLE, Daniel I., notes given at the sale of his property are due. G. H.
WAESCHE & Rushrod POOLE, Trustees.
POULSON, Lee, dec'd., of Carroll County, Samuel EVANS, Administrator.
SELLMAN, Joshua, residing 1 1/2 miles from Warfieldsburg, lost 5 steers.
SHRIVER & TROXEL, new store with cheap goods at the "Forks" in Westminster
in the store room recently occupied by the Rev. Mr. HEAKLE.
SHRIVER, A. K., Secretary, seeking a teacher at Carroll Academy. Apply to
William SHRIVER, P. M., Union Mills.
TRINE, Philip, selling part of farm on which he resides in Carroll County,
4 miles from Westminster, adjoining lands of Jacob TRINE, Caleb STANSBURY
& Joshua ALGIER. Will sell 50, 80, or 100 acres.
TITUS, Theodore & his wife & son, aged 14, last Sunday afternoon were
involved in a Rail Road accident, Mrs. TITUS was killed.
VAN BIBBER, Isaac, delivered an oration at the 4th of July celebration that
John K. LONGWELL, editor of this paper wishes to print.
WARFIELD, J. L., notes due have been given to S. & J. ECKER for collection.
WILLIAMS, Rodney, of Carroll County, petitions for relief of insolvent
debtor, has resided in MD for two years and is detained for debt & for no
other cause. Jesse MANNING, Jacob SHOWER, Clerk.
The undersigned, officers & member of the Jackson Greys of Shrewsbury, PA,
thank the citizens of Manchester & vicinity for the honorable station
they held in the 4th of July celebration. They thank J. F. KOPP, their
host, William CRUMRINE & Col. W. W. GARNER, of Ohio, formerly of
Manchester, MD, for refreshments prior to their departure for home.
Signed: William M'ABEE, Maj.; H. LATIMER, 1st Lt.; Charles PROSSER,

123

21 July 1843
O.S.; Charles DEIGHL; James FULLERTON; John & Samuel GEISEY; Elihu
HENDRIX; Joshua H. HENDRIX, Ensign; Henry HOKE; Daniel & Emanuel
ILGENFRITZ; Jesse & Simon A. KLINEFELTER; Zachariah KOLLER; John & Jacob
NUNAMACHER; Frederick BRANDT; Samuel RUHL; Samuel BRENISE; Charles FRY;
Henry HISE; Peter KLINEFELTER; John SHAFFER, Philip CRAUMER; Nathan
SHAFFER; & William BRENISE, Issac BEEK & Samuel SHEWELL, Musicians.
Camp Meetings: For Westminster Circuit to be held on the old ground, near
Hampstead. Horace HOLLAND & Elias WELTY. United Brethern in Christ to
hold meeting on land of Philip BISHOP, 1/2 mile southeast of Littlestown
(PA). John RUSSELL, Presiding Elder.
List of Letters remaining in the Post Office at Westminster, MD, 1 July
1843. Jaramiah [sic] ARTHUR, Mr. M. D. ALLEN, Samuel BLINSINGER, Abraham
BIXLER, Enoch BAKER, Daniel A. BOWERSOX, Kezekiah CROUT, Elizabeth
CHAPMAN, John DELL, Levi EVANS, Miss M. EVERHART, Jesse FRIZZLE, Jacob
FINKBONE, William GREEN, Francis GROFF, Mrs. Susan GIST, David HARRIS,
Amos G. HAWLEY, Victoria HERSH, James KEEFER, Stephen KEYS, Jacob LYNN,
Lewis G. LINDSEY, Nancy LEISTER, Abraham LAMMOT, Michael LUDWIG, John MC
CORMIC, David MILLER, Jonathan NORRIS, Mr. ORDENSTIEN, Arnat PEIPER,
William SHAFER, J. SHULTZ, Henry SHRINER, Otho SHIPLEY, Mrs. Mary
SHIPLEY, Mary E. SHIPLEY, Elijah WELSH, John T. WARD & George WAGONER.
J. YINGLING, Post Master.
The following are agents for the sale of Stainburn's Vegetable Extract
Anti-bilous Pills: Samuel ORENDORF, Westminster; George BRAMWELL,
Finksburg; J. NELSON, Warfieldsburg; Abraham CASSELL, Wakefield; Michael
SMITH, New-Windsor; Daniel ENGEL, Sams Creek; GORSUCH & POOL, MC
KINSTRY's Mill; Moses SHAW, Union Bridge; W. & J. ROBERTS, Union-town;
Jacob SHRINER, Pipe Creek; SHAW & CRAPSTER, Taney-town; George MEHRING,
Bruceville; George LANDERS, Double Pipe Creek; Jacob YINGLING,
Middleburg.
Candidates for Sheriff: Basil HAYDEN, Michael SULLIVAN, & Lewis TRUMBO.

1 September 1843
MC KENNAN, Hon. T. M. T., appointed delegate to the National Convention
from the Beaver & Washington Congressional district, in PA.
Temperance Procession, assembled at this place Saturday last, under the
direction of David W. NAILL, Esq. as Chief Marshal, assisted by C. W.
WEBSTER, Esq., Richard MANNING, John J. BAUMBARTNER & Peter ENGEL.
Military composed of Capt. MC COLLUM's & Capt. MAULSBY's Rifle & Infantry
Cos. Mr. MASON of Baltimore, Mr. POLLARD & Mr. Christian KEENER of
Baltimore delivered addresses.
Loco Foco Nominations: City of Baltimore in the House of Delegates: Henry
F. FRIESE; Elijah STANSBURY, Jr.; Nathaniel COX; Daniel BENDER & A. J.
RAMSAY. Washington County House of Delegates: Dr. E. L. BOTELER; William
WEBER; Warford MANN; Henry WADE & Joseph HOLLMAN, Esqs. Alleghany County
Nominations: Capt. BUSKIRK, Dr. FITZPATRICK, Patrick HAMMILL & William MC
KAIG, Esqs.
Whig Nominations: Allegany County: House of Delegates John PICKELL; Samuel
P. SMITH; Henry BRUCE & George MC CULLOH, Esqs.

22 September 1843
BOWERS, Joseph, his property seized at suits of Thomas JONES, John & S.
SWOPE, John MC KALEB & others, to be sold one house & lot in Taney-town.
Washington GWINN, Constable.
CARTER, John P. Rev., Principal of New-Windsor Collegiate Institution.
GERNAND, Emanuel, anxious to close his business, notifies persons indebted
to him to pay up immediately.
GROSS, Elizabeth Mrs., a lady of Baltimore, died the 9th instant aged 112
years. She never took any medicine during her long life. She was
followed to the grave by her descendants to the 5th generation.

22 September 1843

M'KALEB, John M., persons indebted to his estate are requested to pay.
A. G. EGE & J. K. LONGWELL, Administrators.

MIDDLEKAUFF, Benjamin, of near Hagerstown, states that a fiend incarnate
entered his field and with a knife so severely cut 4 or 5 of his cows
that 2 of them were found dead the next morning.

NICODEMUS, Philip, his large Switzer Barn about 5 miles from Westminster
was consumed by fire Monday evening last. The fire started when a
lighted candle accidentally fell among the straw which took fire. He has
lost his whole crop of grain, hay, &c.

PARSONS, Samuel, his dead body found Friday last in the cellar of his house
in Pearce Street, (Western Baltimore City) with the throat cut nearly
from ear to ear and a razor with which the deed was perpetrated, lying
close to the corpse. The dec'd. followed the occupation of making
packing boxes & was in easy circumstances. His wife left home several
weeks ago to visit friends on the Eastern Shore.

SMITH, Joshua, Foreman on behalf of the Jury, testified that they have
visited & examined the jail & find it clean & in good order.

SULLIVAN, Michael, Esq., Chief Justice of Orphans' Court of Carroll County
married at Emmitsburg Tuesday last by the Rev. William PHILIPS to Mrs.
Sarah Ann CONWAY d/o the late David HAINES, Esq. of Franklin District.

WATSON, Robert Esq., of Hancock, has been appointed Register of Wills of
Washington County MD, in place of Daniel SCHNEBLY, dec'd.

Independent Candidates for the House of Delegates: Charles W. HOOD, Samuel
ECKER, John K. LONGWELL & Nimrod GARDNER.

Nominated Candidates: Daniel STULL, Jacob POWDER, William SHAW & Thomas B.
OWINGS.

—•◦•—

4 October 1844

BLINTZINGER, Samuel, has commenced the tinning business at the new Brick
House opposite Henry SALTZGIVER's Hatting Establishment.

BUCKINGHAM, Beale & others vs. Ephraim BUCKINGHAM & others: sale made &
reported by C. W. WEBSTER, Trustee for sale of Richard CONDON dec'd.,
(other than sale reported to have been made to Ephraim BUCKINGHAM, which
is hereby absolutely rejected & the property directed to be re-sold)
sales amounted to $1487.85. (No. 105 Court of Equity)

COGHLAN, William, selling 65 acres & house adjoining lands of Frederick
YINGLING, John RUDOLPH & Adam HUPPERT. Also has kitchen (plastered),
smoke house, horse stable, wagon shed, new bank barn.

CONDON, Richard W. & others vs. Abraham WAMPLER & others: sales made &
reported by Richard W. CONDON, Trustee for the sale of real estate of
Thomas CONDON, dec'd., be ratified & confirmed; reported amount of sales
$2356.25. (See Buckingham above) (No. 124 Court of Equity)

DAVISON, John, the farm on which he lives near the head of Bear-branch
containing 230 acres, log house & barn with sheds, lately built. For
sale by C. BIRNIE, of Thorndale, Near Taneytown.

DORSEY, Nicholas, renting new building at Carter's Cross Roads. House is
30' x 16', 2 rooms below & 2 above. On the Liberty Road 100 yds. from
the Westminster & Washington Road. Apply to Henry CARTER or Mr. Lemuel
BUCKINGHAM, living near the premises or Mr. DORSEY 2 miles below Freedom
near the Liberty Road.

EICHELBERGER, Martin, being desirous to curtail his business, offers farm
of 187 acres, large 2-story stone house, new bank barn (45x65'), adjoins
lands of John NULL & Michael ZIMMERMAN. Also selling farm of 150 acres
situated on Owings's Creek within 1/2 mile of the Mills, now owned by the
subscriber & lately owned by George KUHN, dec'd. Improved by 2-story
stone dwelling and log barn. Also selling grist mill above alluded to on
Owings's Creek, known as heretofore belonging to N. SNYDER, Esq., &
lately to George KUHN, dec'd.; connected to mill are a saw mill and
clover-mill. Grist Mill is 35x45'; 1st story stone, upper frame. Can

4 October 1844
  manufacture 30 barrels of Flour daily, all machinery in good repair.
  Comes with dwelling, stone barn & spring house & frame barn.
ECKENRODE, Samuel W., those indebted to him to pay Samuel ORENDORFF.
GALT, Mary, dec'd., of Carroll County, Samuel GAULT, Executor.
GREENWOOD, Ludwick, dec'd., of Carroll County, Josiah & Uriah GREENWOOD,
  Executors.
HIBBERD, Silas, selling stocking yarn at his Factory, Merino Factory.
JORDAN, Zachariah, dec'd., William GORSUCH, Trustee, sale of real estate
  held & amount of sale was $1163. Jacob SHOWER, Clerk.
KERR, Francis T., Esq., Jr., Editor of this Journal married to Miss Mary
  Jane d/o John BAUMGARDNER, Esq., Register of Wills of Carroll county in
  the Cathedral in Baltimore on Monday evening last. The Rev. Mr. HICKEY
  performed the ceremony. (All of Carroll County)
KOONS, Paul, dec'd., of Carroll County his farm of 280 acres for sale 3 1/2
  miles northeast of Taney-town, 1 1/2 miles from the tavern of Messrs.
  Lewis PETERS & Jacob PETERS on road from Taney-Town to Littlestown,
  adjoining lands of Michael NULL & the late Col. William KNOX. Has log
  house with kitchen attached, large stone Switzer barn & stone spring
  house, frame wagon shed & out buildings. John BAUMGARTNER, Trustee.
LEGORE, John, those who held judgments against him to present them.
  Benjamin SHUNK, his trustee.
MURRAY, John, dec'd., of Carroll County, James A. MURRAY, Administrator.
NAILL, N. L., O.S., the New Windsor Guards to meet for parade.
NICODEMUS, John, dec'd., of Carroll County, Elizabeth NICODEMUS Adm.
NICODEMUS, John, (of H.) dec'd., his Administatrix selling at his late
  residence near the Stone Chapel, store goods of dry goods, hardware,
  groceries, household & kitchen furniture, livestock, 1 horse, 1 cow, 1
  gun, &c.
SMEACH, David, left at this office a beet measuring nearly 2' in
  circumference.
WARNER, John selling farm of 143 acres 2 miles East of Taney Town, 1/4 mile
  of ROBERT's mill, adjoining lands of Jacob HILTEBRIDLE & Widow MARKS.
  Has 2-story log house, barn (75' long), stone spring & smoke house.
List of Letters remaining at the Post Office as of 1 October 1844. Mary
  ARMSTRONG, Caleb BORING, Daniel BOWERSOX, John BEGGS, Mr. BARNES,
  Benjamin BROTHINGTON, Joshua BOYER, Jackson BENNET, Miss A. M. BAILE,
  Levin CHALMERS, Jesse CORNELL, Richard DELL, Samuel ECKENROADE, Miss Ann
  E. FRIZZLE, Hester HAINES, John HERISH, Rev. Robert H. JORDAN, John
  MILLER, George F. MILLER, Michael MORELOCK, Jacob MICHAELS, Mrs. Mary
  POOLE, William STANSBURY, Miss Mary STEPHENS, Lydia STEVENSON, William L.
  SHAFFER, Daniel STONER, A. H. SENSENNY, Joseph STOUT, Miss Susan J.
  SINKE, Henry STONESIFER, John D. WOODS, Nathaniel WILLIAMS, John
  WHITTLE Jr. Joshua YINGLING, Post Master.
County Statement shewing amount of charge of Expenditures & Receipts for
  present year ending 9 April 1845: James KEEFER, Court Crier; Jacob
  SHOWER, Clerk County Court; William P. MAULSBY, Deputy Attorney General;
  J. GORE, Acting Coroner; Michael SULLIVAN, Jesse MANNING & John B. BOYLE
  Judges of Orphans' Court; J. KOON, John ADDLESPERGER, Peter HULL, O. H.
  PICKETT, Henry DEWEES, William RANKEES, Jonze SELBY, Samuel ECKENRODE,
  Jacob CHRIST, Joseph MATHIAS, Henry W. DELL for accounts for Coffins for
  paupers; Lloyd SHIPLEY account for damages on road; John L. HEIRD,
  Constable's bill; Adam FEIZER & J. SHAFFER for costs in State case;
  Samuel ORENDORFF's bill for points &c. for Court House; RUNKLES & HALL
  for funeral articles for pauper; Ezra D. PAYNE's bill for medicine for
  paupers; Lovelace GORSUCH for State's business; Samuel LAMMOTT & John
  SYKES for arresting negro; Abraham BAILE's account for pauper; Bennett
  SPURRIER for State business; John COLEMAN for support of pauper; John
  ROOD's account; John MATHIAS' account for Broom to Courthouse (25 cents);
  Jacob ZUMBRUN's account for examining road; C. W. BENNETT, G. W. GORSUCH,

4 October 1844
Abraham LEISTER, B. BOND, William GORSUCH, William WHALEN, Elias BROWN, Moses BARNES, Jacob HOLMES, Moses BARNES Jr., road services; John REIFSNIDER, WIlliam MURRAY, Josiah BAUGHER, for improper assessment; John KRAUNTZ for arresting negroes &c.; Mary EBAUGH for articles furnished; John Henry HOPPE for Jail expenses & Wood to court & repairs; David KUHN constable bill; Joseph M. PARKE & John K. LONGWELL for printing; Henry KELLY for road work; Ann Eliza LIPPY supporting orphan child; Joshua YINGLING for books & stationaries; John S. MURRAY for collector's books; Bridge Repairs: Union bridge for repairing to Mr. STULTZ, as well as Hollingsworth bridge, Piney Creek bridge, Bridge Bear's Mill 5th district, Bridge Pipe Creek next to A. SHRINER's, bridge over Branch to J. WERNER, Bridge over Falls to Jacob HAEFAKER, bridge oover Pipe Creek to J. WENTZ & J. WHITE; bridge over race at EVERLY's Mill near Hampstead; bridge near C. BIRNIE's to James CROUSE as well as WAMPLER's Mill, Sykesville, Patapsco Falls, IRELAND's Meadow, bridge over Piney Creek George RODKEY; John STUDY medicine for pauper; Ellen BYERS for clothes for pauper; L.W. GOLDSMITH medicine for pauper; Stephen R. GORE & Thomas BARTHOLOW for stationary; Jacob GROVE for furnishing Jail; William MINOR digging grave for pauper. Basil ROOT, Clerk.

8 May 1846
BIXLER, Louis A., married in Baltimore City Tuesday the 28th ult. by the Rev. E. HEISER, to Ellen M. d/o the late Greenbury DUHURST, all of Baltimore City.
CLARK, Eben H., Post Master at Cherry Hill, Wayne Co., PA, has for some time been robbing packages of letters which passed through his office.
MILLER, George D., Jr., Editor of the "Westminster Carrolltonian" married in Frederick City on Monday the 4th inst., by Rev. S. W. HARKEY to Miss Christiana d/o Mr. Jacob LITTLE of Frederick City.
RIEMENSNYDER, J. J. Rev. has taken charge of the Lutheran congregations in Westminster lately under Rev. P. WILLARD.
TORREY, Rev. Mr., imprisoned in Baltimore penitentiary for aiding in the escape of slaves, now believed to be on the verge of the grave, sinking fast beyond all hopes. His coffin is built & preparations have been made to take the body home to New England immediately after death. (May 22 issue gives notice of his funeral.)
Mormons in Franklin Co. PA: A number of Mormons have returned from Illinois with Sidney RIGDON at their head & located themselves in Greencastle, near which they are forming a settlement.

22 May 1846
SMITH, F. J. Dr., dissolving partnership with Dr. S. L. SWORMSTEDT, asks persons to settle accounts.
Westminster Temperance Society: Delegation elected to represent interests at County Convention to be held in New Windsor on Whit Monday, June 1st: Otho SHIPLEY, John MILLER, J. J. NELSON, W. H. GREAMMER, H. PRICE, Dr. SWORMSTEDT, S. J. DELL, H. H. WAMPLER, E. F. CROUT, H. L. NORRIS, John MALEHORN, J. J. BAUMGARTNER, N, I. GORSUCH, Amon TIPTON, Francis SHRIVER, C. W. WEBSTER, Isaac SHRIVER, N. BUCKINGHAM, Hez. CROUT, Jer. MALEHORN, R. MANNING, Jesse SHRIVER. W. H. GRAMMER, Sec. pro. tem.

29 May 1846
BUCKINGHAM, Thomas V., died 4 May, in Freedom District at the residence of his father-in-law in the 27th year of his age. He was sick one week, left a wife of 5 weeks.
CLEMSON, John, Sen., at his residence in Frederick County, died Monday last, in the 89th year of his age.

29 May 1846
GORDON, Henry, Saturday evening week during a great freshet along Little
  Conowago creek (PA) his farm greatly injured by the removal in many
  places of the entire soil. (Gettysburg Sentinel)
GROSE, John, of Manchester district, killed last week by the fall of a limb
  of a tree. He resided on the adjoining place to the one on which George
  BORNS was killed last year under similar circumstances. He was 55.
HILTON, Clement, an old citizen of Frederick, MD, died very suddenly at his
  residence Tuesday, supposed from apoplexy.
NECOMER, Henry, of Westminster district, died the 19th instant.
NORRIS, Israel, appointed collector of Direct Taxes for Carroll County.
OGG, Sylvester, died 21 May in the Woolery's district, of Consumption,
  aged 34 years.
SHILLING, Murray, Woolery's district, died Sunday last in his 81st year.
SHRIVER, Francis, of Westminster has fine American Bend Leather, tanned on
  William BROWN's improved Patent process.
SNIDER, Michael, of Westminster district, died about 3 weeks since, aged
  86 years.
SWOPE, John infant son of Dr. John SWOPE of Taney-town, died Sunday last.

5 June 1846
BROWDER, Isaac Maj., of the 20th Regiment MD Militia was in town a few days
  ago making arrangements for reorganization.
SLOTHOWER, John D., of Little Pipe Creek, married in Gettysburg PA at Mr.
  MC COSH's Hotel by the Rev. Benjamin KELLER to Miss Sarah E., youngest
  d/o Joseph HARTSOCK, near Libertytown.
WAMPLER, Henry of Carroll County, married at Baltimore Wednesday the 27th
  ultimo by Rev. J. M. DUNCAN, to Miss Elizabeth B. GRAYSON of Baltimore.

12 June 1846
WILLIAMS, John H., chosen Teller of the Frederick County Bank to fill the
  vacancy occasioned by the death of Mr. TURBUTT.

19 June 1846
Reasons for a Divorce: A divorce has been asked by an aggrived husband out
  West, on the ground that the lady, though often repremanded, will persist
  in using her husband's night-cap to get charcoal in. He says that he has
  broken her of the habit of taking one of his boots to the pump to get
  water for dinner.

—◦◉◦—

THE DEMOCRAT & CARROLL COUNTY REPUBLICAN

9 August 1838
BARNITZ, Michael, selling brewery in Westminster, built of brick &
comprised of between 200 & 300 kegs. There is none other nearer than
Baltimore & Gettysburg. He finds ready sale for as much beer as he can
make; & desires to quit due to ill health. Will teach buyer the art.
BROWN, John, dec'd., late of Carroll County, sale of his 129 acre farm 4
miles from Westminster on Cranberry Creek, it being a fork of Patapsco
Falls, adjoining lands of Abraham SHAFFER and Joshua BROWN. Contains 2
dwelling houses, barn, shedding, springhouse & out buildings. Michael
SULLIVAN, Trustee, residing near the premises & will show same.
BURNS, David, has Saddle & Harness-Making business manufactures to order
Patent Spring Seat Saddles & carriage & wagon harness.
CARTER, Thomas J., has brought before Joseph STEELE, Clerk of the Court, a
stray bay gelding. Inquire 3 miles from Freedom, Liberty Road.
DORSEY, D., having taken the City Hotel in Frederick City informs the
public that he is open & his bar is stocked with Wines & Liquors of the
best quality & his rooms have new & handsome furniture.
EVANS, Levi, cabinet & carpentry, continues his business in Westminster &
has on hand a handsome supply of furniture. He has provided himself with
a Hearse for the purpose of delivering to order coffins.
_____ FRIZZEL, Jr., selling 223 acre farm on which he resides, on the
Washington City & Deer Park roads, within 3 miles of Westminster.
Contains dwelling, barn, stables, grainery & out houses.
GUISHARD, Henry of Uniontown, warns persons not to let any person of his
family have goods on his credit, as his circumstances at this time will
not justify his going farther into debt.
HARTZELL, Jacob, running the Westminster Hotel, thanks the public for their
liberal encouragement & reminds them that the Baltimore & Pitsburgh
stages leave his house daily & his table at all times supplies the
delicacies of the season.
HOPPE, Frederick, constable's sale to be held at William CRUMRINE's tavern
in Manchester, selling all of above HOPPE's right, title, interest, claim
& demand of his to the following property: 1/4 acre of land in the town
of Manchester with 2-story brick dwelling, with shop attached & stable.
Property seized & taken at the suits of George EVERHART & Solomon MYERLY.
John KRANTZ, Constable.
HULL, Abraham & wife, through Jacob GROVE, Trustee selling personal
property and 155 acre farm in Carroll County, formerly property of
Abraham HULL, 1 mile west of Westminster & Littlestown Turnpike, on
Silver Run. Has 2-story brick dwelling house 45x27', a spring & Dairy in
the cellar of the house, brick Switzer barn 82x50'. Farm is within a
short distance of GROFF's Mill & Silver Run Church & adjoins the Tan Yard
of Peter HULL, Esq.
HUTCHINSON, Enoch, selling valuable land in Wisconsin Territory at 75 cents
per acre. Inquire at J. HARTZELL's Hotel or to the editor of this
newspaper.
KELLY, Samuel, desirous of removing to the west, selling the 164 acre farm
on which he now resides within 2 miles of Westminster, at the
intersection of the Washington & Deer Park roads. Contains dwelling
house, barn, stabling & dairy. 2 streams run through the property.
KERLINGER, Jacob, Secretary of Manchester Academy, posting rates.
LECOMPTE, Samuel D., attorney at law, office in Westminster, 3 doors below
the Clerk's office & next door to the Post Office.
MATHER, Michael, has taken in a stray cow at his residence in Manchester.
MAULSBY, William P., attorney at law, his office on Main street in
Westminster opposite Mr. HARTZEL's Hotel.
NELSON, Madison, attorney, his office in west Church Street, Frederick,
next door to the Tannery of Gideon BANTZ, Esq.
NEILSON, Thomas S., selling 256 acre farm in Carroll County, 4 miles from
Manchester, adjoining lands of John HOSOCKER, Thomas SATER, Henry MILLER.

9 August 1838
& Jacob BOWMAN, improved by log dwelling & stable. Also selling woodland tract of 33 1/2 acres 3 miles from Westminster, adjoining lands of Caeb STANSBURRY & Alexander CRAWFORD. Apply to Jacob KERLINGER, Manchester.

ROYER, Jacob & Co., Threshing Machines & horse powers, Uniontown. William SEAFOOSER & Emanuel ROYER, Agents.

RUNKLES, William, announcing the Ridgeville Races.

SHAFFER, Samuel, residing between Westminster & Manchester, sheriff's sale for all right, title, estate and interest at Law his tract of land on which he resides containing 29 acres. Said property was seized & taken at the suit of Mary SHAFFER. Nicholas KELLY, Sheriff.

WARFIELD, George has given a deed of trust to Archibald DORSEY to hold a sale of household goods for the benefit of his creditors to take place at Warfieldsburg in Carroll County. A second sale to be held in Lisbon, Anne Arundel County of 4 improved lots in said town of 1/4 acre each and 1 improved lot in Lewistown, Frederick County.

YOUNG, Dewalt, sherif's sale by Frederick County court at his late residence of livestock, grain and all right, title, interest & estate of said YOUNG of his 60 acre farm in Carroll County on which he lately resided known as "Look about and Keepers Range;" taken at suit of the Westminster Bank.

ZEPP, Solomon, has purchased the Lumber business under the name of ROSE & ZEPP.

Garlegant's Balsam of Health, Prepared only by John S. MILLER at his Drug & Medicine Store, opposite the Market House, Frederick, MD. Testimonials given by Nicholas WEAVER of Gettysburg; the Rev. D. F. SCHAEFFER, Pastor of the Lutheran Church in Frederick; Joseph SNAPP of Frederick County. John F. REESE, Agent.

Road Notice: Henry HOUCK, John FURHMAN, John SMEACH, George WEAVER of Henry, & John WEAVER filed their petition to open a public road in Carroll County to commence at the PA & MD line near the dwelling house of Henry HOUCK & thence running through his land & that of John FURHMAN, John SMEACH, Mrs. Catharine BENDER, J. Henry HOPPE (formerly KILLEA's), George WEAVER & John WEAVER to intersect the Turnpike road from Manchester to Hanover at or near the 34th milestone on said road, opposite John WEAVER's dwelling house. Samuel W. MYERS, John WENTZ & Philip CRUMRINE, Commissioners.

Camp Meeting held by the Church of God, 3 miles from Westminster near the Taneytown Road, a quarter mile above Mr. ROOP'S on the grounds of Leonard POWDER.

Candidates for Sheriff: Jacob GROVE, Benjamin YINGLING, David HAPE, Isaac DERN, Basil ROOT & Henry GEATTY.

Petitioners for benefit of insolvent debtors. All are now in custody for debt and for no other cause, the Petitioner must have resided in the State of MD for two years next preceding date of petition. Francis ANCHERS, Ephraim COOK, Thomas GIBSON, Edward HAYNES, Peter KNIGHT, Henry MATHEWS, Reazin MULLINEAUX, Larkin W. SELBY, and James THOMAS.

20 September 1838
BORING, Ezekiel, dec'd., late of Carroll County, sale of 50 acres of land, part of his estate, lying on the Turnpike from Westminster to Littlestown & 2 miles from Andrew SHRIVER's Mill, improved by 2-story log dwelling house, kitchen, and log stable.

BROWN, Arthur R., wishing to remove to the West selling grist mill & saw mill on 12 acres, lying on waters of Morgan Run, about 8 miles from Westminster & 1/4 from the Washington Road.

BROWN, Nicholas, dec'd., late of Carroll County, sale of 8 3/8 acres of timber land, being part of his estate, lies 2 miles North West of Westminster, near Mr. David ROOP's mill dam. To view call on John ROOPE, Senior or Ruth & N. H. BROWN, Trustees.

20 September 1838

CROUT, Hezekiah, commenced the mercantile business at the store room at the "Forks" recently occupied by Messrs. ROSE & SWORMSTEDT & opposite Mr. TOPPER's tavern.

EASE, Lewis, on 31 August inst. left his family & place of residence, Codorus township, PA, 2 miles from Jefferson, in a state of mental derangement. He has not been seen since. Frederick EASE, his brother, residing near Manchester, Carroll County will gratefully receive news of him, whether dead or alive.

GALLAGHER, Thomas, died, his farm seized & now occupied by Gen. JAMISON containing 218 acres being sold. Located 21 miles from Baltimore on the Turnpike between that city & Westminster. Contains frame dwelling house with barn & stables &c. Previously occupied as a tavern. James M. BUCHANAN & Charles F. MAYER, Trustees.

HAINES/HOLMES?, Jonathan, dec'd., 108 1/2 acre farm for sale 2 miles from Westminster with log dwelling house, barn & spring house. George Gordon BELT & James M. BUCHANAN, Trustees.

KELLY, Nicholas, Sheriff, giving election notice.

PARRISH, John, dec'd., late of Carroll County, Flin GARNER, Acting Exec.

WELCH, Upton D., sale of 300 acre farm on which he resides in Anne Arundel County named "Prospect Hill", adjoins lands of Dr. HOOD, Dr. GOLDSBOROUGH & Dr. HEWETT, 23 miles from the city of Baltimore, 1/2 mile from B&O Railroad & 1 1/2 miles from Mr. SYKES' Mill. Has dwelling house with cellar, barn, stable, 3 tobacco houses, granary, & dairy.

WELLS, Thomas, near Westminster, seeks to employ a miller.

WENTZ, Rachel, dec'd., her house & lot for sale. Jacob REESE, Ex't.

WOOTTEN, John, residing at Rockville, Montgomery County, MD, offers reward for runaway negro named Park who ran away from subscriber's plantation near Queen Anne, Prince George's County. About 35 years old, 5'8-10", well made, yellow complexion, cross-eyed, full suit of hair & broad mouthed; has remarkable scar on stomach.

—•◉•—

20 February 1840

ARNOLD, George, his establishment, The Gettysburg Steam Foundry, is now in full operation doing all kinds of iron & brass castings.

BECK, George Sen., all persons who gave their notes at his sale are notified that they have become due. Daniel J. GUIMAN.

BECK, Nimrod, his property seized and taken in execution at the suit of Joshua YINGLING & others, to be sold 1 lot being in the 7th Election District, being a part of the land called "Winter's Addition" designated & known as Lot No. 4 on the Plat, containing 1/4 of an acre, adjoining the lots of James KEEFER & others, in the town of Westminster, near David KEEFER's Tavern, now occupied by Emanuel GERNAND, said lot fronting on the main street, being in a business part of the town. Also household goods consisting of 1 ten-plate stove & pipe, 2 work benches, 1 lot of crockery ware, a lot of beef in salt, a lot of potatoes, cabbage, onions, lumber, four tubs, 1 cider barrel, &c. All to be sold at the house of Benjamin DAVIS, Innkeeper in Westminster. William GIST, Constable.

BULLER, Cyrus Jr., has taken part of the house at the NW corner of Main & Church Streets, 2d door East of the Bank, where he will keep a chair factory to manufacture rocking, Windsor & table chairs & do repairs.

COVER, Tobias, Tax Collector, having been unsuccessful in making as large collections of Taxes due the county for 1839, will meet taxpayers without fail at the following locations: Uniontown District--POOLE's Tavern, New Windsor & SEGAFOOSE's Tavern, Uniontown. Taneytown District--MARTIN's Tavern, Middleburg & LEADER's Tavern, Taneytown. Myers' District--Peter G. MYERS' Tavern. Manchester District--CRUMRINE's Tavern, Manchester. Hampstead District-- Henry LAMMOTT's Tavern, Hampstead. Finksburg District--HORNER's Tavern, Finksburg & Charles STEVENSON's Tavern (Woolery District). Franklin District--HAUSE's in Ridgeville. Freedom

THE DEMOCRAT & CARROLL COUNTY REPUBLICAN

20 February 1840
District: Henry CARTER's Tavern, John LITTLE's Tavern in Freedom, Thomas
CARTER's Tavern. Westminster District taxpayers can pay Basil ROOT.
CRABB, William, petitions the court for benefit of the insolvent debtors
act. Nimrod FRIZZELL, Justice of Orphans' Court.
CROUT, Hezekiah, renting 2 rooms in the basement of dwelling occupied by
William P. MAULSBY, Esq. Inquire of Basil ROOT, Westminster or the
subscriber at Warfieldsburg. Also selling new 3-story frame building &
lot in fee simple, now occupied by William P. MAULSBY, Esq. in a central
part of the town of Westminster on the main street. Also selling the
adjoining house now occupied by Basil ROOT & George SHEETS.
FISHER, William, Secretary, orders the Taneytown Guards to parade on the
usual ground in full winter uniform for election of officers.
GOLDSBOROUGH, Dr., formerly of Frederick County, offers services, his
office near Mr. MOUL's Tavern and opposite residence of James RAYMOND,
Esq. in Westminster.
GOSNELL, William, dec'd., John WEAVER, Ex'r.
HAPE, David, under arrest for debt, has petitioned for benefit of insolvent
debtors law. John CLABAUGH, Constable.
KEEFER, David, renting well-known tavern stand in Westminster, formerly
occupied by himself, presently occupied by Emanuel GERNAND, Esq. In
business part of town, has excellent Wagon yard, two Granaries, 2 Drover
Lots, & Stabling sufficient for 40 or 50 horses, 2 pumps of excellent
water in the yard.
KERLINGER, Jacob, county surveyor, charges moderate prices.
KESSELRING, Catharine Miss, intends to teach at the residence of Mr. BURNS'
an English School. (Westminster)
MANNING, Nelson, has removed his shop to the brick house opposite David
BURNS' Saddler Shop, opposite Mr. MOUL's Hotel & will continue to carry
on his tailor's business.
MILLER, John, having rented all his land, will sell, at his residence in
Westminster livestock, grain, wagons, ploughs, harrows & cultivators.
Also selling farm of 200 acres.
POLE, William Jr., renting house & lot in town of New Windsor, now occupied
as a Public House.
PRICE, Mordecai & David CROCK, the partnership in the blacksmith business
dissolved. Mr. PRICE to continue the business alone at "The Forks" in
Westminster.
REESE, John F., of Westminster, selling Garlegant's Balsam of Health,
prepared only by John S. MILLER at his Drug & Medicine Shop opposite the
Market House in Frederick, MD. Endorsements by Nicholas WEAVER of
Gettysburg, Rev. D. F. SCHAFFER, Pastor of the Lutheran Church in
Frederick & Joseph S. SNAPP of Frederick County, Va.
RILEY, William, dec'd., Johnzee HOLMES, Adm'r.
SHOWER, Jacob & Henry E. BELTZ, Doctors, have entered into co-partnership
in the practice of medicine, midwifery & surgery at office in Manchester.
SKINNER, S. P., prospectus for publishing in Baltimore City a Daily & Tri-
Weekly Paper to be called the "Baltimore Post & Commercial Transcript."
SMALL, Alexander, 3 miles below York, PA, operates Petraea Sawmill.
STEVENSON, Nimrod, his property seized & taken in execution at the suite of
William SHEEV & Michael BARNETZ, to be sold 2 tracts of land 4 miles
below Westminster, within 1 mile of the turnpike in Carroll County, being
the farm on which the said STEVENSON now lives containing 99 acres. Also
2 tracts of 4 acres and 15 square perches, within 1 mile of Westminster.
Jacob GROVE, Sheriff.
STONESIFER, Jacob, selling 135 1/4 acre farm on which he now resides, 4
miles north-west of Westminster, adjoining lands of Frederick WERBLE,
David GUIMAN, John REESE & others. Improved by stone house, barn,
spring-house & out buildings. Also selling wood lot of 22 3/4 acres

20 February 1840
adjoining lands of Lewis WAMPLER & on the country road from Westminster to Manchestser.
WEISER & ZIEGLER, selling lumber at their Yard on No. George Street, near the Stone Bridge in York, PA.

──●○──

7 August 1845
BOLLINGER, Daniel, sheriff's sale of his property by virtue of suits of John JOHNS, Jacob MYERLY, David HOUCK & Co., Jacob CAMPBELL, William FISHER, George W. WARNER, George EVERHART, Jacob BOWMAN, Daniel BOWMAN & the Bank of Westminster. Selling all that part of a tract of land called "Joseph BOLLINGER's Contrivance" containing 313 acres, being that land conveyed by a certain Catharine BOLLINGER to said Daniel BOLLINGER by deed recorded among the land records of Baltimore County. Land lies 3 1/2 miles from Manchester on road leading to York & 1/2 mile from KROH's mill. Improved by large 2-story log dwelling house, 3 tenant houses, bank barn, spring house & apple orchard &c. Also selling his personal property of livestock, grain, and household goods.
BOOTH, R. R., Surgeon Dentist, will attend to various diseases of the teeth & gums & restore them to their natural beauty & soundness &c.
BROWN, Samuel, a Bankrupt, District Court gives notice to his creditors to file claims. U. S. HEATH, District Judge, Thomas SPICER, Clerk.
EVERLY, Levi, dec'd., sale of his late residence 2 miles north east from Westminster, 160 acre farm on which he resided, lying between the Mills of Abraham WAMPLER & David EVERLY. The Patapsco Falls run through one side of the place & Cranberry Run through the other. Improvements are large 2-story stone house with stone kitchen attached, stone spring house, new stone blacksmith shop, Switzer barn & smoke house, Limekiln, new Still House with two rooms above & a kitchen with a stable. David LEISTER & Rebecca EVERLY, Ex.
FRIZZELL, Joshua, by virtue of writs issued by Richard A. KIRKWOOD, chief justice of the 9th Election District at suits of Isaac BROWER against goods & Chatels, lands &c. of Joshua FRIZZELL the following property to be sold at constable's sale: All that tract called "Caleb's Delight Enlarged" in Carroll County containing 36 1/2 acres, 1/4 mile from Franklinville. New log dwelling thereon. Bennet SPURRIER, Constable.
FULLER, Azariah (Mr.) died on Monday the 29th ult., at his residence in Finksburg, aged about 23 years.
GORE, J., conveyancer & scrivener, always found at the Clerk's office in the Court House, Westminster where he will attend to the drawing of Deeds, Mortgages, Bills of Sale &c. Being Deputy Clerk of Carroll county he has free access to the public records.
GRAMMER, William H., Secretary of the Westminster Union Sabbath School Association gives notice of their monthly meeting.
HOOK, James W., his property seized & up for sheriff's sale by virtue of 3 suits by Jeremiah SLORP & John BEAVER. Selling tract called "Rochester Resurveyed" 3 miles from Westminster, 1 mile to the west of the Reisterstown turnpike, where said HOOK resides, containing 105 acres & a 2-story log dwelling house, stable &c.
KOUTZ, Henry, died the 30th ult., at his residence in Manchester district, in the 39th year of his age.
LEISTER, Israel, sheriff's sale of 49 1/3 acres near Finksburg, being same land conveyed by James ADAMS & wife, Peter GALLAWAY & wife & Peter SHIPLEY to said Israel LEISTER by deed dated 13 December 1841 & recorded in Liber JS No. 1, folios 17 &c., land records Carroll County. Improved by 2-story weather-boarded house, large stable with shedding Also 6 acres & 31 perches in town of Finksburg being part of a tract called "Hooker's Meadow Enlarged" & same land conveyed by Lemuel GARDNER & wife to said LEISTER by deed dated 20 August 1838 & recorded among land records of Carroll County in Liber W.W. No. 3, folios 11 &c. Improved by

7 August 1845

2-story dwelling house with shop & stable in the occupancy of Augustine
MILLER. Also personal property of wagons, livestock, &c. being sold.
Above property seized at the suits of Jeremiah DUCKER & John SUMWALT
against goods & chattels lands & Tenements of Francis S. KEY & Israel
LEISTER & suit of Jacob MATHIAS against Israel LEISTER & George BRAMWWELL
& at suit of Samuel ORENDORFF against Israel LEISTER & Charles BENNETT.

MATHIAS & SHIPLEY, Doctors, offer services.

MATHIAS, Joseph, carpenter & cabiner maker, keeps on hand an assortment of
furniture & makes coffins. He is also prepared with a hearse & will
attend to Funerals.

MOALE, Samuel, selling land part of "Absalom's Chance," part of "Porter's
Pleasant Levels," & Part of "Lawrence's Pleasant Valley" containing 116
1/4 acres. Improvements are an old 2-story log house. Has good stream
of water runnng through & plenty of Limestone within a few miles. 7 1/2
miles from Westminster, adjoins lands of Mrs. YOHN & Joseph FRIZZLE & 1
1/2 miles north of Col. Joshua GIST's farm, who will show property, or
apply to Mr. MOALE in Baltimore

MOTTER, Henry, has purchased the store of his father at Manchester & has
begun business for himself at the same well known stand. Carries dry
goods & groceries, hardware, Queensware &c. Mrs. Rebecca MOTTER still
continues to follow the business of a milliner & Mantau maker & is
prepared to make bonnets & dresses in the most fashionable style.

ORENDORF, Samuel, agent for Clickener's Sugar Coated Vegetable Extract
Pills & Sherman's Lozenges.

PAYNE, E. D. Dr., performs all the important operations in surgery.
Westminster.

PETERS, J. & L., their notes of hand & due bills payable to them were
stolen from their store at Piney Creek, Carroll County by thieves who
entered during the night of 15 July.

REIFSNIDER, Jesse, at the Forks, notifies farmers & blacksmiths that he
has just received 6 tons of iron.

ROOT, Basil to sell without reserve 76 1/4 acres lying 1 mile south of
Westminster, adjoining lands of Jacob GROVE, Esq. & others. There is a
new log house & barn & 2000 bushels of lime has lately been applied.

RUMLER, Perry married Sunday the 3rd inst. by the Rev. P. WILLARD to Miss
Rachel MATHIAS, all of Myers' district Carroll County.

SCARFF, William, Hampstead, has taken in stray bay horse.

SHRIVER, Jesse & Alfred TROXEL, selling dry goods, groceries, hardware, &c.
in the "Forks" in Westminster.

SMITH, Eleanora Virginia, infant d/o Jacob SMITH of Uniontown district died
Friday the 1st inst.

SMITH & SWORMSTEDT, Doctors practicing Botanic Medicine offer services.
Office in new building of J. ORNDORFF. Dr. SMITH resides in Brick
building of John S. MURRAY.

STOUT, Joseph, selling lime at 9 cents per bushel, which he has burned on
Joseph ORNDORF's farm, now occupied by Mr. S. MYERLY, 1 1/4 miles west of
Westminster.

WAGONER, Elijah, selling at his residence, Westminster farming implements.

YINGLING, John M., & John MATHIAS, John M. YINGLINGS's property seized &
taken in execution by Richard MANNING, Deputy Sheriff the following
property to be sold at the suit of Henry W. HISER & Jacob BESORE: all
that tract called "Peggy's Chance," part of a tract called "Denmark," &
part of a tract called "Rochester," all in Carroll County containing 76
1/2 acres, being the same lands described in a deed from Thomas HILLEN &
wife dated 10 July 1843, conveying same to John M. YINGLING, recorded
among the land records of Carroll county in Liber J. S. No. 2, folio 395.
Said land lies 1 mile south of Westminster & has thereon a log dwelling
house &c., in the occupancy of Daniel HUNTER.

THE DEMOCRAT & CARROLL COUNTY REPUBLICAN

7 August 1845
YINGLING, Joshua, agent for Hance's Compound Syrup of Horehound at 50 cents
per bottle, made by Seth S. HANCE, corner of Charles & Pratt streets,
Baltimore & Hance's Sarsaparilla Pills, & numerous other pills.
Candidates for Sheriff: Benjamin YINGLING, Michael SULLIVAN, Lewis TRUMBO,
Jesse MANNING, Horatio PRICE, Samuel MOFFET, Nelson NORRIS, Basil HAYDEN.
Petitioners for benefit of the insolvency debtors act. In custody for debt
and for no other cause, has resided in the State of MD for 60 days next
proceeding the date of petition. William CASH, Michael CLAPSADDLE, John
HAFLEIGH, Henry KELBAUGH, Francis S. KEY, Michael LYNCH, Jacob LOOKING-
BILL, Henry G. MITTEN, Lewis MYERS, John RICKORDS, John WISE, Roger
N. YINGLING, Solomon ZEPP,
Five suits issued: Suit of George RINEDOLLAR, Jr. against John LICHTY, 2
suits of George RINEDOLLAR, Sen. & Andrew DUTTEROW against John LICHTY &
Jacob TROXEL, 1 suit of Jacob BOWER against John LICHTY & Henry BLACK & 1
suit of Jacob STONESIFER & Ephraim SWOPE against John LITCHY. J. Henry
HOPPE, Sheriff has seized & taken in execution all right, title claim
&c. of said John LICHTY of the following property: 82 acres being part of
a tract in Myers District called "Ohio" in Carroll County, heretofore
purchased by John LICHTY from Peter HULL. Improvements are log dwelling
house & log barn & out buildings. Also personal property to be sold.
At the suit of the State of MD, use of Reuben RAICHNER & Matilda his wife,
against goods &c. of Peter HULL & John FLICKINGER. J. Henry HOPPE,
Sheriff has seized & Taken all right, title, claim &c. of Peter HULL to
the following property: 147 acres being part of a tract called "Ohio",
the same land conveyed by the heirs of Peter BROWN, dec'd., to Peter
HULL, now in the occupancy of George LEASE. Property adjoins lands of
David FEESER & Joseph BROWN & has thereupon a log dwelling house & barn.
Also selling livestock & farm implements. Also seized & taken the
following property of John FLICKINGER: 200 acres devised to said
FLICKINGER by the last will & testament of his father Andrew FLICKINGER,
dec'd., which will was recorded by the Register of Wills of Frederick
County. Said land is now occupied by John FLICKINGER & is located on Big
Pipe Creek, on road from Frizzleburg to Silver Run Church, improved by a
log dwelling house & large bank barn. Also selling grain & farm
impliments.
Camp Meeting to be held by the Church of God on the old camp ground
belonging to James CROUSE, 2 miles south east of Taneytown.
Wright's Indian Vegetable Pills agents: Joshua YINGLING, Westminster; SHAW
& CRAPSTER, Taneytown; Peter CHRIST, Uniontown; RUNCKELS & HALL,
Ridgeville; George MATTER, Manchester; Joseph EBAUGH, Hampstead.

135

THE REGULATOR AND TANEY-TOWN HERALD

2 August 1831
BOYLE, James V., at No. 3, East Market Space in Taney-town gives the
  highest price for wool.
DAVIDSON, Samuel P., Taney-town, has new book & stationary store at his
  dwelling, adjoining the Rev. John N. HOFFMAN's, at which he has an
  assortment of school books, family bibles, blank books, paper, inkpowder,
  wafers, slates, slate pencils, lead pencils, crayons, superior black Ink
  & bottles, cork ink-stands, pocket do., quills, &c., &c., cheaper than
  they can be purchased elsewhere. For example: Shorter Catechisms, 4 for
  one cent.
DELAPLANE, Joshua Jr., dec'd, had applied for benefit of insolvent laws.
  John MC CALEB, Adm'r. asks those having claims to present them.
GEISSELMAN, George, late of Germany township, Adams County, PA, by
  authority of his last will & testament, sale of his plantation in the
  township above, 1 mile west of Petersburg (Littlestown) on the great road
  from York to Frederick, containing 187 acres, a large 2-story log
  dwelling, log barn with sheds, & spring house. Also 1-story log
  dwelling-house, small log barn & spring house. The newly-laid out road
  from Emmitsburg to Petersburg (Littlestown) passes through this land. To
  view property apply to Stephen KING, now in possession of same. Daniel
  GEISSELMAN & John BAUMGARTNER, Ex'rs.
GREASON, Nathaniel & William, having leased the Rockdale Woolen Factory
  from William GREASON will manufacture wool into cloth cassinet, &c. Wool
  will be received at the following places: James GOURLEY's, Gettysburg;
  James BLACK's, 'Two Taverns'; John COWNOVER's, near Black's mill; Peter
  EPLEY's mill, Marsh-creek; Frederick CRABB's mill,Toms-creek; Mr. Thomas
  WILLSON's, 'Willson's Ford,' Monococy; John NULL's, Taney-town; Francis
  SPALDING's, Monococy Bridge; Sterling GALT's, Piney creek; Abraham NULL's
  mill,Monococy & John TOPPER's, Alloways-creek.
HEBBARD, Maria Louisa, infant daughter of Dr. E. B. HEBBARD of this place,
  died after a short illness Saturday last, in the first year of her age.
KEY, Francis S., Esq., spoke at 4th of July celebration at Washington City.
MAUS, David R., informs the public that he has rented the merchant mill,
  Centre Mills, on Big Pipe Creek and new saw mill from W. & J. ROBERTS,
  formerly owned by Lewis MOUSE, having it thoroughly repaired & running.
  Has 2 pair of burrs (one entirely new), 1 pair chopping stones, 1 pair of
  rubbers; for cleaning grain.
MERING, William & John SWITZER, their partnership dissolved by mutual
  consent, accounts left in hands of John SWITZER for collection.
MYERS, Joseph, dec'd., trustee's sale of property. 183 acres called "Part
  of Sheer Spring," improved by large log dwelling house, log barn &
  necessary outhouses. Jacob MYERS, Trustee.
O'BRIEN, L., appointed by the Medical & Chirurgical Faculty of MD, agent
  for the preservation & dissemination of Genuine Vaccine Matter. Orders
  from any part of the Union addressed to "Dr. L. O'BRIEN, south-east
  corner of Wilk & Bond streets, Baltimore will be attended to.
ROYER, Jesse, living nigh to Westminster, in Frederick County, offers 6 1/4
  cent reward for runaway boy bound to him named Theodore FOREY. About 11
  years old. Any person securing him so that I get him shall be entitled
  to the reward, but no thanks.
SHELMAN, James M., proposes to publish a Weekly Newspaper in the City of
  Frederick, to be called "The Times." A family newspaper devoted to
  Literature, Science, Agriculture & News.
SHUNK, Benjamin, of Emmitsburg informs the public that he has taken the
  stand occupied by Joseph HANNER to operate a Country Retail Store.
SULTZER, Sebastian, in Taneytown, National Republican voters of the
  district will meet at his house to consider resolutions passed by our
  National Republican friends in Frederick.
SWITZER, John, thanks the citizens at Union Bridge for patronage.

136

2 August 1831
SWOPE, Daniel H., selling dry goods, hardware, medicines, bar iron, plough
    irons, school books, Lutheran Hymn Books, &c.
WELLS, Daniel, whereas his wife Mary WELLS has left his bed & board without
    just cause, he is determined not to pay her debts.
WOODWARY & SPRAG, No. 15 No. 4th street, Philadelphia, PA, have commenced a
    Periodical Journal, "The Saturday Courier" to be published once a week,
    $2 per annun, payable half yearly in advance.
A Camp Meeting to be held for Liberty Circuit on land of Mr. S. WARFIELD,
    about 5 miles north of Liberty, under superintendance of the Presiding
    Elder, Rev. J. HAMBLETON.
Jackson Republican Nominations: For Electors of the Senate--William M.
    BEALL & Roderick DORSEY. For the Assembly--Isaac SHRIVER, Sommerset R.
    WATERS, Richard H. MARSHAL, & Abdiel UNKEFER.
National Republican Nominations: For Electors of the Senate--David KEMP &
    Richard POTTS. For the Assembly--Davis RICHARDSON, Evan MC KINSTRY,
    Abraham JONES & William C. JOHNSON.
List of Letters remaining in the Post-Office at Taneytown, MD, which if not
    taken out before 1 October next, will be sent to the General Post-Office
    Dead Letters: Reuben D. BURGESS, John BAUMGARTNER, Esq., George BRAMWELL,
    Basil CRAPSTER, Samuel P. DAVIDSON, Thomas ESSOM, Simon GEETHING, Jacob
    HAHN Sen., Alley HYTER, Mrs. HELM, Peter KEFFER, Mary Ann LINN, Mary Ann
    MERING, Frederick MERING, Hannah MANSON, David MARTIN, Robert PETTINGALE,
    Rebecca SHUNK, Abraham STANSBURY, Dr. John SWOPE, Mary J. R. SMITH, Lt.
    Jacob WORKING & Henry WOLFE. Hugh SHAW, Jr., Post Master.

23 August 1831
CAMPBELL, Abner, candidate for sheriff of Frederick County.
CROUSE, Daniel, house carpenter of Taney-town, has rented house adjoining
    Dr. John SWOPE's dwelling, for several years occupied as a Doctor Shop,
    where he will sell furniture & coffins made at the shortest notice.
STARR, John N., cabinet maker of Taney-town, has assortment of furniture &
    lumber; also hatters' finishing blocks & coffins.
TALBOTT, Mahlon, candidate for sheriff of Frederick County.
WARFIELD, Alexander, eldest s/o Surratt D. WARFIELD, died at his father's
    residence near Liberty on Wednesday the 17th inst. after a short illness,
    aged about 18 years.
ZOLLICKOFFER, Daniel, of Lauderdale, near Union-town, is cheered by
    progress of the Temperance cause.
A Camp Meeting of the Methodist Protestant Church to be held on land of Mr.
    NICODEMUS, 1 mile from the Sulphur Springs or New-Windsor the 26th ult.

137

BLIZZARD, Isaac 74
Jackson 20
James 4, 41, 64, 74
Rachel 110
Sarah 110
Stephen 43
BLOCHER, Daniel 39
BLOOM, (?)am 67
Mary (DUDDERAR) 67
Blooming Plane 107
BOBLINE, Michael 29
BOBLITZ, Peter 107
BOCKER, G. W. 93
BODEN, Samuel M. 64
BOGGS, Harmanus 10
Jane Alricks 10
BOLINGER, Daniel 106
BOLLAND, Ben 91
BOLLINGER, Catharine 133
Daniel 133
Mathias 51
BOLTON, Robert 105
BOMGARTNER, Henry 46
Peter 3
BOND, Ann C. 118
B. 127
Benjamin 19, 41, 49, 120
Elijah 1, 34, 37, 58, 86, 110,
114, 120
Elisha 39
Mary Ann 46
Bond's Meadow Enlarged 97, 106
Bond's Tavern 53
BONNER, John 40
BOOL, Henry W. 84
BOOM, John 46, 113
Rachel 113
BOON, Dianh 43
John R. 62
BOONE, Benedict 31
Benedict I. 38
BOONSOCK, Nathaniel 82
BOOS, Catharine (FREED) 110
Josiah 110
BOOTH, R. R. 133
BORING, Caleb 70, 126
Ezekiel 130
Ezekiel, Sr. 106
Jacob W. 48
Josiah 106
Boring's Range 106
BORNS, George 128
BOSLEY, Joshua 91, 93, 95
Shadrack 93
BOSLY, Shadrack 91
BOSSERMAN, Polly 46
BOSSOM, Rachel 107
BOSST, Nicholas 3
Boston 105
BOTELAR, Elias W. 3

BOTELER, E. L., Dr. 124
Edward 33
Henry 4, 33
Thomas 24
BOULTON, William 84
BOURING, Jacob 72
BOWER, (?) 13
Jacob 135
Rachel (PANNEBECKER) 82
Samuel 82
BOWERS, Adam 59
Barbara 38
Christian 12
John 105
Joseph 117, 124
Peter 105
Samuel 86, 105, 121
BOWERSOX, Daniel 126
Daniel A. 124
BOWIE, Richard I. 6, 38, 70
Richard J. 6, 90, 91
BOWLEY, (?) 94, 122
BOWLUS, George 9, 20, 36, 37, 44
BOWMAN, Ann Elizabeth (DERN) 109
Daniel 133
Jacob 130, 133
James L. 96
John 96
John D. 109
Matilda (LOVEALL) 96
William H. 64, 85
BOWSER, Joseph 106, 112
BOYD, J. J., Dr. 85
John G. 102
Reuben T. 21
Robert 14
William 85
BOYER, (?), Dr. 13
Francis H. 86
Jacob 17
Joshua 126
Peter 34, 36
Thomas, Dr. 30
BOYERS, Catharine 20
Gabriel 5
BOYLE, (?), Rev. 73
Daniel 3, 105
J. B. 32
James V. 136
John B. 1, 19, 35, 39, 40, 41, 43,
48, 49, 63, 88, 119, 120, 126
Joseph R. 43
P. Rev. 105
Philip, Rev. 64, 81, 95, 109, 118
Boyle's Retreat 105
BRADDEE, (?), Dr. 83
BRADDOCK, John 91
BRADENBURG, William 118
BRADENBURGH, Lemuel 3
BRADFORD, A. W. 26

143

CHILCOTE, Richard 24
CHILDS, Nathaniel 6, 7
CHOATE, Solomon 84
CHRIST, Ann (DEVILBISS) 66
  Jacob 66, 73, 117, 126
  Peter 58, 116, 120
  Christopher's Lot 77
CHRISTS, Peter 135
CHURCH, S. S. 22, 24
CIRCLE, Barbara 15
  David 15
CLABAUGH, E. A. 116
  Edwin A. 96
  Elizabeth M. (DELAPLANE) 96
  Hanson 72
  James 53
  John 22, 32, 35, 44, 48, 59, 93,
    132
CLAGETT, Samuel 89
CLAGGET, Henry 20
  Julia 20
CLAPSADDLE, Elmira 96
  Michael 51, 135
CLAPSADLE, Margaret Ann 91
CLARK, Augustus 27
  Eben H. 127
  George 15
CLARY, Solomon 3
CLAY, George 95
  John 30
  Lemuel 3
  Martha M. (KING) 95
CLAYTON, Thomas G. 21
CLEMANS, John M. 15
CLEMSON, H. T. 91, 92
  James 34, 36, 91, 92
  John 30, 89
  John, Jr. 35
  John, Sr. 127
CLINE, Peter 90
CLINGAN, Winchester 120
CLOPPER, F. C. 70
CLOSE, Elijah 61
  Susan (BIGGS) 61
CLOUGH, (?) 2
  Clover Hill 106
CLUNK, Jacob 53, 92, 120
  Lydia 59
CLUTZ, Jacob 3
  Joseph 43
COAD, John 106
  William 84
COALE, J. M., Col. 95
  James 84, 94
  James M. 4, 21, 22, 37, 86
  Richard 88
  Richard, Capt. 63
  Richard, Maj. 95
  William, Dr. 35, 103
COBBS, J. G. 25

COBLENTZ, John 24
COBLER, Mary 12
S. 12
COCHRAN, Thomas 103
  William 38
COCKEY, J. 9, 19, 31, 88
  J. H. F. 30
  J. H. T. 70
  J. Robert 27
  Johsua 20
  Joseph C. 34
  Joshua 3
  Joshua F. 107
  M. G. 5, 70
  Mordecai G. 44, 48, 50, 59, 72,
    77, 78, 92, 114
  S. 106
  S. G. 23
  William H. 15
  Cockey's Hotel 25
COCKEYS, (?), Miss 89
COFFIN, George B. 15
COGHLAN, William 125
COHEN, Mendez J., Col. 31
COLE, (?), Dr. 98
  A. G. 31, 36
  John 22
  Luther 48
  Maria 10
  Richard 88
COLEGATE, (?), Dr. 42, 108
  George, Dr. 29
  Georgiana Parker 29
  Mary 106
COLEHEN, John C. 3
COLEHOUR, John C. 59, 105, 120
COLEHOUSE, Susan A. (ROSENBERG) 113
  W. H. 113
COLEMAN, Edward 121
  John 14, 121, 126
  Nicholas 34
COLHOUN, John 104
COLLIER, Daniel 71
  William 21, 71
COLLINS, Asa 38
  Charles S. 15
  Isaac 69
  L. A. 71
  Robert 51
  William H. 122
COLLUM, William 85
  Colross 49, 106
COLTRIDER, Frederick 50
  Come by Chance 65
  Come By Chance 107
COMINGS, Robert 46
CONDON, Arey 92
  Richard 64, 92, 125
  Richard U. 93
  Richard W. 125

147

CONDON, Thomas 44, 64, 70, 92, 110, 125
CONELLEY, Frances 96
CONGHLAN, William 44
CONISE, Jacob 23
CONN, James C. 110
Robert 15
Silas W. 15
Thomas 62
Conn's Tavern 110
CONNELLY, Frances 96
CONNER, (?) 17
CONOWAY, Charles W. 122
Reuben 59
Solomon 106
CONRADT, G. M. 2
George M. 108
CONROE, Thomas H. W. 87
CONSTABLE, A. 26
CONTEE, John 67
Contrivance 106
CONWAY, Sarah Ann (HAINES) 125
COOK, Andrew 106
Columbus E. 84
Eber F. 78
Elizabeth 12
Ephraim 130
Ephraim, Capt. 80
George W. 86
Israel 89
John 12
Lucy 46
Nancy 70
Nicholas 106
Regin 7
Resen 100
Resin 89
Rezin 29, 70, 118
Sarah Matilda 82
Thomas 38
COOKERLY, William 37
COOKSON, J. 117
Joseph 34
COONCE, Jacob 3
COONS, Jacob 49
COOPER, Samuel 35, 38
COPPERSMITH, Sophia 41
CORBIN, Catharine 53
Joshua 53
CORDAINER, N. Louis 105
CORMAN, (?) 83
CORNELL, Jacob 35
James 35, 76
Jesse 126
John 35
Smith 34
William 35, 76
Cornhill 107
COROTHERS, (?) 100
CORRELL, (?) 89

CORRELL, Jacob 85, 86, 91, 100
Jacob, Jr. 12
COST, Henry 24
John 24
COUL, C. 89
COVELL, Frederick 32
COVER, Alson 53
Elizabeth 12
Ephraim 120
John 35, 51, 76, 97
Tobias 1, 33, 34, 39, 59, 82, 89, 105, 120, 131
COWNOVER, John 136
COX, E. G., Dr. 108, 111
Ephraim G., Dr. 85
George 22
James H. 83
Joseph 70
Mary (KETTLEWELL) 111
Nathaniel 124
CRABB, Frederick 136
George 12, 19
William 132
Crabb's Mill 50
CRABBS, David 20
F. 48
George 5, 16, 48, 58, 61, 120
George, Capt. 1, 35, 39
CRABSTER, William 35
CRADDICK, C. 29
T. W. 29
Thomas 29
CRAIN, P. W. 88
Smith 101
CRAMER, Helpher 58, 70, 120
Jacob, Col. 23
CRAPSTER, (?) 124, 135
Basil 137
Jesse 47
John 29, 47, 55
W. L. 68
William L. 29, 43, 105
Crapster's Tavern 40
CRAPSTSER, William L. 17
CRAUMER, Philip 124
CRAVEN, Ishi 67
CRAWFORD, A. F. 107
Alexander 130
E. L. 79, 116
Evan L. 5, 49, 61, 66, 68, 114
Jacob 59, 72, 86
Robert 11, 58, 120
CRAY, James Z. 118
CREAGER, Jonathan P. 6
CREERY, R. 112
CREGLOW, John 53
CREIGH, John 107
CRINER, Henry 64
CRISE, Elizabeth 58
CRIST, Conrad C. 88

149

DAVIS, Elias 31
Ellen (PENNINGTON) 103
Francis P. 49
Francis T. 88, 110, 114, 116
Henry S. 72
James 59, 72, 86
James L. 25
John 103, 106
John A. 67
Luke 3
Mary 89
Phineas 26
Thomas 107
Thomas J. 30
Thomas L. 25
Thomas, Sr. 51
Ureth 89
Walter 19
Davis' Tavern 80, 83
Davis's Hotel 37
DAVISON, John 125
DAWSON, George W. 70, 88
DAY, (?) 14
DAYHOFF, James M. 32
Mary 103
Peter 30
DAYHUFF, Alexander 84
DE LA ROCHE, William F. 15
DEAHOFF, Margaret 61
DEAL, Daniel 59
David 58
Jonas 51, 72
DEAN, (?) 83
William F. 15
DEBART, (?), Rev. 28
Deep Valley 105
DEER, Elizabeth (CRISE) 58
Israel 58
DEFENBAUGH, (?), Mrs. 108
DEFFENBAUGH, Catharine 109
DEIGHL, Charles 124
DELAPLANE, Elizabeth M. 96
John 5, 19, 22, 27, 35, 38, 76, 96
Joseph 23
Joshua, Jr. 136
DELL, Adam 46
George Washington 111
Henry 11
Henry W. 51, 60, 114, 120, 126
Jacob 105
John 124
John K. 99, 109
John Nicholas 1
Naomi 43
Richard 126
S. J. 57, 127
Samuel J. 110
Samuel Jackson 56
Sarah (MILLEKEN) 111
Sarah (WEAVER) 11

DELL, William 2
DELOLANE, Eliza 12
DEMAN, John 12
DEMESS, Thomas 38
Denmark 134
DENNING, Charles 58, 120
DERENPORT, Moses 100
DERIES, John 70
DERN, Ann Elizabeth 109
George 80
Isaac 5, 35, 43, 44, 57, 76, 109,
120, 130
Juliann 80
Zacheus 28
DESHON, John C. 27, 28
DEVENPORT, Moses 53
DEVILBISS, Adah Zillah 97
Ann 66
C. 63
C. Harr. Samuel 121
Charles 4, 21, 44, 59, 86, 112,
121
Charles, Capt. 66
Charles, Jr. 95
George 35
Harriet 85
Louisa (SMITH) 95
W. 28
DEVIT, David B. 37
DEVRIES, Christian 70, 103
Christian, Jr. 72
Christian, Sr. 74, 105
Devries Mills 76
Devries' Mills 53
DEWALL, Daniel 7
DEWEES, Henry 126
DEWEESE, Samuel 62
DICE, Perry, Sr. 24
DICKENSHEETS, Frederick, Sr. 100
DICKINSON, Samuel S., Dr. 87
DICKSON, Isaac N. 15
Louis L. 15
DIEHL, Daniel 92, 121
Jacob 109
Mary 109
DIFFENBAUGH, Catharine 43
DIFFENDALL, John 70
Samuel 35
DILL, H. G. 69
John 11
Joshua 32
Nicholas 9, 64
DILLEY, Joseph 39
DILLINGER, H. W. 88
DITTERT, Charles 47
DIXON, (?) 4
James 1, 2, 39
DIXSON, George 70
DODDERO, John 9
DODDS, Robert, Dr. 2

152

GAULT, Samuel 126
GAUMER, Amos 62
GEATTY, Henry 5, 46, 57, 130
GEATY, Henry 38, 86
GEDDINGS, (?), Rev. 111
GEESERD, Mathias 93
GEETHING, Simon 137
GEIGER, (?), Rev. 23, 97, 110
  J., Rev. 45, 60, 73
  Jacob 27
  Jacob, Rev. 2, 28, 96
GEIMAN, (?), Mrs. 105
  Christian 98
  D. J. 87
  Daniel 58, 112
  Daniel J. 42, 75, 120
  David 12, 22, 43, 75, 86
  John 76
GEISEY, John·124
  Samuel 124
GEISSELMAN, Daniel 136
  George 136
GELWICKS, David 97
GENT, Joshua 15
  William 15
GEORGE, Enoch 40
GERAND, Emanuel 16
GERE, (?), Rev. 89
  J. A. 104
  John A. 69, 84
  John A., Rev. 108
GERNAND, (?) 23
  Charlotte 20
  E. 51, 117
  Emanuel 2, 8, 12, 16, 20, 21, 39,
    42, 44, 48, 49, 57, 61, 64, 68,
    71, 78, 82, 124, 131, 132
GETELIUS, S., Rev. 77
GETT, Jacob 40
GETTIER, Jacob 94
GETTINGER, Michael 104
  William 62
GETTY, Henry 43, 106
GETZENDANNER, Christian 40
  Daniel 34, 37
  Jona. 25, 37
GEYER, George, Jr. 10
  J. W., Dr. 37
  John W. 36, 90
  John Wesley 36
  Maria (COLE) 10
GIBB, John 105
GIBSON, Thomas 29, 46, 130
GIEMAN, David 34
GILBERT, Adam 109
  B. 92
  David 106
  James 89, 97
  John 92
Gilbert's Tavern 104

GILEM, Jacob 34
GILES, William Fell 62
GILL, George M. 122
  Jetson L. 51, 72
  R. W. 9, 26
GILLESPIE, Hamlet 1
GILLIS, Hamlet 106
GILLMYRE, G. 119
GILT, Jacob T. 2
GINTLING, (?) 70
GIRTY, Jacob 7
GISE, Adam 9
GISH, Jacob W. 119
GIST, David R. 107
  G. W. 78
  George 15
  J. 13
  J. C., Col. 78
  Joshua 16, 55
  Joshua C. 44, 69, 71, 122
  Joshua C. Jr., Col. 122
  Joshua C., Col. 17, 72
  Joshua G. 4
  Joshua, Col. 68, 99, 134
  Richard 15
  States L. 59
  Susan 124
  Thomas 107
  William 131
  William B. 29, 46, 59, 72
GITT, Jacob 44, 58
GITTINGER, Daniel 80
  George 34, 37
GITTINGS, John S. 83
  Thomas 91
GLASE, Henry 98
GLASS, Cadeel Ann 108
GLAZE, William T. 70
GLAZIER, Jacob 25, 32, 34, 39, 47,
  49
Glazier's Tavern 9, 40
GLEIM, Jacob 34, 39
Glendock & John 105
GLENN, (?), Judge 23
Globe Inn 55, 103
GOAL, Simon 109
GOBLE, George 11
GOLDSBOROUGH, (?), Dr. 23, 131, 132
  Alexander W. 110
  L. W., Dr. 68, 117
  Nicholas W. 84
GOLDSMITH, L. W. 127
GOLLY, David 35
  David S. 47, 86
GONDER, Joseph 47
GONTER, Joseph 2
GOOD, Henry L. 75
  W. A. 22
Good Intent 14
GOODMAN, Ann E. (RICHARDSON) 111

GRIFFITH, Thomas 15
GRIFFY, (?) 91
GRIMAN, David 1
GRIMES, Cornelius 58, 121
  Elias 4, 5, 23, 35, 44, 51, 76
  Frederick 32
  Gasaway S., Dr. 72
  George G. 35
  Jahael 70
  John 3
  Nicholas 27
  Warner T. 23, 32
  William H. 23
GROFF, D. 35
  Doras 39
  Dorious 120
  Francis 29, 34, 124
Groff's Mill 129
GROGG, Eve 107
GROSE, John 128
GROSH, (?), Mrs. 112
  Jonathan 112
GROSS, Elizabeth 124
  Henry, Jr. 24
  Henry, Sr. 24
  John 89
  John I. 84
Ground Oak Hill 106
GROVE, Augustus G. 21
  Jacob 1, 34, 38, 48, 50, 52, 57,
    59, 62, 73, 75, 87, 92, 97, 102,
    114, 120, 120, 127, 129, 130,
    132, 134
  Jacob, Lt. 117
  Lewis J. P. M. 45
Grove's Mill 24
GROVER, (?) 22
  George 47
GRUMBINE, Jacob 12
  John 81
  William 8, 24, 44, 47, 48, 57, 89,
    116, 117
GRUMBLE, George 81
GRUNDY, (?) 54
GUIMAN, Daniel J. 131
  David 132
GUISHARD, Henry 129
GUMMELL, Jacob 98
GURLEY, Amanda (STULL) 10
  Thomas 1, 6, 7, 19, 20, 24, 28,
    32, 34, 116, 120
  Thomas, Jr. 10
GUSH, M., Mrs. 63
GUTELIUS, (?), Rev. 10
GUYER, George 104
GUYTON, Henry 27
GWIN, Washington 72
GWINN, (?), Dr. 35, 39
  W. G., Dr. 48

GWINN, Washington 59, 86, 117, 121,
    124
  William B. 48, 55
  William B., Dr. 1, 4
GWYNN, John R. 27
  William 83
  William B. 35
Gytsylvania 106
HAASE, Jacob 57
HAEFAKER, Jacob 127
HAEN, David 53
HAFLEIGH, George 89
  John 135
HAFLLEIGH, Peter 105
HAGEN, Richard 3
HAGERTY, James 114, 114
HAHN, Benjamin 78
  Jacob 77
  Jacob, Jr. 3, 29, 35, 45
  Jacob, Sr. 137
  James 51, 71
  John 21
  Mary Ann (STONEBRAKER) 78
  Samuel 34
HAIDEN, William 109
HAINES, Catharine 18, 26
  Daniel 10
  David 125
  Eli 118
  Elizabeth 118
  Francis 86
  Harriet 118
  Henry 57, 59, 92
  Hester 126
  Isaac 55, 112
  Job 68
  Job C. 46, 118
  Joel 68
  Jonathan 131
  Joseph 4, 60
  Lewis 66
  Margaret 60
  Mordecai 18
  Nathan 55, 58, 64, 105, 117, 118
  Reuben 55
  Samuel 52, 64
  Sarah Ann 125
  Sarah Jane 60
  Susan 10
  Thomas 1, 18, 26
  William 34, 39, 55, 64, 86
Haines Inheritance 105
Haines' Mill 4, 24
Haines' Mills 18
Hale's Adventure 107
Hales Addition 105
Hales Adventure 105, 106
HALL, (?) 112, 126, 135
  E. E. 55, 72
  E. J. 42, 55

HALL, Edward E. 51, 64, 65, 79, 106
Elisha J. 15, 30, 64, 65, 79
Elisha J., Dr. 70, 108
George W. 15
Jacob 105
Joel 3
R. W. 120
Susan I. 108
Warfield 107
HALLER, Daniel 32
J. B. 24
Jacob B. 33
HALVERSTADT, Peter 19
HAMBLETON, J., Rev. 137
John 49
Thomas E. 31, 36, 49, 107
HAMBURG, Frederick 43
HAMILTON, G. D. 71
George D. 21, 31
J. S. 119
John 92
HAMMILL, Patrick 124
HAMMOND, Grafton 52, 88
Harriett 107
Nathan 23, 30
Ormond 23
Philip 107
Thomas 4, 6, 7, 24, 93
Thomas, Maj. 4, 35
V. 30
William T. 59
HAMMONDS, H. 89
HAMNER, J. G., Rev. 57, 66
HAMOND, Thomas 36
Hampton Court 107
HANCE, Seth S. 135
HANES, Reubin 118
HANKEY, (?), Rev. 122
HANN, Henry 43
John 21
Philip 51, 96
Phillip 74
Sophia (ROBINSON) 96
William 61
William, Jr. 48
HANNA, Joanna (WARNER) 109
Nathan 109
William 90, 94
HANNER, Joseph 136
HANSHEW, John 37
HANSON, Contee 110
HAPE, David 1, 19, 35, 39, 46, 47,
 48, 57, 58, 93, 104, 120, 120,
 130, 132
Jacob 39, 52, 72, 86, 97, 118, 122
John 45, 80
HAPENER, Catharine 74
HARBAUGH, John 97
HARDCASTLE, E. 112
HARDEN, James 38

HARDEN, Joseph 49, 59, 106
Nathan M. 15
Nicholas 51, 52
William 31, 36
William, Rev. 119
HARDING, Henry 44, 70
James 32
James M. 7, 8, 18
John 3
HARDY, John H. 91
HARE, John 107
HARKEY, S. W., Rev. 127
HARLEN, James W. 31
HARMAN, Daniel 49, 51
John 11
Joseph 55
Harne's Old Field 20
HARNER, Frederick 114
John 21
HARON, Jacob 89
HARPEL, (?), Rev. 53, 54, 76, 81
HARPER, Amelia Caroline 71
R. G. 71
Richard 97
HARR, Jane 86
Harriett's Retreat 107
Harris 107
HARRIS, (?) (FOREMAN) 81
David 81, 124
Ellxis 89, 118
Richard 59
Sarah 104
Washington 26
William 35, 104
HARRISON, (?), Gen. 40
H. S., Rev. 98
Nicholas 114
William G. 84
HARRITT, (?) 34
Cecilia Loretta 20
John 16, 20, 31, 32
John, Maj. 20, 47
HARROD, John J. 32, 43
HARRY, George L. 59
J. K. 119
Parmenio R. 119
HARRYMAN, George 35, 37
HARSNEPE, Alice 20
HARTLEY, S. 27
HARTSOCK, Ephraim 42
John A. 75, 85
Joseph 128
Sarah E. 128
HARTSTOCK, Ephraim 65
HARTZELL, (?) 38
J. F. 57
Jacob 8, 34, 37, 42, 45, 48, 49,
 57, 65, 129
John 79
L. W. 57

159

HESSON, Benjamin 86
  Catharine (YINGLING) 28
  John 28, 53, 104
  Peter 49, 59, 70, 75, 120
HETBAUGH, Henry H. 74
Hetrick's Tavern 79
HEWETT, (?), Dr. 131
HEWIT, Eli 82
HEWITT, Eli 58, 91
  Elil 73
HIBBERD, Silas 126
HIBBERT, (?), Mrs. 19
HICKEY, (?), Rev. 126
HICKLEY, Thomas 1, 17, 35, 39, 104
HICKLY, Thomas 48
HICKOK, J. H. 9
HICKS, Charles G. 27
HICKSON, (?) 116
  Mary E. 29
  William C. 38, 47
Hilbert's Mill 73
HILL, Arthur 15
HILLEARY, J. H. 6
HILLEN, Solomon, Col. 118
  Solomon, Jr. 6, 7
  Thomas 134
HILLMAN, H., Mrs. 118
  Samuel 46
Hills & Valley 105
HILSCOMP, Henry 43
HILTEBRIDLE, David 57
  Jacob 58, 120, 126
HILTERBREAK, John 39
HILTERBRECK, John 48
HILTERBRICK, John 66, 81
  William 66
HILTERBRIDLE, David 29
  Jacob 48
HILTLEBRIDLE, Jacob 11
HILTON, Clement 128
HIMES, (?) 111
HINAMEN, Albert 69
HINCKLE, Eli, Rev. 40
HINER, Henry 65
HINES, Anthony 62
  B., Miss 89
  David 23
  Philip 22
HINKLE, (?), Rev. 105
  Barbara 77
  Eli 21, 51
  Eli, Rev. 82
  George 77
HIPSLEY, Catharine 48
  John 48, 53, 76
HINOH, John 109
HIRST, William L. 102
HISE, Henry 124
HISER, Henry W. 134
  J., Rev. 119

HITCHCOCK, I. Irvine 15
HITE, Joseph 118
HITESHUE, Abraham 53, 105
  Elizabeth (HULL) 108
  Ephraim 47
  Israel 10, 32, 47, 48, 86
  William 108
HOBBS, Charles 49
HOFFMAN, George 24, 26, 107
  John 21
  John N., Rev. 136
  Margaretta 110
  Nelson 24
  S. 84
  William 106, 107, 110
HOFOCKER, John 59
HOGG, William 84
HOKE, Henry 124
  Lot 9
HOLLAND, Horace 124
HOLLENBERG, Peter, Jr. 95
  Susan (STEM) 95
HOLLINGSWORTH, Ed. J. 15
  Fr. 15
  Horatio 15, 88
  J. M'H. 15
  J., Col. 88
  John 15, 99
  Mary Ann 99
HOLLMAN, Joseph 124
HOLME, Jonathan 106
HOLMES, (?), Rev. 103
  Abraham 1
  Elias 29
  Francis 11
  Jacob 100, 109, 118, 121, 127
  Jacob, Rev. 96
  John 105
  John B. 6, 7, 27, 28, 63
  Johnzee 132
  Jonathan 8, 131
  Richard 91
  Susan 11
  Victor 27, 28
HOLTZ, Nicholas 31
Home Place 56
HOOD, (?), Dr. 131
  Charles W. 104, 125
  J. 107
  James 61
  John 61
Hood's Mill 53, 82, 89
HOOK, (?), Col. 74, 76
  James W. 133
  Marcus R. 27, 90
  Paul 93
  Sol. 27
  T., Col. 100
  Thomas 4, 5, 44, 45, 48, 53, 54,
    66, 69, 77, 78, 99

Joshua's Fancy 106
JUDEK, (?) 23
KARNEY, Thomas 83
KAUFFMAN, David 81
Fanny 81
Henry, Sr. 40
KEAFAUVER, John 30
KEEFER, (?), Mrs. 96
(?), Widow 85
Catharine 55
Christian 4
David 1, 7, 9, 12, 34, 51, 57, 96,
112, 131, 132
Frederick 22
George 3
Henry 27, 36, 37
James 38, 57, 58, 99, 102, 103,
116, 120, 124, 126, 131
Joseph 5, 16, 18, 21, 47, 70
Lewis 85
Peter 21
Samuel 53, 55
Keefer's Tavern 21, 61, 64, 82
KEENE, Nathaniel B. 84
Tobert T. 40
KEENER, Caroline Susan 60
Christian 124
David 60
KEFAUVER, John, Capt. 24
KEFFER, Peter 137
KEGEL, Christian 89
KEIM, Jacob 12
KEISER, Ann M. 28
Eckard 28
KEITH, (?) 104
William M. 21
KELBAUGH, C. 107
Henry 135
KELLAR, Jacob 121
KELLER, (?), Rev. 73
Adam 37
Benjamin, Rev. 128
David 24
Ezra, Rev. 74
Henry 24, 53, 92
Isiah, Rev. 61
Jacob 5
John 18, 57, 71, 91
M., Rev. 74
Samuel 63
KELLEY, James 58
John A. 57, 117
John C. 58
Joseph 56, 60
Nicholas 48, 59, 106, 106, 107
Patrick 117
KELLY, Caroline (CHENOWETH) 101
Deborah 97
Henry 127
James 70, 101

KELLY, John 51, 86, 116
John C. 5, 47, 59, 68, 104
John Greenbury 58
John Somerfield 58
Joseph 97
Nicholas 5, 27, 44, 57, 62, 84,
120, 130, 131
Patrick 59, 80
Rachel (MORRIS) 58
Samuel 53, 101, 129
William 86
Kelly's Old Fields 27
Kelly's Tavern 67
KEMP, Abraham 25, 37
Barnard 3
Daniel 31
David 37, 137
Henry 25
Henry, Col. 12
Jacob 3
Jacob H. 32, 44, 48, 59, 86, 121
John R. 106
Lewis 31, 36
Lewis, Col. 4
Mary Ann 118
Peter 56
KENDALL, Amos 110
KENEY, George W., Rev. 12
KENKE, E., Rev. 97
KENNAN, James 38
KENNEDY, John P. 61
KEPHART, David 1, 3, 5, 18, 22, 23,
44, 48, 53, 72, 80
David, Jr. 32, 35
George 25, 53, 80, 93
Margaret 53, 80
P. 109
Peter 100
Philip, Dr. 4
KEPPLER, Samuel 69
William McK. 63
KERLINGER, Conrad 106
Henry 48
Jacob 27, 40, 44, 50, 58, 62, 87,
120, 129, 130, 132
John 86, 104
Samuel 107
Kerlinger's Mill 79
KERNAN, Leonard 84
KERR, F. T. 94, 96
F. Thomas 90
Francis T. 85
Francis T., Jr. 126
Mary Jane (BAUMGARDNER) 126
KESELRING, John 49
KESLEY, William 71
KESLY, William 21
KESSELRING, Catharine 132
KESSLER, Jacob 116
KETTLEWELL, Charles 111

164

KETTLEWELL, Mary 111
KEY, F. S. 26, 57, 66
  F. S., Jr. 118
  F. S., Mrs. 7
  Francis 105
  Francis S. 134, 135, 136
  Jeremiah 89
  John 43
KEYS, (?) 112
  Abner, Jr. 27
  David 73
  Elizabeth 3, 12, 29, 46, 53
  Stephen 73, 86, 100, 105, 124
KEYSER, C. M. 19
KIEFFER, Justes 21
KILBURN, E. G. 88
KILER, David 79, 85
  Simon 67, 85
KILGORE, David 112
KILGOUR, (?) 44
KILLEA, (?) 130
KIMMEL, (?), Col. 87
  A., Col. 70, 89
  Anthony 21, 22, 85
  Anthony, Col. 20, 60, 91
KIMMELL, Anthony 30
KINER, Jesse 21, 22
Kinfawn 106
KING, Adam 46
  Herculus 43
  Jacob 53, 100
  Jane A. 112
  John 35, 46
  Martha M. 95
  Nicholas 45
  Robert 92
  S. S. 92
  Samuel 45
  Stephen 136
  Thomas R. 25
  W. R. 25
  William 15, 111, 117
King's Tavern 71
KINNEY, J. K. 76
KINSEY, Elizabeth 64
KINZER, Ann (GORE) 17
  John 27, 36
  John Jr. 17
KIRK, (?) 100, 105
KIRKWOOD, R. A. 81
  Richard A. 47, 49, 58, 59, 78,
    120, 133
KIRTZ, Isaac 27
Kitchen 106
KLAY, John 23
KLINE, Henry 118
  Peter 112, 118
KLINEFELTER, Benjamin 2
  Jesse 124
  Peter 124

KLINEFELTER, Samuel 2
  Simon A. 124
KLING, (?) 121
KLOCKINGATER, Diedrick 111
KNAPP, Frederick H. 78
KNELIER, Godfrey 2
KNIGHT, Jacob 46, 112
  John 72
  John B. 15
  Peter 46, 105, 130
KNOPPLE, David 105
KNOTE, Henry 12
  Henry, Sr. 29
KNOX, Margaret 82
  William 12, 25, 65
  William, Col. 8, 126
KOLB, Daniel 34, 37
  W. W., Dr. 40
KOLLER, Zachariah 124
KONE, Henry 26
  William 3
KONIG, Bos 90
  Frederick 90, 95
  Samuel 5
KONING, Frederick 94
KOON, J. 126
  Joseph 21
KOONS, Abraham 35
  H. 105
  Henry 19, 35
  Jacob 53
  John 29
  Margaret 3
  Paul 126
  Peter 35
  William 7, 35, 105
KOONTZ, Abraham 18, 86
  Eliza (LOWMAN) 109
  Emanuel L. 109
  George 18, 37
  John 9, 86, 120
Koontz's Tavern 40
KOONZ, John 70
KOPP, J. F. 123
  Joshua 40
  Joshua F. 48, 104, 120, 121
KOUTZ, Henry 133
KRANIZ, John 59
KRANTZ, John 48, 72, 86, 121, 129
KRAUNTZ, John 127
KRAUZER, Catharine (STUMP) 116
  Jacob 116
KREIDER, Elmira (CLAPSADDLE) 96
  Jeremiah 96
KRENSE, Wilhelm 112
KRENTZ, John 44
KRILLEY, Michael 94
KRISHER, Elizabeth 86
KROH, Lewis 43
  Martin 54, 59, 79, 85, 86, 121

167

LOVEALL, John 96
 Matilda 96
 Susanna 12
 Zebulon 46
LOWDENSLAGER, Evey 38
LOWDENSLEAGER, Margret 53
LOWE, Betsy 118
 David 48
 Elizabeth 89
 John 30
 John M. 32
 William 5, 6, 7
LOWMAN, Eliza 109
LOWNES, L. 22
 R. T. 22
LOWRY, P. W., Lt. 95
Lowrys Lot 106
LUCAS, Basel 43
 Basil 12
 F., Jr. 13
 Margaret 106, 108
 Robert 3
 Samuel 83
LUCKET, M. B. 25
LUCKETT, Lloyd 24
 Mountjoy B. 37
 N., Col. 24
LUDWIG, Michael 124
LUGENBEEL, Louisa (NAILL) 41
LUGENBELL, Basil 93
 William 101
LYFORD, Henry 2
LYNCH, Edward A. 31, 32, 37, 87
 John 118
 Michael 59, 70, 112, 114, 120, 135
 Thomas 54, 112
 William 24
LYNN, Isaac 22
 Jacob 124
LYON, James E. 40
M'ABEE, William, Maj. 123
M'ALLISTER, James 35
 John W. 75
M'BIAR, (?) 6
M'BLAIR, (?) 7
M'CALEB, John 1
M'CLELLAN, (?), Col. 117
 George W. 34
 William 92
M'COLLUM, (?) 23
 John 57, 67, 91, 93, 116
M'COLUM, John 59
M'COMBS, (?) 4
M'CONACHY, Robert 80
M'COOK, Daniel 105
M'Divitt's Mill 46
M'ELFRESH, John 96
 John H. 90
M'GEE, (?), Rev. 11
M'GUIGAN, James 5

M'IHENNY, A. 13
M'ILVAIN, William 44
M'KALEB, J. A. 4
 John 5, 34
 John M. 125
 John, Maj. 5
 William 34
M'KALEN, William 7
M'KILIP, Henry 13
 James 13
M'KILLIP, James 1, 48
 John 5, 15
M'KINNEY, (?), Maj. 11
 Jane Louisa 11
M'KINSTRY, Evan 5, 25, 36, 44
 S. 25
M'KINZIE, Margaret 38
M'MEAL, (?), Dr. 42
M'MURDIE, David 92
M'PHERSON, David M. 2
 J. B. 92
 John, Col. 84
 William 8
MACFARLANE, J. F. 92
MACGILL, Charles, Dr. 39
MACKELFRESH, M., Mrs. 46
MacKey's Choise 97
Mackey's Luck 83
MACLAY, Robert 14
MADDOX, W. W. 71
MAGEE, Isaac 61
 Margaret (DEAHOFF) 61
MAGILL, Charles 39
MAGINLY, Amos 92
MAGREE, Barnard 7
MAHANEY, M. M. 25
MALAY, M., Rev. 96
MALEHORN, (?) 4, 12
 Ann 46
 Jer. 127
 John 3, 5, 17, 27, 31, 58, 61, 85, 93, 120, 127
 John, Rev. 117
MALLALIEU, (?) 54
MALLALINE, William 72
MANAHAN, Aaron 74
Mancle's Purchase 107
MANN, Warford 124
MANNING, Jesse 10, 47, 53, 57, 58, 103, 114, 120, 123, 126, 135
 Jessie 2
 John 7, 17
 N. 57
 Nancy 56
 Nelson 102, 120, 132
 R. 127
 Richard 56, 124, 134
MANRO, G. W. 86, 88
 George W. 58, 86, 120
 J. Dr. 30

168

MEYERLY, Jacob 100
MICHAEL, John 112
  Samuel 42
MICHAELS, Jacob 126
MICHAIL, John 87
MIDDLECOFF, David 21
MIDDLEKAFF, A. 119
  D. 119
MIDDLEKAUFF, Benjamin 125
  D. M. 11
  J. A. 11
Middlesburg 105
MIDDLETON, R. W. 79
MIERLY, Solomon 112
MILER, George 58
Mill Right's Design 65
MILLEKEN, Sarah 111
MILLER, (?), Gen. 73
  Abraham 72
  Augustine 134
  Charles 2
  Christiana (LITTLE) 127
  Conrad W. 82
  David 124
  George 10, 47, 48, 120
  George D., Jr. 127
  George F. 126
  H. 71
  Henry 59, 77, 81, 114, 129
  J. H., Prof. 73
  Jacob 72
  Jacob N. 2
  Jacob T. C. 90
  John 5, 26, 33, 37, 47, 59, 61,
    68, 73, 97, 106, 120, 121, 126,
    127, 132
  John S. 130, 132
  John, Jr. 28
  John, Sr. 25, 28
  Margaret 77
  Martin 24
  Mary Ann 42
  Michael 5, 54, 70
  Sarah Matilda (COOK) 82
MILLS, Robert 78
MILLVAIN, William 8
MILRAY, Thomas 12
MILTMORE, Ebenezer 6
MINOR, John W. 84
  William 127
MITCHELL, Gideon 106
  Margaret 67
  Thompson 69
MITTAN, Miles 89
MITTEN, Catharine (EBAUGH) 108
  Henry G. 75, 108, 135
  John 110
  Mary Ann H. (SMELSER) 42
  Susannah 21
  William 42, 78

MOALE, Samuel 107, 134
MOBBERLY, E. M., Dr. 4
  Eli 37
MOCK, Peter 19
MOFFET, Samuel 104, 135
MOFFETT, Samuel 109
MOFFIT, (?) 119
  Samuel 100, 117, 120
Molly's Delight 77
Molly's Fancy 34, 105
MONKUR, John C. S., Dr. 23
MONROE, (?), Rev. 17
  T. H. 104
  T. H. W. 69, 84
  Thomas H. W. 116
  William, Rev. 97, 98
MONTELL, (?) 56
MONTGOMERY, John, Jr. 116
  W. A. 38
MOORE, Corydon K. 97
  Jason 7
  Jehu 97
  Joseph 4, 104
MOREHEAD, Susan 12
MORELOCK, Jacob 22, 46, 85, 86, 102
  Michael 1, 29, 34, 38, 70, 126
  Michael, Jr. 29
  Michael, Sr. 40
MORES, James 31
MORGAN, Gerald 69
  James 58, 86, 105, 120
  James B. 46
  John 101
  T. A. 69, 84, 104
MORLOCK, Jacob 98
MORNINGSTAR, Elizabeth 78
MORRIS, Rachel 58
MORRISON, Robert 35
  Sally 43
MORSELL, D. 101
  William 23
MORT, Margaret 95
  Peter 112
MORTER, George 64
MORTIMER, John 103
MORTON, (?), Mr. 46
MOSHER, E. J. 27
MOTT, Edward 15
  Richard, Dr. 4
MOTTER, Andrew 103
  George 103
  Henry 20, 134
  Isaac 97
  Joshua 47
  Lewis 3
  Lewis M. 97
  Rebecca 134
MOUER, Henry 29
MOUL, Conrad 57, 63, 65, 69, 71, 91
Moul's Hotel 76, 86, 103, 108, 132

171

RINEHART, George 3, 12, 34, 59, 120
  Hannah (ENGLAR) 119
  Israel 68, 101, 114
  John 53, 120
  Magdalina 29
  Rinehart's Tavern 28
RINEMAN, John 57
RING, Ezekiel B. 104
RINGGOLD, Tench 84
RIPLE, Jacob 105
RISTEAU, T. C., Dr. 63
  Thomas C. 90
  Thomas, Dr. 27, 37
RISTOR, John 29
RITCHIE, (?), Rev. 89
RITSCHHART, Elizabeth 92
  John 95
RITTER, Anna 1
  Frederick 5, 27, 40, 58, 62, 98,
    120
  Jesse 27
  Joseph 13
  Lewis 1
  Michael 29, 30, 59, 62, 86, 104
ROACH, James 120
  Sarah 59
  William 78
Roanoke Farm 16
ROBBINS, J. L. B. 53
Robert's Mill 126
ROBERTS, Ann 71, 97
  Basil 111
  Hester 111
  J. 36, 49, 84, 89, 124, 136
  John 4, 5, 19, 25, 27, 29, 31, 33,
    44
  W. 49, 84, 89, 124, 136
  William 1, 5, 19, 22, 29, 31, 33,
    36, 60, 72, 92, 97
ROBERTSON, Elias 13
  George 29
  Hunter 29
  J. 119
  Jeremiah 29
  John 36, 59, 111
  Mary 111
  W. 119
ROBINSON, Charles 43
  David 43
  Henry 87
  Jeremiah 89
  Samuel 43, 105
  Sophia 96
  William H. 84
ROBY, Washington 71
Rochester 105, 106, 106, 107, 134
Rochester Resurveyed 133
Rockland 107
RODERICK, Lewis 24
RODFELTZ, David 75

RODGER, John 76, 78
RODKEY, George 49, 127
ROETHICKEN, Unit 7
ROGAN, James 29
ROGERS, James 39, 48, 62, 104, 120
  Micajah 69, 92
ROHR, Philip 34, 37
ROHRBACK, (?), Col. 116
  Otho W. 116
ROHRBAUGH, Joseph 96
  Maria E. (BANKERD) 96
ROLLISON, J. 71
ROLOSON, William H. 78
ROMAN, (?) 102
  J. Dixon 88
RONEY, William 84
ROOD, John 126
ROOP, (?) 130
  David 21, 50, 60, 102, 120, 130
  Jacob 114
  Jesse 67
  John 8, 12, 21, 34, 39, 45, 58,
    82, 87
  John, Sr. 48, 92, 105
  Joseph 58
  Michael 92
  Urith (GOSNELL) 67
Roop's Mill 52, 109
ROOPE, John 130
ROOT, Basil 34, 39, 43, 44, 57, 59,
    83, 88, 93, 100, 107, 117, 120,
    127, 130, 132, 134
  Bazil 58
  Daniel 32, 35
  Jacob 23
ROSE, (?) 52, 130, 131
  John 6, 13, 45, 50
  John, Dr. 32, 38, 43, 48
ROSENBERG, Susan A. 113
ROSS, (?), Rev. 41, 81
  William J. 25, 34, 37, 41, 50, 88,
    108
ROTTEKEN, Charles E. 12
ROUTSONG, Henry 39
  Jacob 105
ROUZER, Henry 51
ROWL, David 100
ROYER, Christian 42, 75
  Emanuel 50, 92, 130
  Jacob 50, 66, 83, 130
  Jesse 136
  Peter 113
RUBEY, H. 26
RUCKMAN, Thomas 3
RUDISEL, George 51
  John 51
  Ludwick 51, 111
  Sarah 95
  T. W. 47
  Tobias W. 72

178

SELBY, Jonze 126
  Larkin W. 130
Sell's Place 56
SELLER, Jacob 2
SELLERS, Jacób 62
  Peter 95
  Sarah 54
SELLMAN, Beal 45
  Henry 106
  Joshua 5, 92
  Mary Barbara (WEAVER) 45
SELMAN, John S. 39
SENCE, Carroll 85
SENSENEY, A. H. 68
SENSENNY, A. H. 126
SENSENSEY, (?) 107
SENTMAN, S. 109
  S., Rev. 92, 95
SENTZ, Peter·98
SETTLE, William 92
SEVOYER, Joshua 12
SEWALL, Charles B. 7
  Charles S. 6, 28
  Charles S., Col. 4
  Sewall's Belief 106
SEWELL, Charles S. 105
SEWER, Philip 7
SEXSMITH, William 21, 31
SEYMAN, R. M. 105
  William 105
SHADE, Catharine 99
  George 99
SHAEFFER, Barbara 93
  John 24, 53, 93
  Joseph 38, 100
SHAFER, Abraham 55, 75
  George 24, 33, 79
  H. G. 34
  Henry I. 34
  Jacob 58, 120
  John 21, 44, 60, 118
  Joseph 57, 120
  Nicholas 67
  William 100, 124
SHAFFER, Abraham 129
  Andrew 53, 100
  Elizabeth 108
  George 87, 100
  J. 126
  Jacob 1
  John 30, 47, 89, 118, 124
  John R. 77, 108
  Joseph 48, 86, 86
  Mary 130
  Nathan 124
  Samuel 130
  Susannah 77, 108
  William L. 126
SHAMER, John 7, 29, 38
SHANER, Adam 3

SHARER, Daniel, Sr. 106
  Joseph 105
SHAROTS, Catharine 12
SHARP, Caroline R. (SNIDER) 11
  George W. 11
SHARRAR, Joseph 113, 116
SHATER, Peter 24
Shauch's Mill 54
SHAUCK, Henry 59, 66, 79
  John 66, 79
  Mary 89
SHAW, (?) 116, 124, 135
  Ann (SHEPHERD) 38
  Fanny 60
  Hugh 5, 19, 21, 29, 32, 33, 34,
    38, 43, 46, 47, 48, 49, 84, 105
  Hugh, Jr. 3, 12, 137
  John G. 85, 90
  Moses 30, 32, 38, 60, 74, 90, 124
  Moses, Jr. 1
  Moses, Sr. 4
  William 1, 5, 35, 36, 39, 44, 48,
    51, 58, 59, 117, 125
SHAWEN, Daniel, Jr. 40
SHEAFER, Jonathan 97
SHEAN, John 29, 89
SHEARER, F. A. 97
  L. V. 97
SHEELY, Caleb 120
SHEEN, Benjamin 7
SHEETS, George 46, 57, 107, 132
  John 11
SHEETZ, Jacob 86
SHEEV, William 132
SHEFFER, John R. 92, 95
SHEILDS, Jefferson, Dr. 76
SHELLMAN, James M., Col. 48
SHELMAN, (?), Col. 74
  J. M., Col. 72, 100
  James M. 34, 37, 45, 48, 53, 57,
    69, 71, 78, 78, 93, 102, 136
  James M., Col. 34, 44, 77
  James M., Lt. Col. 4
SHEPARD, Solomon 45
SHEPHER, N. 22
SHEPHERD, Ann 38
  Harriet (HAINES) 118
  Solomon 30
  Susanna 30
  Thomas 46, 78
  Thomas F. 86, 118
  Thomas, Jr. 72
  William 4, 5, 25, 30, 33, 38, 39,
    44, 46, 87
  Shepherd's Factory 19
SHERMAN, Elizabeth 1, 111, 112
  Jacob 63, 111
  John 118
  Sherman's Retreat 107
SHETER, G. 69

STANSBURY, Micajah 47, 107
  Rebecca (STEVENSON) 61
  Tobias E. 40
  Tobias E., Gen. 27, 33
  William 44, 48, 126
STARR, Edward 13
  J. N. 109
  John N. 35, 53, 74, 100, 137
  Mary 34
  Thomas 27
STARY, George 7
  Susannah 46
STEAVENSON, Charles 19
  Harriet Frances 19
STECK, (?) 122
STEDMAN, (?) 10
STEEL, Joseph 5, 44
STEELE, Catherine Ann (LITTLE) 69
  David 69, 104
  J. N. 122
  J. Nevett 96
  Joseph 69, 72, 77, 78, 86, 129
STEINER, M. Henry 28
STEM, David 20, 24, 44, 80
  Juliet 57
  Reuben 95
  Susan 95
STEPHEN, Ann P. 100
STEPHENS, Mary 53, 87, 126
  Reason 43
STEPHENSON, Robert 89
STEUART, George H., Gen. 95
  William M. 7
  William M., Maj. 25
Steven's Meadow 107
STEVENS, Andrew 107
  George 107
  John 3
  Rezin 7
  Samuel 3
  T. 10
  Thaddeus 14
  Thomas H. 92
STEVENSON, Basil D. 18, 98, 99
  Bazel D. 5
  Charles 11, 40, 45, 58, 61, 78,
    80, 82, 86, 107, 131
  H. 51
  J. M. 92
  Lydia 126
  Mary Ann 1
  Nimrod 22, 47, 64, 107, 132
  Rebecca 61
  Samuel 73
  Thomas 98, 99
  William 21
STEWART, Benjamin 54
  J. Erskine 78
  John 94, 95
  Mary 3, 7

STEWART, Sarah 95
  Thomas 54
  William 54, 118
  William M. 88
Stick's Tavern 79
STIER, Frederick 71, 100
  H. 26
  Hamilton 30, 70
STIERS, Henry 22
STILTS, Nicholas 27
STIMMEL, E. H. 118
STIMMELL, Jacob 118
STOCK, Frederick 28
STOCKDALE, Solomon 3
STOCKMAN, David 24
STOCKSDALE, Edmund H. 77
  Edward 56, 90
  John 56
  Nathan 77
  S. 48
  Solomon 72
STOCKTON, T. H. 71
  Thomas H. 21, 31
STONE, Jacob 100
  Jacob, Jr. 29
  John, Jr. 12
STONEBRAKER, Mary Ann 78
STONER, Augustus 78
  Daniel 74, 126
  Hannah 78
  Jacob, Sr. 101
  John 46, 79, 85, 92
  Polly (BOSSERMAN) 46
  Upton 82
STONESIFER, Abraham 38, 73, 120
  Adam 69
  Benjamin 59, 120
  Daniel 42, 70, 121
  David 72
  Henry 126
  Jacob 21, 59, 70, 132, 135
Stonesifer's Place 56
Stoney Ridge 106
STORM, Ann 38
  Maryann 7
  Peter 84
STORME, Mary Ann 118
STORMS, George 43, 103
  Naomi 103
STOUFER, Elizabeth 99
STOUFFER, David 21, 54
STOUT, C. 92
  Joseph 126, 134
STRAUSBAUGH, John 35
STRAWSBURG, John 19
STRAYER, (?) 83
STRICKENHOUSER, G. 92
STRICKLAN, Joshua 121
STRICKLAND, Jacob 116
  Joshua 116

WEBSTER, George 78, 92, 107
  Isaac 21, 31, 71
  Isaac, Rev. 67
  James J. 43
WEED, Alonzo F. 84
WEISEL, (?) 102
WEISER, (?) 133
  Charles 60
  D. P. 20
WEIST, Jon 88
WELCH, Mary 56
  Robert 59
  Robert, Jr. 63
  Upton D. 131
WELLER, J. 16
WELLS, Daniel 137
  John 10
  Mary 137
  Thomas 21, 53, 58, 69, 90, 92, 99,
    104, 108, 131
  Thomas, Dr. 72, 78
Wells' Mill 114, 115
WELSH, Elijah 124
  Ferdinand 78
  Mary 78
  Prudence 106
  Robert, Sr. 40
WELTY, Andrew 85
  Elias 124
  H. C. 27
  Joseph 11, 47, 89
  William 111, 115
WENTS, George 1, 62
WENTZ, Catharine 53
  David 50
  Frederick 50
  George 3, 8
  J. 127
  Jacob 109
  John 104, 114, 130
  Philip 57
  Rachel 16, 43, 51, 131
  Valentine B. 79
WERBEL, R. 112
WERBLE, Andrew 21, 104
  Frederick 113, 115, 132
WERNER, J. 127
  Joseph 64
WERTENBAKER, William 3, 4, 31
WERTZ, John 59
WEST, (?) 10
  Joseph 31
WEVER, James S. 84
  Mary M. 47
WEYGANDT, William 95
WHALAN, William 58
WHALEN, Henry 106
  William 53, 61, 120, 127
WHARTON, John O. 86
Wheatfield Inn 19

WHEELER, Edward 15
  Hannah 7
WHESKLEY, Isabelah 53
WHITBECK, John 84
WHITE, (?) 96
  Charlotte (PEDICORD) 41
  David H. 100, 103
  Eliza Ann 69
  Elizabeth (MYERS) 29
  Ephraim, Capt. 27
  George W., Dr. 29
  J. 92, 127
  Jacob 84
  John 1, 66, 92
  Martin 34
  Nicholas 109
  William 34
White Hall 65
WHITELOATHER, John 21
WHITELY, (?) 54
  Anthony 84
WHITINGHAM, (?), Rev. 74
WHITMAN, George 43
WHITRIDGE, (?), Dr. 96
WHITTINGHAM, (?), Rev. 117
WHITTLE, J. W. 87
  John, Jr. 126
WICKARD, Jacob 58
WICKET, Jacob 120
WIER, John 106
WIESCHE, George H. 11
WIEST, (?) 121
WIGHT, William J. 83
WIGNAL, James 49
WILDT, George 44
WILES, M., Rev. 56
WILEY, Bill 100
WILKINS, C. P. 112
WILKINSON, (?) 44
  (?), Judge 47, 70, 104, 114
  William H. 121
WILLARD, (?), Rev. 108, 109, 113,
    116
  O., Rev. 96
  P., Rev. 127, 134
WILLET, (?), Miss 40
WILLIAM, George 24
WILLIAMS, (?) 96, 117
  Ann (WAPPING) 46
  Bemjamin 86
  Benjamin 59, 86, 117, 120
  Elias 21
  George 86, 120
  Henry 100
  Henry J. 83
  J. T. 118
  James 47, 90
  James W. 84, 87
  John 27, 51
  John H. 34, 37, 128

189

WILLIAMS, John, Sr. 114
 Levin 120
 Levin, 2nd. Lt. 41
 Lovelace 107
 Nathaniel 126
 Nathaniel F. 84
 Nicholas 105
 Onom 47
 Phyllis 107
 Prudence 38
 Robert 46
 Rodney 123
 S., Rev. 101
WILLIAMSON, James 32
WILLIS, (?), Capt. 94
 (?), Dr. 2, 22, 38, 42, 57, 75
 (?), Mrs. 10, 23
 Emily Georgiana 13
 Joseph 106
 W., Dr. 105
 William 5, 8, 12, 19, 20, 26, 27,
  33, 44, 46, 51, 60, 85, 89
 William, Dr. 13, 25, 32, 36, 38,
  43, 44, 48, 72, 83, 99, 100, 102
 William, Lt. Col. 4
WILLS, William, Dr. 4, 21
WILLSON, G. W. 74
 Mary 92
 Thomas 136
WILSON, (?) 19
 Charles 59
 Greenberry 47, 122
 Henrietta 50
 Henry R., Rev. 11
 Horace, Dr. 6
 Isaac 32
 J. G. 71
 James C. 43
 John 44, 49, 74, 87
 R. 72
 R. C. 27
 Robert 21
 Victor 21
 William 87
Wilson's Intent 106
WILT, George 22, 35, 38
 Jacob 49, 58, 104, 120
WIMMS, Frances 7
WINCHESTER, (?), Gen. 13
 David 25, 26
 E. 31
 Elizabeth 26
 Hiram 7
 L. 31
 Lydia 26
 W. 21
WINDER, William S. 28
Windfaw 77
WINDSOR, Z. S., Lt. Col. 95
 Z. T. 25

WINDSOR, Zadock 25
Windsor Forrest 106
WINE, Jacob 63
WINEBRENNER, (?), Rev. 41
 George 14
 Mary Ann 14
WINK, George 77
 Susan 77
WINTER, Catharine 112
 Winter's Addition 131
WINTERODE, Levi S. 121
WINTERS, Earhart 104
 Lewis 117
 Magdalena 36
WINWOOD, Ebenezer 15
 Thomas 13
WIREMAN, (?) 10
WIRT, William, Hon. 14
WISE, (?) 17, 34, 117
 John 90, 91, 114, 115, 135
 John M. 27
WISNER, Joshua 57
WITHERODE, C. 89
WITHERS, Emanuel 12
WITMER, John 83
WIVEL, G. 57
 George 110
 Joseph 39, 104
WODBRIDGE, (?), Rev. 29
WOETTON, Singleton 23
WOLD, David 86
WOLF, (?), Rev. 105
 Daniel 93
 David 59, 72
 John 4
 William 53, 110, 115
WOLFE, (?), Rev. 102
 Henry 137
WOLFGANG, Jacob 86
WOOD, Joel 32
 John 32, 34, 36, 93
 Joseph, Capt. 31
 Thomas 10
Wood's Tavern 9
WOODALL, James 74
WOODS, Elias 74
 John D. 61, 126
 Josiah 79
 Nathan 121
WOODWARD, E. T J. 33
 E. T. J. 6, 7, 27
 William 31, 36
WOODWARY, (?) 137
WOOLERY, Christopher 36
 Elijah 58, 59, 80
 Honor 106
 Nimrod 58, 59, 72
 Noah 92, 113
 Sarah (RICHARDS) 113
Woolery's Tavern 31, 54

ZEPP, (?) 45
  Christopher 106, 107
  Lawrence 57
  Leonard 107
  Mary Ann 57
  Michael 57
  Solomon 57, 90, 115, 130, 135
  William 57
ZIEGLER, (?) 133
  David 92
  Emanuel 60
ZILE, John 3, 34, 99, 122
ZIMMERMAN, (?) 40
  Ann 71
  C. 106
  Catharine 77
  Frederick 77
  Henry 98
  J. 22
  Jacob 5, 8, 71

ZIMMERMAN, John 8, 43
  Michael 125
ZINCCHI, (?), Rev. 101
ZITE, John 29
ZOCCHI, N., Rev. 36, 59
  Nicholas, Rev. 108
ZOLLICKEFER, Daniel, Rev. 74
ZOLLICKEFFER, William 21
ZOLLICKOEFER, William, Dr. 47
ZOLLICKOFFER, (?), Rev. 58, 95
  D., Rev. 100
  Daniel 32, 77, 103, 137
  Daniel, Rev. 4, 10, 52, 60, 66,
    109, 110
  H. F. 109
  M., Rev. 96
  William, Dr. 35, 51, 79
ZOLLICOFFER, (?), Rev. 78
ZUMBRUN, Jacob 23, 35, 51, 70, 126

Other Heritage Books by Marlene Strawser Bates

Abstracts of Carroll County Newspapers, 1831–1846
Marlene Bates and Martha Reamy

Early Charles County, Maryland Settlers, 1658–1745
Marlene Strawser Bates, F. Edward Wright

Other Heritage Books by Martha and Bill Reamy:

*Erie County, New York Obituaries as Found in the Files of
The Buffalo and Erie County Historical Society*

*Genealogical Abstracts from Biographical and
Genealogical History of the State of Delaware
Volumes 1 and 2*

History and Roster of Maryland Volunteers, War of 1861–1865, Index

Immigrant Ancestors of Marylanders, as Found in Local Histories

Pioneer Families of Orange County, New York

*Records of St. Paul's Parish, [Baltimore, Maryland]
Volumes 1 and 2*

St. George's Parish Register [Harford County, Maryland], 1689–1793

St. James' Parish Registers, 1787–1815

St. Thomas' Parish Register, 1732–1850

The Index of Scharf's History of Baltimore City and County [Maryland]

Other Heritage Books by Martha Reamy

*1860 Census Baltimore City: Volume 1, 1st and 2nd Wards
(Fells Point and Canton Waterfront Areas)*

*Abstracts of South Central Pennsylvania Newspapers
Volume 2, 1791-1795*

Early Families of Otsego County, New York, Volume 1

Early Church Records of Chester County, Pennsylvania, Volume 2
Martha Reamy and Charlotte Meldrum

Abstracts of Carroll County Newspapers, 1831–1846
Martha Reamy and Marlene Bates

www.ingramcontent.com/pod-product-compliance
Lightning Source LLC
Chambersburg PA
CBHW070914270326
41927CB00011B/2569